Mirjam Schmalz, Manuela Vida-Mannl, Sarah Buschfeld, and Thorsten Brato (Eds.)
Acquisition and Variation in World Englishes

Studies on Language Acquisition

Series Editors
Luke Plonsky
Martha Young-Scholten

Volume 69

Acquisition and Variation in World Englishes

―

Bridging Paradigms and Rethinking Approaches

Edited by
Mirjam Schmalz, Manuela Vida-Mannl, Sarah Buschfeld, and Thorsten Brato

DE GRUYTER
MOUTON

ISBN 978-3-11-221380-3
e-ISBN (PDF) 978-3-11-073372-3
e-ISBN (EPUB) 978-3-11-073380-8
ISSN 1861-4248

Library of Congress Control Number: 2023942310

Bibliographic information published by the Deutsche Nationalbibliothek
The Deutsche Nationalbibliothek lists this publication in the Deutsche Nationalbibliografie;
detailed bibliographic data are available on the internet at http://dnb.dnb.de.

© 2025 Walter de Gruyter GmbH, Berlin/Boston
This volume is text- and page-identical with the hardback published in 2024.
Typesetting: Integra Software Services Pvt. Ltd.
Printing and binding: CPI books GmbH, Leck

www.degruyter.com

Contents

Manuela Vida-Mannl, Mirjam Schmalz, and Sarah Buschfeld
1 The current role of children and adolescents in World Englishes research —— 1

Part I: Language in the family

Guyanne Wilson
2 Language among Trinidadian-heritage children raised in diaspora —— 13

Teresa Wai See Ong and Su-Hie Ting
3 Language use patterns and strategies for children's English language development: Insights from Chinese descendant mothers in multilingual Malaysia —— 37

Kamolwan Fairee Jocuns and Andrew Jocuns
4 Family language policies in Thailand: Multiliteracy practices and Global Englishes —— 59

Manuela Vida-Mannl
5 Parental language ideologies and children's language use in Singapore – raising speakers of "Standard" English? —— 83

Part II: Language acquisition and language learning in multilingual contexts

Zeynep Köylü and Kenan Dikilitaş
6 Syntactic and lexical complexity in CLIL and EFL written production: Evidence for ELF as a WEs paradigm in Turkey —— 111

Sarah Buschfeld and Gerold Schneider
7 Investigating child language acquisition from a joint perspective: A comparison of traditional and new L1 speakers of English —— 133

Giuliana Regnoli and Thorsten Brato
8   Speech rhythm in Cameroon English: A cross-generational study —— 159

Patricia Ronan and Sarah Buschfeld
9   From second to first language: Language shift in Singapore and Ireland —— 177

Part III: Attitudes and identity

Mirjam Schmalz
10   Children's language attitudes in a World Englishes community: A focus on St. Kitts —— 205

Jette G. Hansen Edwards
11   Youth identity as linguistic identity: Political engagement and language acquisition and use in Hong Kong —— 227

Bianca Vowell
12   Varieties of English and Third Culture Kids in Hong Kong —— 255

Philipp Meer
13   Variation and change in the NURSE vowel in Trinidadian English: An apparent-time analysis of adolescent and adult speakers —— 279

Stefan Dollinger, Vanessa Chan, Kate Pasula, and Anthony Maag
14   How linguistically tolerant or insecure are school-aged children? A matched-guise, gamified approach for 6- to 12-year-olds in Canada —— 307

Naashia Mohamed
15   Caught between languages and cultures: Exploring linguistic and cultural identity among Maldivian adolescents —— 335

Part IV: **Summary and discussion**

Simone E. Pfenninger
16 **Conclusion and envoi: Language acquisition at the intersection of sociolinguistics and World Englishes research** —— 361

Index —— 379

Manuela Vida-Mannl, Mirjam Schmalz, and Sarah Buschfeld
1 The current role of children and adolescents in World Englishes research

English is currently the most widely used language around the globe; it is used in a multitude of contexts, by various and diverse speaker groups, and for an increasingly wide scope of purposes. As a result, the English language is not a homogenous entity but various realizations of the language have developed around the globe, some of which have been considered individual (learner) variations while others have been categorized as full-fledged varieties, i.e. indigenous first- and second-language varieties, of English. These varieties have been traditionally described by the relatively young field of World Englishes (WEs). Over the last two decades, the focus in WEs has gradually shifted away from a synchronic interest in classifying and describing the linguistic inventory of static and clearly delimitable varieties of English towards assessing the status, functions, and characteristics of such varieties as result and part of their evolution and development (Schneider 2003, 2007; see also Schreier, Hundt, and Schneider 2020). Consequently, modeling in WEs had to follow suit: after early synchronic models of WEs (e.g. Kachru's 1985 Three Circles Model or Görlach's 1990 Circle of International English[1]) had been used to compare and classify varieties of English, for example into "norm-providing" ENL (English as a native language), "norm-developing" ESL (English as a second language), and "norm-dependent" EFL (English as a foreign language) used in the Inner, Outer, and Expanding Circle, respectively (cf. Kachru 1985; Strang 1970 for the ENL–ESL–EFL division), models such as Mesthrie and Bhatt's (2008) English Language Complex were introduced to reflect the heterogeneity of English around the globe. These more flexible models were indicative of a change in perspective on WEs. While in these subsequent models varieties of English were no longer discussed only as being bound to their geographical location but rather as being based on their functions and uses, i.e. English can serve as a first language (L1), second language (L2),

---

[1] This is the way McArthur (1998: 98) refers to Görlach's model. Since Görlach (1990) does not provide a name for his model, we use the label introduced by McArthur.

Manuela Vida-Mannl, TU Dortmund University, Germany
Mirjam Schmalz, University of Zurich, Switzerland
Sarah Buschfeld, TU Dortmund University, Germany

https://doi.org/10.1515/9783110733723-001

and foreign language for different speaker groups within one country,[2] these new models did not assess the development of these varieties. This changed with what Buschfeld and Kautzsch (2020b) have called the "diachronic turn". In the course of the diachronic turn, WEs research has turned towards assessing and highlighting the interrelation between speaker groups and the identification of "new" speakers with "their" variety of English. By including new speaker groups, i.e. speakers of English in postcolonial contexts as rightful first language users of English, the field of WEs has been complexified and widened in scope while still offering a fruitful field to test sociolinguistically motivated hypotheses. The most widely recognized and accepted model reflecting this turn is Schneider's (2007) Dynamic Model that shows the uniform development of postcolonial varieties of English. To further the scope of the WEs paradigm even more and include non-postcolonial Englishes, Buschfeld and Kautzsch (2017, 2020a, 2020c) introduced the Extra- and Intra-Territorial Forces Model (EIF Model). It builds on the Dynamic Model and expands it in a way so that it can include both postcolonial as well as non-postcolonial varieties of English. In shifting from anecdotal observations in its earliest days to structured investigations of linguistic characteristics and contexts of language use, from static to dynamic perspectives including diachronic dimensions, and, finally, from including postcolonial to including any type of English, the WEs paradigm has enhanced and opened up towards shedding light on the full multiplicity of the English language. Investigating English as a dynamic and evolving concept has offered a new understanding of the nature and role of English around the globe.

Despite this more holistic approach to WEs, three paradigm gaps persist, two of which are based on the strict separation of WEs and the field of Language Acquisition research (Buschfeld 2020b): the integration of research (1) in second and foreign language acquisition and (2) in children's first language acquisition. The need to bridge the gap between WEs and (second) language acquisition research was first highlighted by Sridhar and Sridhar (1986). Only more recently, empirical studies followed suit (cf. e.g. the contributions to Mukherjee and Hundt 2011; Laporte 2012; Percillier 2016). The EIF Model (Buschfeld and Kautzsch 2017) was the first model developed to include all types of English, aiming to close the first paradigm gap.

However, even though they are much more flexible in their approach and assessment of the process of second and foreign language acquisition, current research in WEs still mostly focuses on adults' use of English (see, for example, the makeup of existing ICE corpora). Since children and young adolescents are widely

---

[2] While Kachru has always argued for this reality, his model is often criticized for not reflecting this nation-internal variation of English (Bolton [2006] 2020).

neglected in data collection processes and their language use and attitudes are, consequently, not explicitly included in the most recent models of WEs, the second paradigm gap has yet to be addressed. First language acquisition processes observed in children and adolescents as well as the conceptual changes these might create for the English language, i.e. the development from a postcolonial L2 variety into an L1 variety, have only been taken up and discussed occasionally and very recently as part of the WEs paradigm (cf. Buschfeld 2020a, 2020b). Traditionally, studies in the field of first language acquisition focus on western, mainly monolingual societies, in which children acquire the sociolinguistic norms of their community usually from their parents before peer influence takes over and teenagers dissociate themselves from their elders (cf. Sharma 2017: 234 on the "peers over parents" principle). That this assumption may not necessarily be true for children growing up in a different context has been shown by several studies on a British-Asian context (cf. e.g. Alam and Stuart-Smith 2011; Sharma 2011, 2017). Consequently, the need for a joint approach of WEs and Language Acquisition theory to fully understand and adequately represent current English(es) and the rapidly emerging generations of new L1 English speakers becomes increasingly clear (see Buschfeld 2020a for an argument based on the context of Singapore).

A further paradigm gap can be identified between WEs, the field of Language Acquisition, and sociolinguistics. While traditional sociolinguistic theory is concerned with reflecting the reality of language variation and change, its core generalizations and principles have predominantly been developed based on immobile, monolingual, English-speaking communities located in the global north (cf. Sharma 2017). The robustness of these principles and generalizations is put to the test by WEs scholars who apply them to English in multilingual, multicultural, and heterogeneous contexts in the global south (e.g. Bolton 2020; D'Arcy 2020). Even more so, sociolinguistically informed studies of first and second language acquisition constitute a rather recent development. The acquisition of structured variation and community norms (e.g. Foulkes, Docherty, and Watt 1999; Smith and Durham 2019; Snell 2008) and second dialect acquisition (e.g. Tagliamonte and Molfender 2007; see Siegel 2010: 23–37 for an overview) has so far almost exclusively looked at L1 varieties. Sociolinguistically motivated studies of L2 WEs communities are rare (for some exceptions, see Beckford Wassink 1999; Lacoste 2012; Youssef 1991a, 1991b, 1991c, 1993, 2005). However, a sociolinguistically informed look into children's and adolescent's language perception, production, and acquisition in different contexts is needed to broaden our understanding of current changes in WEs.

The volume at hand is the first of its kind and addresses the paradigm gaps we introduced above. To close these gaps and to understand the pivotal role children and young adolescents play in the diffusion of innovative linguistic variants in language and dialect contact situations (e.g. Kerswill and Williams 2000; Trudgill 1986), research must consider a joint and more flexible treatment of variety types (e.g. native, second, and learner Englishes) and a stronger integration of other linguistic subdisciplines. The volume at hand takes new research avenues to understand how current changes in WEs proceed: It brings together sociolinguistically informed studies of L1- and L2-Englishes in WEs contexts and focuses on their acquisition and use by children and adolescents, adding valuable insights and therefore going beyond the traditional focus and knowledge in both language acquisition research and sociolinguistics. The diversity of the contributions may offer a first impression of the extent of language use and acquisition contexts that have not yet been investigated. The contributions include topics such as first and second language acquisition, sociolinguistic variation and awareness, language use and choice, governmental and family language policies, language attitudes and perceptions, modeling children's and adolescents' language in WEs, and the role of child language acquisition in processes of language change. Drawing on psycholinguistic, corpus-linguistic, ethnographic, and sociolinguistic methods, the volume includes various qualitative and quantitative methodological approaches to eliciting spoken and written language data from children and adolescents in a variety of WEs communities around the globe. Geographical settings included in the volume range from Trinidad and St. Kitts to the USA, Cameroon, Ireland, the Maldives, Hong Kong, and Singapore. Despite their diversity, all contributions to the volume address the theoretical implications of a joint approach towards WEs, sociolinguistics, and language acquisition and/or identify best-practice methods for collecting and analyzing children's and/or adolescents' linguistic data. Together, this volume and each of its contributions show why a joint approach is fruitful and how it can contribute to a better and deeper understanding of the different research paradigms and the reality of language use and acquisition in WEs contexts.

The first part of this volume focuses on language use in the family. It includes several contexts of the global south, i.e. Malaysia, Singapore, Thailand, and Trinidad. In Chapter 2, Wilson explores "Language among Trinidadian-heritage children raised in diaspora," focusing on the linguistic characteristics of English used by five Trinidadian-heritage children (aged 4–9) in the USA. She investigates if characteristic features of Trinidadian English or Creole can be found in these American-born, second-generation immigrants' use of English. She finds a tendency towards Standard American English in the phonological and lexical aspects of her participants' speech.

Ong and Ting, in Chapter 3, introduce "Language use patterns and strategies for children's English language development," focusing on children's language choice and maternal strategies to enhance the acquisition of English in their bilingual children of Chinese ethnicity in Malaysia. Based on parental questionnaires, the authors find that the societal and global importance of the English language has led the mothers to include it into their home language use. This, consequently, has facilitated English to become the language of choice of children in Malaysia in many domains.

The global role of English and its effect on family language politics is also in focus in Chapter 4. Jocuns and Jocuns' study "Family language policies in Thailand: Multiliteracy practices and Global Englishes" focuses on five families in Thailand, who state to have introduced English as one of their home languages to make its acquisition more natural for their children. Furthermore, the authors find that translanguaging and the use of a local variety of English are accepted practices and conclude that the standard language ideology is less strongly followed than expected.

Examining governmental language policy and parental language ideologies in Singapore in Chapter 5, Vida-Mannl shows that the reality of children's language use diverges from their parents' preferences. When investigating "Parental language ideologies and children's language in Singapore – raising speakers of 'Standard' English?," she finds that, while parents state that their children would use Standard Singapore English predominantly, the children use a considerable amount of Colloquial Singapore English characteristics in their speech.

Part two of the volume presents studies on language acquisition and language learning in multilingual contexts across continents and cultures. In Chapter 6, Köylü and Dikilitaş study "Syntactic and lexical complexity in CLIL and EFL written production" in Turkey using a timed written production task. Their study aims to investigate the effects of CLIL (Content and Language Integrated Learning) on written L2 development and compare them to the linguistic outcomes in an English as a Foreign Language high school classroom in which an integrated skills approach is implemented. The results show that the quantitative analysis has not revealed any significant effects of learning context, except for an increase in the range of lexical diversity, while the qualitative analysis has revealed English as a Lingua Franca (ELF) compatible lexical frequency profiles and syntactic and word-level characteristics typical of ELF as a WEs variety.

In Chapter 7, Buschfeld and Schneider investigate "child language acquisition from a joint perspective" and compare "traditional and new L1 speakers of English". To that end, they study past tense realization patterns in four groups, i.e. simultaneous bilingual English-Chinese children in Singapore, in Hong Kong, and in the US, and monolingual children who acquire English in the US. Their findings suggest that important differences indeed exist between past tense marking between the different groups, depending on the children's acquisitional background and the linguistic input they receive in their immediate social environment.

Zooming in on the African continent, Regnoli and Brato investigate "Speech rhythm in Cameroon English". To contribute to the existing paradigm gap, they analyze patterns of rhythmic variation among pre-adolescents and their parents, drawing on conversational data collected by means of different elicitation methods. Their results have revealed a more syllable-timed speech rhythm for the children than for their parents, which is interpreted as evidence for the children's accommodation towards an L2 speech rhythm, i.e. an adaptation of their English speech rhythm towards the syllable-timed speech rhythm of their L2, French.

In the final chapter of Part 2 of the volume, Ronan and Buschfeld compare "Language shift in Singapore and Ireland" from L2 to L1 English-speaking nations. Even though the motives and driving forces for such a shift differ substantially between the two countries and they are currently at different stages of this shift, both analyses show differences in frequency between the child and adult data investigated and, therefore, suggest that children have indeed played an important role in further rooting the contact language characteristics as widely used characteristics of Irish and Singapore English.

The third part of the volume focuses on attitudes and identities in various communities in Hong Kong, the Maldives, Trinidad, St. Kitts, and Canada. In Chapter 10, Schmalz investigates language attitudes of children in St. Kitts in the eastern Caribbean towards different local and non-local varieties of English. In her study "Children's language attitudes in a World Englishes community," the results point at strong favoritism of exonormative varieties from the US and England in formal contexts. However, a change amongst the children in the participant group to more positive attitudes towards endonormative varieties, such as Kittitian English or Jamaican English can be detected.

In Chapter 11, Hansen Edwards studies "Youth identity as linguistic identity" in Hong Kong, based on attitudinal data of a large-scale longitudinal study. In Hong Kong, a place where language is highly politicized, the author investigates the connection of social movements on youth language acquisition and language use. Hansen Edwards finds considerable changes since 2014, such as a significant increase in the perception of Hong Kong English as an English variety in its own right and thereby shows that studies on language acquisition in multilingual contexts have to take sociocultural and sociopolitical circumstances into account.

In Chapter 12, staying with the topic of Hong Kong, Vowell focuses on "Varieties of English and Third Culture Kids in Hong Kong". Third Culture Kids (TCKs) are children of expats, who live outside of the culture of their parents as well as of the host culture. This community, created by globalization, is characterized by its high degree of variability and short-livedness. The paper presents a close-up analysis of a number of lexical features as well as various phonological analyses (e.g. vowel qualities and rhoticity) of seven TCKs with parents from New Zealand

and England. Vowell finds a high degree of variation in the children's speech, which illustrates the high levels of variability in the feature pool of the individual members of this community.

In Chapter 13, Meer focuses on the "Variation and change in the NURSE vowel in Trinidadian English" of 65 secondary school students and 35 teachers. He finds that NURSE-rhoticization is led by younger speakers associated with prestige schools. Moreover, he finds a multi-layered pattern of change that goes beyond a pure assimilation to an AmE norm. These results illustrate the complexity of sound changes in WEs contexts and that binary distinctions such as endo- or exonormative orientations do not always apply in WEs contexts.

In Chapter 14, Dollinger, Chan, Pasula, and Maag investigate the question "How linguistically tolerant or insecure are school-aged children?" in Canada. The accents presented in the gamified matched-guise experiment, which the authors conducted in 2021, were Cantonese, Mandarin, Finnish, and (East) Indian. The authors find that in their participant group, eight- to nine-year-olds are the least tolerant of all age groups tested when it comes to the rating of the accents in question on their friendliness, easiness of understanding, interstingness, cuteness, smartness, and correctness. Seven-year-olds, on the other hand, exhibit the highest degree of linguistic tolerance. These findings illustrate the different stages of the acquisition of attitudes.

Rounding off part three of the edited volume, Mohamed explores the "linguistic and cultural identity among Maldivian adolescents" in Chapter 15. Based on a mixed-methods study, Mohamed finds differing associations connected with English and Dhivehi, two of the different languages present in the community. In her findings, English is frequently associated with progress and global economic possibilities and occupies a more prominent position than Dhivehi in various language domains.

In the final chapter of the volume, Pfenninger brings together the various contributions and offers a synopsis and discussion of their main findings. In particular, she points out how the contributions in this volume represent and make use of current developments in the fields of second language acquisition and WEs and, thus, help further our understanding of how different speaker groups in various contexts around the world use and acquire English. With reference to the complex dynamic system theory (see e.g. Larsen-Freeman and Cameron 2008), she shows how the various chapters unveil the dynamic – and often bi-directional – interactions between the variables that influence language acquisition. In particular, Pfenninger points towards the necessity of considering the social and physical contexts of language acquisition and use to comprehensively understand (longitudinal) language development. Language acquisition is rarely linear and its understanding calls for inter- and transdisciplinary research and broadened horizons. With this volume we take a first step in this direction.

References

Alam, Farhana & Jane Stuart-Smith. 2011. Identity and ethnicity in /t/ in Glasgow-Pakistani high-school girls. In Proceedings of the 17th International Congress of Phonetics Sciences (ICPhS), 216–219. Hong Kong.

Beckford Wassink, Alicia. 1999. Historic low prestige and seeds of change: Attitudes toward Jamaican Creole. *Language in Society* 28 (1). 57–92.

Bolton, Kingsley. 2020 [2006]. World Englishes: Current debates and future directions. In Cecil L. Nelson, Zoya G. Proshina & Daniel R. Davis (eds.), *The handbook of World Englishes*, 2nd edn., 743–760. Hoboken, NJ: Wiley-Blackwell.

Buschfeld, Sarah. 2020a. *Children's English in Singapore: Acquisition, properties, and use*. New York: Routledge.

Buschfeld, Sarah. 2020b. Language acquisition and World Englishes. In Daniel Schreier, Marianne Hundt & Edgar W. Schneider (eds.), *Cambridge handbook of World Englishes*, 559–584. Cambridge: Cambridge University Press.

Buschfeld, Sarah & Alexander Kautzsch. 2017. Towards an integrated approach to postcolonial and non-postcolonial Englishes. *World Englishes* 36 (1). 104–126.

Buschfeld, Sarah & Alexander Kautzsch. 2020a. Introduction. In Sarah Buschfeld & Alexander Kautzsch (eds.), *Modelling World Englishes: A joint approach to postcolonial and non-postcolonial varieties*, 1–15. Edinburgh: Edinburgh University Press.

Buschfeld, Sarah & Alexander Kautzsch. 2020b. Theoretical models of English as a world language. In Daniel Schreier, Marianne Hundt & Edgar W. Schneider (eds.), *Cambridge handbook of World Englishes*, 51–71. Cambridge: Cambridge University Press.

Buschfeld, Sarah & Alexander Kautzsch (eds.). 2020c. *Modelling World Englishes: A joint approach to postcolonial and non-postcolonial varieties*. Edinburgh: Edinburgh University Press.

D'Arcy, Alexandra. 2020. The relevance of World Englishes for variationist sociolinguistics. In Daniel Schreier, Marianne Hundt & Edgar W. Schneider (eds.), *Cambridge handbook of World Englishes*, 436–458. Cambridge: Cambridge University Press.

Foulkes, Paul, Gerard Docherty & Dominic Watt. 1999. Tracking the emergence of sociophonetic variation. In Proceedings of the 14th International Congress of Phonetic Sciences, 1625–1628. San Francisco.

Görlach, Manfred. 1990. The development of Standard Englishes. In Manfred Görlach (ed.), *Studies in the history of the English language*, 9–64. Heidelberg: Carl Winter.

ICE 2016. International corpus of English. www.ice-corpora.uzh.ch/en.html (accessed 22 November 2021).

Kachru, Braj B. 1985. Standards, codification and sociolinguistic realism: The English language in the Outer Circle. In Randolph Quirk & Henry G. Widdowson (eds.), *English in the world: Teaching and learning the language and literatures*, 11–30. Cambridge: Cambridge University Press for The British Council.

Kerswill, Paul & Ann Williams. 2000. Creating a New Town koine: Children and language change in Milton Keynes. *Language in Society* 29 (1). 65–115.

Lacoste, Véronique. 2012. *Phonological variation in rural Jamaican schools*. Amsterdam: John Benjamins.

Laporte, Samantha. 2012. Mind the gap!: Bridge between World Englishes and Learner Englishes in the making. *English Text Construction* 5 (2). 264–291.

Larsen-Freeman, Diane & Lynne Cameron. 2008. Research methodology on language development from a complex systems perspective. *The Modern Language Journal* 92 (2). 200–213.

McArthur, Tom. 1998. *The English languages*. Cambridge: Cambridge University Press.

Mesthrie, Rajend & Rakesh M. Bhatt. 2008. *World Englishes. The study of new linguistic varieties*. Cambridge: Cambridge University Press.

Mukherjee, Joybrato & Marianne Hundt (eds.). 2011. *Exploring second-language varieties of English and learner Englishes: Bridging a paradigm gap*. Amsterdam: John Benjamins.

Percillier, Michael. 2016. *World Englishes and second language acquisition: Insights from Southeast Asian Englishes*. Amsterdam: John Benjamins.

Schneider, Edgar W. 2003. The dynamics of New Englishes: From identity construction to dialect birth. *Language* 79 (2). 233–281.

Schneider, Edgar W. 2007. *Postcolonial English: Varieties around the world*. Cambridge: Cambridge University Press.

Schreier, Daniel, Marianne Hundt & Edgar W. Schneider. 2020. World Englishes: An Introduction. In Daniel Schreier, Marianne Hundt & Edgar W. Schneider (eds.), *Cambridge handbook of World Englishes*, 1–21. Cambridge: Cambridge University Press.

Sharma, Devyani. 2011. Style repertoire and social change in British Asian English. *Journal of Sociolinguistics* 15 (4). 464–492.

Sharma, Devyani. 2017. World Englishes and sociolinguistic theory. In Markku Filppula, Juhani Klemola & Devyani Sharma (eds.), *The Oxford handbook of World Englishes*, 232–251. Oxford: Oxford University Press.

Siegel, Jeff. 2010. *Second dialect acquisition*. Cambridge: Cambridge University Press.

Smith, Jennifer & Mercedes Durham. 2019. *Sociolinguistic variation in children's language: Acquiring community norms*. Cambridge: Cambridge University Press.

Snell, Julia. 2008. *Pronouns, dialect and discourse: A socio-pragmatic account of children's language in Teeside*. Leeds: University of Leeds dissertation.

Sridhar, Kamal K. & Shikaripur N. Sridhar. 1986. Bridging the paradigm gap: Second language acquisition theory and indigenized varieties of English. *World Englishes* 5 (1). 3–14.

Strang, Barbara M. H. 1970. *A history of English*. London: Methuen.

Tagliamonte, Sali A. & Sonja Molfenter. 2007. How'd you get that accent?: Acquiring a second dialect of the same language. *Language in Society* 36 (5). 649–675.

Trudgill, Peter. 1986. *Dialects in contact*. Oxford: Blackwell.

Youssef, Valerie. 1991a. 'Can I put – I want a slippers to put on': young children's development of request forms in a code-switching environment. *Journal of Child Language* 18 (3). 609–624.

Youssef, Valerie. 1991b. The acquisition of varilingual competence. *English World-Wide* 12 (1). 87–102.

Youssef, Valerie. 1991c. Variation as a feature of language acquisition in the Trinidad context. *Language Variation and Change* 3 (1). 75–101.

Youssef, Valerie. 1993. Children's linguistic choices: Audience design and societal norms. *Language in Society* 22 (2). 257–274.

Youssef, Valerie. 2005. 'May I have the bilna?': The development of face-saving in young Trinidadian children. In Susanne Mühleisen & Bettina Migge (eds.), *Politeness and face in Caribbean Creoles*, 227–254. Amsterdam: John Benjamin.

Part I: **Language in the family**

Guyanne Wilson
2 Language among Trinidadian-heritage children raised in diaspora

Abstract: Previous work on language use in Caribbean diaspora communities has focussed on language use by teenagers (Sebba [1993] 2013) and adults (Hinrichs 2014), but little attention has been paid to the language of children with Caribbean parentage raised outside the region, particularly in their pre-adolescent years. This chapter is an attempt to fill this gap by documenting the language use of five pre-adolescent children with Trinidadian parentage being raised in the United States. Using data collected via a series of interviews and elicitation tasks, the chapter examines the children's knowledge of Trinidadian English lexical items as well as Trinidadian English phonological patterns in their speech. In contexts where Trinidadian English and Standard American English differ from each other phonologically, the children employ Standard American English pronunciation, except in the case of lexical items which are specific to Trinidadian English. Moreover, the children show low awareness of Trinidadian English lexical items. Nevertheless, sounding Trinidadian and having knowledge of Trinidadian English vocabulary is important to the children and their parents, and is a key aspect of their identity as Trinidadians living in the United States.

Keywords: Trinidadian English/Creole, children's language in diaspora, dialect maintenance and shift, identity

1 Introduction

Although there have been sizable populations of immigrants from the English-speaking Caribbean in the United States since 1965 (Tsuji 2011: 2147), studies on language use in Caribbean diaspora communities continue to focus on the United Kingdom (UK), especially London (Sebba [1993] 2013), and Canada (Hinrichs 2014). However, Caribbean immigrant communities in New York and Florida, where the largest Caribbean immigrant populations reside (Tsuji 2011: 2148), have not been studied. This is despite the cultural impact that Caribbean immigrants have had in these communities, not least through events such as Miami Carnival and Brooklyn Caribbean Literary Festival, which can be taken as evidence of an en-

---

Guyanne Wilson, University College London, UK

https://doi.org/10.1515/9783110733723-002

during community which possibly uses language as another means of retaining their identity.

The current paper is a first attempt to systematically study the language of Caribbean immigrants in the United States. It focuses not on first generation immigrants but on their American-born children and the language practices of this group. The principal research question directing the current study is: What features of Trinidadian English/Creole are present in the speech of Trinidadian-heritage children raised in the United States? Specifically, this paper will look at the children's use and awareness of selected Trinidadian and Standard American English phonological features and lexical items and attempt to make connections between these and their Trinidadian/American identity. Thus, this paper contributes to discussions of children's language in diaspora.

The paper proceeds as follows: in the Section 2, previous work on language in immigrant communities, with a special focus on language in the Caribbean diaspora, is discussed, and the features of Trinidadian and American Englishes are compared. After this, the modified sociolinguistic interview used in this study is presented, and readers are introduced to the children whose language is the focus of the current study. This is followed by a presentation of the phonetic and lexical features of the children's language, and a discussion of what these results tell us about the studying World Englishes in diaspora.

2 Background

2.1 Language acquisition and migration

Among immigrant populations in the United States of America (USA), the focus of studies on language maintenance or shift has focused upon how heritage languages are replaced by English, often in the course of one generation (Fishman 2014). With regard to accents and dialects of English, however, little research has been undertaken, and Labov (2008: 317) notes that there is a dearth of research focussing on the question of how young children of second language English speakers do not acquire the accents of their parents in the USA. However, there has been some research undertaken in this vein in the UK, involving children whose parents speak English as either a first or subsequent language. In Milton Keynes, for example, Kerswill and Williams (2000) find that four-year-old children's speech more closely resembles that of their primary caregivers than the speech of eight- or twelve-year-olds, whose speech is more similar to that of their peers and the community. Indeed, the importance of caregiver speech in early language acquisition is well documented, but so is the fact that in the process of language acquisition, children neither completely copy nor completely reject the variation patterns that their parents use (Hazen 2002: 511), and this is particularly true of children whose families settle in a dialect area different from that of their parents. However, even though children's speech does not always resemble that of their parents, and parents may be able to identify differences in their child's speech, children perceive their parents as sounding the same as they do (Hazen and Hall 1999 in Hazen 2002).

Furthermore, while it was previously believed that second generation and subsequent immigrants completely lost the accent features that defined their parents' English (e.g. Chambers 2002; Labov 2008), Sharma and Sankaran (2011) show that this is not necessarily the case. In their study on the language of Indian English speakers in London, the pair finds that older second-generation speakers exhibited bidialectalism in Indian English and in London English, though they more frequently employed London English features since Indian English features are stigmatised in the community. Younger second-generation speakers, however, are not bidialectal, and instead used a select repertoire of Indian English features stylistically and as part of their British Asian identity. Sharma and Sankaran's (2011) study thus highlights the importance of identity in the acquisition process, since bidialectalism develops with age.

If we shift our attention to Caribbean immigrant communities, Sebba's (2013) landmark study on London Jamaican looks at how Caribbean Creoles change across generations. With a distinct focus on the second generation, i.e., British-born people of Caribbean descent, Sebba notes that this generation speaks British English and so do not use Creole for communicative purposes. Instead, building on previous work by Hewitt (1986), who found that primary-school aged children make less use of Creole than their teenaged counterparts, Sebba argues that adolescents use Creole as an identity marker. Within families, Sebba notes that Creole is spoken among members of the first generation to one another and to members of the second generation, their children, who do not necessarily use the variety with each other or peers. Thus, Mair (2003: 234) claims that the "variation of type found in the Caribbean will not survive an immigrant generation" in London.

Beyond Great Britain, Hinrichs (2014) studies the Jamaican diaspora in Canada. He shows that Jamaican Creole in Toronto, despite the large population of speakers, has not gained the stronghold and influence that the variety enjoys in London. This is seen in the speech of four adult speakers, who, although they are rooted in the Toronto Jamaican community and are committed to the promotion of Jamaican culture in the city, often adopt Canadian English pronunciations of vowels, especially in the TRAP and MOUTH lexical sets, though they do use Jamaican Creole FACE vowels.

In the United States, studies of language among Caribbean immigrants are usually limited to possible problems arising due to language issues in education (e.g. Nero 2006; Winer 2006; Winer and Jack 1997) or in healthcare encounters (Winer and Jack 1997). Within this field, Winer and Jack (1997) note that different generations of speakers within the same family may have access to and proficiency in different varieties of English and Creole, and they note that Caribbean Creoles cannot only be heard in New York City but can also be seen and read, particularly in newspapers and menus in restaurants owned by people of Caribbean heritage. With specific reference to immigrants from Trinidad, Carlin (2006), in a series of qualitative interviews, notes that her Trinidadian-born, Maryland-based participants view language as an important element of their identity that connects them to Trinidadian culture. However, she does not discuss any specific linguistic elements.

This overview thus shows that much work still needs to be done on language in the Caribbean diaspora, specifically Trinidadians in the USA.

2.2 Differences between Trinidadian and American Englishes

In Trinidad and Tobago, a local variety of Standard English is spoken alongside an English-lexicon Creole. In reality, the differences between the two varieties are not clear cut, which has led to some researchers preferring to use the term Trinidad English/Creole (TE/C) to encompass all of the varieties (e.g. Winer 2009). Since the aim of this study is to investigate whether children of Trinidadian parentage display any features of Trinidadian speech in their own speech, the distinctions between Trinidadian Standard English and Creole are not the main focus, and therefore the term TE/C will be used here as well. In the USA, too, there are several varieties of English, and the children whose language will be studied here reside in New Jersey, California, and Virginia. Because, or perhaps in spite of their different places of residence, Standard American English (AmE) will be used as the basis for comparison. It is possible to view potential speakers of these varieties together because New Jersey and Virginia both belong to the Mid-Atlantic dialect region of the United States (Labov, Ash, and Boberg 2008), and this region shares many features with the West dialect region, to which California belongs. These features include, for instance, the retention of distinct vowels in the DRESS and KIT lexical sets and as well as merger of the NORTH and CURE lexical sets (Labov, Ash, and Boberg 2008: 52). Of course, there are differences between these dialect regions. Notably, the low back merger is a feature of the West dialect but not a feature of the Mid-Atlantic. However, this study is not concerned with the low back merger. Critically, however, these varieties share a number of features with Standard American English (AmE), and in terms of the phonological and lexical features which form the focus of this study, the three varieties overlap considerably.

2.2.1 Phonetic and phonological differences

AmE TE/C and AmE differ systematically from each other on all levels of the linguistic system, though this overview focuses on selected phonological and lexical features only. The main consonantal differences between TE/C and AmE involve the realisation of /ɹ/, dental fricatives, and /t/. TE/C is generally regarded a non-rhotic variety (Youssef and James 2008: 330), though recent work by Carrington (2018) suggests that there is increasing semi-rhoticity among university students, and Barclay (2017: 32) found that upper-class seven- and eight-year-olds in an elite private primary school use "r colouring of the open-mid central unrounded vowel [i.e. the NURSE vowel] where all informants rhotacised this vowel in every instance except for one informant in the word 'third'". AmE, however, is consistently rhotic (Schneider 2020: 84), so that a word such as *car* is realised as [kɑː] or [kaː] in TE/C but as [kɑːɹ] in AmE. With regard to dental fricatives, both /θ/ and /ð/ may be stopped in TE/C, so that *thin* and *then* may be realised as [tɪn] and [dɛn]. This is not a feature of AmE, though it may occur in some contexts in African American English (Thomas 2007: 453), with which the participants in this study may have contact. Finally, in AmE, "intervocalic *t* is most often realised as a tap or flap, frequently with voicing" (Kretzschmar 2008: 48). Thus, the medial sound in words like *water* are likely to be pronounced as [ɾ]. This does not occur in TE/C, where it is realised as [t].

The vowel inventories of TE/C and AmE are markedly different. In this paper, I focus only on the TRAP, NEAR, SQUARE, GOAT, FACE, MOUTH, and LETTER lexical sets, though there are differences to be found in other lexical sets as well. Table 2.1 captures the differences in pronunciation for the lexical sets under examination.

TE/C and AmE differ from each other not only at the segmental level but also at the suprasegmental level. TE/C has a lexical stress system with "intonationally marked prominences," meaning that fundamental frequency "aligned with prominent syllables is not contrastive" (Gooden and Drayton 2017: 422). Moreover, the "main stress in TrE [Trinidadian English] falls on the leftmost or only syllable in a word with closed syllables, with syllables containing a long vowel or diphthong having metrical weight" (Ferreira and Drayton 2015: 27). With regard to stressed and unstressed syllables, differences in stress are marked by vowel duration, with stressed syllables having significantly longer durations that unstressed syllables,

Table 2.1: Realisation of lexical sets in TE/C and AmE (based on Youssef and James 2008: 328; Kretschmar 2008: 44).

Lexical Set	TE/C	AmE
TRAP	/a/	/æ/
NEAR	/ɛː/	/iɚ/, /ɪɚ/
SQUARE	/ɛː/	/ɛɚ/
FACE	/eː/	/eɪ/
GOAT	/oː/	/oʊ/
MOUTH	/ɔʊ/	/aʊ/
LETTER	/ə/, /ʌ/	/ɚ/

but the difference in intensity between the two stressed and unstressed syllables is not significant (Gooden and Drayton 2017: 424).

2.2.2 Lexical differences

TE/C is an English-lexicon creole, whose basic English vocabulary is derived from British English (BrE) due to the country's colonial past (Winer 1993). More recent work, however, has found that Trinidadian newspaper writing makes use of more AmE than BrE word types, although there are overall more BrE (53%) than AmE (47%) tokens (Hänsel and Deuber 2013: 342). In terms of register, Wilson (2023) found that while there is a clear preference for American variants in spoken language, corpus results suggest that in written language the balance is more equal. Furthermore, in a survey study of Trinidadian respondents, Wilson (2023) found that American variants were overwhelmingly preferred over British variants, though this differs depending on the lexical item. In addition to this, TE/C contains a sizable vocabulary drawn from the indigenous languages of the early Taino and Arawak settlers, or else from the (forced) migrations of people from the African continent, India, Portugal, Spain, the Middle East, and France, some of which may refer to referents which are unique to Trinidad, such as *doubles*.[1]

---

[1] Doubles, n. two "flat round flat fried bread made with urdee dal" (Winer 2009: 53) with a curried chick pea filling. It is an extremely popular street food (Winer 2009: 309).

3 Data and method

3.1 The ethics of interviewing children

In order to interview the children, their parents were approached and asked whether they might be interested in having their child participate. An invitation was placed in the Facebook group "Expats from Trinidad and Tobago," inviting parents of young children to join another group, "Trini parents with children in foreign countries". Parents from the Trinidadian diaspora in the United States, United Kingdom, the Netherlands, Canada, Australia, and New Zealand responded to the call and, though children from each of the above-mentioned locations were interviewed, this paper focuses only on those living in the United States. Parents were briefed on the purposes of the research and asked to give explicit permission, in writing, for their child or children to participate. They were also given a background information form which gathered basic information about the children and the families' language practices. Parents were asked to explain to their children what they were being asked to do in advance of the meeting.

Kortesluoma, Hentinen, and Nikkonen (2003: 437) advocate for children being told clearly what they are being asked to do and being allowed to choose whether they would like to participate. Thus, at the start of each interview, each child was briefed on what they were being asked to do and was asked if they still wanted to participate. The children responded enthusiastically and generally enjoyed the interviews. To ensure child safety, pseudonyms are used both for parents and children.

3.2 The participants

The current paper is part of a larger study on children's language in diaspora. The data in this paper represents the language of five children residing in the USA: three girls and two boys. Given the strong links established between children's language and the language of their primary caregiver, the main criteria used in selecting the children was that their primary caregiver was from Trinidad; for three children, the primary caregiver was their mother, and for another two children, siblings, their father (though their mother came from the neighbouring island of Grenada). The Trinidadian parent should have lived in Trinidad up to their eighteenth birthday and migrated to the USA in the first instance to pursue tertiary-level education before settling there permanently either immediately after graduation or after a brief sojourn in Trinidad. Table 2.2 contains a summary of the children, giving their ages and socioeconomic information about their parents.

Table 2.2: Child participants and their parents.

Child's name	Child's age	US state of residence	Parental information	Other important childcare notes
Amy	6	Virginia	Tamara (mother, primary, BSc) David (father, military, African-American)	
Isabel	8	New Jersey	Marcus (father, primary, MD) Helen (mother, MD, from Grenada, also present at interview)	Maternal and paternal grandmothers visit regularly from the Caribbean for long periods
Luke	4	New Jersey	As for Isabel (siblings)	As for Isabel (siblings)
Maggie	9	California	Jessica (mother, primary, MSc) George (father, BArch, also from Trinidad)	
Jonathon	7	California	As for Maggie (siblings)	

All the children who participated in the study had contact with Trinidad and TE/C via regular contact with grandparents via phone or video chatting technologies, regular visits from grandparents or other relatives to the USA, and frequent visits to Trinidad with their parents. All parents reported exposing the children to Trinidadian media either through children's storybooks, particularly for pre-schooled aged children, and encouraging them to view videos and streamed events from Trinidad, particularly around Carnival time.

3.3 The interview process

Research on stylistic variation rooted in the Labovian notion of attention to speech has traditionally relied on a battery of tests that elicit different speech styles, i.e. the minimal pair task, the wordlist task, and reading passage (Labov 1972). However, these methods rely on literacy, a feature that has been criticised previously for possibly contributing to participant discomfort (see Schilling 2013: 109). This criticism is particularly true of children, particularly young children, who are only just acquiring literacy. Nevertheless, such stylistic elicitation methods have the potential to yield a substantial amount of data on a variety of speech styles by an individual speaker in a relatively short period of time. Moreover, the minimal pair and wordlist tasks ensure that tokens of key phonetic features are obtained, which is not guaranteed in recordings of free speech.

The current study therefore used a series of modified elicitation tasks. First, the minimal pair and wordlist tasks were merged into a single, picture-based wordlist task. This was divided into three parts. In the first part, children were shown pictures of common objects which had the same name in both TE/C and AmE and asked to name what they saw. This part of the task was designed to elicit specific phonetic features of TE/C and AmE. The task was presented to the children in the form of a PowerPoint presentation. After they named the item, the children were shown the next slide on the PowerPoint using the formula, "And this one?" to introduce each slide.

The aim of the second part of the task was to see whether the children were aware of and actively employed TE/C lexical variants in naming items. Children were shown pictures of objects which had different names in TE/C and AmE or were unique to Trinidad. They were asked to name the objects and then asked if they had ever heard a word different from the one they had given. For example, when shown a picture of an avocado, the children could say *avocado* or the TE/C allonym, *zaboca*.

In the third part of the modified wordlist task, children were shown pictures of people engaging in different activities and asked to describe what was happening. As in the second part, this part of the interview was designed to see if children produced TE/C items or AmE items. Whereas in the naming parts of the task, children were expected to produce one-word utterances, the pictures of people engaging in different activities were meant to trigger utterances of at least three words, e.g., "They are playing football". The target words in parts two and three could be divided into two categories:

1) referents for which TE/C and AmE have different words (AmE in brackets). Nominal referents were *football* (*soccer*), *zaboca* (*avocado*), and *soft drink/ sweet drink* (*soda, pop*). Verbal referents for which TE/C and AmE have different words, such as *liming* (*hanging out/ relaxing*) and *boufing* (*yelling, reprimanding*).
2) referents which are unique to Trinidadian culture and have no AmE equivalent. These were largely food items, such as *doubles* and *callaloo*, but also extended to include cultural events like *cricket* and *Carnival/playing mas*. Arguably, Carnival could be equated with New Orleans' Mardi Gras celebrations or with events like Miami Carnival or Labour Day celebrations in New York. However, since none of the families lived in Louisiana, and since Miami Carnival and Labour Day are spinoffs of Caribbean carnivals, this is still included in this analytic category. Furthermore, one could argue that *cricket* and *football* are BrE terms, and not strictly TE/C. However, in the context of this study, they were better understood in juxtaposition to TE/C rather than BrE.

In total, the children were shown 30 pictures: 11 for phonetic features, 11 for lexical items, and 9 distractors. However, some of the pictures were unclear, and so this paper presents the results only for the 10 phonetic items and 9 of the lexical items.

In addition to the modified wordlist task, the traditional reading passage task was replaced by two story telling tasks. The first story telling task involved the children re-telling their favourite story. If the children could not think of a story, they were asked to recount the story of "Goldilocks and the Three Bears". In the second task, the children used picture prompts to re-create the story of "Anancy and the Magic Pot".[2] Since each pair of siblings was interviewed together, the two children worked together on the story. I started by asking if they had heard about Anancy, and then telling them that I had found some pictures of an Anancy story but there were no words and so I was trying to figure out what had happened in the story. The children then had to describe what they felt was happening in the story.

The final element of the interview was designed to elicit casual speech. The children were asked questions about themselves, their siblings, and their hobbies. A danger of death question, or a similar stimulus, was not included. This was because without this question, the interviews lasted between 35 and 45 minutes; as the children already grew restless in this timeframe, it was felt that a further question would be too much. This was especially true for the younger children, Luke and Jonathon, who both had to be prodded by their mothers to return to the interview after drifting away. The older children, however, were very talkative, and tended to produce quite a lot of casual speech. Moreover, in sharing about their interests, children often started to tell stories of "something funny" which had happened with their pets, siblings, or parents. In the final part of the interview, I asked the children what they thought about their accents versus those of their parents and other adults they knew. This type of meta-discussion was difficult for the children, and only one child, Maggie (age 9), in the current study could participate meaningfully at this stage.

The use of pictorial stimuli for the wordlist and reading passage task was generally successful in obtaining spoken data. Nevertheless, these adaptations presented new challenges. The first was that, in the wordlist task, one could not be sure that the children would produce the target word based on the picture. For example, when shown a picture of the house, most of the children said *house*. However, one child, Isabel, said *home*. In the future, researchers can circumvent this by including the word alongside the picture. Of course, this would only aid

---

2 Anancy is a folklore character from Africa and the Caribbean.

literate children. Another potential shortcoming of this method was that although asked to say only the word for the first part of the task, the school-aged children, who were probably used to being expected to describe pictures with attention to detail, often stated more than required. When attempts were made to have them list only the word, by moving on to the next picture, one child even requested that I return to the previous picture because they were not yet finished. Because the children's comfort and confidence were tantamount, I allowed children to explain as little or as much as they liked. Thus, the "attention to speech" element that is so critical to the success of sociolinguistic interviews was compromised. At the same time, the children's behaviour suggested that they associated the task with school-related activities, and so were likely to be using the more formal codes associated with speech in education settings.

The interviews took place online using the web conferencing tool Zoom. Parents were asked to be present for the interview since, as I was physically distant from the children, support was needed to keep the children focussed. Because the period of data collection coincided with international closure of school buildings as part of the precautions taken to dampen the spread of the coronavirus disease (COVID-19), the older children were familiar with Zoom and web conferencing. The pictures for the tasks were shared using the share screen option on Zoom.

Where siblings were interviewed, both children[3] were interviewed together on the basis of the advantages of interviewing respondents with members of their peer group reported in previous works (e.g. Labov 1972). However, sibling relationships are slightly different from friendship groups, and so in both cases of sibling interviews, the younger sibling (in both cases the brother), had to be encouraged not to let his older, more garrulous sister dominate the interview.

3.4 Data analysis

The tasks in the interview were designed to elicit tokens of all of the vowel and consonant features listed in Section 2.1, as well as to check the children's knowledge of TE/C lexical items. For the vowel and consonant features, each child's pronunciation of the wordlist items was transcribed using an impressionistic analysis. In addition to these, two tokens of words containing each of the vowel and consonant features produced by the child either during the storytelling phase or the casual conversation were extracted and phonetically transcribed using the IPA. Thus, for each child, three tokens of each feature were transcribed, giving a total of 27 tokens

---

[3] In families with more than two children, only two children were included.

per child. Although an instrumental analysis was possible for both the wordlist and the storytelling/conversation phase, it was not deemed necessary since the children's pronunciations were clear.

For the analysis of lexical items, the children's answers were coded into two categories, depending on the etymology of the word used: AmE and TE/C. Some objects proved to be difficult for the children to identify, or were unfamiliar, and some objects were misidentified.

Although the focus of this study is on the children's language, attention will also be paid to the comments that parents made about their children's language and throughout the interview. Such comments give insights into the role of the primary caregiver's language and identity on the children's language.

4 Results

4.1 Phonological realisations

Table 2.3 contains an overview of the children's productions of each of the target sounds both in the wordlist and casual speech segments of the interview. Results are merged since there was rarely any difference in pronunciation of the variables under consideration. Primary pronunciations (1°) show the first pronunciation the children used. The secondary pronunciations (2°) show alternates the children produced. A slot is marked (-) indicates that the child did not produce any useable tokens either from the wordlist (e.g., because they said another word) or from the casual speech part of the interview. Although the voiced dental fricative was not on the wordlist, the children produced it so often in their casual speech, and indeed more often than the voiceless counterpart, that the tokens were counted. Finally, the NORTH and START lexical sets were used to ascertain whether the children used a rhotic pronunciation outside of NURSE, since this is potentially rhotacized in their parents' speech.

For the variables under consideration, it is clear from Table 2.3 that the children employ the AmE features almost categorically. Specifically, with regard to the consonants, children consistently make use of flap, not only in *water* (the wordlist item), but also in their free speech in words such as *shouting* (Isabel), *bottles* (Maggie), or even across word boundaries, as in *but I* (Jonathon) or *spit it* (Amy). The only exception to the flapping rule is a single token by Isabel, who misidentifies the food item *doubles* as *roti*, which she pronounces as [ɹoti:] and not as [ɹouɾi], which her otherwise consistent use of flap might predict. The use of flap in the children's speech is markedly different from their parents' speech

Table 2.3: Phonetic realisations in children's speech.

	Maggie (9)		Jonathon (7)		Isabel (8)		Luke (4)		Amy (7)	
	1°	2°	1°	2°	1°	2°	1°	2°	1°	2°
TRAP	[æ]	[æ]	[æ]	–	[æ]	[a]	[æ]	[a]	[æ]	[æ]
NEAR	[ɪɚ]	–	[iɹ]	[ɛɚ]	[ɪɚ]	–	[ɪɚ]	–	[ɪɚ]	[ɪəɹ]
SQUARE	[ɛɚ]	[ɛɚ]	[ɛɚ]	[ɛɚ]	[ɛɚ]	[ɛɚ]	[ɛɚ]	[ɛəɹ]	[ɛɚ]	[ɛɚ]
FACE	[eɪ]	[eɪ]	[eɪ]	[eɪ]	[eɪ]	[eɪ]	[eɪ]	[eɪ]	[eɪ]	[eɪ]
GOAT	[oʊ]	[oʊ]	[oʊ]	[oʊ]	[oʊ]	[o]	[oʊ]	[oʊ]	[oʊ]	[o]
MOUTH	[aʊ]	[aʊ]	[aʊ]	[aʊ]	[aʊ]	[ɔʊ]	[aʊ]	[aʊ]	[aʊ]	[aʊ]
LETTER	[ɚ]	[ɚ]	[ɚ]	[ɚ]	[ɚ]	[ɚ]	[ɚ]	[ɚ]	[ɚ]	[ɚ]
NORTH/START	[ɔɹ]	[ɑɹ]	[ɑɹ]	–	[ɔɹ]	[ɑɹ]	[ɔɹ]	[ɔɹ]	[ɔɹ]	[ɑː]
WATER	[ɾ]	[ɾ]	[ɾ]	[ɾ]	[ɾ]	[t]	[ɾ]	[ɾ]	[ɾ]	[ɾ]
[θ]	[θ]	[θ]	[θ]	[θ]	[θ]	–	[θ]	–	[θ]	[θ]
[ð]	[ð]	[ð]	[ð]	[ð]	[ð]	–	[ð]	[d]	[ð]	[ð]

and, when during the interview Luke asks his mother for a drink of water, his parents both begin to laugh at his AmE pronunciation of the word as [wɒɾɚ]. Children also regularly realise dental fricatives as fricatives [θ] and [ð]. Only one child, Luke, ever produces the TE/C feature [d] in a /ð/ context, and then only one token is produced. Finally, children are categorically rhotic in the wordlist task and also consistently make use of rhotic /ɹ/ in their free speech. The only exception to this is Amy, who on one occasion produces *Carnival* as [kɑːnɪvl] though she subsequently produces [kɑɹnɪvəlz].

In their realisation of vowels, too, the children's speech more closely resembles AmE than TE/C. In TRAP contexts, children consistently use [æ], again with the exception of Luke, who produces a token of [a] in [kɹabz]. In the FACE and GOAT lexical sets, the children all use diphthongs, rather than the TE/C monophthongs. There is only one instance on the wordlist in which a child does not use a diphthong in one of these sets, which is when Isabel produces *roti*. In the lexical items task, both Isabel and Amy pronounce tokens of *coconut* as [kokonʌt]. In MOUTH, children consistently produce [aʊ], though Isabel has a single [ɔʊ] token in *girl scout*.

Unlike their parents, and other speakers of TE/C, none of the girls have a NEAR-SQUARE merger, realising words in the two sets with two distinct vowels. Jonathon, however, pronounces the wordlist item *ear* as [ɛɚ] on two occasions. However, in his free speech, he produces *year* as [jiɹ] and *weird* [wɪəɹd].

Finally, in words belonging to LETTER lexical set, such as *paper* and *water*, children use the AmE pattern for first syllable stress followed by an unstressed second syllable.

4.1.1 Exceptions

As seen in 4.1, children consistently used AmE consonant and vowel realisations, except in a few, scattered instances, linked not so much to a particular lexical set but rather a semantic field, notably *Trinidadian food*. Whenever a child uses a TE/C pronunciation, it is in reference to a food item which is part of Trinidadian cuisine: *roti, crab, coconut*.

In her interview, Isabel misidentifies *doubles* as *roti and channa*, which she pronounces [ɹoti ən tʃanə], thus missing three opportunities to use an AmE feature: [oʊ], [ɾ] and [æ] in *chana*, in favour of the TE/C variants. It should also be noted that, in this instance, she uses the TE/C word *chana* (Winer 2009: 190) and not *chickpeas*, as Maggie does. Luke, when shown a picture of Trinidadian dish *crab and callaloo*, identifies the *crab* as [kɹab] rather than [kɹæb], which would be more consistent with his other realisations of words in the TRAP lexical set.

The children's responses for *coconut* are also very telling. Maggie pronounces the word [ˈkəʊkənʌt] and points out that you can get it at the [səˈvænə];[4] although her pronunciation is AmE, she accurately identifies the item and the cultural space in which the activity of buying coconuts takes place. Isabel also immediately identifies coconuts, which she pronounces with a TE/C pronunciation, including syllables in which all vowels are equally stressed, as [kokonʌts]. Unlike the other two girls, Amy misidentifies the picture first as *mangoes* and then refuses to believe that the items are, indeed, coconuts (1), which she first pronounces with the AmE pronunciation. However, when her mother and I convince her that they are coconuts, she modifies her pronunciation towards our TE/C pronunciation, although she retains her flap in *water*.

(1) <Amy><#>*Mango*
   <Tamara><#>*No* <#>*You don't know what that is* <#>[kokʌnʌt]
   <Amy><#>[ˈkoʊkənʌt] <#>*That looks nothing like* [ˈkoʊkənʌt]
   <Tamara><#>*That's the* [kokʌnʌts] *you get water from*
   <Amy><#>[kokənʌt waɾɚ]
   <Tamara><#>*Yeah*
   <Amy><#>*I don't like* [kokənʌt waɾɚ]

---

[4] The Queen's Park Savannah is a large park in Port-of-Spain, Trinidad. It is popular with fitness enthusiasts, but is also regarded as a good location to try local delicacies such as coconut water and snow cones.

One possible explanation for the children's use of TE/C phonetic variants only when producing lexical items associated with Trinidadian food items might be because the only pronunciation model they receive for these words is from their parents, whereas for other words, they also receive AmE inputs in their schools and communities.

4.2 Lexical items

Table 2.4 gives an overview of the children's performance in the tasks that required them to name different items. The first word the children give is always listed first, regardless of whether it was the TE/C variant or AmE variant. The second word, represented in brackets, is the word the children gave if they provided a second option.

Table 2.4: Children's responses to lexical naming task.

	Maggie	Jonathon	Isabel	Luke	Amy
Target word	Given (alternate if given)	Given (alternate if given)	Given (alternate if given)	Given (alternate if given)	Given (alternate if given)
Zaboca	avocado	avocado	avocado	avocado	avocado
Football	soccer (football)	soccer (football)	football (soccer)	football	soccer
American football	football	football	football	football	football
(Cricket) bat	cricket bat	bat	bat	bat	–
Soft drink	soda	soda	drinks juices soda	juices and soda	drinks and stuff, sodas
Boufing	getting told you've done something naughty	getting mad at someone	she is mad at the girl	I think putting her in time-out	the child is frowning because he's in trouble
Doubles	patty with chickpeas –	–	Roti with channa		(doubles)

Table 2.4 (continued)

	Maggie	Jonathon	Isabel	Luke	Amy
Liming	they look like they're relaxing	– – –	sitting down eating	sitting	eating and drinking (lime)
Playing mas'/ Carnival	Carnival	–	Carnival	they're dancing	Carnival

Table 2.4 shows that the children use AmE terms over Trinidadian ones. For items where the TE/C word and the AmE word are different (*zaboca~avocado, football~ soccer, soft-drink~soda*) the children almost always use the AmE variant, and rarely seem to know the TE/C variant. The only exception to this is *football~ soccer*. Isabel and Luke give *football* as their preferred choice in their interview, although Isabel quietly adds "or soccer". When, later in the interview, the children are shown a picture of children playing different games in a park and asked to describe all the activities the children undertake, Luke also answers "playing football". This suggests that for this sibling pair, *football* is the default term, and this is unsurprising. The children's primary caregiver is their father, Markus; for many years he was a stay-at-home parent and often spends time watching the sport with his children. He has enrolled Luke in a local children's football club. Maggie and Jonathon give *soccer* as their default term, but both give *football* as an alternate variant. When asked where they have heard the word *football*, the children reply "grandma and papa," referring to their Trinidadian grandparents, who often visit the children in San Francisco and the children see on their yearly visits to Trinidad. Their mother also reports that the children's grandparents insist on the children calling the sport *football*. Only Amy says *soccer* and claims not to use *football*, saying "oh, but football is a different game" when her mother tells her that people in Trinidad name the sport thus. Amy's mother, however, explains that "before she started school she used to say *football* and *American football*. But now that she's in school and she splits her time between her daddy and here, she started saying more things like what they say in school".

With regard to verbal referents, the children display no familiarity with *boufing*. This could have been due to poor photo quality. However, the children unanimously understood that the child in the picture was being admonished for some misdemeanour, as evidenced by the use of words like *naughty*, *time-out*, and *mad*. For the target word *lime/ liming*, i.e., "an informal gathering characterized by semi-ritualized talking and socializing, drinking and eating" (Winer 2009: 532) only Amy, with considerable help from her mother, eventually produces the target word. Isabel's parents say that she does know the word, but is being shy during the interview.

In the category of lexical items which refer to cultural items, only one child, Maggie, correctly identifies the *cricket bat*, and she and her brother are the only ones who know about the sport. Isabel also identifies it as a bat, but is at first uncertain, and needs her father's extra encouragement ("What does it look like?") to produce an answer, which her brother echoes. Amy seems to have been exposed to the sport before although she has forgotten, as can be seen in (2). When her mother asks her if she remembers, Amy confuses the sport with the polysemous animal.

(2) <Amy><#>*I have no idea*
<GW><#>*Do you know what cricket is?*
<Tamara><#>*Remember what cricket is* <#>*I can't tell you.* <#>*You have to remember*
<Amy><#>*The the uhm the bug the insect*

In contrast, all of the girls correctly identify *Carnival*, though none of them produce the target *playing mas*. For the boys, Jonathon had grown distracted at this point and had wondered off briefly, before being brought back by his mother, and Luke provided the answer *they're dancing*.

The food items are the items best identified by the children. All the children except Luke identify snow cones, pictured in the way they are served in Trinidad, in a Styrofoam cup and served with condensed milk and guava syrup, and both Maggie and Isabel comment on how much they enjoy this treat. At the other extreme, none of the children identify *crab and callaloo*, though Luke is able to name *crab*. However, when Amy's mother tells her that the picture shows callaloo, she expresses dislike of the food and her mother says "yes I know, that's why I don't cook it". Amy identifies *doubles* correctly, and Isabel misidentifies it as the closely related *roti*. Maggie, whose grandmother is Jamaican, identifies *doubles* as *patty*, a Jamaican pastry, possibly because of the bright yellow colouring of the two foods.

Tamara's response to Amy's reaction to *callaloo* lends an important insight into how children in diaspora acquire TE/C lexical items: they are introduced to them through their parents. Amy is not familiar with the dish because after introducing her to it once and discovering she did not like it, Tamara has not done so again. On the other hand, the children are to some extent more familiar with *doubles* and *roti*, which have been identified as embodiments of "the cultural identity of what it means to be authentically Trinidadian" (Plaza 2014: 483). This may be why, when Isabel gets *doubles* wrong, her father tries to correct her by asking, "are you sure that's *roti*?".

5 Discussion

Questions of language use in diaspora contexts are inevitably questions of language and identity, and the case of Trinidadian children in the USA is no different. That the children show little evidence of retention of TE/C phonological features as their default speech style is very much in keeping with Sharma and Sankaran's (2011) work on the language of second generation British Asian speakers, and Sebba's (2013) work among Caribbean immigrants in London. For both groups, second generation speakers were competent in London English, even while using Indian English or Creole features to do identity work. The children in this study are perhaps too young to draw on TE/C in this way; Hewitt's (1986: 107) participants are adolescents, and this type of identity work seems linked to their age and peer group interactions. In addition, Hewitt (1986: 106) stresses the importance of "meeting more black children" for the acquisition of British Creole forms, but the participants in this study do not seem to have regular interactions with other Trinidadian or Caribbean children. For example, Maggie points out that, "I don't think anybody knows about Trinidad in our school except for us". There is evidence of TE/C pronunciations when referring to Trinidadian foods in particular, such as *roti* and *coconut,* and this limited performance is similar to Hewitt's (1986: 107) respondents, whose use of Creole is sometimes limited to "creole tokens and formulaic expressions" which are used symbolically.

Sounding Trinidadian is important to the children. They acknowledge themselves as isolated from the larger Trinidadian speech community. When we talk about different accents, Maggie acknowledges that she sounds different from her parents, reports the differences between her teachers' accents and adults in Trinidad (3), and then concludes that she has both accents – even though this claim is contrary to all the evidence in this paper. Nevertheless, her hybrid identity, as part Trinidadian and part American, is important to her, and is something she believes can be heard in her speech. It may be that Maggie, the eldest participant, is on the cusp of discovering how she can draw on features of TE/C to do identity work. Longitudinal studies would be required to see whether this suggestion is true.

(3) <Maggie><#> *I'm not sure how they sound different because we look alike* <#>*And well our teachers have American accents and Trinidad have Trini accents*

<GW><#> *And your parents*
<Maggie<#>*They have both.*
<GW><#>*And you have*
<Maggie><#> *I have both as well*
<Jonathon><#>*Both*

Beyond accent, knowledge of TE/C lexical items is also linked to Trinidadian identity. The children's parents are very invested in their children showing that they are familiar with Trinidadian lexical items. Knowledge and use of Creole lexical items, whether with Jamaican or London pronunciations were also an important resource in indexing Caribbean identity among Sebba's (2013) informants in London. Whenever children do not know the TE/C lexical item, their parents may prod them to try to recall, as seen above with both Amy and Isabel. But it is not simply a case of parents encumbering their children with a vocabulary item they do not wish for. The children are eager to learn new TE/C words. For example, when I reveal to them what *callaloo* is, Maggie and Jonathon seem pleased to have learned a new word (4). Similarly, Amy does not remember the TE/C word *soft drink*, but is keen to learn it (5).

(4) <Maggie><#>*Something to do with crab but I don't know what the green stuff on the outside is.*
<GW><#>*It's callaloo*
<Maggie><#>*I've never heard of that*
<Jonathon><#>*Me either*
<Maggie><#>*That's new*

(5) <Amy><#>*Juices and sodas*
<Tamara><#>*What do people in Trinidad call it*
<Amy><#>*Sodas*
<Tamara><#>*So you don't remember?*
<Amy><#>*But I wanna know*

The present study also provides insights into the tension between caregiver and community inputs in the language of immigrant children. The children use mostly AmE phonology, and their language behaviour most closely matches that of Kerswill and Willams' (2000) eight-year-olds, i.e. school-aged children whose peers and larger community also serve as models for their speech. Their parents are aware of the effect of the AmE speech community of which they are now a part on their children's speech; consider Tamara's observations on Amy's use of *football* and *soccer* (Section 4.2). The parents are aware that, as the children attend school, join Girl Scout troops, and play on sports' teams, they will adopt AmE ways of speaking. Nevertheless, it is important to the parents that their children are provided with sufficient contact with TE/C through their grandparents' visits or engagement with Trinidadian culture through books and online audio and visual materials. At the end of the interview, all of the parents express frustration or embarrassment with their children's performance in the interview: "You probably think we are the worst Trini parents," say Maggie and Jonathon's parents. "They have all the books and we are always reading these things to them. Maybe they were shy," explains Isabel and Luke's mother. "Does she sound too American?" asks Amy's mother. Their children's ability in TE/C is important for their identity as Trinidadian parents, even as they raise them in the US, away from any of the areas populated by large populations of Caribbean people. This is a perspective which future work on language in diaspora families may want to explore further.

The study made use of a modified sociolinguistic interview to gather the children's data. For the variables under consideration, however, the different speech styles did not produce any variation in the children's pronunciation. This does not mean that there is no variation in the data. Luke, for instance, shows variation in the use of [ŋ] and [n], though the only pattern that could be found was that [ŋ] was always used after word medial [ɾ] as in *sitting* [sɪɾɪŋ] and [n] in other words, such as *dancing*. This suggests that second-generation Trinidadian children do not use the presence or absence of TE/C features to differentiate between formal and informal speech, in contrast to the speakers in Winford's (1978) study on hypercorrection in Trinidadian English.

6 Conclusion

Outside of educational contexts, the language of Caribbean immigrants to the United States has hitherto gone undocumented, and so this study represents a first step towards filling this research gap. It provides a first look at the language of second-generation Trinidadian immigrants in the United States. Despite having TE/C speaking primary caregivers, the five Trinidadian-heritage children whose language was studied employed mostly AmE phonological patterns and lexis, though they were sometimes aware of TE/C vocabulary, particularly in the semantic field of food. Nevertheless, TE/C worked alongside personal relationships, books, media, and knowledge of specific places and customs to create the Trinidadian aspect of the children's complex national identities. Further research in this field should therefore consider TE/C in light of other sociocultural elements.

The five children who participated in this study may not be representative of other Trinidadian-heritage speakers. They do not live in areas with large Caribbean and especially Trinidadian populations, such as New York or Miami. However, studies of child language among Caribbean immigrants in these areas do not currently exist, and future research in this regard would reveal whether a linguistic situation similar to that reported by Sebba (2013) for London exists in US metropoles, or whether, perhaps, Caribbean Englishes and their speakers are subsumed into larger groups of African American speakers of African American Vernacular English. Given the high mobility between the Caribbean and the US, studying the language of English-speaking Caribbean immigrants in the US is crucial for the discussions of World Englishes in the context of globalisation. Moreover, the inclusion of studies on the language of children and adolescents in diaspora settings within the World Englishes paradigm brings new perspectives on the relationship between language and identity. Exposure to and competence in other varieties, such as AmE, means that children's linguistic repertoires are in many ways distinct from that of their parents. How subsequent generations are able to use language to index their identity thus changes over time. Studying how this change develops is surely a worthwhile endeavour.

References

Barclay, Keneisha C. 2017. *Semi-rhoticity in Trinidadian English of 7–8 year olds: Based on Dunross Preparatory School*. St. Augustine: University of the West Indies BA thesis.
Carlin, Cherisse. 2006. The role of language in cultural identity: Trinidadian immigrants to the United States. *LCC Review* 6 (1). 69–79.
Carrington, Justin. 2018. *The patterns of changing rhoticity in Trinidadian English among students of The University of the West Indies, St. Augustine campus*. St. Augustine: University of the West Indies BA thesis.
Chambers, Jack K. 2002. Dynamics of dialect convergence. *Journal of Sociolinguistics* 6 (1). 117–130.
Ferreira, Jo-Anne S. & Kathy-Ann Drayton. 2015. *A phonological description of Trinidadian English*. uwispace.sta.uwi.edu/dspace/handle/2139/46335 (accessed 2 February 2022).
Fishman, Joshua A. 2014. Language maintenance, language shift, and reversing language shift. In Tej K Bhatia & William C. Ritchie (eds.), *The handbook of bilingualism and multilingualism*, 466–494. Oxford: Blackwell.
Gooden, Sheloome & Kathy-Ann Drayton. 2017. The Caribbean – Trinidad and Jamaica. In Raymond Hickey (ed.), *Listening to the past: Audio records of accents of English*, 414–444. Cambridge: Cambridge University Press.
Hänsel, Eva Canan & Dagmar Deuber. 2013. Globalization, postcolonial Englishes, and the English language press in Kenya, Singapore, and Trinidad and Tobago. *World Englishes* 32 (3). 338–357.
Hazen, Kurt. 2002. The family. In Jack K. Chambers, Peter Trudgill & Natalie Schillig-Estes (eds.), *The handbook of language variation and change*, 500–525. Oxford: Blackwell Publishing.

Hewitt, Roger. 1986. *White talk, black talk: Inter-racial friendship and communication amongst adolescents*. Cambridge: Cambridge University Press.

Hinrichs, Lars. 2014. Diasporic mixing of World Englishes: The case of Jamaican Creole in Toronto. In Eugene Green & Charles Meyer (eds.), *The variability of current World Englishes*, 169–198. Berlin & Boston: De Gruyter Mouton.

Kerswill, Paul & Ann Williams. 2000. Creating a new town koine: Children and language change in Milton Keynes. *Language in Society* 29 (1). 65–115.

Kortesluoma, Riita-Liisa, Maija Hentinen & Merja Nikkonen. 2003. Conducting a qualitative child interview: Methodological considerations. *Journal of Advanced Nursing* 42 (5). 434–441.

Kretzschmar, William A. 2008. Standard American English pronunciation. In Edgar W. Schneider (ed.), *Varieties of English 2: The Americas and the Caribbean*, 37–51. Berlin & New York: De Gruyter Mouton.

Labov, William. 1972. *Language in the inner city: Studies in the Black English vernacular*. University of Pennsylvania Press.

Labov, William. 2008. Mysteries of the substrate. In Miriam Meyerhoff & Naomi Nagy (eds.), *Social lives in language sociolinguistics and multilingual speech communities: Celebrating the work of Gillian Sankoff*, 315–326. Amsterdam/Philadelphia: John Benjamins.

Labov, William, Sharon Ash & Charles Boberg. 2008. *The Atlas of North American English: Phonetics, phonology and sound change*. Berlin & New York: De Gruyter Mouton.

Mair, Christian. 2003. Language, code, and symbol: The changing roles of Jamaican Creole in diaspora communities. *AAA: Arbeiten aus Anglistik und Amerikanistik* 28. 231–248.

Nero, Shondel. 2006. Language, identity, and education of Caribbean English speakers. *World Englishes* 25 (3–4). 501–511.

Plaza, Dwaine. 2014. Roti and doubles as comfort foods for the Trinidadian diaspora in Canada, the United States, and Britain. *Social Research* 81 (2). 463–488.

Schilling, Natalie. 2013. Surveys and interviews. In Robert Podesva & Devyani Sharma (eds.), *Research methods in linguistics*, 96–115. Cambridge: Cambridge University Press.

Schneider, Edgar W. 2020. *English around the world: An introduction*, 2nd edn. Cambridge: Cambridge University Press.

Sebba, Mark. 2013 [1993]. *London Jamaican: Language system in interaction*, 2nd edn. London: Routledge.

Sharma, Devyani & Lavanya Sankaran. 2011. Cognitive and social forces in dialect shift: Gradual change in London Asian speech. *Language Variation and Change* 23 (3). 399–428.

Thomas, Erik. R. 2007. Phonological and phonetic characteristics of African American vernacular English. *Language and Linguistics Compass*, 1 (5). 450–475.

Tsuji, Teruyuki. 2011. Trinidadian and Tobagonian immigrants. In Ronald H. Bayor (ed.), *Multicultural America: An encyclopedia of the newest immigrants*, 2137–2191. California: ABC–CLIO/Greenwood Press.

Wilson, Guyanne. 2023. British and American norms in Trinidadian English lexicon. *World Englishes* 42 (1). 73–90.

Winer, Lise. 1993. *Trinidad and Tobago* (Varieties of English Around the World 6). Amsterdam: John Benjamins Publishing.

Winer, Lise. 2006. Teaching English to Caribbean English creole-speaking students in the Caribbean and North America. In Shondel Nero (ed.), *Dialects, Englishes, creoles, and education*, 105–118. London: Routledge.

Winer, Lise. 2009. *Dictionary of the English/creole of Trinidad & Tobago: On historical principles*. Quebec: McGill-Queen's Press.

Winer, Lise &Lona Jack. 1997. Caribbean English Creole in New York. In Ofelia García & Joshua A. Fishman (eds.), *The multilingual apple: Languages in New York City*, 300–337. Berlin & New York: De Gruyter Mouton.

Winford, Donald. 1978. Phonological hypercorrection in the process of decreolization: The case of Trinidadian English. *Journal of Linguistics* 14 (2). 277–291.

Youssef, Valerie & James Winford. 2008. The creoles of Trinidad and Tobago: Phonology. In Edgar W. Schneider (ed.), *Varieties of English 2: The Americas and the Caribbean*, 320–338. Berlin & Boston: De Gruyter Mouton.

Teresa Wai See Ong and Su-Hie Ting
3 Language use patterns and strategies for children's English language development: Insights from Chinese descendant mothers in multilingual Malaysia

Abstract: Through the lens of bilingual first language acquisition, this study examines languages used by Chinese descendant children in various domains and home language strategies taken by their mothers to enhance the children's English language learning. Data were collected by means of an open-ended questionnaire answered by three Chinese descendant mothers living in Penang, Malaysia. The findings reveal an overarching trend of the children speaking English as their principal language of communication in the domains of home, extended home, and school, thus hampering the acquisition of Chinese dialects as their ethnic languages. Because their mothers see the importance of English in light of today's competitive educational landscape, they provided reading materials, educational television, and tutoring programmes to improve their children's English proficiency. The findings suggest that children's simultaneous dual language acquisition and the resulting use of code-mixing is due to parental home language policies.

Keywords: bilingual first language acquisition, language use patterns, improvement strategies, multilingual families, Chinese, Malaysia

1 Introduction

English plays a crucial role in past and present Malaysian society. Although it is not an official language in Malaysia, its status and functions have grown over the years. The 1980 census found that: (i) 30% of Malaysians were literate in English; (ii) 46% of those living in urban areas were literate in English; and (iii) 20% of those living in rural areas were literate in English (Tan 2003). Four decades later, literacy in English among Malaysians has increased from 30% to 50% of the general

---

Teresa Wai See Ong, National University Hospital, Singapore
Su-Hie Ting, Universiti Malaysia Sarawak, Malaysia

https://doi.org/10.1515/9783110733723-003

population due to the widespread use of English in private education, the impact of internet technology, and globalisation (Bolton and Bacon-Shone 2020). The key point here is that English language acquisition is considered salient in Malaysian society as the country heads towards becoming a developed nation (Gill 2014). A case in point is that many parents from urban areas believe that speaking English at home will boost their children's English proficiency (Hashim 2014), and give them access to academic advancement and promising career opportunities.

However, the family domain is the bastion of ethnic language use, and the encroachment of English into family communication inevitably causes the role of ethnic languages to diminish. When such a situation happens, parental beliefs influence the children's choice of language, thereby shaping the family language use. Past studies conducted in urban areas in Malaysia have already demonstrated that English is taking over as the language for family communication among many Indians (Ting and Mahadhir 2009) and Chinese (Ong 2021). With the younger generation choosing English over ethnic languages, the cultural worldviews reflected in these ethnic languages will be lost in the future. In the Malaysian context, the probability of language shift is greater in urban areas, where children have the privilege of being exposed to different languages, often simultaneously, at a very young age. Although findings on imminent language shift in the Chinese community concur on how urbanisation and functions of ethnic languages vis-à-vis English lead to the preference for English, these are macro-level factors. Little is known about how parental practices and ideologies affect day-to-day decisions in language choices. The few studies on children's simultaneous language acquisition in Malaysia (Mohamed Salleh, Di Biase, and Kawaguchi 2021; Mohamed Salleh, Di Biase, and Ramlan 2020; Mohamed Salleh, Kawaguchi, and Di Biase 2019; Mohamed Salleh et al. 2016) generally demonstrate that both children's language aptitude and home and school language environments influence their English and Malay lexical and morphological development. Additionally, their linguistic structures, such as plural expressions and negative constructions, exhibited bidirectional interactions between both languages. To our knowledge, there are no studies examining parents' views on children's simultaneous acquisition of English and Chinese dialects. Understanding the perceptions of language value has important political and cultural implications for ethnic communities such as the Chinese in Malaysia.

Considering that urban areas are the site of rapid change in language use patterns, this study examined the languages used by children of Chinese descendants living in urban areas and the home language strategies adopted by their mothers to enhance their English language learning. It is guided by two research questions:

1. What language(s) do children of Chinese ethnic descent speak to different people in different domains?
2. What home language strategies do the mothers use to improve their children's English language learning?

The next section presents an overview of how English[1] came into use in Malaysia, the language policies, and current status and role of English to contextualise the language use of Chinese descendant families. This is followed by theoretical frameworks and the method of the study. In the findings section, we show that children in the three families included in the study made strategic languages choices to fulfil their needs despite their mothers' home language management strategies and use of ethnic languages. The chapter wraps up with a discussion and conclusion.

2 Overview of the status and role of English in Malaysia

Malaysians of Chinese and Indian descent living in Malaysia respectively account for 22.4% and 6.8% of the total population of 32.7 million people; the majority group is the *Bumiputra* (69.8%, 'sons of the soil') comprising people of Malay ethnicity and the Indigenous groups (Department of Statistics 2021). The Chinese migrated from China and speak Chinese dialects such as Hokkien, Cantonese, Hakka, Teochew, Hainan, and Foochow. They later learnt Mandarin Chinese, which is used as a medium of instruction in some schools and taught as an optional subject in public schools. "National" schools use Malay as the medium of instruction, while Chinese- and Tamil-medium schools were categorised as "national-type" schools (Constitutional Commission 1957). In addition to Chinese schools, there are Chinese newspapers, radio and television programmes, and associations that reinforce the Chinese identity.

English was introduced to Malaysia by the British who first arrived in 1771. During that time, Malay was the language of diplomacy and trade, and Bazaar Malay (colloquial Malay) was used with foreigners. In addition to the Chinese immigrants who came on their own, the British also arranged for the import of Chinese labourers to work in the tin mines in the late 19th century. They came

---

1 English in this study refers to the standard Malaysian English taught and learnt in schools. It does not refer to either British or American English or *Manglish* (colloquial variety of Malaysian English).

mainly to escape war and poverty in China. The divide-and-rule policy practised by the British kept people of Chinese ethnicity in the tin mines, Indians in the rubber estates, and the Malays to be fishermen and farmers, which led to "an identification of a racial group with a particular type of vocation or industry, and hence its identification with wealth or poverty" (Omar 1987: 63). English was seen as a vehicle for upward mobility, providing access to jobs in the civil service and scholarships in the UK. The English-medium schools were attended by Chinese and Malay children from wealthy families. Malay- and Tamil-medium schools were established in rural areas, while the Chinese set up schools that used Chinese dialects but switched to Mandarin Chinese in the early 20th century. Nevertheless, Chinese dialects continue to be spoken today, mainly in private domains (Ong 2019, 2020).

However, when British Malaya gained independence in 1957 and became Malaysia, the role and status of English was reduced, which suppressed its value as a tool for social mobility (Gill 2005). Malay was ratified as the sole national language of Malaysia and a change from English to Malay as the medium of instruction was put in place. When the transition was completed at Form Five level throughout Malaysia by 1989, English continued to function as the second most important language of Malaysia because it was used for international trade and continued to provide access to higher education and career opportunities in English-speaking countries.

English and Malay competed for prominence with English having the advantage of being an international language and Malay being the language for education and governmental communication. The Third Malaysia Plan (1976–1980) states that "Bahasa Melayu [Malay] is the basis for national integration" but "measures will be taken to ensure that English is taught as a strong second language" (Government of Malaysia 1976: 386). In both "national" and "national-type" schools, English became a compulsory subject to study but not necessarily to pass (Omar 1997). Instead, Malay is a must-pass subject when students complete secondary school.

Malaysia could not afford to neglect English because it was needed "to keep abreast of scientific and technological developments in the world and to participate meaningfully in international trade and commerce" (Government of Malaysia 1976: 391). Therefore, exceptions to Malay as the medium of instruction were made for the teaching of mathematics and science two times, first in 2003 and again in 2018. The first attempt was reversed in 2012 due to pressure from various quarters citing identity and academic performance issues. Additionally, the national examination results showed poor performance in mathematics and science, especially in rural areas dominated by Malay students (Hashim and Leitner 2017). To compensate for the switch back to Malay for teaching mathematics and science, the "Upholding the Malay language and strengthening the English language"

(MBMMBI) policy was introduced in 2012 to allow extra hours for teaching English. In 2018, another policy of the "Dual Language Programme" (DLP) was instituted to allow students to choose either English or Malay to study mathematics and science. This policy change concerning the medium of instruction indicates that Malaysia is acting to strengthen the mastery of English among Malaysians, particularly when English opens the door for global scientific, technological, economic, and cultural developments (Graddol 1997).

3 Theoretical frameworks

The theoretical frameworks used in this study are the concepts of domain and bilingual first language acquisition (BFLA). Fishman's (1964) concept of domain has been employed in studies on language use patterns in indigenous, bilingual, and multilingual communities. Fishman (1972: 82) defines domain as "[a] sociocultural construct abstracted from topics of communication, relationships between communicators, and locales of communication in accord with the institutions of a society and the spheres of activity of a culture, in such a way that individual behaviour and social patterns can be distinguished from each other and yet related to each other". Fishman (1972) also states that there are five domains of language use: family, friendship, religion, education, and employment. Of these, the family domain is considered the bastion of ethnic language use (Spolsky 2012), and this domain is commonly studied along with other domains relevant to the individuals.

The family domain is also where most of the language acquisitional process takes place. One of the prominent forms of language acquisition in Malaysia is BFLA, which refers to children simultaneously acquiring two languages from birth (Genesee and Nicoladis 2006). Interest in this field began with Ronjat's (1913) and Leopold's (1939, 1947, 1949a, 1949b) publications on their children's simultaneous acquisition of dual languages. Leopold (1954) claimed that children go through an initial unified stage before gradually differentiating the two languages. Different timeframes have been proposed to what counts as children's simultaneous bilingual acquisition as this acquisition context falls within the sensitive periods for language acquisition (Locke 1997). The maximal age of onset for bilingual language acquisition is said to range between one month from birth (De Houwer 1995) and a little younger than three years (McLaughlin 1978).

Although there were many concerns that BFLA may strain children's linguistic development (Bialystok 2001), increase children's risk for academic delay/failure (MacNamara 1966), and cause sociocultural problems among children (Diebold 1968), research on BFLA continued developing, particularly with the unitary language system hypothesis. The hypothesis, proposed by Volterra and Taeschner (1978), considers children's acquisition of two languages as one hybrid system. Today, as researchers become more aware of the complexities involved in the earliest stages of bilingual development, the Separate Development Hypothesis (De Houwer 2005) is believed to explain children's acquisition of dual languages more accurately. The hypothesis states that children who are simultaneously exposed to two languages from birth develop two distinct morphosyntactic systems, so that "the morphosyntactic development of the one language does not have any fundamental effect on the morphosyntactic development of the other" (De Houwer 1990: 66). This means that utterances with words from language A[2] have morphosyntactic features that are related to input in the same language. The same goes for language Alpha that the children are simultaneously acquiring. In other words, bilingual first language learners have the additional skills to manage two languages simultaneously and from a very young age, which is regarded as a "highly functional communication skill" (Genesee 2008: 12). They are able to "differentiate between the grammatical systems they are exposed to from very early on" (Haznedar 2007).

Managing two languages simultaneously, however, often leads to mixing languages. Code-mixing refers to the use of phonological, lexical, and morphosyntactic elements from two languages in the same utterance or stretch of conversation or in different situations (Genesee 1989). While mixing languages used to be perceived as a sign of lacking knowledge and ability to separate languages, it has been shown that this might actually be a strategy of language use. Still, the use of code-mixing may be due to children's limited vocabulary in language Alpha (Deuchar and Quay 2000; Genesee 1989), since it enables the speaker to incorporate vocabulary or transfer knowledge from language A into language Alpha (Yip and Matthews 2007). When such a situation takes place, language A is interpreted as the language in which the child is more proficient. In other words, language A resembles the child's stronger/first language while language Alpha, which is far less developed, is regarded as their weaker/second language (Paradis 2010). Additionally, children's code-mixing may be a result of the input they hear from adults (Rowland 2014). Scholars such as Hernandez, Li, and MacWhinney (2005) view code-mixing positively. They argue that children code-mix because languages influence one another during their development as one word utilises the conceptual packaging raised by a word from another language, resulting in language interaction. In simpler terms, code-mixing is a strategy children use to extend their communication competence

---

2 Because De Houwer (2005) mentions that there is no "second language" in the chronological sense in BFLA, the terms of language A and language Alpha are used to refer to the two languages that play a similar role in BFLA. These terms are borrowed from Wölck (1984).

when their mastery of two languages is incomplete (Genesee 2008) and should not be regarded as a result of grammatical or lexicon confusion (Genesee, Nicoladis, and Paradis 1995).

Bilingual children's understanding of appropriate language choices develops from the fundamental processes of language socialisation (Lanza 1997a). Bilingual children were found to demonstrate sensitivity when interacting with strangers with whom they have had no prior experiences (Genesee, Boivin, and Nicoladis 1996) and adjusting their rates of code-mixing to match those unfamiliar speakers who also code-mix from one occasion to another (Comeau, Genesee, and Lapaquette 2003). Parents are sometimes surprised to hear of their children's language socialisation practices because they do not realise that their children are usually very responsive to the sociolinguistic norms that appear in their surrounding environment in regards to language choice (De Houwer 1990). This implies that children are "active and creative social agents" (Lanza 2007: 47) who employ strategies of their own during language socialisation, and they do not need any form of preparation to do so.

4 Method of the study

This descriptive study involved data collected from three ethnic Chinese mothers living in Penang – a Malaysian state that has a 90.8% level of urbanisation (Mok 2016). The population statistics show that 42.3% of the 1.77 million people living in Penang are Chinese, 47.2% are Malay, 10.2% are Indian, and 0.3% are from other ethnic backgrounds (Department of Statistics Malaysia 2020). Most of the Chinese in Penang belong to the Hokkien dialect group (63.9%), and fewer speak Teochew (17.8%), Cantonese (8.3%), Hakka (5.2%), Hainan (1.5%), and others (3.2%) (Penang Monthly 2017).

The participants of this study were Chinese descendant mothers living in an urbanised area in Malaysia with at least an academic degree and are married to Chinese descendant spouses, though not necessarily from the same Chinese dialect group. The mothers are referred to as VC, RW, and SL for anonymity and all three hold a university degree, obtained either locally or abroad. VC's husband is from Hong Kong while RW's and SL's husbands are from Malaysia. Table 3.1 shows their demographic background.

The data were collected using open-ended questionnaires. This decision was made to avoid limiting the participants' choice of responses (cf. Krosnick and Presser 2010; Schuman 1972). On the first page of the questionnaire, there was a

Table 3.1: Demographic background of participants.

Demographic features	VC	RW	SL
Occupation	Researcher	Accountant	Housewife
Age group	40–49	40–49	30–39
First language(s)	English	English	Hokkien
Additional language(s)	Cantonese, Malay	Malay, Hokkien, Cantonese, Mandarin	English, Malay, Cantonese, Teochew, Mandarin
Husband's first language(s)	Cantonese	Hokkien	Hokkien
Number and gender of children	1 male 1 female	2 males 1 female	1 male
Age of children	Male – 10 Female – 8	Male – 12 Male – 11 Female – 8	Male – 7
Children's first language(s)	English	English	English
Children's additional language(s)	Cantonese	Mandarin, Malay, Hokkien, Cantonese	Hokkien, Malay, Cantonese, Teochew
Children's medium of education in school	English (private school)	Mandarin, Malay, English (national-type school)	Malay, English (national school)

section for the participants to insert their names and provide consent for participation in the study. The main questions in the questionnaire were as follows:
1. What language(s) do your children speak to you, your husband, parents, in-laws, and their siblings and friends?
2. What do you think are the reasons behind their choice of language(s)?
3. What strategies do you take to improve your children's English language learning?

The data were collected during the lockdown period of the COVID-19 pandemic from December 2020 to January 2021, which prevented face-to-face interactions. Potential participants were identified by the first researcher and contacted to seek their willingness to participate in the study. The purpose of the study, voluntary participation, and anonymity of identity in research reports arising from the study were explained to the participants. After the three mothers gave verbal consent for the study, the questionnaires were sent via email. As the mothers are computer literate, they agreed to type their responses because typing responses is easier than writing them by hand (Reja et al. 2003) and would generate richer open-ended responses (Gonier 1999; Kwak and Radler 1999). The mothers were given two weeks to complete the questionnaires. Reja et al. (2003) warned that open-ended questionnaires tend to suffer higher rates of incompletion. Therefore, after the first week, the researcher contacted the mothers to check if they understood the questions. Before the end of the second week, the mothers were gently reminded via Whatsapp regarding the submission deadline.

5 Findings

The children's language use patterns are presented in three domains: home, extended home, and education. Following this, the results on the home language strategies adopted by the mothers to enhance their children's English language learning are presented.

5.1 Home domain

In this study, the home domain refers to interactions within the nuclear family. Based on the three mothers' responses, the general trend was that all six children spoke English with their mothers, while with their fathers they spoke English with limited use of Chinese dialects (Hokkien or Cantonese). Their mothers claimed that the children were exposed to two languages from birth (English from mother, English and Chinese dialects from father). RW practised the one-parent-one-language policy, as seen in the following extract:

> English was the first language taught to them [my children]. We were also comfortable expressing ourselves in English and occasionally Hokkien. After all, they picked both languages up. It's maybe because of the upbringing. I was brought up speaking English with my siblings. For my husband, he feels it's important to maintain his first language, Hokkien, because it actually gives him an identity of being a Hokkien.

In RW's case, her bias towards English is due to her own experience of growing up in an English-speaking environment and she wanted to replicate it for her children. On the other hand, her husband's choice of speaking both English and Hokkien is attributed to the maintenance of his family's cultural heritage. He is seen as holding strong beliefs in constructing his heritage identity. It is deduced that RW's family bilingualism arises as a result of a careful decision made by RW and her husband, who grew up with a different first language, to bring up their children bilingually (Bretteny and de Klerk 1995).

The next case, VC's family, shows the use of English as a first language. Although VC's husband is from Hong Kong and his first language is Cantonese, the couple chose to raise their children mainly in English despite their children's early exposure to Cantonese. This is seen in VC's statement:

> *I speak English to my children. My husband speaks English with limited Cantonese to them. We live in a globalised world so it is essential that we are fluent in English for work, education, and everyday purposes.*

Their choice of English for family communication arises from a mutual recognition of the importance of English for practical purposes and preparation of their children's future. This decision reflects the increasing demand for English in primary and secondary schools not just across the Association of Southeast Asian Nations (ASEAN) but worldwide, alongside its role in facilitating communication between the ASEAN and international regions (Kirkpatrick 2020). VC considered English as her children's first language:

> *English is their [the children's] mother tongue[3] because it's the first language taught and they have the ability to read, write, and speak.*

At the time of the interview, VC's children were speaking only English among themselves; so were the other four children in the study although they could speak two languages (albeit having a limited vocabulary in the weaker language).

The final case, SL's family, demonstrates English taking over from Chinese dialects as the child's stronger language of communication with his parents:

> *My son speaks English, Cantonese, Teochew, and Hokkien. He automatically uses more and more English after he picks it up officially at school. The switch takes place because he learns the dialects orally and they are not written form.*

For SL's son, the shift from Chinese dialects to English took place after he began nursery school at the age of three. English soon became his stronger language, which was his choice of language, even though his parents spoke Chinese dialects to him. Nevertheless, the home domain still acts as a critical space for him to develop his multilingualism. This situation indicates that although SL's son was raised simultaneously in a multilingual language environment from birth, divergence still took place at three years old, which is the age children begin schooling. His stron-

---

3 VC used the term, mother tongue, in reference to first language.

ger language (English) will probably overtake his weaker language (Chinese dialects) and subsequently act as his first language in the future (Paradis 2010).

5.2 Extended home domain

In this study, the extended home domain refers to the home of the children's maternal or paternal grandparents and relatives. The three mothers said that their children largely chose to speak Chinese dialects with their grandparents and older relatives, who mostly spoke Chinese dialects. These elders could speak some English but they preferred to speak Chinese dialects with family. With their cousins who were of similar age, the children spoke English only. This pattern aligns with most researchers' findings that bilingual children tend to associate language(s) with different speakers (De Houwer 1990; Deuchar and Quay 2000).

With the maternal grandparents, VC's and RW's children chose to speak a mix of English and Cantonese while SL's son spoke a mix of Cantonese and Teochew. When asked the reason why the children chose to speak Chinese dialects with their maternal grandparents, SL stated:

> Cantonese is the mother tongue[4] of my mother and Teochew is the mother tongue of my father. They [My mother and father] will speak [those dialects] among themselves, so my son, who was taken care by them when young, have early exposure to the dialects.

Interestingly, with the paternal grandparents, almost no English was spoken by the six children. They mainly used Chinese dialects (Cantonese or Hokkien) but their proficiency was low due to occasional use, according to the three mothers. English came in when they did not know the exact words in Cantonese, as seen in VC's statement:

> My mother-in-law doesn't speak English, she speaks only Cantonese. My children speak Cantonese and some English to her. They will point to the things they want when my mother-in-law doesn't understand.[5]

Based on VC's statement, it is deduced that her children code-mix on a lexical level in either the same utterance or a stretch of conversation with their grandmother. Cantonese is their less proficient or weaker language, and thus they adopt the code-mixing strategy to extend their communication competence (Genesee 2008). Although empirical studies (e.g., Genesee 1989, 2001) indicate that bilingual child-

---

4 SL refers to first language as mother tongue, similar to VC in Footnote 3.
5 The researcher was curious why VC did not mention her father-in-law and so she asked VC verbally. VC mentioned that he has health issue and thus, he does not really talk much to the grandchildren.

ren's code-mixing declines with age, the individual levels of proficiency among the children in the present study led to the continued use of code-mixing. At home, the children had shifted to mostly using English. Their choices have led to them receiving less input in Chinese dialects, and thus, their development of the dialects has become slower when compared to English language development.

When the children visited or played with their cousins, from the time when they were toddlers until about 10 years old, all three mothers claimed that they spoke only English. To RW, their use of English was natural:

> *Most naturally English as they [RW's children] were exposed and taught the language at the early age.*

Since English has taken over RW's children's weaker language (Hokkien), consequently they perceived English as their more proficient and comfortable language to use when speaking to their cousins during playtime. It is possible that RW's children had a great awareness of their language choice during interactions with different people (De Houwer and Nakamura 2022). In this case, they knew that their cousins could speak English and thus, they switched to English for interactions.

5.3 Education domain

In this study, the education domain refers to the space where the children study, interact, and play with their classmates. Because the six children were educated in different types of schools, they spoke different languages with their school friends, depending on the medium of instruction. VC's children spoke only English as they were educated in a private school that used English as the medium of instruction. RW's children spoke English and Mandarin Chinese with their school friends because they were educated in the national-type school where the medium of instruction was Mandarin Chinese. As for SL's son, it was English and Malay because he attended a national school where the medium of instruction was Malay.

Nevertheless and regardless of the respective school type, the children used English with their school friends because the foundation for this had already been established when they started using English upon going to nursery or, even earlier, at home and with their cousins. All three mothers claimed that English remained the principal language of communication for their children when socialising with friends. The mothers offered different explanations for the use of English. SL said, *"We are educated in English so it is easy for my son to express himself"*. It was more convenient for SL's son to express himself in English since he was raised mostly using English. Although he could speak Chinese dialects, he was not proficient in them. On the other hand, RW decided to encourage her children to speak English because they did not like Mandarin Chinese despite it being the medium of instruction:

> My children didn't develop the love for Mandarin although they spent a large part of their weekdays in school which is Mandarin based. So I encourage the use of English.

RW had the one-parent-one-language policy whereby she spoke English and her husband spoke Hokkien. As Mandarin Chinese was not spoken at home, this might explain her children's adverse feelings towards Mandarin Chinese. As a result, RW's children developed the strategy of communicating in the language with which they have a stronger bond. These findings demonstrate that parental discourse strategies may influence bilingual children's language choice.

5.4 Home strategies for English language development

Thus far, we have observed a trend of all six children growing up as bilingual or multilingual speakers while preferring to speak English as their dominant language for various reasons: (i) the children are most comfortable using English, (ii) their acquisition of English was more advanced than the acquisition of their other language(s), and therefore, they lack lexicon and grammar in the weaker language (Hokkien, Cantonese, or Teochew). Because the mothers consider English as an important language for the children's future, they have employed two home language strategies to enhance their children's English learning.

5.4.1 Reading in English

The principal strategy taken by all three mothers is reading, as evidenced in SL's statement:

> The mother provides as much opportunity for her children to practise the use of the language by reading to them and asking them to read to her or having them reading to her. . . . Whenever I come across any books that are helpful, I will buy them. I will go through them first before purchasing. It is compulsory that children borrow books from the school or state library.

SL believed that the action of reading, i.e. when a mother reads to her children or when children are able to read on their own, will offer more opportunities for the children to use English. SL's and VC's children also borrow books from the school or library. VC began by reading aloud to her children and when they could read, she took turns reading a chapter with each of them every night. This means that their children had diverse reading materials to nurture their language development. VC hoped that the reading habit would last through adulthood.

5.4.2 Fun extra-curricular activities in English

Other fun extra-curricular activities served as a commonly-adopted home language strategy for improving the children's English proficiency. RW described hers:

> I sent my children to private and group tutoring. They used online website for revision such as Vschool. They love watching educational videos [on] YouTube too.

Adding on, VC illustrated her strategy:

> My daughter enjoys watching TV Playschool and the Australian Broadcasting Corporation educational programs as well as singalong (Baby Shark for one example) and storytelling programs. My son plays 'choose your adventure' and interactive games (e.g., Minecraft where the children talk to friends by typing to each other as the game progresses) to assist him with learning activities.

SL gave further examples:

> I enrol my son for camp activities and Bible study group organised by the church. They [the organisers] speak English so he gets more opportunities to practise English.

The three mothers engaged their children with various activities to improve their English language learning. This indicates the mothers have seriously considered the importance of English for academic purposes and their children's future, particularly in a multilingual country within the ASEAN region where English is not predominantly spoken.

6 Discussion

The study produced three noteworthy findings. First, the results showed that the language(s) used in the home domain within the nuclear family does not set the pattern of language use in the extended home and education domains. On the contrary, it is the school language that powerfully determines the main language spoken by the children. The results reveal that even if the parents used a one-parent-one-language policy to encourage the use of Chinese dialects and English as the first language, the children ended up speaking English as their main language. Furthermore, this study reveals that the point at which English transitions into the main language of communication is when children begin formal education.

The formal exposure to English begins at nursery school and is later reinforced at primary school. The children predominantly speak English to their parents, which aligns with Hager and Müller's (2015) explanation that children frequently develop a preference for the language taught in school over ethnic language(s) at school age. Nicoladis and Grabois (2002) found that adopted children who originated from China and lived in monolingual English-speaking homes in the USA before the age of two to three years old first spoke English as a second language before eventually having English become their only first language. However, children who lived in Chinese-speaking homes and were exposed to English in the community developed some form of bilingualism, with both English and Mandarin Chinese acquired together (Yip and Matthews 2010). The children in Nicoladis and Grabois's (2002) study had no further contact with Chinese languages but the children in the present study were exposed to two or more languages from birth until they were teenagers. Despite the contact with Chinese dialects, English replaced Chinese dialects as their main language of communication when they entered the education domain, signified by the nursery and primary schools, where they found that English is "the" language to speak.

Second, the present study reveals that the mothers were ultimately in favour of their children learning and speaking English well, as shown by their home language strategies for English development of their children – despite what they say about speaking Chinese dialects at home. The mothers talked about encouraging their children to read and having them join activities held in English such as tutoring classes, online programmes, and church activities. This is why it appears that attempts of one or more parents, or the grandparents, to speak the Chinese dialects failed to improve the children's proficiency in the dialects to a satisfactory level for them to communicate comfortably in the dialects. The pervasive use of English in school, introduced since nursery school or even earlier at home, sets the foundation for the children of the three Chinese urban families to use English as their primary language of communication. The mothers placed stronger emphasis on the children's English language learning due to its importance in the educational and economic sectors. They adopted these home language strategies with full awareness of the growing demand of English in the Malaysian society in order to create a conducive English-speaking environment for the children's language development. The mothers did not rely on the school to teach their children English but "took matters into their own hands" to ensure that their children mastered English.

Finally, the findings suggest that the languages of the children in the three families might have developed in correspondence with the Separate Development Hypothesis proposed by De Houwer (2005). Their inability to communicate effectively in two languages should not be interpreted as evidence of a fused system

(Volterra and Taeschner 1978) or a reflection of one underlying language system (De Houwer 1990). Instead, their code-mixing of English in conversations conducted in Chinese with their grandparents can be explained as an "integral part of early bilingual development" (De Houwer 2005: 42). Admittedly, we did not collect linguistic data to show whether they could differentiate between the two grammar systems, but we have circumstantial evidence based on the mother's reports of their children using English when they did not know the appropriate lexis in Chinese dialects. When the children code-mix, they are seen as drawing on all their known linguistic resources to express themselves and their message across during communication. Their lexicons in the weaker language may not have sufficiently developed, and they still lack certain words. However, such behaviour should not be regarded as the children experiencing "linguistic confusion" (Lanza 1997b: 315) but rather a reflection of the kind of output the children present when their mastery of both the stronger and weaker languages is still in progress (Genesee 2008).

However, what the study has shown definitively is that the children associate languages with interlocutors, knowing when to make appropriate language choices. This is valuable experiential knowledge when interacting in a multilingual community where certain groups of people may be more proficient in certain languages and making appropriate language choices is important for communicative efficiency. Children are able to adjust the use of both languages (English and Chinese dialects) in accordance to preference and competency of interlocutors (Genesee 2008). Although the children in this study cannot speak the Chinese dialects fluently, the finding still indicates that "bilingual children have the cognitive capacity to identify and respond appropriately on-line to important communicative characteristics of their interlocutors" (Genesee 2001: 156).

7 Conclusion

Through the employment of BFLA framework, this study has shown that the children in this study are bilingual speakers/learners (English and Chinese dialects) since birth due to the language policy their parents have adopted at home. However, the children's preferred language is English due to them having more exposure to it and thus, acquiring it as their stronger language through their schooling experience and in the home domain. In fact, their mothers have regarded English as the children's first language and adopted home language learning strategies in favour of English, which indicates the uphill challenges in maintaining heritage languages. Although the children may have used Chinese dialects less in most circumstances, they are still able to switch to those dialects when meeting other dialect speakers, albeit using them in a limited way. Such switching is mainly due to Penang being a Malaysian state where people of Chinese descendant comprise almost 40% of the state population. Nevertheless, what these children have experienced may not be similar to what children living in other states in Malaysia may experience due to different input factors, childhood language environment, and parental ideologies and educational approaches. For example, in Sarawak, a Malaysian state on Borneo where people of Chinese descendant constitute about a quarter of the state population, Lee and Ting (2016) found that the English-, Mandarin Chinese-, and Malay-educated Chinese parents[6] influence their children's language choice. A majority (81.17%) of the Mandarin Chinese-educated parents and over half (58.75%) of the Malay-educated parents are inclined to speak Mandarin Chinese with their children. Among the Malay-educated parents, only 22.50% speak English with their children. The parents who are more likely to speak English with their children are English-educated parents (49.38%), but 27.16% of them speak Mandarin Chinese while another 23.46% speak Chinese dialects as their home language. Another study in the Malaysian state of Johor, Ting and Hoo (2022) found that there is no significant relationship between the Hakka youth's use of Hakka and their socio-economic status. In their study, socio-economic status was estimated based on the educational level and monthly income of the youth's parents. They found that both parents being Hakka and Buddhist are factors that influence the use of and proficiency in Hakka. However, these studies report outcomes of the processes of language socialisation that lead the Chinese youth to speak languages other than the Chinese dialects. These studies did not investigate children's language acquisition process and whether they use code-mixing as a strategy to extend their communication competence when their mastery of two languages is incomplete. Thus, further research on the manifestation of children's BFLA in the form of code-mixing utterances should be conducted to understand when and how the children are able to differentiate both languages lexically and syntactically. "By extending the database from pairing English and European languages to typologically unrelated languages with very different structures such as Chinese languages, childhood bilingualism will be better understood" (Yip and Matthews 2010: 128). Chinese is a tonal language whereas English is a non-tonal language, the interaction between tone and intonation may produce code-mixing patterns that have yet to be researched. The findings of such studies will also provide empirical data to test the Separate Development Hypothesis proposed by De Houwer (2005). By doing so, the findings will also en-

---

[6] Medium of education refers to language of instruction used for teaching various subjects in primary school.

hance our understanding of children's language use when growing up with two languages simultaneously (e.g., English and a home language), particularly when English has become a significant language to learn in many parts of the world today. This form of bilingualism leads to the development of new first language varieties of English, which have to be included in the World Englishes paradigm.

References

Bialystok, Ellen. 2001. *Bilingualism in development: Language, literacy, and cognition*. New York: Cambridge University Press.

Bolton, Kingsley & John Bacon-Shone. 2020. The statistics of English across Asia. In Kingsley Bolton, Werner Botha & Andy Kirkpatrick (eds.), *The handbook of Asian Englishes*, 49–80. Hoboken: Wiley Blackwell.

Bretteny, Beverley & Vivian de Klerk. 1995. Bilingualism: The one-person one-language bond. *Studies in the Languages of Africa* 26 (1). 40–58.

Comeau, Liane, Fred Genesee & Lindsay Lapaquette. 2003. The modeling hypothesis and child bilingual code-mixing. *International Journal of Bilingualism* 7 (2). 113–126.

Constitutional Commission. 1957. *Report of the Federal of Malaya Constitutional Commission [The Reid Report]*. London: Her Majesty's Stationery Office.

De Houwer, Annick. 1990. *The acquisition of two languages from birth: A case study*. Cambridge: Cambridge University Press.

De Houwer, Annick. 1995. Bilingual language acquisition. In Paul Fletcher & Brian MacWhinney (eds.), *The handbook of child language*, 219–250. Oxford: Blackwell.

De Houwer, Annick. 2005. Early bilingual acquisition: Focus on morphosyntax and the Separate Development Hypothesis. In Judith F. Kroll & Annette M. B. De Groot (eds.), *Handbook of bilingualism: Psychological approaches*, 30–48. New York: Oxford University Press.

De Houwer, Annick & Janice Nakamura. 2022. Developmental perspectives on parents' use of discourse strategies with bilingual children. In Robert Blackwood Robert & Unn Røyneland (eds.), *Multilingualism across the lifespan*, 31–55. New York/Abingdon: Routledge.

Department of Statistics. 2020. *Population statistics*. www.dosm.gov.my/v1/index.php?r=column/cthree&menu_id=UmtzQ1pKZHBjY1hVZE95R3RnR0Y4QT09 (accessed 1 March 2022).

Department of Statistics. 2021. *Current population estimates, Malaysia, 2021*. www.dosm.gov.my/v1/index.php?r=column/cthemeByCat&cat=155&bul_id=ZjJOSnpJR21sQWVUcUp6ODRudm5JZz09&menu_id=L0pheU43NWJwRWVSZklWdzQ4TlhUUT09 (accessed 1 March 2022).

Deuchar, Margaret & Suzanne Quay. 2000. *Bilingual acquisition: Theoretical implications of a case study*. Oxford: Oxford University Press.

Diebold, Richard A. 1968. The consequences of early bilingualism on cognitive development and personality formation. In Edward Norbeck, Douglass Price-Williams & William M. McCord (eds.), *The study of personality: An inter-disciplinary appraisal*, 218–245. New York: Hold, Rinehard & Winston.

Fishman, Joshua A. 1964. Language maintenance and language shift as a field of inquiry. *Linguistics* 9 (2). 32–70.

Fishman, Joshua A. 1972. Language maintenance and language shift as a field of inquiry: Revisited (1968). In Anwar S. Dill (ed.), *Language in sociocultural change: Essays by Joshua A. Fishman*, 76–134. Stanford: Stanford University Press.

Genesee, Fred. 1989. Early bilingual development: One language or two? *Journal of Child Language* 16 (1). 161–179.

Genesee, Fred. 2001. Bilingual first language acquisition: Exploring the limits of the language faculty. In Mary McGroarty (ed.), *21st annual review of applied linguistics*, 153–168. Cambridge: Cambridge University Press.

Genesee, Fred. 2008. Bilingual first language acquisition: Evidence from Montreal. [special issue] *Diversité urbaine* 8. 9–26.

Genesee, Fred & Elena Nicoladis. 2006. Bilingual acquisition. In Erika Hoff & Marilyn Shatz (eds.), *Handbook of language development*, 324–342. Oxford: Blackwell.

Genesee, Fred, Elena Nicoladis & Johanne Paradis. 1995. Language differentiation in early bilingual development. *Journal of Child Language* 22 (3). 611–632.

Genesee, Fred, Isabelle Boivin & Elena Nicoladis. 1996. Talking with strangers: A study of bilingual children's communicative competence. *Applied Psycholinguistics* 17 (4). 427–442.

Gill, Saran Kaur. 2005. Language policy in Malaysia: Reversing direction. *Language Policy* 4 (3). 241–260.

Gill, Saran Kaur. 2014. *Language policy challenges in multi-ethnic Malaysia*. Netherlands: Springer.

Gonier, Dennis E. 1999. The emperor gets new clothes. Paper presented at the Advertising Research Foundation's On-line Research Day.

Government of Malaysia. 1976. *Third Malaysian plan 1976–1980*. Kuala Lumpur: Government Press.

Graddol, David. 1997. *The future of English: A guide to forecasting the popularity of the English language in the 21st century*. London: The British Council.

Hager, Malin & Natascha Müller. 2015. Ultimate attainment in bilingual first language acquisition. *Lingua* 164 (4). 289–308.

Hashim, Azirah. 2014. English and the linguistic ecology of Malaysia. *World Englishes* 33 (4). 458–471.

Hashim, Azirah & Gerhard Leitner. 2017. English as a Malaysian and ASEAN language: Implications for language policy and planning. In Suseela Malakolunthu & Nagappan C. Rengasamy (eds.), *Policy discourses in Malaysian education*, 71–85. Singapore: Routledge.

Haznedar, Belma. 2007. Crosslinguistic influence in Turkish-English bilingual first language acquisition: The overuse of subjects in Turkish. In Alyoa Belikova, Luisa Meroni & Mari Umeda (eds.), *Proceedings of the second conference on generative approaches to language acquisition North America (GALANA)*, 124–134. Somerville: Cascadilla Proceedings Project.

Hernandez, Arturo, Ping Li & Brian MacWhinney. 2005. The emergence of competing modules in bilingualism. *Trends in Cognitive Sciences* 9 (5). 220–225.

Kirpatrick, Andy. 2020. English as an ASEAN lingua franca. In Kingsley Bolton, Werner Botha & Andy Kirkpatrick (eds.), *The handbook of Asian Englishes*, 725–740. Hoboken: Wiley Blackwell.

Krosnick, Jon A. & Stanley Presser. 2010. Question and questionnaire design. In Peter V. Marsden & James D. Wright (eds.), *Handbook of survey research*, 263–314. Bingley: Emerald.

Kwak, Nojin & Barry T. Radler. 1999. A comparison between mail and web-based surveys: Response pattern, data quality, and characteristics of respondents. Paper presented at the 1999 Annual Research Conference, Midwest Association for Public Opinion Research, 19–20 November.

Lanza, Elizabeth. 1997a. Language contact in bilingual two-year-olds and code-switching: Language encounters of a different kind? *International Journal of Bilingualism* 1 (2). 135–162.

Lanza, Elizabeth. 1997b. *Language mixing in infant bilingualism: A sociolinguistic perspective*. Oxford: Oxford University Press.

Lanza, Elizabeth. 2007. Multilingualism and the family. In Peter Auer & Wei Li (eds.), *Handbook of multilingualism and multilingual communication*, 45–66. Berlin & New York: De Gruyter Mouton.

Lee, Diana Phooi Yan & Su-Hie Ting. 2016 Language environment and educational background of Chinese parents in Sarawak, Malaysia: ESL or EAL? *The English Teacher* XLIV. 1–12.

Leopold, Werner. F. 1939. *Speech development of a bilingual child: A linguist's record* (Vol. 1: Vocabulary growth in the first two years). Evanston: Northwestern University Press.

Leopold, Werner. F. 1947. *Speech development of a bilingual child: A linguist's record* (Vol. 2: Sound learning in the first two years). Evanston: Northwestern University.

Leopold, Werner. F. 1949a. *Speech development of a bilingual child: A linguist's record* (Vol. 3: Grammar and general problems). Evanston: Northwestern University Press.

Leopold, Werner. F. 1949b. *Speech development of a bilingual child: A linguist's record* (Vol. 4: Diary from age 2). Evanston: Northwestern University Press.

Leopold, Werner. F. 1954. A child's learning of two languages. In Hugo J. Mueller (ed.), *Fifth annual Georgetown University round table on languages and linguistics*, 19–30. Washington: Georgetown University Press.

Locke, John L. 1997. A theory of neurolinguistic development. *Brain and Language* 58 (2). 265–326.

MacNamara, John. 1966. *Bilingualism and primary education*. Edinburgh: Edinburgh University Press.

McLaughlin, Barry. 1978. *Second language acquisition in childhood*. Hillsdale: Lawrence Erlbaum.

Mohamed Salleh, Rabiah Tul Adawiyah, Bruno Di Biase & Satomi Kawaguchi. 2021. Lexical and morphological development: A case study of Malay English bilingual first language acquisition. *Psychology of Language and Communication* 25 (1). 29–61.

Mohamed Salleh, Rabiah Tul Adawiyah, Bruno Di Biase & Wan Nur Madiha Ramlan. 2020. The acquisition of English grammar among Malay-English bilingual primary school children. *GEMA Journal of Language Studies* 20 (4). 166–185.

Mohamed Salleh, Rabiah Tul Adawiyah, Satomi Kawaguchi & Bruno Di Biase. 2019. A case study on the acquisition of plurality in a bilingual Malay-English context-bound child. *GEMA Journal of Language Studies* 19 (3). 22–42.

Mohamed Salleh, Rabiah Tul Adawiyah, Satomi Kawaguchi, Caroline Jones & Bruno Di Biase 2016. The development of plural expressions in a Malay-English bilingual child. *Asiatic* 10 (2). 60–81.

Mok, Opalyn. 2016. *Massive projects in place to alleviate urbanisation in Penang*. www.malaymail.com/news/malaysia/2016/10/29/massive-projects-in-place-to-alleviate-urbanisation-in-penang/1238453 (accessed 9 November 2021).

Nicoladis, Elena & Howard Grabois. 2002. Learning English and losing Chinese: A case study of a child adopted from China. *The International Journal of Bilingualism* 6 (4). 441–454.

Omar, Asmah Haji. 1987. *Malay in its sociocultural context*. Kuala Lumpur: Dewan Bahasa dan Pustaka.

Omar, Asmah Haji. 1997. From imperialism to Malaysianisation: A discussion of the path taken by English towards becoming a Malaysian language. In Halimah Mohd Said & Ng Keat Siew (eds.), *English is an Asian language: The Malaysian context*, 12–21. Kuala Lumpur: Association of Modern Languages, Malaysia and The Macquarie Library Pty. Ltd.

Ong, Teresa Wai See. 2019. A language maintenance project in Malaysia: Efforts to use Chinese community languages in everyday life. *TEANGA, the Journal of the Irish Association for Applied Linguistics* 26. 107–115.

Ong, Teresa Wai See. 2020. Safeguarding Penang Hokkien in Malaysia: Attitudes and community-driven efforts. *Linguistics Journal* 14 (1). 122–153.

Ong, Teresa Wai See. 2021. Family language policy, language maintenance and language shift: Perspectives from ethnic Chinese single mothers in Malaysia. *Issues in Language Studies* 10 (1). 59–75.

Paradis, Johanne. 2010. Bilingual children's acquisition of English verb morphology: Effects of language dominance, structure difficulty, and task type. *Language Learning* 60 (3). 651–680.

Penang Monthly. 2017. *Dialects and languages in numbers*. https://penangmonthly.com/article/7447/dialects-and-languages-in-numbers-1 (accessed 27 December 2021).

Reja, Urša, Katja Lozar Manfreda, Valentina Hlebec & Vasja Vehovar. 2003. Open-ended vs. close-ended questions in web questionnaires. Metodološki zvezki – *Advances in methodology and statistics* 19. 159–177.

Ronjat, Jules. 1913. *Le développement du langage observé chez un enfant bilingue*. Paris: Champion.

Rowland, Caroline. 2014. *Understanding child language acquisition*. New York: Routledge.

Schuman, Howard. 1972. Two sources of anti-war sentiment in America. *American Journal of Sociology* 78 (3). 513–536.

Spolsky, Bernard. 2012. Family language policy – The critical domain. *Journal of Multilingual and Multicultural Development* 33 (1). 3–11.

Tan, Ying Ying. 2003. Reading the census: Language use in Asia. In Jennifer Lindsay & Ying Ying Tan (eds.), *Babel or behemoth: Language trends in Asia*, 178–210. Singapore: Singapore University Press.

Ting, Su-Hie & Hui-Yee Hoo. 2022. Vitality of Hakka Chinese in Johor, Malaysia. *Taiwan Journal of Linguistics* 20 (2). 1–50.

Ting, Su-Hie & Mahanita Mahadhir. 2009. Towards homogeneity in home languages: Malay, Chinese Foochow and Indian Tamil families in Kuching, Sarawak, Malaysia. *Australian Review of Applied Linguistics* 32 (2). 11.1–11.22.

Volterra, Virginia & Traute Taeschner. 1978. The acquisition and development of language by bilingual children. *Journal of Child Language* 5 (2). 311–326.

Wölck, Wolfgang. 1984. Komplementierung und Fusion: Prozessenatürlicher Zweisprachigkeit. In Els Oksaar (ed.), *Spracherwerb – Sprachkontakt – Sprachkonflikt*, 107–128. Berlin & Boston: De Gruyter.

Yip, Virginia & Stephen Matthews. 2007. *The bilingual child: Early development and language contact*. Cambridge: Cambridge University Press.

Yip, Virginia & Stephen Matthews. 2010. The acquisition of Chinese in bilingual and multilingual contexts. *International Journal of Bilingualism* 14 (1). 127–146.

Kamolwan Fairee Jocuns and Andrew Jocuns

4 Family language policies in Thailand: Multiliteracy practices and Global Englishes

Abstract: Elective English bilingualism has become popular among Thai families in Thailand who seek to have an educational edge amidst a deficient public education system. Our interest in this study is in how Thai families with varying degrees of proficiency in L2 English introduce bilingual practices among children under the age of 5. While there has been a lot of research regarding English in Thailand there has been little research attention paid to Thai/English bilingualism especially among Thai families who have acquired English as an L2. To fill this gap this research is developed from two questions: 1) What are the practices that are salient within family language policies promoting elective bilingualism with English in Thailand? 2) How do these family language polices reflect practices that are inclusive or exclusive of a global variety of English in Thailand? To answer these questions we had five Thai families participate in semi-structured interviews and a journal task. The variety of practices that emerged illustrates how family language policies among Thai families reveal a nexus of practice that is inclusive of Thai English that includes: translanguaging, co-reading, role play, and others.

Keywords: elective bilingualism, Thai English, family language policy, translanguaging, Global Englishes

1 Introduction

Recently, there has been a growing interest in elective bilingualism in Thailand. This interest is evidenced in the number of social media sites on Facebook and YouTube devoted to promoting English and/or elective bilingualism in the Thai Netscape. However, there has been little research interest from the Thai applied linguistics community into this issue. To address this issue, this study examines the practices that are salient within family language policies promoting Thai and English elective bilingualism in Thailand. Our interest lays in what variety of English is being developed in households where the English-speaking parent(s) ac-

Kamolwan Fairee Jocuns, Thammasat University, Thailand
Andrew Jocuns, Wenzhou-Kean University, China

https://doi.org/10.1515/9783110733723-004

quired English as a second language (L2). The data reveal a nexus of practices that is inclusive of Thai English.

English in Thailand has been researched extensively, yet the focus of the majority of this work has drawn attention to language teaching (Hayes 2009; Wongsothorn, Hiranburana, and Chinnawongs 2002), student perceptions of English (Snodin and Young 2015; Thanosawan and Laws 2013), native speakerism (Boonsuk and Ambele 2019; Savski 2021), and more recently English as a lingua franca (Jaroensak 2018; Jaroensak and Saraceni 2019). The present study adds another dimension to research on English in Thailand which we find has been largely overlooked – the role of English in Thai families. The necessity of filling this gap is due in part to the importance of English in Thai education (Foley 2019; Hiranburana et al. 2017) where it is a compulsory subject beginning in grade 1. Despite English being introduced so early in Thailand, English proficiency of Thai students is consistently low. Therefore, examining contexts where English is used outside of Thai classrooms among families adds to the larger context of how English is used in Thailand.

Our interest in family language policy in Thailand is informed by two theories: global stances towards English (Rose and Galloway 2019) and, more analytically, nexus analysis (Scollon 2001; Scollon and Scollon 2004). For the latter, the unit of analysis is mediated action – a social actor performing an action with a mediational means (e.g., language, gesture, inscription, or other tools used in literacy events). This orientation towards action is important for the present study as it broadens the scope of actions and practices involved in English in Thailand. By using the term "Global Englishes," we are aligning with recent trends in the study of World Englishes which suggest that varieties of English transcend national boundaries (Jenkins [2003] 2014) and combine terms such as English as an international language, English as lingua franca, and World English under one term (Rose and Galloway 2019: 3). This is important because even though several researchers have argued and shown evidence for an emergent localized variety of English in Thailand (Huebner 2006, 2009; Jocuns 2018; Trakulkasemsuk 2012), Thai English lacks a strong community of speakers (Jocuns 2021). Therefore, its status as a variety is contested. Furthermore, Thai English does not fit the standard English varieties model; while features are identifiable, they most certainly are not uniform. Recent research suggests that although modelling English based on features and variables does not work for Thai English, there are ideological stances within the community of Thai English speakers that suggest the variety is enregistered (Jocuns 2021). These ideological stances are reflective of what Scollon and Scollon (2004) note as a nexus of practice, the intersection of multiple practices that are used to perform social actions. Some speakers identify Thai English as a variety of English, but there are stereotypes among this community, namely that speakers of Thai English are uneducated and work in certain occupations such as taxi drivers and restaurant workers. In examining the family language policy practices that emerge among Thai families, we are concerned with how they perceive the status of Thai English as a variety and the practices involved in using it.

This research sought to examine the practices that are salient within family language policies promoting elective bilingualism with English in Thailand. To explore and capture such practices, we had families participate in semi-structured qualitative interviews enabling us to discern the families' attitudes towards a global variety of English. We also had participants engage in a weekly journal task over a one-month period in which they responded to prompts asking them to offer an example of an English language communicative practice with their child in the form of a video or photograph. The range of practices that the study uncovered illustrates how family language policies among Thai families reveal a nexus of practice that is inclusive of Thai English. In the sections that follow, we discuss Global English in Thailand, child language acquisition, bilingualism, Global Englishes, and family language policy.

2 Literature review

The theoretical framework for this research is derived from nexus analysis (Scollon 2001; Scollon and Scollon 2004) which focuses on social action as a unit of analysis in a combination of ethnographically focused micro and macro data and uses discourse analysis to discern situated social practices (Wohlwend 2020). This orientation towards action is important for the present study as it broadens the scope of analysis beyond verbal language to include nonverbal communication as well as the use of space in early childhood literacy practices (Rainbird and Rowsell 2011; Whittingham 2019). A focus on action, furthermore, helps examine English in Thailand because there is not a uniform variety of Thai English that is in use. Yet there are ideological stances within the community of Thai English speakers that suggest the variety is enregistered (Jocuns 2021). Because of this, there are practices involved in the use of Thai English which transcend language which aligns with Seargeant and Tagg's (2011) discussion of "post-varieties" of English. The linguistic ecology of Thailand includes somewhere between 51 (Ethnologue 2023) and 91 (Smalley 1994) languages, and both authors note that the standard Thai language is based on the Central Thai dialect. In terms of bi- or multilingualism in Thailand, Smalley (1994) discusses how many minority languages in the peripheral areas of Thailand (i.e., outside of Bangkok) engage in situational bilingualism and identifies some diglossic situations where minority languages and Thai language are used for different purposes. Trakulkasemsuk (2012) notes there are roughly 6.5 million speakers of English in Thailand; however, this count is deceptive given the status of English in Thailand and the fact that children begin learning English in Thailand in grade 1. Based on these facts, the definition of a "speaker" of English is a vague one. Trakulkasemsuk (2018) recently noted that Thai speakers of English seldomly speak to one another in English which influences how bilingualism is introduced in families. While Trakulkasemsuk (2018) is correct in that one may not witness Thai people speaking English amongst themselves in public with great frequency, this assumption ignores the fact that there are Thai families who introduce English to their repertoire of home languages through elective bilingualism as part of their family language policy (Kamalanavin 2011, 2015).

Family language policy is a field of study which is still in its infancy having only just recently emerged as an object of inquiry in the early 2000s (King, Folge, and Logan-Terry 2008). The goal of many family language policy studies is to explore the perceptions and ideologies that families develop towards languages and the practices that are promoted in developing bilingual or multilingual language behavior. The study of family language policy intersects with two other well-established fields of inquiry in linguistics: national language policy (Spolsky 2004) and child language acquisition. The approach developed in this research adds another dimension to family language policy by also considering Global Englishes and the stances that Thai speakers of English take up towards Thai English (Bennui and Hashim 2014; Jocuns 2018, 2021; Trakulkasemsuk 2012, 2018). In addition, more recent conceptualizations of multilingualism (Blackledge and Creese 2010) which emphasize how languages are not separate entities but rather a part of a complete linguistic repertoire (García and Li 2014) increasingly offer new insights into how family language policy can include translanguaging (Danjo 2021).

2.1 Methods of raising bilingual children

The most popular method for raising a bilingual child has been the one person-one language or one parent-one language (OPOL) approach to child bilingual language acquisition (Baker and Wright [1993] 2021; Crisfield 2021). One study of the OPOL approach found that the success of the acquisition process was related to how the parent approached language use as child-centered and positioned the child as a conversational partner (Döpke 1992). This suggests that the successful implementation of the OPOL approach is not just a matter of one person speaking one language, but that the interactive quality of the language's use is integral.

Döpke (1992) shed light on the amount of effort involved for parents who implement OPOL, especially among the minority language parent. OPOL as a strategy for raising a bilingual child is effective, but it should be noted that the reality of its implementation varies widely. Furthermore, factors such as the local language context as well as the status of a minority language in the home are equally important to consider.

While OPOL is often known as a highly successful strategy, there is no one size fits all-model for how bilingual language use may emerge in the family context. The forms of bilingualism found in the present research were more aligned with García's (2009) dynamic concept of bilingualism in which bilinguals make use of their entire linguistic repertoire during communication. In a similar vein, Kamalanavin (2015) points out that the kind of bilingualism focused on in this study is commonly referred to by several terms: i.e., artificial, non-native, elective, additive, and even elite bilingualism (King and Fogle 2006; King, Folge, and Logan-Terry 2008; Pearson 2008). Following Kamalanavin's (2015) suggestion, the present research employs the term elective bilingualism as its connotation is neutral. Kamalanavin found elective bilingualism to be used by Thai families when searching for advice through an online message board, while King and Fogle (2006) found that families introducing elective bilingualism mostly drew on their own experiences in language learning as opposed to expert advice. These differences are interesting in that they highlight how elective bilingualism is dynamic in terms of context and how seeking advice from experts, online message boards, or relying upon one's own experiences may also be cultural factors. The subject of the role of the family in developing bilingualism is the subject of the next section.

2.2 Family language policy

Spolsky (2004) notes that one of the domains of language policy is the family and that the family domain focuses on language as practice, language ideology, and language management. He further finds that bilingual families follow/implement more explicit family language policy than families with only one home language. Language as practice refers to the variety of ways in which language is used within the context of the family. Language ideology refers to the beliefs and values that are placed upon linguistic choices (Woolard 1998; Woolard and Schieffelin 1994). Language choice within the family is determined in part by language proficiency as well as attitudes towards a language. Spolsky (2004) also suggests that within the home, language policy is not always explicit but rather ideologically honed through language practices. An issue that Spolsky touches upon is the role of children in determining language choice in the home (see, e.g., De Houwer 2021 for a recent overview; Tuominen 1999).

In an ethnographic study of bilingual Japanese and English families in the UK, Danjo (2021) noted how one family's OPOL policy was navigated by their children in ways which ultimately mitigated the "double monolingualism" that bilingual family language policies that promote OPOL establish. The bilingual children in Danjo's study were creative and flexible in their use of both languages, thereby negating the seemingly negative effects of double monolingualism embedded within OPOL strategies exemplified in translanguaging. Translanguaging refers to how speakers use their entire linguistic repertoire during communication as well as several epistemological distinctions, for example, the lack of named languages, the lack of common underlying proficiency, and that languages that are invented are not countable (García and Li 2014; García et al. 2021). For the latter languages are not countable because the understanding of languages as separate entities is an invention. Translanguaging contrasts with traditional views of code-switching which tend to suggest that speakers utilize two disparate codes (Baker and Wright 2021). Danjo focused upon translanguaging and translingual practices (Canagarajah 2013) and found that in family multilingual interactions, notions of language as a resource and language as a social practice emerged in such a way as to enable creativity in the face of the monolingual ideal of code-switching, which tends to perceive languages as separate entities.

While there are a number of studies that examine language choice in family language policies, another group of studies focuses on the role of parenting. One such study (Piller and Gerber 2018) examines modern western parenting and finds it to entail a high level of anxiety amidst the backdrop of self-help literature. We will add social media as an additional medium to provide self-help for parenting and raising bilingual children, keeping in mind that web 2.0 sources can be authored by anyone, not necessarily experts. Piller and Gerber's (2018) discussion focuses on an Australian online parenting forum where topics emerged with regards to raising bilingual children and bilingual parenting. Their findings show how members of the forum encourage a narrow view of bilingualism which is effectively English-centric; one acquires English and a language other than English (LOTE). The notions of bilingualism in this forum entailed hints of neoliberal ideology as well, where bilingualism was discussed as a gift that entails both academic and economic success. In some discussions, they found that a LOTE was at times presented as a threat to the acquisition of English-first. In short, Piller and Gerber (2018) revealed how an ideology of family language policy in Australia was in effect promoting double monolingualism and that the praise given towards bilingualism on the forums did not equate with fully valued multilingual repertoires.

Another interesting aspect of family language policy studies is children's agency and creativity. Similar to Tuominen (1999) and Danjo (2021) who noted the role of children in family language policy, Said and Zhu (2019) found that children play both an agentive and creative role in their own bi- or multilingual development when studying the context of one Arabic and English speaking family in the UK. Said and Zhu (2019) found such agency and creativity to be related to three factors: flexible language policies, the children's understanding of their parents' preference for Arabic, and the child-centric nature of language interactions at the dinner table. These findings are related to what De Houwer (2015, 2020, 2021) has described as harmonious bilingual development which refers to a positive or neutral experience that family members have in a bilingual context.

Purkarthofer (2019) offers an alternative approach to family language policy which included the developing family language policies of three couples who were expecting their first child. One of the differences with this study compared to other family language policy studies is that it also focused on how these families were constructing a social space for their respective policy. To accomplish this, Purkarthofer utilized a production of space analysis derived from Lefebrve (1991). Results indicate how representations of social space, space in family language policy, and how family language policies are negotiated, can change, and develop over time. One area of research in family language policy that requires further attention is its relationship to contexts of Global Englishes, the subject of the next section.

2.3 Global Englishes and family language policy

As noted in Section 1, we prefer the term Global Englishes aligning ourselves with researchers who contest the idea that varieties may be attributed to nations and with recent trends in Global Englishes Language Teaching to merge several terms (Jenkins 2014; Rose and Galloway 2019). This is important for the present study since the variety status of Thai English is itself contested. This contestation is in part ideologically driven as, in some cases, Thai English is perceived negatively (Jocuns 2021) whereas others believe that it is to be granted "ownership" by Thai users of English (Boonsuk and Ambele 2019). In short, some studies suggest that Thai English is an owned variety whereas others suggest that Thai speakers of English are apprehensive of owning it. Such differences could have to do with the different regions of Thailand in which the studies were conducted and the educational differences in the local population. While it goes beyond the scope of the present study to go into the minute details of whether Thai English should be considered a distinct variety, it should be noted that it does share similarities with

Jenkins' (2000, 2014) discussion of postcolonial English (e.g. interdental fricatives /θ, ð/ emerging as /t/ and /d/ and many localizations and borrowings from Thai language). Thai English is the variety that is emergent among the families in our study. To date, there have been only a few studies that have explored issues of Global Englishes and family language policy, but there have been studies of family language policy that have examined English in the context of former British colonies and contexts of English as a second language.

Jenks (2020) makes some interesting points regarding the relationship between the recent translingualism movement (Pennycook 2016), which advocates an approach to bi- and multilingualism by drawing attention to how the epistemology of translanguaging does not always take the variety of contexts with which multilingualism can emerge and family language policy into consideration. Using his own experience as a bilingual Korean/(American) English speaker, Jenks (2020) notes how the rigid family language policy that his family employed was specific to the challenges of his family's linguistic and social situation in Hong Kong. This suggests that, as far as family language policies are concerned, there is no one model, as with OPOL, that is universally successful. Family language policies, like the languages they promote, are localized and dependent upon the context and situation for their implementation and success.

Other studies of Global Englishes and family language policies include Mirvahedi and Cavallaro (2020) who examined Singapore English in family contexts. They found that the parents in their study adopted an OPOL strategy, wishing to maintain Malay but also to use English in the home because it is the language of wider communication in Singapore.

The gap we are filling in this research is the lack of family language policy studies in Thailand and in Global Englishes. Our approach to Global Englishes is in line with recent trends in applied linguistics which give preference to translanguaging (García and Li 2014), multilingualism (Blackledge and Creese 2010), and Rose and Galloway's (2019) approach to Global Englishes in English language teaching, which contest the idea that varieties of English are attributed to nations. Of particular relevance to the present study is how Rose and Galloway's (2019) approach epistemically aligns with a range of topics that are important to current trends in bi- and multilingual research. For example, Rose and Galloway (2019: 19–26) emphasize that the target speakers are all users of English; they emphasize that the ownership of English is a global enterprise and the goal of learning is to to have multicompetence; they follow an ideology that is inclusive of Global Englishes, and, lastly, see the orientation for using English as being multilingual/ translingual. Such attitudes are an attempt to rectify ideological issues in English language teaching and English ideologies, which still persist in Expanding Circle countries, such as Thailand, that privy English as a lingua franca (Jaroensak and

Saraceni 2019) and a foreign language. Such ideologies also emerge in the hiring practices of English teachers which entail aspects of race and native-speakerism (Savski 2021), but it should also be noted that that local ideologies regarding varieties of English (Thai English and native varieties) vary considerably. At the same time, there seems to be some suggestion that positive attitudes towards a local variety of English have already begun to take hold in Thailand. Boonsuk and Ambele (2019) found that Thai university students in Southern Thailand believed in the local ownership of English. The next section presents how we implemented a nexus analysis to investigate family language policies and practices in five Thai families in Thailand. Then, we will present the findings and discussion, which also include how Global Englishes emerged among the five families.

3 Methodology

In order to examine how a nexus of family language policies in Thailand is oriented towards Global Englishes, we implemented two data collection methods: a semi-structured interview and a weekly journal task conducted over a one-month period. We organized a semi-structured interview with five families in Bangkok, Thailand with children aged from one to three years old. The following criteria were included during an initial screening session:
1. The family has children under the age of five.
2. The family performs activities at home using English and Thai.
3. Both parents are L1 Thai speakers.

Table 4.1 shows the family background information of the families who participated in the study. The names of the parents and children are pseudonyms.

Table 4.1: Summary of the five families.

Parents' names (mother & father)	Child's name	Age (Y;M)
Ying & Chaiya	Wan	3;1
Dao & Kitti	Ploy	2;5
Mali & Narong	Kla	2;5
Tida & Pichai	Nicha	2
Kanya & Den	Akin	2;10

The families were recruited as a sample of convenience, four of whom were friends of one of the authors, and one was acquired via a word-of-mouth recommendation. This sample represents highly educated Thai citizens. Three participants have obtained a bachelor's degree, four participants have obtained a master's degree, and two participants have obtained a PhD. They persued their education beyond grade 9 which is more than the requirements of the basic education system in Thailand. Thus, they are considered highly educated Thai citizens. These educational backgrounds may suggest their social status as "educated middle class" and may also affect literacy practices at home. However, this is not to suggest that only "highly-educated" Thai people have access to English in Thailand. The status of English in Thailand is two-fold as it is used as a foreign language (EFL) and as a lingua franca (ELF). As for EFL, English is introduced as a part of the common Thai core curriculum as early as grade 1 (The Ministry of Education 2008). However, it is not uncommon for English to be introduced earlier in kindergarten or preschool where students are taught the alphabet and/or phonics. Despite this early introduction of English and its continual study throughout primary and secondary school, Thailand continuously ranks very low with regards to English proficiency (Education First English Proficiency Index 2021). In terms of ELF in Thailand, English is used in several communities of practice, including the tourism industry, international businesses, and the private "international" education sector. Because the status of English in Thailand is that of EFL and ELF as well as Thailand's continual low ranking regarding English proficiency, we note that our sample of families who introduce English through elective bilingualism is extraordinary in terms of being able to introduce English literacy to their children by themselves.

The interviews were conducted in Thai and translated into English by one of the authors. The interview questions were built around three main topics including: 1) the participants' English learning experience and their attitudes toward the importance of English; 2) their family language policy and English literacy practices at home; and 3) their attitudes towards English and the local variety of Thai English. After the interview, we asked the participants to make video or audio recordings of their activities with their children and to write a short journal entry about their daily conversations based on a series of prompts. The objective of this data collection was to observe how the ideologies of family language policy that were identified during interviews matched up with their actual use of language and other communicative practices. To examine these matches, we implemented a nexus analysis of the family language policies.

Nexus analysis is an approach to research that enables a critical examination of action by unpacking the various practices, ideologies, and discourses that make up a nexus (Scollon and de Saint-Georges 2012; Scollon and Scollon 2004; Wohlwend 2020). There are three steps in a nexus analysis: engaging, navigating, and changing the nexus. Engaging the nexus, as Wohlwend (2020) notes is a matter of seeking out literacy practices. Navigating the nexus is where we begin to analyze the practices that emerged from the data; this analysis focused upon actions and practices that emerged in both the interviews and the journal task. Changing the nexus was not carried out in the study because the present study is reporting on initial findings. An additional focus of nexus analysis states how action resides at the intersection of three components: the historical body, the interaction order, and discourses in place. In our analysis, we focus on two of these concepts: the interaction order (Goffman 1983; Scollon and Scollon 2003) which is the social arrangements embedded in family language policies (e.g. the child acting alone, or one parent interacting with the child) and the discourses in place which includes languages present and literacy tools (e.g. the languages used in the family, children's picture books, and literacy toys like wooden English letters).

4 Findings and analysis

In this section, we present the findings and data analysis from both the interviews and journal entries which are devided in two main themes: 1) the parents' English learning experience and their attitudes toward the importance of English, and 2) family language policy and English literacy practices at home.

4.1 The parents' English learning experience and their attitudes toward the importance of English

The data of this section is based on the interview task only. All five families perceive the importance of English for their child's education. For example, Ying and Chaiya said English is a tool to explore new things and they gave priority to learning English over other academic success even though their child has not yet reached the age of school assessment. They also emphasized how they feel that English is a tool for their child to be an autonomous learner. Dao specifically mentioned that being literate in English is important because it will give children access to more literature.

One family discussed how their perspectives towards English have changed over time. One participant expressed this by comparing his attitude when he was a student and his present attitude toward the status of English. Den said that when he was a student, being good at English gave him opportunities for a better education abroad. Both he and his wife received Thai government scholarships to study at universities in the Netherlands, such scholarships are granted partly because recipients have good grades in all subjects including English. Another important factor for English in education that they mentioned was that it is an important language that is used at university. Although the medium of instruction was Dutch, they were required to read English textbooks. His perception has changed from seeing English as a language of opportunity to a language of necessity. As Den discussed in an interview, he believes that it is hard to live without knowing English now, "[i]f you don't know English, you will be left behind. You see English (in Thailand) in news, services, phone applications and so on". Both of these ideas of having access to English fit within a larger ideology of English being related to future success or access to resources in the future.

4.2 Family language policy and English literacy practices at home

The data of this section is based on both the interview and journal tasks. All five families started using English at home because they believed that it is the most natural and effective way for their child to learn a language. They want to familiarize their children with the language and want them to learn it naturally just like when the parents learned Thai as children. Narong said that using English with his child at home is not the only important factor to develop their child's English skills. He pointed out that he has known people who are fluent in English who are from families where there was no English at home. For him, the reason why English is nonetheless used in his family is that he thinks a child at this young age can absorb languages very easily. The interview data shows that four families are very flexible about their language policies at home. They speak English when they feel like speaking it and do not have any formal policy about language use in their homes. Consequently, the amount of English used in the four families varies. Tida, for example, reported using English with her child during 60–70% of their daily conversations while Dao reported using English with her child during approximately 10% of their daily conversations. Dao also reported that, initially, she wanted to use an OPOL approach so that she would speak English and her husband would speak Thai to their child. She learned this method from her Thai friend in the UK but did not know it was called OPOL. However, she did not think this method would work well in her family because she was concerned that she would not be able to get her intended meanings across in English. One family in the study (Kanya and Den) implemented an OPOL strategy where the father only speaks English and the mother speaks Thai, but as the journal data shows, they are much more flexible in practice, see Excerpt (3). Regardless of the policies, the families implemented similar elective bilingualism practices. Table 4.2 lists the activities in which English emerged in communicative practices from both interviews and journal entries.

Table 4.2: English activities.

English Communicative Practices
Roleplay
Listening to music
Reading aloud
Singing
Talking along with daily routines
Talking during mealtime
Talking during a day out
Watching cartoons or other media

The practices that emerged from analyzing the journal entries included the use of translanguaging, no accent preference, repairing pronunciation idiosyncratically, and, most importantly, no inhibition when speaking English with their children. The English being developed in these households aligns with Global Englishes as none of the families are promoting one single standard variety of English, and they allow their children to speak with Thai accented English. Either or both parents read English storybooks and talk in English during their respective storytimes. Some families reported they read and talk to their children about the book. Excerpt (1) is an example of such a practice reported during the interview. Dao gave some example of questions she would ask her child during the story times both when reading Thai and English books.

(1) Dao: *I not only read, but also ask, "what color is this?," "where are they going?," "who is this?," something like that. I do the same both when reading Thai and English books.*

English language structures used in their conversations are not complex – mostly simple sentences and phrases. In the following section, we present the journal data which include both video and audio data recordings. The journal data offer examples of: 1) the use of translanguaging, 2) English pronunciation practices, and 3) the participanting families' attitudes towards English and the local variety of Thai English. Translanguaging is used both by the children and their parents to smooth out the conversation. From the video recordings, we were able to get a glimpse of how English is pronounced within the family as well. What emerged from both the interviews and journal entries was that families showed positive attitudes towards Thai English which was also reflected in their practices of translanguaging because their pronunciation patterns were more consistent with pronunciation related to Thai English. While this may be a sign of language transfer, we wish to emphasize that parents did not correct children's pronunciation of English to favor a specific variety, which may indicate their positive attitude toward local varieties of Thai English.

4.2.1 Translanguaging in conversations

In this section we discuss some instances of translanguaging that emerged in the journal entry data (video and audio recordings) where the parent and the child were drawing on their communicative repertoires during interactions. There was one family that submitted only audio recordings and because the data were not used in the present paper, we refer to all recordings as video recordings. Kanya and Den are the only family that implemented OPOL. Using OPOL, they have assigned themselves clear roles where Den, the father, communicates in English and Kanya, the mother, communicates in Thai. They implemented OPOL since Akin, their child, was born, and they said this approach works quite well for their family. However, as noted in Section 2, OPOL is not a one size fits all-model of bilingual language acquisition. While Kanya and Den try to maintain a strict OPOL strategy, translanguaging occurs because they are both proficient speakers of both English and Thai. Excerpt (2) entails an example – it shows Akin using a lexical item from English to fill a gap in his linguistic knowledge of Thai in Line (2.1) while his mother is trying to direct his language use to Thai in Line (2.2).

(2) 1. Akin: อคินมี *grapes*. . .. [I have *grapes*. . .]
    2. Kanya: อันนี้เรียกภาษาไทยว่าอะไรนะ [What do you call this in Thai?]
    3. Akin: Grapes
    4. Kanya: อันนี้ภาษาอังกฤษเรียกว่า grapes ภาษาไทยเรียกว่าอะไร [It is called *grapes* in English. What is it called in Thai?]

Excerpt (2) shows that the use of translanguaging was implemented by Akin's mother as well: Although Akin's parents have separate roles in using Thai and English, his mother – whose initial role is to speak Thai – introduces books and songs in both languages. Excerpt (3) shows Kanya using an English book but talking in both Thai and English. Kanya is using translanguaging to give her child more English input by reading the book and making a conversation.

(3) 1. Akin: นี่คืออะไร [What's this?]
2. Kanya: แล้วอคินว่าคืออะไรนะครับ [What do you think it is?]
3. Akin: *cup, green cup*
4. Kanya: *green cup, yes, excellent* ต่อไป [Next]

Kanya speaks Thai with her child but reads and initiates conversations in both English and Thai as noted in Lines (3.2) and (3.4). Both parents believe that reading aloud to their child will help develop his English listening skills and pronunciation.

Another example of the use of translanguaging can also be seen during interactive reading in Ying and Chaiya's family who do not use an OPOL strategy. One video shows Ying's daughter, Wan, reciting an English children's story book *The Hungry Caterpillar*. Excerpt (4) shows both mother and child using translanguaging as Wan initiates questions in Thai in Line (4.1) and Ying responds in English in Line (4.2) in order to direct their conversation towards the use of English. Wan starts to use translanguaging in Line (3); however, the response from her mother is in Thai.

(4) 1. Wan: ทำไมหนอนมันทำงี้อะหม่าม้า [Why did the caterpillar act like that, mama?]
2. Ying: Oh, he is too full.
3. Wan: หม่าม้าขา ทำไม he eat better, he eat อันนี้อะ [Mama, why did he eat better [when] he eat this one?]
4. Ying: เพราะว่าใบไม้อะ มันย่อยง่ายใช่ไหม มันเป็นผักไง มันเหมือนผักไง [Because the leaf is easy to digest, right? It's a veg. It's like a veg.]

Ying explains in a follow-up interview that she tries to initiate conversations in English, but sometimes, due to the complex sentence structures and vocabulary, it was difficult for her to produce English spontaneously. That is why she responded in Thai. The practice of translanguaging either through spoken discourse or through literacy events, represented in all examples from Excerpt (1) to (4), are conducive to developing and fostering Thai English, as both parents and children equally use English creatively.

4.2.2 The parents' English pronunciation practice and attitudes towards English and the local variety of Thai English

Another insight that emerged from the interview and video recording data was that the parents do not promote one accent or a specific variety of English and many of them emphasized that a specific English accent was not their priority. All families agreed that parents should demonstrate clear pronunciation. At the same time, such attitudes and practices exemplify these families' positive attitudes towards Thai English. There has been a long-held value of สำเนียงดี /sǎm-nian di:/ 'good accent' among Thai people. 'Good accent' is a Thai phrase that is used as a compliment for Thai L1 speakers who have a near-native pronunciation when they speak a foreign language. The participating families said intelligibility is most important which also is aligned with Rose and Galloway's (2019) precepts for Global Englishes Language Teaching (GELT). Excerpt (5) shows Den talking in English with his child Akin while they are stuck in traffic. Den uses simple English sentences and phrases alongside clear pronunciation.

(5) 1. Den: *A lot of cars. Ooh, many motor**cy**cles.* [primary stress on "cy"]
    2. Akin: *Papa, a lot of cars.*
    3. Den: *Yes, a lot of cars. . .stuc**k**, stuc**k** in traffic.* [noticeable /k/ final consonant release]
    4. Akin: *Akin is also stuc**k**.* [noticeable /k/ final consonant release]
    5. Den: Yes, Akin is also stuc**k**. We all are stuck in traffic. [noticeable /k/ final consonant release]

Den tried to pronounce words as clearly as possible. In Line (5.3), he tried to emphasize the final sound /k/ of the word *stuck* and in Line (5.4) we could hear his son pronouncing the word *stuck* the same way. Dropping final sounds in English is one of the pronunciation features that Thai people often miss because final consonants in Thai are inaudible (Suntornsawet, 2019). At the same time, some of Den's pronunciation includes features that resemble Thai pronunciation, for example the primary stress on the syllable "cy" instead of "mo" in the word *motorcycle*. Despite errors in word stress, the conversation was smooth and comprehensible.

Excerpt (6) shows how a parent repairs her child's English. All three videos Ying's family shared with us entailed interactions in both Thai and English. One video showed her daughter reciting the English storybook *The Hungry Caterpillar*. During this video, a continuation of Excerpt (4), her daughter initiates questions in Thai and Ying responds in both English and Thai. Ying helps her daughter to fill lexical gaps that she cannot remember as well as to talk about the book. Excerpt (6) also shows how Ying repairs her daughter's use of English.

(6) 1. Wan: *Orange juice* (pointing at pictures of oranges)
    2. Ying: *Oranges.* (repairing the word)
    3. Wan: *And he is a beautiful butterfly!*
    4. Ying : *Oh, how he fly?*
    5. Wan: *Flap, flap, flap*
    6. Ying : *Flap, **frap**, **frap**, the end.*

Ying repairs an error in her child's speech by replacing an incorrect word with the correct one. Though the lexical item was correct, Ying's pronunciation is not. Ying puts the stress on the second syllable instead of the first one: "o*ra*nges". Another error is found in the production of a consonant cluster *fl-* in *flap*. However, it is not a repetitive error as she pronounces it correctly in *fly*. Apart from those noticeable errors, most of Ying's pronunciation is clear. We can hear clear final consonant sounds, for example, when she says, "Let's see the next pa*ge*". The Thai language codes for final consonant sounds much differently than the English language. Therefore, the production of English word-final sounds can be problematic for some Thai speakers and learners of English (Iwasaki and Ingkaphirom 2009). Ying's video shows that she tries her best to use clear pronunciation as much as possible.

In the interview, Den, Ying, and other parents in the study emphasized their belief of being good models in showing their children clear pronunciation. Narong and Chaiya pointed out that the phrase สำเนียงดี /sămniaŋ diː/ 'good accent' is usually used to compliment those who have an American-like accent because Thai people are familiar with American entertainment such as Hollywood movies. At the same time, they emphasized that they do not mind if their children do not meet this social expectation. There are several studies that indicate that American, British, and Canadian English are the preferred varieties of Thai students (Choomthong and Manowong 2020; Jindapitak and Teo 2013). In other words, native English speaker accents are still highly valued in Thailand. However, it seems to be unrealistic for the families that their children would acquire one of these accents.

(7) Chaiya: *Supposing that "good accent" is what most people speak in the world. What if one day all the Chinese spoke English? Do we all need to do that? I don't mind accent differences. I focus on understanding.*

When we asked whether they have heard of the variety of English known as Thai English and who speaks Thai English, most parents were not sure what Thai English refers to. However, their responses included "speaking English with a Thai accent". Chaiya described in detail that speaking English with a Thai accent includes such features as lengthening vowels in English words, and that Thai English probably includes the influence of Thai sentence structure on English sentence structure. Again, Excerpt (7) and its affective stance with regards to English pronunciation indexes a Global Englishes perspective. Other families have similar views. The families are aware of the preference in terms of sounding "American" or สำเนียงดี /sămniaŋ diː/ 'good accent' but at the same time draw our attention to the importance of being effective communicators as opposed to native pronouncers of English.

Challenges in communicating in the family seem to be at the lexical level rather than pronunciation. Some families reported both looking a word up and replacing it with words/phrases with similar meaning in English. Most of them said that they learn English as their children learn it. They learn new words because they see the need to fulfill the conversational needs of their children. Excerpt (8) shows examples of words that parents had never encountered before.

(8) a. Chaiya: *We know the phrase brushing the teeth, but we don't know how to say spitting the water.*
 b. Ying: *button up, roll up your sleeves, tie your shoelaces – we need to look them up.*
 c. Den: *Like, a bucket and a shower, I only use one word: water container.*

Excerpts (5) to (7) reflect practices where parents believed in being a good role model for clear pronunciation. They tried their best to give enough English input at home. They embraced their pronunciation and their accents. Excerpt (8) reflects challenges that families faced at home while using English during daily routines with their children. Even though they know they might have some pronunciation and lexical errors, they do not refrain from using English at home nor are they afraid of being a bad example for their children.

5 Discussion

The present study has shown how some practices that the five families implemented in using English in their respective family language policies reflect global stances towards English (Rose and Galloway 2019). One of the findings regarding their family language policies is that the implemented practices were not fixed but fluid; even the family that claimed to use OPOL was found to be more flexible in practice. The communicative practices that emerged through implementation of elective bilingualism included: using translanguaging, not having an accent preference, repairing pronunciation idiosyncratically, and, most importantly, not being afraid to speak English with their children. In terms of language ideology, the families did not have a negative attitude towards the local variety of English, Thai English.

In terms of nexus analysis (Scollon 2001; Scollon and Scollon 2004), we will discuss the three concepts in a nexus analysis that note that a social action lays at the intersection of the interaction order, the historical body, and discourses in place. Our analysis informs discourses in place more directly as a part of this nexus analysis, this is due in part to the size of our sample and the amount of data collected.

Interaction order refers to the way social arrangements emerge during social interaction. The different social arrangements that we observed among the families in the study included one parent and one child interaction, or both parents interacting with their child in their car and home. These interaction orders also reflect the flexible family language policies that emerged in the data where there were not strict boundaries placed around Thai or English, and participants used their respective linguistic repertoires.

The historical body refers to a social actor's accumulation of bodily actions which includes actions such as opening a children's English storybook or initiate conversations about things that were going on around them. We also observed many practices of reading, interacting, and role play. However, the one practice which stands out in terms of our interest in the presence of positive attitudes towards Global Englishes was the use of translanguaging in several of the excerpts, including among the family who established an OPOL policy.

Discourses in place refer to the various discourses that are present within a given social action which can range from different languages as well as larger orders of discourse. The discourses in place that emerged from the interview data revealed how the families in our study did not have a negative attitude towards Thai English, they were open to its use in the home, and this was reflected by the media that they shared with us in the journal entries and the interviews. For example, parents initiated converations based on children's storybooks, e.g. Excerpts (1) and (3), and the immediate events and contexts that they were engaged in, e.g. Excerpts (2) and (5). Specifically initiating questions in English while reading the *Hungry Catepillar*, Excerpts (4) and (6) offered an example of how parents incorporated a variety of discourse strategies while implementing elective bilingual family language policies: not overcorrecting pronunciation and using their full linguistic repertoires. Also showing a tendency towards an understanding of English as a global language is the fact that the participants were more concerned with communicative competence than with native-like pronunciation in their use of elective bilingualism, e.g. Excerpt (7). This is, for example, indicated by the fact that parents did not overcorrect their children's pronunciation nor did they have accent preferences. Other discourses that emerged around English pertained to how English is ideologically perceived as a language that increases learning, opportunities, overall educational benefits, and is a language that one cannot live without.

6 Conclusion

The study at hand has explored family language policies among Thai families living in Bangkok, Thailand. The families introduced English in different amounts and through different practices to their children. Both the interviews and the journal entry data informed our understanding of salient practices within family language policies. These policies were found to be fluid in practice. The interview data revealed the practices that parents were aware of at a metalevel. These practices were mentioned in Table 4.2 and include practices such as role-play, listening to music, singing songs, reading aloud, and others. The families in our study revealed that they had positive attitudes towards the local Thai variety of English being used in the home. What is interesting about this is that while the interview data suggested some seemingly neoliberal ideology regarding English – English is a language of opportunity, English is about education (Piller and Cho 2013, Alarcón Utrera and Nieto Moreno de Diezmas 2023) – this ideology did not emerge in practice. While there were instances of repair in the data, the child's language that was being repaired was not repaired towards a specific variety of English. In addition, the practice of translanguaging, i.e. using their entire linguistic repertoires, suggests that the families in our study were liberal in terms of how they viewed the boundaries between these two disparate languages.

The present study adds to the paradigm of World Englishes as it shows how families in an expanding circle context incorporate English into their family language policies through elective bilingualism. The study not only included young children, but the research sites were not educational or classroom contexts. To that end, we find studies of children in World Englishes and outside of educational settings under explored in the World Englishes paradigm. By investigating the acquisitional practices of English as an additional language among family language policies in Thailand, we observe how such practices challenge the status of varieties in the expanding circle. Both children and out of school contexts are important research areas for World Englishes as we are able to see how learners use World Englishes in novel ways and novel contexts. Young children in the expanding circle will be future users of English and it is important to capture how their parents nurture and influence use and attitudes. At present, we feel that we have only just scratched the surface of elective bilingualism in Bangkok, Thailand. Future research would need to cast a wider net in terms of different age groups, number of participants, educational background of participants, and deeper investigation in English language used in Thai families and children in the study of World Englishes.

References

Alarcón Utrera, Ana Belén, and Esther Nieto Moreno de Diezmas. 2023. *Speaking in Nobody's Mother Tongue: English Immersion at Home as a Family Language Policy*. Ampersand 11.

Baker, Colin & Wayne E. Wright. 2021 [1993]. *Foundations of bilingual education and bilingualism*, 7th edn. Bristol & Blue Ridge Summit: Multilingual Matters.

Bennui, Pairote & Azirah Hashim. 2014. English in Thailand: Development of English in a non-postcolonial context. *Asian Englishes* 16 (3). 209–228.

Blackledge, Adrian & Angela Creese. 2010. *Multilingualism: A critical perspective*. London & New York: Bloomsbury Academic.

Boonsuk, Yusop & Eric A. Ambele. 2019. Who 'owns English' in our changing world? Exploring the perception of Thai university students in Thailand. *Asian Englishes* 22 (3). 297–308.

Canagarajah, Suresh. 2013. *Translingual practice: Global Englishes and cosmopolitan relations*. Milton Park, Abingdon, Oxon & New York: Routledge.

Choomthong, Daranee & Supaporn Manowong. 2020. Varieties of English accents: A study of the degree of preference and intelligibility among second-year English major students at Maejo University. *Manusya: Journal of Humanities* 23 (2). 151–169.

Crisfield, Eowyn. 2021. *Bilingual families: A practical language planning guide*. Bristol & Blue Ridge Summit: Multilingual Matters.

Curdt-Christiansen, Xiao Lan. 2016. Conflicting language ideologies and contradictory language practices in Singaporean multilingual families. *Journal of Multilingual and Multicultural Development* 37 (7). 694–709.

Danjo, Chisato. 2021. Making sense of family language policy: Japanese-English bilingual children's creative and strategic translingual practices. *International Journal of Bilingual Education and Bilingualism* 24 (2). 292–304.

De Houwer, Annick. 2015. Harmonious bilingual development: Young families' well-being in language contact situations. *International Journal of Bilingualism* 19 (2). 169–184.

De Houwer, Annick. 2020. Harmonious bilingualism: Well-being for families in bilingual settings. In Andrea C. Schalley & Susana A. Eisenchlas (eds.), *Handbook of Home Language Maintenance and Development: Social and Affective Factors*, 63–83. Berlin & Boston: De Gruyter Mouton.

De Houwer, Annick. 2021. *Bilingual development in childhood*. Cambridge University Press.

Döpke, Susanne. 1992. *One parent – one language: An interactional approach*. Amsterdam & Philadelphia: John Benjamins.

English First. 2021. *The world's largest ranking of countries and regions by English skills – EF English Proficiency Index 2021*. www.ef.co.th/epi/ (accessed 16 November 2021).

Ethnologue, Languages of the World. 2023. *Thailand*. www.ethnologue.com/country/TH (accessed 10 August 2023).

Foley, Joseph A. 2019. Issues on assessment using CEFR in the region. *LEARN Journal: Language Education and Acquisition Research Network Journal* 12 (2). 28–48.

García, Ofelia. 2009. *Bilingual Education in the 21st Century: A Global Perspective*. 1st edition. Malden, MA; Oxford: Wiley-Blackwell.

García, Ofelia & Wei Li. 2014. *Translanguaging: Language, bilingualism and education*. New York: Palgrave Pivot.

García, Ofelia, Nelson Flores, Kate Seltzer, Wei Li, Ricardo Otheguy & Jonathan Rosa. 2021. Rejecting abyssal thinking in the language and education of racialized bilinguals: A manifesto. *Critical Inquiry in Language Studies* 18 (3). 1–26.

Goffman, Erving. 1983. The interaction order: American Sociological Association, 1982 Presidential Address. *American Sociological Review* 48 (1). 1–17.

Hayes, David. 2009. Learning language, learning teaching: Episodes from the life of a teacher of English in Thailand. *RELC Journal* 40 (1). 83–101.

Hiranburana, Kulaporn, Pramarn Subphadoongchone, Supong Tangkiengsirisin, Supakorn Phoochaeoensil, Jaroon Gainey, Juthamas Thogsngsri, Piyaboot Sumonsriworakun, Monnipha Somphong, Pattama Sappapan & Pimsiri Taylor. 2017. A framework of reference for English language education in Thailand (FRELE-TH) — based on the CEFR, the Thai experience. *LEARN Journal: Language Education and Acquisition Research Network Journal* 10 (2). 90–119.

Huebner, Thom. 2006. Bangkok's linguistic landscapes: Environmental print, codemixing and language change. *International Journal of Multilingualism* 3 (1). 31–51.

Huebner, Thom. 2009. A framework for the linguistic analysis of linguistic landscapes. In Elana Shohamy & Durk Gorter (eds.), *Linguistic landscape: Expanding the scenery*, 70–87. New York: Routledge.

Iwasaki, Shoichi & Preeya Ingkaphirom. 2009. *A reference grammar of Thai*. Cambridge: Cambridge University Press.

Jaroensak, Tiraporn. 2018. *ELF on a tropical island: The use of pragmatic strategies in touristic ELF in Thailand*. Portsmouth: University of Portsmouth PhD Dissertation.

Jaroensak, Tiraporn & Mario Saraceni. 2019. ELF in Thailand: Variants and coinage in spoken ELF in tourism encounters. *rEFLections* 26 (1). 115–133.

Jenkins, Jennifer. 2000. *The Phonology of English as an International Language*. Oxford: Oxford University Press.

Jenkins, Jennifer. 2014 [2003]. *Global Englishes: A resource book for students*, 3rd edn. London & New York: Routledge.

Jenks, Christopher. 2020. Family language policy, translingualism, and linguistic boundaries. *World Englishes* 39 (2). 312–320.

Jindapitak, Naratip & Adisa Teo. 2013. Accent priority in a Thai university context: A common sense revisited. *English Language Teaching* 6 (9). 193–204.

Jocuns, Andrew. 2018. English in Thai tourism: Global English as a nexus of practice. In Sandhya Rao Mehta (ed.), *Language and literature in a glocal world*, 57–76. Singapore: Springer.

Jocuns, Andrew. 2021. 'Uhh I'm not trying to be racist or anything': exploring an indexical field of Thai English. *Asian Englishes* 23 (3). 1–23.

Kamalanavin, Varisa. 2011. Raising bilingual children. *Bangkok Post*. www.bangkokpost.com/print/268363 (accessed 15 November 2020).

Kamalanavin, Varisa. 2015. เลี้ยงลูกให้เป็นเด็กสองภาษา (ไทย-อังกฤษ): สมควรลอง หรือเสียเวลา. *ภาษาปริทัศน์ ฉบับที่* [Raising Thai-English bilingual children in a native Thai family: Worth a try or waste of time?]. *Pasaa Paritat Journal* 30. 251–279.

King, Kendall A. & Lyn Fogle. 2006. Bilingual parenting as good parenting: Parents' perspectives on family language policy for additive bilingualism. *International Journal of Bilingual Education and Bilingualism* 9 (6). 695–712.

King, Kendall A., Lyn Fogle & Aubrey Logan-Terry. 2008. Family language policy. *Language and Linguistics Compass* 2 (5). 907–922.

Lefebvre, Henri. 1991. *The production of space*. Oxford & Cambridge, MA: Blackwell.

Mirvahedi, Seyed Hadi & Francesco Cavallaro. 2020. Siblings' play and language shift to English in a Malay-English bilingual family in Singapore. *World Englishes* 39 (1). 183–197.

Pearson, Barbara Zurer. 2008. *Raising a bilingual child*. New York: Living Language.

Pennycook, Alastair. 2016. Mobile times, mobile terms: The trans-super-poly-metro movement. In Nikolas Coupland (ed.), *Sociolinguistics: Theoretical debates*, 201–216. Cambridge University Press.

Piller, Ingrid, & Jinhyun Cho. 2013 Neoliberalism as Language Policy. *Language in Society* 42 (1). 23–44.

Piller, Ingrid & Livia Gerber. 2018. Family language policy between the bilingual advantage and the monolingual mindset. *International Journal of Bilingual Education and Bilingualism*. 1–14.

Purkarthofer, Judith. 2019. Building expectations: Imagining family language policy and heteroglossic social spaces. *International Journal of Bilingualism* 23 (3). 724–739.

Rainbird, Sophia & Jennifer Rowsell. 2011. 'Literacy nooks': Geosemiotics and domains of literacy in home spaces. *Journal of Early Childhood Literacy* 11 (2). 214–231.

Rose, Heath & Nicola Galloway. 2019. *Global Englishes for language teaching*, 1st edn. Cambridge University Press.

Said, Fatma & Hua Zhu. 2019. "No, no Maama! Say *'Shaatir ya Ouledee Shaatir*'!" Children's agency in language use and socialisation. *International Journal of Bilingualism* 23 (3). 771–785.

Savski, Kristof. 2021. Dialogicality and racialized discourse in TESOL recruitment. *TESOL Quarterly* 55 (3). 795–816.

Scollon, Ron. 2001. *Mediated discourse: The nexus of practice*. London & New York: Routledge.

Scollon, Ron & Suzie Wong Scollon. 2003. *Discourses in place: Language in the material world*. London: Routledge.

Scollon, Ron & Suzie Wong Scollon. 2004. *Nexus analysis: Discourse and the emerging Internet*. New York: Routledge.

Scollon, Suzie Wong & Ingrid de Saint-Georges. 2012. Mediated discourse analysis. In James Paul Gee & Michael Handford (eds.), *The Routledge handbook of discourse analysis*, 66–78. New York: Routledge.

Seargeant, Philip & Caroline Tagg. 2011. English on the internet and a 'post-varieties' approach to language. *World Englishes* 30 (4). 496–514.

Smalley, William A. 1994. *Linguistic diversity and national unity: Language ecology in Thailand*. Chicago: University of Chicago Press.

Snodin, Navaporn Sanprasert & Tony J. Young. 2015. 'Native-speaker' varieties of English: Thai perceptions and attitudes. *Asian Englishes* 17 (3). 248–260.

Spolsky, Bernard. 2004. *Language policy (Key topics in sociolinguistics)*. Cambridge & New York: Cambridge University Press.

Suntornsawet, Jirada. 2019. Problematic Phonological Features of Foreign Accented English Pronunciation as Threats to International Intelligibility: Thai EIL Pronunciation Core. *Journal of English as an International Language* 14(2). 72–93.

Thanosawan, Prapassara & Kevin Laws. 2013. Global citizenship: Differing perceptions within two Thai higher education institutions. *Journal of Higher Education Policy and Management* 35 (3). 293–304.

The Ministry of Education Thailand. 2008. *The Basic Education Core Curriculum*. https://academic.obec.go.th/images/document/1525235513_d_1.pdf (accessed 29 March 2022).

Trakulkasemsuk, Wannapa. 2012. Thai English. In Ee-Ling Low & Azirah Hashim (eds.), *English in Southeast Asia: Features, policy, and language in use*, 103–111. Philadelphia: John Benjamins.

Trakulkasemsuk, Wannapa. 2018. English in Thailand: Looking back to the past, at the present and towards the future. *Asian Englishes* 20 (2). 96–105.

Tuominen, Anne. 1999. Who decides the home language? A look at multilingual families. *International Journal of the Sociology of Language* 140 (1). 59–76.

Whittingham, Colleen E. 2019. Geosemiotics←→Social Geography: Preschool Places and School(ed) Spaces. *Journal of Literacy Research* 51 (1). 52–74.

Wohlwend, Karen. 2020. *Literacies that move and matter: Nexus analysis for contemporary childhoods.* New York, NY: Routledge.

Wongsothorn, Achara, Kulaporn Hiranburana & Supanee Chinnawongs. 2002. English language teaching in Thailand today. *Asia Pacific Journal of Education* 22 (2). 107–116.

Woolard, Kathryn A. 1998. Introduction: Language ideology as a field of inquiry. In Bambi B. Schieffelin, Kathryn A. Woolard & Paul V. Kroskrity (eds.), *Language ideologies: Practice and theory*, 3–50. Oxford: Oxford University Press.

Woolard, Kathryn A. & Bambi B. Schieffelin. 1994. Language ideology. *Annual Review of Anthropology* 23 (1). 55–82.

Manuela Vida-Mannl

5 Parental language ideologies and children's language use in Singapore – raising speakers of "Standard" English?

Abstract: Language ideologies mediate between language and social construction. In this chapter, the interrelation between language attitudes and ideologies and child language acquisition and perceived home language use will be examined. Furthermore, it will be shown that these ideologies may differ widely from the observable reality of language use. Based on Buschfeld's (2020) study of child language acquisition of English in Singapore, the alignment between parents' language preference and children's actual language use is investigated. To this end, the questionnaire data on the language use and attitudes of 34 families collected for Buschfeld's study are analyzed and the parents' statements on their children's language acquisition and use are interpreted in a new light. The open preference of Standard Singapore English, which is firmly rooted in Singapore's social fabric and governmental language policies, e.g. through campaigns like the Speak Good English Movement (cf. Leimgruber 2013), is shown and the influence of these political and societal language attitudes and ideologies on the language attitudes and ideologies reported by parents is revealed. Hereby, the gap between (child) language acquisition, language policies, World Englishes, and language attitudes and ideologies will be bridged, finding an ideology-based discrepancy between the parents' preferences and the reality of their children's L1 acquisition.

Keywords: parental language attitudes, language ideologies, Singapore English, language policy, home language use, Standard English, standard language ideology

1 Introduction

Current research within the World Englishes paradigm has taken a shift and refocused from assessing (standard) varieties of English to centering on successful communication and speaker equality. While this is an important development, this shift

---

Manuela Vida-Mannl, TU Dortmund University, Germany

https://doi.org/10.1515/9783110733723-005

has not yet been realized outside of linguistics, e.g., through adapting governmental language policy or changing language ideologies. In many societies, the ideology of the standard varieties' hegemony has been maintained and is strengthened by political campaigns and decisions. Language ideologies reflect a conscious or subconscious positioning of speaker groups towards each other that is based on (shared) beliefs about language, i.e. the rightfulness of specific speaker groups or the level of prestige of a certain variety (c.f. Woolard 1998; Wortham 2001). Consequently, the maintenance of an ideology, e.g. the ideology of the hegemony of standard varieties, can cause existing social stratification to be reinforced. When investigating the dynamics of language ideologies and their reproduction within a society, the social groups that immediately affect the prestige and contexts of use of English are particularly relevant, i.e. policymakers, teachers, and parents concerned with the practical or theoretical implementations of (first or second) language acquisition. This chapter focuses on the ideologies affecting the use of English in Singapore by examining parental language ideologies, their influenceability through governmental language policy, and their relation to the reality of child L1 acquisition of English.

Singapore, located just off the Malay Peninsula in Southeast Asia, has long been of interest to World Englishes scholars. In recent times, however, the focus has shifted from investigating Singapore English as an L2 towards considering the transformation of English in Singapore functioning as an L1 (e.g. Bolton & Ng 2014; Buschfeld 2020; Tan 2014). As is often the case, colonization initiated the growing entrenchment of English in Singapore and its current transition between traditional categories and paradigms of English. While most Singaporeans might be defined as L2-variety users of English, Buschfeld (2020) has found that Singapore English is changing and that children are currently acquiring an emerging L1 variety. This variety appears to be a hybrid and cannot be categorized clearly as being Standard Singapore English (SSE) or Colloquial Singapore English (CSE). While this itself presents the World Englishes paradigm with a challenge to digest and include such a not-clear cut but hybrid and changing new variety of L1 English, it, furthermore, presents parents with an ideological challenge. Based on their – government-supported – belief that correct English is "Standard (Singapore) English," they appear to not have adapted to the reality of their children's L1 acquisition process. Parents seem to still expect and wish for their children to acquire SSE, although their children, as Buschfeld (2020) has shown, frequently produce features that are considered to be markers of CSE. This discrepancy between the actual child language acquisition process and the expectations and hopes of the parents will be presented in the following chapter.

2 The ideology of "standard" language

"Representations, whether explicit or implicit, that construe the intersection of language and human beings in a social world are what we mean by 'language ideology'" (Woolard 1998: 3). Functioning as mediators between language and social constructions (see Piller 2015; Woolard 1998; Wortham 2001), language ideologies are immanent, co-existing, and competing in all social groupings, independent of their size, the composition of members, or the involved languages. Language ideologies reflect concepts, understandings, and interpretations of any specific language as well as of the concept of language in general. In doing so, they comprise interpretations, attitudes, and beliefs about properties, meanings, functions, and use of (a) language (Gal 1998; Song 2019; Woolard 1998; Wortham 2001). Language ideologies, furthermore, are at the basis of social differentiation; they might blur or highlight them (Piller 2015) and, thereby, influence the construction of communities, prestige, and relations of power (Park 2009). Maintaining existing language ideologies supports the perceived rightfulness of the social structures they produce since they serve as rationalizations of language users' positioning within a social group (Wortham 2001: 256) and as justification for a specific way of using and valuing (a) language (Silverstein 1979). Since ideologies are traditionally a tool to preserve the power of the powerful, one might expect them to be reproduced only by those social groups who benefit from their implementation. However, they are commonly shared by various social groups and, therefore, also reproduced and supported by those language users who do not benefit from the structures they produce. As they are potentially supported across social classes, ideologies might gain power within a society – become hegemonic (Woolard 1998) – and become instrumentalized by politics. One ideology that is hegemonic in various societies and has been utilized by political authorities and governments in numerous cases is the *standard language ideology*.

The standard language ideology, which reflects the belief that a particular variety, i.e. the – often artificially constructed – so-called standard, is superior to any other variety of a particular language (Piller 2015: 4), is one of the most commonly shared ideologies. Like all language ideologies, the standard language ideology guides language users "to value and recognize particular ways of using language and discourse styles (Blackledge 2008; Kroskrity 2007)" (Song 2019: 255). Individuals are aware of co-existing and competing ideologies and adopt them to position themselves as members of a particular social group. The standard variety of a language is commonly spoken by only a comparably small group of speakers; however, this group is of high prestige and associated with a high level of education, formality, and success. Therefore, language users position themselves as rightful members of this prestigious group of speakers by supporting and practicing the standard language ideology and by, ideally, using a standard variety themselves. While this discrepancy between language use and prestige of standard varieties holds in (almost) every language, the case of English is somewhat more complex. Although the hegemonic standard variety of English is still most often Standard British English (BrE; due to the United Kingdom's colonial history), the global spread of English caused other standard varieties – and standardized varieties – to emerge. Although the categorization and recognition of language use as reflecting only one variety have increasingly been recognized as potentially problematic (see Wee 2018 for a discussion) – from an ideological and linguistic perspective – we do recognize standard varieties, e.g., of Indian English, Nigerian English, and Singapore English which tend to co-exist with a more colloquial use of English in the respective countries. In these contexts of New Englishes, the standard language ideology has been adopted, as the local standard variety is associated with correctness, good English, international understandability, and a high level of education and, consequently, is more highly valued than the colloquial variety. In addition to the ideological considerations of the standard language ideology, this belief also includes practical implications when it comes to language acquisition: A standard variety tends to be decreasing in its use as it is only spoken by a comparably small number of L1 speakers – if at all. This means that the majority of speakers choose to adhere to an ideology that reproduces the linguistic superiority of a few speakers. While this acceptance of the standard language ideology might be an unconscious process for most users of English, parents might be especially accessible for its practical implications and consciously determine and consciously determine which variety their children should learn.

Since child L1 acquisition is highly dependent on the input the child receives, it appears to be influenceable – at least to a certain degree. Due to the ideological superiority awarded to the standard variety and the advantages its use offers in social contexts, parents might be tempted to influence their children's language acquisition process so that their children become L1 users of a standard variety. This holds especially true in contexts of New Englishes, i.e. in contexts in which children learn English in addition to one (or more) local language(s): parents might expect their children to have more promising choices and opportunities in their educational and professional future as standard English speakers and want to prevent them from being perceived as low proficient speakers when using CSE (Chew 2007). Again, language use and prestige are highly emotional and ideologically-laden concepts – especially in post-colonial contexts – and parents might choose to raise their children in a way that provides them with the utmost options and possibilities and the fewest obstacles. This choice might even be independent of whether parents agree with the hegemony of the standard variety or its reproduction within global or local social structures. Being responsible for their children's future seems to increase the parents' tendency to choose the "safe" and socially agreed-upon procedure: raising speakers of Standard (Singapore) English. However, while parents certainly share this hope, it might diverge from reality. I will discuss this phenomenon using Singapore as an example.

3 English in Singapore

Singapore, an island-state in Southeast Asia, is approximately 710 km^2 big and home to 5.69 million people (SingStat 2021: 4). Of these, 74.3% are Chinese, 13.5% Malay, 9% Indian, and 3.2% are of other ethnicities (SingStat 2021: 7). To reflect the multi-ethnic composition of Singapore's inhabitants, four official languages have been pronounced: Malay, Mandarin, Tamil, and English. While the former three languages serve as so-called "mother tongues" for the three major ethnic groups and Malay is, furthermore, the state's national language, English has been brought to Singapore during its almost 150 years of (interrupted) British rule. Similar to many other former British colonies, English is unique within Singapore's linguistic landscape as it is considered to be ethnically neutral and, as the language of globalization, it is Singapore's inter- and intra-national lingua franca of choice (Blommaert 2010; Leimgruber 2013; Wee 2004; Wong 2014).

3.1 A comparison of Standard Singapore English and Colloquial Singapore English

In Singapore, like in many other former British or American colonies, more than one realization of English has emerged, i.e. SSE and CSE. Recent studies have shown that the two varieties cannot clearly be distinguished from one another and that English in Singapore might better be understood as a continuum between the two Singaporean Englishes (e.g. Buschfeld 2020; Leimgruber 2013; Siemund and Li 2020). However, the identification of linguistic variables is still understood as helpful in modeling the complex linguistic reality in Singapore in which the two varieties are considered to be – and treated as – distinct from one another. Since the differentiation between SSE and CSE is commonly maintained, linguistic characteristics, which are supposed to indicate which variety is in use, have been identified in numerous studies. While scholars appear to agree that SSE "does not exhibit major differences from other versions of Standard English around the globe" (Leimgruber 2011: 47; see also Gupta 1992; Pakir 1991; Wong 2014), CSE "differs significantly from Standard English at all levels (i.e. phonology, intonational, morphological, syntactic, semantic and pragmatic)" (Wong 2014: 6) and linguistic characteristics, i.e. the use of zero subjects or objects, vowel shortenings, copula deletion, and zero past tense marking (amongst others), have been agreed upon to function as markers of CSE (see, e.g., Buschfeld 2020; Deterding 2007; Leimgruber 2013; Lim 2004). While we have come to understand the properties of CSE and SSE, i.e. their phonological, morphological, and syntactic characteristics, their roles in child L1 acquisition and their impact on family language use is yet to be unveiled. Buschfeld (2020) has taken a first step towards this understanding and has found that children produce features of CSE more extensively during their acquisition process than had been expected. I will follow suit in untangling the role of "English" in child L1 acquisition in Singapore by assessing the parental language ideologies and attitudes which accompany this acquisition process. To understand the influential factors in the production and recreation of language ideologies and beliefs, the social and cultural aspects and properties of CSE and SSE are of central importance. Therefore, the varieties' roles within Singapore's society, their contexts of use, as well as in the attitudes their speakers hold towards them are to be considered.

Singapore follows a somewhat complex policy of societal bilingualism. Officially, every Singaporean has to acquire the official language that is considered their father's "mother tongue:" Indians acquire Tamil, Malays acquire Malay, and people of Chinese ethnicity are to acquire Mandarin. However, in addition to their respective mother tongue, Singaporeans are expected to acquire English. Consequently, English is the only shared language and the language of interracial communication. While SSE, the officially promoted language variety, is structurally quite similar to Standard British English and therefore considered to be culturally neutral, CSE is understood as culturally-laden and used to be associated with speakers of low proficiency in English and limited formal education (Chew 2007). While an increasing number of Singaporeans understand CSE to be the language of their national identity and a marker of Singaporean culture and, therefore, support its use, others feel that CSE is an inferior and improper variety whose use should be avoided (Siemund and Li 2020; Wee 2018). Some might even follow the government's concerns about CSE hindering Singaporeans being able to acquire "good" English – which there is no evidence for. These critics of CSE fear that a lack of "good" English might cause difficulties in international communication and economic repercussions for Singapore on the global market. Yet, Singaporeans' attitudes towards SSE and CSE cannot be based on their own language use: although, especially in higher social classes, SSE is still considered to be more prestigious than the still strongly stigmatized CSE (Buschfeld 2020), only very few Singaporeans sustain speaking SSE (Wong 2014). Independent of whether its users consider CSE to represent good or bad language use – and therefore to be desired or avoided – it is a "deeply entrenched cultural category" (Wong 2014: 4). Nonetheless, Singaporeans appear to agree that CSE is to be used, if at all, in informal settings and only amongst Singaporeans (cf. Wee 2018 for an extensive elaboration on the Singlish controversy). CSE holds a culturally important but controversial position in Singapore's society, which is (at least partly) caused and fueled by the choices of the government. While attitudes towards CSE are mixed on the societal level, on the political level CSE clearly holds negative connotations and is considered to be a "problem" (Wee 2018).

3.2 Language policy and home language use in multilingual Singapore

Language policy and planning are quite extensive in Singapore as the government is heavily involved in deciding who should speak which languages. Rather than promoting multilingualism, the general language policy in Singapore is English-based bilingualism. Officially, the mother tongue of a Singaporean is determined based on the father's ethnic group, i.e. Mandarin, Tamil, or Malay. As often the case, the reality of language acquisition differs from the government's wishes: Mandarin appears to be the most prestigious mother tongue in Singapore and is sometimes acquired as a substitute-L1 by Singaporeans of ethnicities other than Chinese as well (Buschfeld, personal communication in March 2021). In addition to one of the mother tongues, all Singaporeans are required to learn English, which is ensured through its implementation in the education system as the major language of instruction. English, however, is not only essential in educational contexts. It, furthermore, serves as a major home language (Siemund and Li 2020).

In domestic contexts, the use of English is increasing; while, in 2010, for 32.3% of the residents in Singapore, who were older than five years, English was the language used most frequently at home, in 2015, it increased to 36.9% (SingStat 2016: 18) and further to 48.3% in 2020 (SingStat 2021: 26). The increasing use of English as the most frequent home language also holds across the major ethnic groups – from 2015 to 2020, the use of English as the most frequently used home language increased by 15% in Chinese homes, by 22% in Malay homes, and by 17.6% in Indian homes (SingStat 2021: 27–28). While for Indians, English remains the most frequently used language at home, for Malays, English remains the second most frequently used language at home and Malay the most frequently used language (SingStat 2016: 19; SingStat 2021: 28). However, in Chinese households the order of most frequently used languages has changed so that, in 2020, for the first time, English became used at home more frequently than Mandarin. In 2015, only 37.4% of Chinese households used English at home most frequently and the majority (46.1%) used Mandarin (SingStat 2016: 19). In 2020, English was used at home most frequently (47.6%) in these households and

Mandarin became the second most frequently used language (40.2%) (SingStat 2021: 27). While these numbers show the increasing significance of English within domestic Singapore, they also reflect that Singaporeans are strictly allocated to one ethnic group, which serves as a reflection of social belonging in Singapore. However, language policy and planning are not only based on social aspects in Singapore, language is also linked to economic factors.

Two of the most expressive examples of the economic considerations behind the language policy in Singapore might be the Speak Mandarin Campaign (SMC) and the Speak Good English Movement (SGEM). The SMC was established in 1979 and promoted the use of Mandarin Chinese as a substitute for the many different Chinese dialects, i.e. Cantonese, Hokkien, Teochew, which served as the home languages of the Chinese population of Singapore (Siemund and Li 2020). After a problematic initiation phase, the SMC has successfully increased the use and positive attitudes towards Mandarin. However, in so doing, the Chinese population of Singapore has also weakened their multilingualism and diversity and became more homogenous. Still, unity amongst the Chinese population has only been a side effect, as the SMC was established to facilitate Singapore's access to the economically promising Chinese market (Siemund and Li 2020). Another example of Singapore's institutional exertion of influence is the SGEM. The SGEM was initiated in 2000 and aimed at Singaporeans to speak Standard English (or "Good English") rather than Singlish or CSE. It states that "[t]he role of the Speak Good English Movement is to encourage Singaporeans to speak and write standard English and provide resources to learners who wish to improve their English. [. . .] [It] aim[s] to help those who speak only Singlish, and those who think Singlish is English, to speak standard English" (SGEM n.d.–a). In its understanding, Singlish is a deficient form of English that should be avoided as it hinders Singaporeans from acquiring "good English" and being understood internationally. For policymakers, the use of Singlish appears to be a handicap that is not to be supported. However, while the SMC has been initiated and executed by governmental institutions, the SGEM is "a movement steered by a quasi-government committee comprising a number of government and professional parties" (Wong 2014: 8) as well as academics. As mentioned before, the SGEM provides "learners who wish to improve their English" (SGEM n.d.–a) with resources, i.e. book recommendations, common English mistakes, grammar rules, idioms, pronunciation guide, spelling tips, and quizzes on their homepage. Specifically, they provide "Tips for Parents" (SGEM n.d.–b), i.e. activities to promote SSE and advice on how to use (and not to use) the English language with children. In doing so, the movement takes prescriptive measures to alter the use and acquisition of English by Singaporeans. Consequently, on a political and institutional level, SSE appears to be considered more valuable and more prestigious. This is partly adopted on a societal level, as the previously-described negative attitudes towards CSE show. To understand parental ideologies and attitudes more comprehensively, the societal positions on CSE and SSE must be assessed in greater detail.

While attitudes towards CSE and SSE are not uniform in Singapore's society, the use of English is essential within the social structures of Singapore. Consequently, it has entered Singapore's homes. Between 2010 and 2020 the use of English as the most frequently used home language has increased by 16% (SingStat 2021: 23); a tendency that holds across age groups, educational level, and ethnic belonging (SingStat 2021: 28–30). With the exception of Indians, the numbers show increasing use of English as the main home language in all ethnic groups from the lowest to the highest level of education. While the numbers for Chinese (61.2%) and Malays (61.4%) climax in the group with university education, for Indians the group with the highest users of English as the most frequent home language are those with diplomas and professional qualification (63.9%), followed by those with post-secondary but non-tertiary education (61.1%), and those with university education (59.5%) (SingStat 2021: 30). These numbers corroborate a trend that has already been perceivable in 2010 (cf. Buschfeld 2020): the educational level of the parents appears to be a decisive factor of parents' decision to implement English as their home language. However, Singaporeans hardly use SSE for prolonged utterances or without code-switching to and from CSE (Wong 2014). Furthermore, the politically induced negative attitudes towards CSE have only partially been adopted into Singapore's society (Leimgruber 2013; Siemund and Li 2020); especially in higher social classes and by highly educated speakers, CSE is perceived less negatively than expected. I will now turn to the analysis of parental language attitudes to show how the presented ideologies and policies might affect their actual home language use and to see whether they express similarly positive attitudes towards CSE as found in previous research.

4 The study

The findings presented here are based on questionnaire data collected as part of Buschfeld's (2020) study on child L1 acquisition of English in Singapore. While Buschfeld centered the children and found new insight into the acquisition process, I will focus on parental language ideologies and how they are reflected by the parents of Buschfeld's participants using information that has been provided in complementary parental questionnaires. Subsequently, I will examine possible interrelations between these parental language ideologies and Buschfeld's (2020) findings of child L1 acquisition of Singapore English.

4.1 Methodology

This study is based on information collected as part of Buschfeld's study of first language acquisition in Singapore (cf. Buschfeld 2020). Specifically, it centers information provided through questionnaires by 34 parents (mean age mother 35.76, range 25 to 42.42; mean age father 39.05, range 25.83 to 47.17) of 38 children (mean age 4.79, range 1.33 to 12.08). These questionnaires served as complementary parental questionnaires to collect relevant background information about the participating children. Four parents filled in two questionnaires each – one for each of their participating children. For these parents, only one of these questionnaires is considered, since the relevant answers matched for both of their children. Therefore, the following analyses will be based on the information provided about 34 (rather than 38) children and parents.

The parts of the questionnaire which are relevant for the study at hand include each child's and both parents' biographical and linguistic information as well as the parents' attitudes and beliefs about their respective child's language use and acquisition. To elicit biographical information, the parents were asked to provide the dates and places of birth (PoB), sex, and ethnicity of themselves and their children as well as their highest level of education and current occupation. To understand the linguistic background of the children and their parents, the parents were asked, among other questions, to name or pick the languages they and their child(ren) acquired from birth, the languages they learned at a later time, the languages that are used at home, as well as the language which is most dominant in their child. While the biographical information has been elicited mostly through open questions, the linguistic background has been examined predominantly using closed questions. In these closed questions, parents were asked to choose between languages widely spoken in Singapore, i.e. English, Mandarin, Cantonese, Hokkien, Tamil, Teochew, and Malay, or adding any other language that they felt was missing.

In addition to the biographic and linguistic background of the children and their parents, Buschfeld elicited information about which variety (or varieties) of English the parents believe their children are acquiring, use most often, and are exposed to most often. To do so, parents were given four varieties of English to choose from, namely SSE, CSE, BrE, and American English (AmE; in this order). Furthermore, they could add another variety of English or tick "I am not sure". These data, which to this point have not been analyzed comprehensively, reflect the parents' language ideologies and their attitudes towards the varieties of English at use in Singapore and are most crucial for this study. Consequently, they function as my dependent variables *acquisition*, *use*, and *exposure*. I will examine the parents' statements concerning their home language use and their children's language acquisition, use, and exposure by use of frequencies, statistical independence, and conditional inference trees (c-trees, cf. Gries 2020; Hothorn, Hornik, and Zeileis 2006; Tagliamonte and Baayen 2012) to show interrelations and dependencies between the three dependent and twelve independent variables.

4.2 Assessing parents' language ideologies

As mentioned before, to assess the linguistic background of the participating children, their parents were asked to provide information about their child's language use, acquisition, and exposure. These answers reflect the parents' language ideologies – their beliefs and attitudes towards their own and their child's language use. When stating which language variety/ies their children are acquiring, are exposed to most often, and use most often, parents were asked to choose between SSE, CSE, BrE, and AmE. For the analysis, the parents' answers were categorized as referring to "non-standard" or "standard:" in the case that the parents indicated their children would acquire, use, or be exposed to (one or more) standard varieties, i.e. SSE, BrE, or AmE, the answer was categorized as "standard". However, in case the parents indicated their children would acquire, use, or be exposed to CSE – only or in combination with one or more standard varieties – the answer was categorized as "non-standard," as this recognizes the role of non-standard English in Singapore. Furthermore, provided answers concerning the independent variables *home language*, *L1_mother*, and *L1_father* were subsumed on the language level. Specifically, Chinese languages were subsumed under "Chinese," since all but four mothers and four fathers of Chinese ethnicity have stated to be L1-speakers of another Chinese language than Mandarin, and Indian languages were subsumed under "Indian," since all but two mothers and two fathers of Indian ethnicity have stated to be L1-speakers of another Indian language than Tamil. The parents' level of education has been categorized as "'uni" in the case of a university degree and as "non-uni" in all other cases. Missing values are indicated by "N_A". Based on this coding, I analyze the parental questionnaires.

For a deeper understanding of parental language ideologies in Singapore, the parents' statements are analyzed in three steps: First, for a general understanding, a descriptive analysis based on frequencies will be presented. Second, potential dependencies between the three dependent variables *use*, *acquisition*, and *exposure* and the twelve independent variables, namely *home language*, *L1_mother*, *L1_father*, *age_mother*, *age_father*, *age_child*, *PoB_mother*, *PoB_father*, *ethnicity_mother*, *ethnicity_father*, *education_mother*, and *education_father*, are examined using Fisher's exact test of independence. Finally, c-trees are executed to examine the potential dependencies indicated by the results of Fisher's exact tests and potentially unveil further variables that influence parental language ideologies concerning children's language acquisition, use, and exposure.

The first analysis of the dependent variables acquisition, use, and exposure is based on the frequencies of the provided answers. For all three, I found a strong tendency towards standard varieties: 24 parents (70.59%) state that their children are acquiring only (one or more) standard varieties (Figure 5.1), while 19 parents (55.88%) believe their children to use (Figure 5.2) and 26 parents (76.47%) to be exposed (Figure 5.3) to only (one or more) standard varieties most often. Amongst these, three parents (8.82%) and four parents (11.76%) respectively stated that their children were acquiring or exposed to British and/or American English and therewith exclude Singaporean varieties. In comparison, seven parents (20.59%, Figure 5.1) state their children are acquiring (also) CSE, while nine parents (26.47%) believe their children to use (Figure 5.2) and eight parents (23.53%) to be exposed to (also) CSE (Figure 5.3).

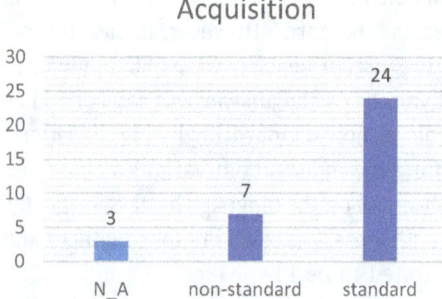

Figure 5.1: Frequencies "Acquisition".

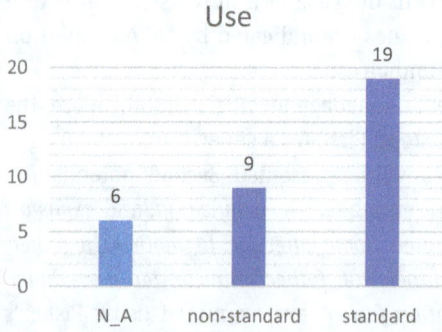

Figure 5.2: Frequencies "Use".

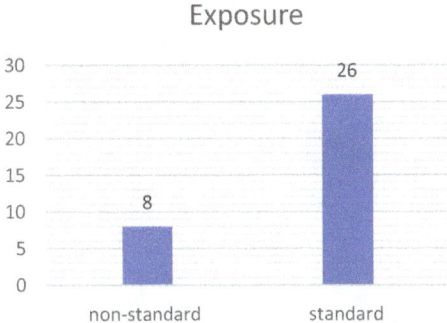

Figure 5.3: Frequencies "Exposure".

Concerning the independent variables, I found English to be the dominating language: English is (one or the only) home language in all homes. It is the most frequently used language in 27 families (79.41%), while for the remaining 20.59% the respective racial mother tongue is most frequently used, directly followed by English (Figure 5.4). This corroborates the findings published in Singapore's *Census of Population 2020* (SingStat 2021). Furthermore, English is (one of) the L1(s) of 15 mothers (44.12%, Figure 5.5) and 17 fathers (50%, Figure 5.6). Although the presented frequencies show strong tendencies, a more detailed analysis is necessary.

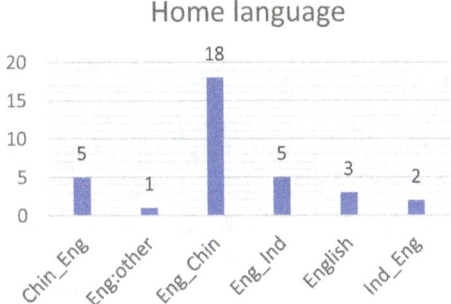

Figure 5.4: Frequencies "Home language".

To examine potential interdependencies between the dependent variables *acquisition*, *use*, and *exposure* and the twelve independent variables, two-sided Fisher's exact tests with confidence intervals of 0.05 were executed. Unlike other commonly used tests, Fisher's exact test of independence does not approximate but exactly calculates the probability of getting the observed data. Therefore, its validity is not bound to data in any kind of distribution or of any minimum size. The results of

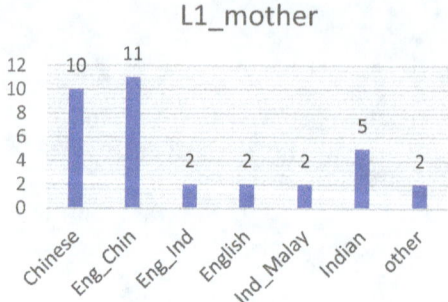

Figure 5.5: Frequencies "L1_mother".

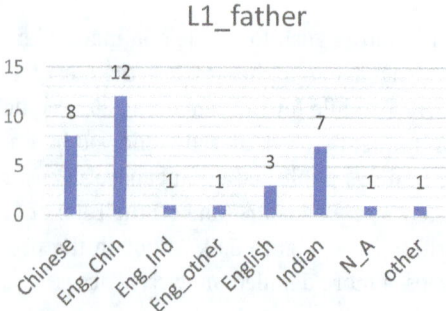

Figure 5.6: Frequencies "L1_father".

these tests are presented in Table 5.1, the cases in which the independence of the tested variables should be rejected are underlined for easier understanding.

When assessing the variety of English that the parents believe their children to be acquiring, the only factor for which the assumed independence has to be rejected is the mother's level of education (p-value = 0.01132). The variety of English the parents state their children would use most often appears to also be connected to the mothers' characteristics, as the variable *use* cannot be assumed to be independent of the mother's L1(s) (p-value = 0.03545) and the mother's age (p-value = 0.04962). Furthermore, it appears to be not independent of the father's place of birth (p-value = 0.01381). Finally, Fisher's exact test has shown that the variety of English that the children are exposed to most often cannot be assumed to be independent of the father's level of education (p-value = 0.00352) and the mother's age (p-value = 0.03697).

In addition to the potential dependencies unveiled in Table 5.1, c-trees were executed using the software R (R Core Team 2019), specifically the R-package "partykit".

Table 5.1: Results of Fisher's exact tests.

	Acquisition	Use	Exposure
age_child	0.3549	0.004742	0.1418
L1_mother	0.8276	0.03545	0.2618
age_mother	0.06625	0.04962	0.03697
ethnicity_mother	0.5658	0.2175	0.2806
education_mother	0.01132	0.438	0.6488
PoB_mother	1	0.328	0.5641
L1_father	0.3413	0.2449	0.341
age_father	0.5916	0.1988	0.09443
ethnicity_father	0.6971	0.5107	0.3474
education_father	0.1033	0.2766	0.00352
PoB_father	0.5255	0.01381	0.5653
home language	0.699	0.0745	0.7924

By using c-trees, the dependencies indicated in Table 5.1 are reviewed and the impact of the independent variables on the realization of the dependent variables are assessed. To do so, in a first step, c-trees were created that consider all variables to see which one(s) are most significant for the realization of each dependent variable. In a second step, every possible permutation of these variables was considered as well as each independent variable separately. Starting with modeling *exposure*, Figure 5.7 represents the c-tree created considering all independent variables. It can be considered highly accurate as it has a balanced accuracy of 0.774. The model shows that *education_father* is the only variable that is significant for the realization of *exposure* (node 1), reflecting that parents believe their children to be exposed to CSE significantly more often if her/his father's educational level is lower than a university degree. Further modeling has corroborated the father's education to be decisive while its significance decreased the more other variables were considered. All models were of the same balanced accuracy as Figure 5.7 and separated the data in the same manner. However, and contrary to what might have been expected based on Fisher's exact test of independence, *age_mother* has not been found to be significant for the realization of the dependent variable *exposure*.

Concerning the parents' statements about the variety of English their children use most often, Figure 5.8 represents the c-tree considering all variables. The model has a balanced accuracy of 0.503, which, although being quite low, is considered to be acceptable for a non-binary dependent variable. It shows that the parents of children with mothers aged 32.67 years or younger either believe their children to only use (one or more) standard varieties or did not specify. Most parents of children with mothers older than 32.67 years also believe their children to use standard varieties of English most often (59.26%), however, 33.33%

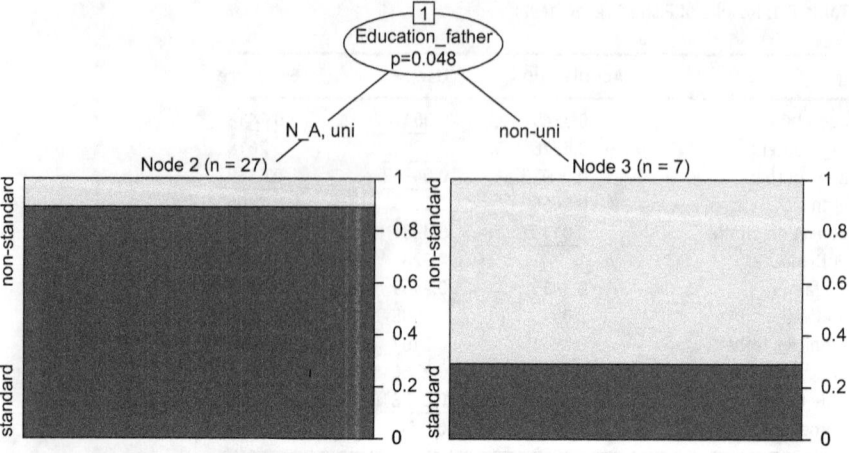

Figure 5.7: C-tree exposure ~ all independent variables.

of these parents believe their children to use non-standard English most often (Figure 5.8). Again, the fewer other variables are combined with *age_mother*, the more significant the latter is for the realization of the dependent variable *use*. The balanced accuracies of the models including *age_mother* remain the same.

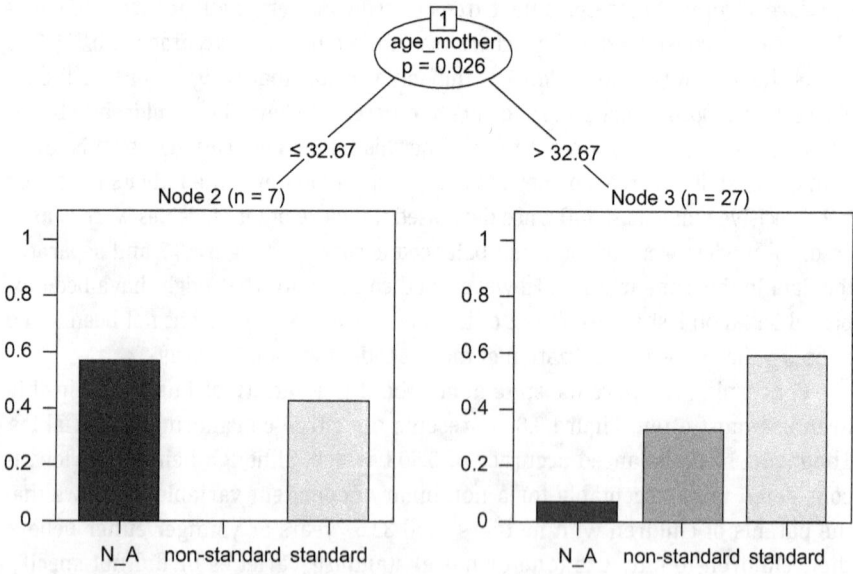

Figure 5.8: C-tree use ~ all independent variables.

As the variable *use* is expected to also not be independent of the variable *L1_mother* (see Table 5.1), I have created c-trees centering this variable while excluding *age_mother* (Figure 5.9). Considering the significance of *L1_mother* on *use*, the c-tree shows that the parents believe their children to use standard varieties of English more often in case the mother's L1s are English and Chinese or English and Indian as well as in case her L1 is Indian (node 3). In the case that the mothers' L1s are Indian and Malay, Chinese, English, or a language other than Chinese, English, or Indian, the parents more often believe their children to use non-standard English (node 2). The balanced accuracy of this model is 0.505, which is again low but acceptable for this variable. Again, the two-level structure and the balanced accuracy of the model do not change once other variables are added. However, the significance of *L1_mother* decreases the more variables are considered.

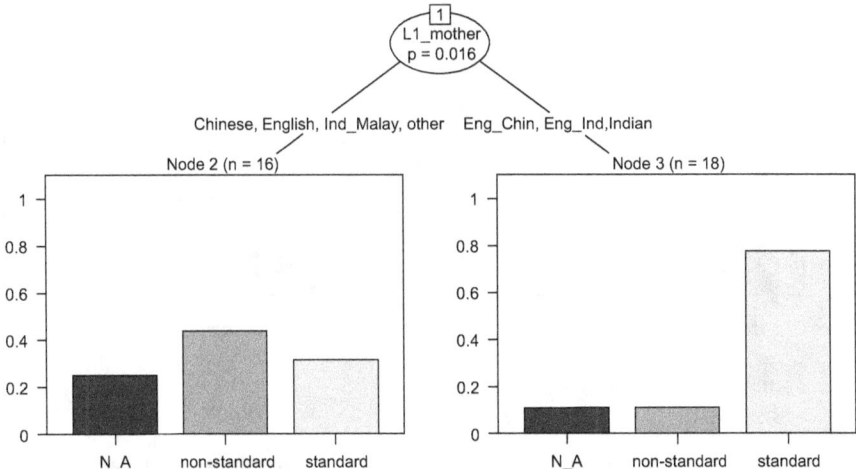

Figure 5.9: C-tree use ~ L1_mother.

Following Fisher's exact test of independence, the dependent variable *use* is expected to also not be independent of the variable *PoB_father* (see Table 5.1). To examine potential relations between these two variables, I have created another c-tree centering *PoB_father* while excluding *age_mother* and *L1_mother* (Figure 5.10). Considering the significance of *PoB_father* on *use*, the c-tree shows that the parents of children whose father has been born in Singapore believe their children to (also) use non-standard varieties of English more often than only standard varieties (node 3). The parents of children whose father has been born in countries other than Singapore believe their children to use only standard varieties of English considerably more often than (also) non-standard varieties of English (node 2). The balanced accuracy of this model is 0.54191, which is, as explained above, low but acceptable for this variable. Similar to the variable *L1_mother*, the two-level structure and the balanced accuracy of the model do not change once other variables are added. However, the significance of *PoB_father* decreases as more variables are considered as long as *L1_mother* and *age_mother* are excluded.

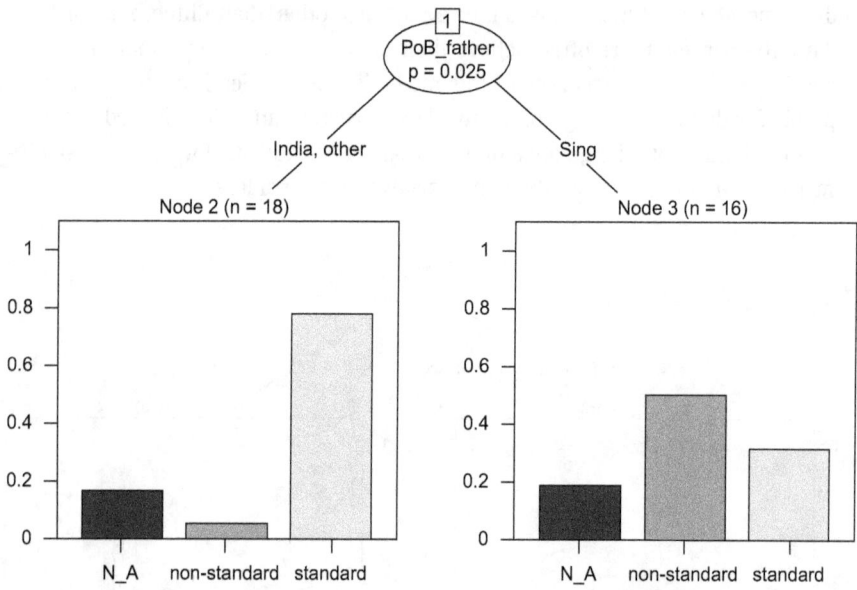

Figure 5.10: C-tree Use ~ PoB_father.

Finally, I proceeded the same way in assessing the third dependent variable, *acquisition*. Unlike for the other two dependent variables, in this case, no variable has shown to be significant when all independent variables were considered. Furthermore, considering the influence of the variable *education_mother*, which has been found to not be independent of the variable *acquisition* (cf. Table 5.1), on *acquisition* a model with a balanced accuracy of 0.482 has been created, which is considered to be too low to be included here. The only variable that has been found to be significant for the realization of the variable acquisition is *age_father* (Figure 5.11). Figure 5.11 shows that, in case the father is 37.83 years or younger, slightly more parents believe their children to also acquire non-standard English than that they acquire only standard varieties of English (node 2). Parents of children whose father is older than 37.83 years are more often convinced that their children acquire solely standard varieties of English (node 3). The balanced accuracy of Figure 5.11 is 0.597, which is considered to be acceptable.

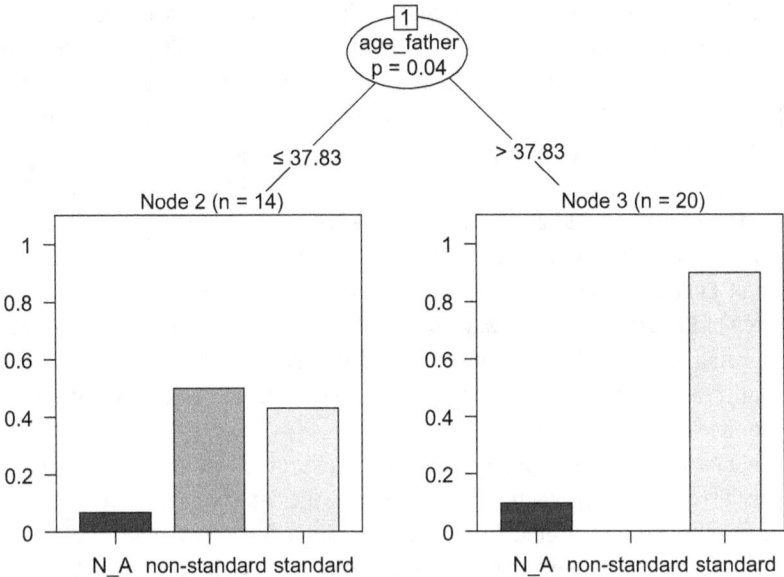

Figure 5.11: C-tree acquisition ~ age_father.

I will now turn to broadly summarize Buschfeld's (2020) findings on the linguistic features used and acquired during early child L1 acquisition of English in Singapore and show how the presented tendencies and interrelations of the parents' statements reflect the parents' wishes rather than the reality of their children's L1 acquisition.

5 Discussion – child language acquisition and use: reality versus parents' preferences

After analyzing parental questionnaires concerned with the linguistic background and language use of 34 families in Singapore, I found that the vast majority of parents state that their children were acquiring, use most often, and are primarily exposed to (one or more) standard varieties of English, i.e. SSE, AmE, or BrE. In so doing, these parents background the use of the less formal CSE – only or in combination with standard varieties – from their assessment. However, Buschfeld (2020) found that the acquisition of L1-English by children in Singapore is more complex than my results indicate the parents believe. She found that especially young children in Singapore realize structures that serve as markers for CSE, e.g. zero subjects, copula deletion, and zero past tense marking. While these structures are also observable in children's L1 acquisition process of British and American English, Buschfeld found them to be realized more often and more consistently by children in Singapore. She assumes that the fact that children in Singapore receive positive feedback when realizing these structures might lead to this increased realization, which, in turn, gives reason to expect a structural divergence of child English from adult English in Singapore (Buschfeld 2020). This positive feedback is likely to be rooted in the use of non-standard characteristics in the children's primary input, i.e. the parents' use of English, which indicates that the parents do not primarily use a standard variety of English. However, I have shown that parents do claim to expose their children primarily to standard varieties of English, unveiling an important gap between reality and parental perception concerning child L1 acquisition in postcolonial contexts, and potentially beyond.

As the data set includes a comparably low number of tokens and the participating parents are quite homogeneous in their answers, the dependencies and interrelations found must be interpreted cautiously. Although this study might not offer inerrant revelations, clear tendencies and interrelations have been unveiled. When compared to Buschfeld's (2020) findings, the frequencies presented here paint a clear picture: In general, the parents' statements about their children's language acquisition, use, and exposure diverge from the reality of their children's language acquisition process, suggesting that these statements reflect parental language attitudes and ideologies. In this study, I have found different indicators of this discrepancy for the three variables in question. Concerning the varieties of English children are exposed to most often, the father's level of education appears to be an indicator (Figure 5.7). Parents of children whose father has received a university-level education more frequently stated exposing their children only to (one or more) standard varieties of English than those who have achieved a lower level of education. Therefore, a tendency towards the use of CSE by highly educated parents is not reflected in my study, although it has been found that CSE is less negatively connotated in this social class (e.g. Siemund and Li 2020). However, these results might reflect probability rather than dependency, as the vast majority of parents in this study have received a university education (73.53% of the mothers, 76.47% of the fathers). While, in other studies, the father's level of education has been shown to function as a predictor for children's language use, i.e. for migrated children's vocabulary scores (e.g. Western et al. 2018), my results have not followed suit in reflecting an effect on child language use.

I have found the mothers' characteristics to be the main influential variables when assessing *use*, specifically her age and L1(s), followed by the father's place of birth. My analysis has shown that the mother's age has a significant influence on the varieties of English used by her children (cf. Figure 5.8). However, this finding should be considered related to the often-occurring correlation between the mother's and the child's age: In the data at hand, the women in the younger age group are all mothers to children younger than three years. The young age of their children, and, consequently, the children's early stage within their language acquisition process, is likely to have caused more than 57% of participants in this group to not state which varieties of English their children use most often. A more valid and unsurprising predictor for the language use of children in my dataset, therefore, is the mothers' L1(s) (Figure 5.9). The parents of children whose mothers are speakers of Indian languages or bilingual speakers of English and another language believe their children to use only standard varieties of English more often than those who are speakers of other L1s. This tendency appears to also be represented by the effect of father's place of birth on the parents' beliefs about their children's language use (Figure 5.10). While parents of children with Singapore-born fathers believe their children to (also) use non-standard varieties of English more often than only standard varieties, those of children with fathers born outside Singapore (India and others) believe their children to use only standard varieties of English considerably more often than (also) non-standard varieties of English. Concerning the parents' statements about the varieties their children are acquiring, the father's age has been found to be the most influential variable. Much like the effect of the mother's age on the parents' statements about the varieties their children use most often, this has to be interpreted having the children's age in mind. Oftentimes, younger parents have younger children which speak and have acquired less language than older children. Consequently, the younger group must be considered to be of restricted informativity. Parents of children with fathers older than 37.83 years, however, believe more often that their children are acquiring only standard varieties of English than (also) CSE (Figure 5.11). The found tendencies towards standard varieties of English can be understood as a reflection of the effectiveness of campaigns like the SGEM. Singapore's language policy causes language ideologies to be reproduced, which, in turn, can explain the divergence between the parents' perceptions or beliefs and the reality of their children's language acquisition and language use.

While a comprehensive discussion of the complex interactions of language ideologies in and across societies would exceed the scope of this paper,[1] some light has been shed on the impact of governmental language policy in Singapore. It has been found that, while dominant language ideologies are often implemented in a top-down approach, they are instrumentalized, reproduced, and strengthened on various social levels in Singapore: Governmental language policy influences the language attitudes of Singaporeans and causes the reproduction of language ideologies

---

1 Thanks to Jakob Leimgruber for his feedback.

on a societal and domestic level. Since "language policy is deeply connected to sets of beliefs about language use and forms in social interactions, language ideology is central to language policy (Hill, 2001)" (Song 2019: 255). In the context at hand, the standard language ideology is most relevant. Campaigns like the SGEM show that the government embraces and supports the use of the standard variety SSE, causing the ideology of its hegemony to spread and be accepted in Singapore's society. Based on this ideology and its propagation through, e.g., the SGEM, SSE is – and continues to be – more highly valued within Singapore's society than the local non-standard variety CSE. Consequently, and although attitudes of Singaporeans towards CSE become increasingly positive (cf., e.g., Leimgruber 2013; Siemund and Li 2020; Wee 2018), SSE is oftentimes more desirable in Singapore's society than CSE. This, in turn, affects the ideology's mediating function between language use and the social structures it is used in, causing SSE to be associated with – and potentially granting access to – prestigious high social classes. Based on the language ideologies, especially the standard language ideology, promoted in language policy and reproduced in Singapore's society, parents might actually believe that their children acquire and use SSE as much as they believe to be exposing them to SSE by using it themselves, although this is not necessarily the reality of their children's language acquisition process. While the actual language use of the parents has not been assessed, research suggests that sustained use of SSE is unlikely (cf. Wong 2014). Based on this assumption that the input the children are provided with is not exclusively SSE, the fact that the children in Buschfeld's (2020) study show frequent use of CSE characteristics in their L1 acquisition of English could be explained.

In case the parents were not aware of their actual language use but merely reproducing and adhering to the language ideologies propagated by the government, they would honestly believe their children to acquire and use a standard variety of English. However, in case the parents knew that their children do not acquire and use primarily standard varieties of English, the presented answers would suggest them to be aware of the effects of language ideologies on social structures, i.e. the gatekeeper function of standard varieties to certain social classes and the respective prestigious positions and educational opportunities (Block 2015 on dimensions of social class). They would be hoping for their children to acquire SSE – to become members of the group of L1 speakers of the standard variety – as they would expect their children to be commonly respected and more highly valued than speakers of the non-standard variety. While the data does not reflect why parents answered in the presented manner, both possible scenarios strengthen my assumption that the parents' preference of standard varieties of English is not self-motivated but appears to reflect societal conventions and subconscious social positioning.

Bridging the gap between (child) language acquisition, language policies, World Englishes, and language ideologies has revealed a picture of the role, use, and acquisition of English(es) in Singapore which would not have been unveiled using one perspective alone. To understand this complex context of language use and change, insights from various fields must be considered, i.e., the conceptualization of L1 Singapore English as different from adults' English in Singapore, the subconscious impact of language ideologies on various levels of society, and the divergence of parental beliefs and the linguistic realities of their children (amongst others). The increasing global connectedness causes language use to become more complex and language acquisition processes to be increasingly interwoven with locally and globally induced variation and ideologies. Rather than putting linguistic, social, or political pressure on parents to raise "native speakers" of "the right" English or describing local Englishes as deficient, we enable a realistic, unbiased, and open-minded assessment of Englishes around the globe by incorporating various perspectives in linguistic research.

6 Conclusion

I have shown that the children's language use diverges from their parents' beliefs, as children frequently use structures associated with CSE (cf. Buschfeld 2020) while their parents clearly favor standard varieties of English, i.e. SSE, BrE, and AmE, over CSE when describing their children's language acquisition, use, and exposure. This discrepancy between the parents' assumptions and their children's language use, however, is not self-chosen but based on the ideologically-laden language policy at work in Singapore. In Singapore, language ideologies are prescribed by the government and followed and reproduced by the Singaporean society. My findings suggest that the language ideologies that are implemented through campaigns like the SGEM cause parents to assess their children's language acquisition process unrealistically; the open support of SSE over CSE on a political level is internalized by parents who wish for their children to become speakers of "Standard" English. Consequently, language ideologies appear to be used as a tool to maintain social structures and language use that are politically desired. Although the ideology of a standard variety and its global hegemony is adhered to, in local contexts the colloquial variety is believed to also be important and valuable. Much like other social groups (cf. Wong 2014), however, parents in general still appear to hold more positive attitudes towards standard varieties of English than towards CSE and wish for their children to acquire the globally understood variety of SSE. The integrated approach at use in the work at hand has enabled a first important step towards an unbiased understanding of the complex interrelations between language policy, language ideologies, and language use and their effects on parental language attitudes in contexts of language change.

References

Block, David. 2015. Social class in applied linguistics. *Annual Review of Applied Linguistics* 35. 1–19.
Blommaert, Jan. 2010. *The sociolinguistics of globalization*. Cambridge: Cambridge University Press.
Bolton, Kingsley & Bee Chin Ng. 2014. The dynamics of multilingualism in contemporary Singapore. *World Englishes* 33 (3). 307–18.
Buschfeld, Sarah. 2020. *Children's English in Singapore: Acquisition, properties, and use*. Oxon & New York: Routledge.
Chew, Phyllis Ghim-Lian. 2007. Remaking Singapore: Language, culture, and identity in a globalized world. In Amy B. M. Tsui & James W. Tollefson (eds.), *Language Policy, Culture, and Identity in Asian Contexts*, 73–93. Mahwah, NJ: Lawrence Erlbaum Associates.
Deterding, David. 2007. *Singapore English*. Edinburgh: Edinburgh University Press.
Gal, Susan. 1998. Multiplicity and contention among language ideologies. In Bambi B. Schieffelin, Kathryn A. Woolard & Paul V. Kroskrity (eds.), *Language ideologies: Practice and theory*, 317–331. Oxford, UK: Oxford University Press.
Gries, Stefan Th. 2020. On classification trees and random forests in corpus linguistics: Some words of caution and suggestions for improvement. *Corpus Linguistics and Linguistic Theory* 16 (3). 617–647.
Gupta, Anthea F.1992. Contact features of Singapore Colloquial English. In Kingsley Bolton & Helen Kwok (eds.), *Sociolinguistics Today: International Perspectives*, 323–345. London: Routledge.
Hothorn, Torsten, Kurt Hornik & Achim Zeileis. 2006. Unbiased recursive partitioning: A conditional inference framework. *Journal of Computational and Graphical Statistics* 15. 651–674.
Leimgruber, Jakob R. E. 2011. Singapore English. *Language and Linguistics Compass* 5 (1). 47–62.
Leimgruber, Jakob R. E. 2013. *Singapore English: Structure, variation, and usage*. Cambridge: Cambridge University Press.
Lim, Lisa. 2004. *Singapore English: A grammatical description*. Amsterdam: John Benjamins.
Pakir, Anne. 1991. The range and depth of English-knowing bilinguals in Singapore. *World Englishes* 10 (2). 167–179.
Park, Joseph S. 2009. *The local construction of a global language: Ideologies of English in South Korea*. Berlin & New York: De Gruyter Mouton.
Piller, Ingrid. 2015. Language ideologies. In Karen Tracy, Cornelia Ilie & Todd Sandel (eds.), *The international encyclopedia of language and social interaction*, vol. 1, 1–10. West Sussex: John Wiley & Sons.
R Core Team. 2019. R: A language and environment for statistical computing. *R Foundation for Statistical Computing*, www.R-project.org/. (accessed 21 December 2021).
Siemund, Peter &Lijun Li. 2020. Multilingualism and language policy in Singapore. In: Henning Klöter & Mårten Söderblom Saarela (eds.), *Language Diversity in the Sinophone World*, 205–228. London: Routledge.

Silverstein, Michael. 1979. Language structure and linguistic ideology. In Paul R. Clyne, William F. Hanks, and Carol L. Hofbauer (eds.), *The elements: A parasession on linguistic units and levels*, 193–247. Chicago, IL: Chicago Linguistic Society.

Singapore Department of Statistics (SingStat). 2016. General household survey 2015. www.singstat.gov.sg/-/media/files/publications/ghs/ghs2015/ghs2015.pdf (accessed 4 March 2021).

Singapore Department of Statistics (SingStat). 2021. Census of population 2020 – statistical release 1: Demographic characteristics, education, language and religion. www.singstat.gov.sg/-/media/files/publications/cop2020/sr1/cop2020sr1.pdf (accessed 5 October 2021).

Song, Kwangok. 2019. Immigrant parents' ideological positioning on bilingualism. *Theory Into Practice* 58. 254–262.

Speak Good English Movement (SGEM). n.d.–a. About us. www.languagecouncils.sg/goodenglish/about-us (accessed 2 February 2021).

Speak Good English Movement (SGEM). n.d.–b. Tips for parents. www.languagecouncils.sg/goodenglish/resources/tips-for-parents (accessed 2 February 2021).

Tagliamonte, Sali A., & R. Harald Baayen. 2012. Models, forests, and trees of York English: Was/were variation as a case study for statistical practice. *Language Variation and Change* 24. 135–178.

Tan, Ying-Ying. 2014. English as a 'mother tongue' in Singapore. *World Englishes* 33 (3). 319–39.

Wee, Lionel. 2004. Singapore English: Phonology. In Edgar W. Schneider & Bernd Kortmann (eds.), *A handbook of varieties of English, Volume 1: Phonology*, 1017–1033. Berlin & Boston: De Gruyter Mouton.

Wee, Lionel. 2018. *The Singlish controversy: Language, culture and identity in a globalizing world*. Cambridge: Cambridge University Press.

Western, Ingelin, Anne-Marie Halberg, Heloise M. Ledesma, Astri H. Wold & Brit Oppedal. 2018. Effects of mother's and father's education level and age at migration on children's bilingual vocabulary. *Applied Psycholinguistics* 39 (5). 811–833.

Wong, Jock O. 2014. English in Singapore. In Jock O. Wong (ed.), *The culture of Singapore English*, 1–37. Cambridge: Cambridge University Press.

Woolard, Kathryn A. 1998. Introduction – Language ideology as a field of inquiry. In Bambi B. Schieffelin, Kathryn A. Woolard & Paul V. Kroskrity (eds.), *Language ideologies: Practice and theory*, 3–47. New York & Oxford: Oxford University Press.

Wortham, Stanton. 2001. Language ideology and educational research. *Linguistics and Education* 12 (3). 253–259.

Part II: Language acquisition and language learning in multilingual contexts

Zeynep Köylü and Kenan Dikilitaş

6 Syntactic and lexical complexity in CLIL and EFL written production: Evidence for ELF as a WEs paradigm in Turkey

Abstract: This study aims to investigate the effects of Content and Language Integrated Learning (CLIL) on written second language (L2) development in the Turkish context over one semester compared to an intensive integrated skills English as a foreign language (EFL) programmed high school. Drawing on Schneider's Dynamic Model (2012) and Edwards' (2016) notion of "foundation-through-globalization," this study aims to see the relationship between the type of linguistic exposure and how it affects written performance, as the participants have been exposed to a mixed variety of English including both native-speaker English and English as a lingua franca (ELF)/World Englishes (WEs) forms and features in a non-postcolonial context. The data analyzed were collected from two schools: a CLIL-based and an EFL-based private secondary school. Thus, there are two groups of participants: (1) the CLIL group (N = 15) and the EFL group (N = 18). A written task was used twice to collect performance data which were analyzed in terms of syntactic and lexical complexity and lexical profiling. This dataset was also qualitatively analyzed to discern ELF features following a coding scheme by Dewey (2007) and Schneider (2012). The quantitative results indicated no significant effects of time or context on all measures, except for significant gains detected in the range of lexical diversity, while the qualitative data revealed ELF-compatible lexical frequency profiles and syntactic and word-level characteristics typical of ELF as a WEs variety. Our results highlight the need to accentuate the dynamic link between CLIL and written L2 development in relation to EFL in a non-postcolonial context, namely Turkey (Edwards 2016).

Keywords: Content and Language Integrated Learning (CLIL), written L2 development, Turkish context, Schneider's Dynamic Model, syntactic and lexical complexity, lexical profiling

Zeynep Köylü, University of Basel, Switzerland
Kenan Dikilitaş, University of Stavanger, Norway

https://doi.org/10.1515/9783110733723-006

1 Introduction

In an attempt to prepare young generations for the communicative requirements of the English-dominated globalized world (Goris, Denessen, and Verhoeven 2019), educational institutions across Europe have switched to Content and Language Integrated Learning (CLIL) or English-Medium Instruction (EMI), two different instructional designs rooted in Content-Based Instruction (CBI; Lightbown 2014), aimed at promoting the simultaneous acquisition of language and content in meaningful contexts. Commonly practiced across the world, CLIL is underexplored in terms of its comparative linguistic gains in writing to non-CLIL environments. Therefore, we aim to address this gap by exploring the potential qualitative and quantitative impact of CLIL as an instructional design on the writing development of K12 students in CLIL and non-CLIL contexts in Turkey. The rationale behind the potential effectiveness of CLIL on target language (TL) proficiency gains lies in the fact that learners would be exposed to large amounts of authentic input combining content and language in a domestic immersion context without allotting extra time on separate TL instruction. By the same token, this dual focus is expected to help learners not only develop themselves in a curriculum subject to further their education, but also their TL performance and proficiency (Goris, Denessen, and Verhoeven 2019). The advantages of CLIL over traditional formal instruction settings have long been echoed in the literature (Goris, Denessen, and Verhoeven 2019), especially for higher education settings given the contextual focus of the current study, the Turkish context (Kırkgöz and Dikilitaş 2018). The dual focus of CLIL positively affects lexical diversity and creativity, communicative skills, and reading and listening performance, while no clear evidence has been put forward for syntax, writing, or pragmatic development (Dalton-Puffer 2008).

In addition, our knowledge about the variety of English acquired with the help of CLIL is very limited. Given its popular implementation in continental Europe, where English holds the status of a lingua franca, it is quite debatable that pupils are always exposed to native speaker varieties of English (NSE)[1] through authentic content materials and that they are being taught by L1-users of English (Dafouz and Hibbler 2013; Yalçın, Bayyurt, and Alahdab 2020). Drawing on Schneider's (2012) Dynamic Model and Edwards' (2016) notion of "foundation-through-globalization," this study considers the variety of English in the Turkish context as a learner variety, reflecting the lingua franca status of the target language (English as a lingua franca, ELF) in the given setting, under the general forces of globalization. ELF features (Schneider 2012) are thus hypothesized to be apparent especially in pupils' written syntactic and lexical choices. Since written development in CLIL and EFL settings

---

[1] Here we refer to Anglophone varieties as native speaker varieties of English.

has received very limited attention with inconsistent results showing significant development for performance constructs, such as complexity, accuracy, and fluency (Gené-Gil, Juan-Garau, and Salazar-Noguera 2015), further research is needed. There is still a dearth of studies comparing CLIL with traditional formal instruction settings in terms of EFL development, which might lead the reader to consider that the advantages of CLIL are rather inflated (Goris, Denessen, and Verhoeven 2019; Sylven 2013). This paper, thus, aims to retest such hypotheses in a different context through the comparison of students in a CLIL program with those in an intensive EFL program in two private high schools located in the west of Turkey. More specifically it reports results from the analyses of their writings to trace and identify the ELF-related morphosyntactic and lexical features in their production. In what follows, we first present the literature review and our methodology and then discuss the results and conclude with the limitations and pedagogical implications.

2 Literature review

2.1 CLIL and written CAF development

CLIL refers to "an educational approach where curricular content is taught through the medium of a foreign language, typically to students participating in some form of mainstream education at the primary, secondary, or tertiary level" (Dalton-Puffer 2011: 183). The effects of CLIL on written development, especially in secondary school settings, have so far received limited attention in the literature and studies have shown inconclusive results (Gené-Gil, Juan-Garau, and Salazar-Noguera 2015; Whittaker, Llinares, and McCabe 2011). In her review, Ruiz de Zarobe (2011) underscored the empirically confirmed positive influence of CLIL on written fluency and lexical and syntactic complexity. Yet, the results that pertain to the development of written accuracy and discourse skills were not statistically significant. To exemplify, Llinares and Whittaker (2006) examined the written development of a group of Spanish L1 pupils (aged 12–16) receiving English CLIL instruction in social sciences. Their results confirmed significant gains for subject-specific lexis use, while the participants showed no significant development in written complexity (i.e., modality and clause expansion) (Llinares and Whittaker 2006). Taking a longitudinal perspective, Whittaker, Llinares, and McCabe (2011) reported similar positive results for academic register and written coherence and cohesion for a group of secondary school CLIL students.

Taking a comparative perspective, several studies attempted to determine a better teaching methodology to develop L2 writing. Contrasting two CLIL groups with a non-CLIL group of secondary school pupils (N = 198) from Basque Country, Lasagabaster (2008) reported that the CLIL participants outperformed the non-CLIL pupils on holistic written measures, such as content, organization of ideas, vocabulary, language use and accuracy, and mechanics (i.e., punctuation). Within a similar comparative design, Ruiz de Zarobe (2010) investigated written development of secondary school pupils using a holistic rubric and controlling for the amount of exposure to the TL. Ruiz de Zarobe's (2010) results aligned with Lasagabaster (2008) as the CLIL participants had significantly more gains in vocabulary use, target-like language use, and mechanics.

Few studies have employed a complexity, accuracy, and fluency (CAF) assessment framework to measure written development in CLIL settings, which we address in our study. Saladrigues and Llanes (2014) examined the case of 39 Spanish/Catalan bilinguals in their 4th year of obligatory secondary education in terms of written and lexical development through the analysis of a written picture-narration task and a pictured vocabulary test. The authors could only confirm significant gains in written syntactic complexity and fluency for CLIL participants as opposed to the non-CLIL group, showing only a modest advantage for the former. In a similar vein, Gené-Gil, Juan-Garau, and Salazar-Noguera (2015) longitudinally compared the effectiveness of CLIL over EFL, eliciting data from 50 secondary school students at four data collection points over three academic years. The participants completed a timed composition task. Although no differences were discerned at the end of the first academic year, the CLIL group outperformed the EFL group on written syntactic and lexical complexity and fluency, while the latter group only had gains in lexical complexity and accuracy.

By the same token, Roquet and Pérez-Vidal (2017) looked into the effects of age and type of instruction, CLIL and non-CLIL (EFL), among a group of Catalan/Spanish bilingual adolescents over two academic semesters. The authors were unable to detect significant gains in written CAF measures, except for accuracy and lexicogrammatical ability (measured via a grammar test) in the CLIL context, especially for those older than 14 years old. Given the results of the relevant literature, no strong evidence has been articulated favoring CLIL over EFL instruction. Thus, further research is still needed to see whether and in what ways the development of L2 writing through CLIL might have an advantage over that through EFL.

2.2 CLIL and lexical profiling

Vocabulary and lexical development have been popular performative constructs in CLIL research (Augustín Llach 2014; Gierlinger and Wagner 2016). Empirical evidence has confirmed that CLIL students develop the most in terms of TL vocabulary (especially subject-specific) and lexis-related skills when compared to EFL settings (Lagasabaster 2008; Saladrigues and Llanes 2014). In comparative designs, the advantage of CLIL pupils over non-CLIL peers on lexical gains has been investigated. However, this advantage was levelled out by non-CLIL students within two years of receiving EFL instruction from a longitudinal perspective (Mewald, Prenner, and Spenger 2004).

CLIL students' lexical profiles have received limited attention in the areas of their frequency, depth, and range of their lexical choices (Jiménez Catalán and Augustín Llach 2017). Gierlinger and Wagner (2016) drew on the effects of increased input in the TL in CLIL settings as the major cause for lexical growth. By the same token, the authors examined frequency effects of teacher input, over 428 hours of instruction, on pupils' lexical gains in three CLIL classes (chemistry, geography, and history). The data from this teacher vocabulary-input corpus were analyzed in terms of word-frequency bands (the most frequently used 1000 [k1], 2000 [k2], and 3000 [k3] words in English), academic words (AWL), and a residual category called *off-list* (Lexical Frequency Profile, LFP, Laufer and Nation 1995), along with type/token rations and Guiraud's index for lexical complexity and diversity. The results indicated that the majority of the type of teacher input consisted of high-frequency words from the k1 list with low Guiraud's index rates showing the repetitive nature of the high-frequency words, quite similar to EFL or ELF input (Gierlinger and Wagner 2016). That being the case, the authors could not confirm significant gains in receptive vocabulary for CLIL students, except for those within the k1 band.

Focusing on learners' output in terms of productive vocabulary, Jiménez Catalán and Augustín Llach (2017) compared a group of CLIL students (N = 24) with two non-CLIL EFL groups (N = 45) with similar amounts but different types of exposure (1189 hours for CLIL and EFL I; 839 hours for EFL II) to the TL. The authors also analyzed participants' lexical profiles in terms of word frequency, lexical availability, and world level through Lexical Frequency Profiles (Laufer and Nation 1995) and Cambridge Vocabulary Profiles (CVP); additionally, participants' productive vocabulary was classified in terms of Common European Framework of Reference for Languages (CEFR) levels. The data were elicited from a writing task, for which the participants were asked to list all the words that come to their minds when prompted with several topics, such as "Parts of the Body," "Dirty," "Hold," and "Food and Drink". The results of the study indicated that all groups had similar performances in terms of word frequency with the dominant use of items from the most frequent 1000 and 2000-word lists in English (more than 75% of their total production) within a range of A1 to B1 proficiency levels. The only major difference was reported to come from the 10th-grade, non-CLIL group on the topic "Hold," as 43% of all words produced by this group belonged to the off-list words. These vocabulary profiling studies have indicated the fact that the type of exposure and thus the output in CLIL contexts across Europe significantly display characteristics of ELF.

2.3 The overlap between CLIL and ELF as a WEs paradigm

Schneider (2012) and Seidlhofer (2009) highlight the need to classify English as a Second Language (ESL), EFL, and ELF as varieties of the same kind within the World Englishes (WEs) paradigm. Interactions in an ELF context show typicalities of learner Englishes in an EFL setting (Schneider 2012); this is also the case with the inclusion of native speakers (and teachers) in CLIL settings. Turkey is a country where English is mainly taught in formal settings and mostly used as a contact language with NSEs and nonnative speakers of English. Therefore, Turkey provides a suitable context for such a classification as a non-postcolonial (Edwards 2016) country in the expanding circle (Kachru 1985). "ELF describes a situation-bound interaction type which cross-sects the ENL-ESL-EFL categorization, but in practice it overlaps more with EFL than with the others: for most speakers their EFL competence constitutes the prerequisite of their ability to interact in ELF situations" (Schneider 2012: 61).

The pedagogical interplay between ELF and CLIL is closely linked to how CLIL is implemented by teachers who might position themselves differently as CLIL practitioners (Hüttner 2018). English is the primary medium of instruction in most CLIL programs in the context in question. As explained above, it holds the status of a contact language in the broader context and serves mainly a functional purpose as a lingua franca (Yalçın, Bayyurt, and Alahdab 2020). CLIL programs in Turkey do not build on native speaker-oriented pedagogies. Hence, they integrate content into language instruction, resulting in non-native teachers overlooking erroneous production, accepting such production as instances of deviation, and thus shifting "ultimate attainment" expectations to those of meaningful interaction and successful communication in or outside of class (Yalçın, Bayyurt, and Alahdab 2020). This perspective itself suffices to clarify the link between CLIL and ELF in the given context. A CLIL setting in Turkey replicates an ELF setting.

Yalçın, Bayyurt, and Alahdab (2020) also highlight the fact that content classes in CLIL settings are instructed by English language teachers in most primary and secondary schools in Turkey. This leads to a serious deficiency in content taught in science and art classes seeing that the language teachers are not competent in subjects other than EFL (Yalçın, Bayyurt, and Alahdab 2020). Thus, the type of CLIL practiced in Turkey is one that is "language-driven rather than content-driven" (Yalçın, Bayyurt, and Alahdab 2020: 388). This also strengthens the major aim of CLIL programs in Turkey: helping learners emerge as efficient lingua franca users of the TL to communicate in the broader global ELF, EFL, ESL, or native speaker

(NS) contexts (Yalçın, Bayyurt, and Alahdab 2020). That being the case, the current study draws on the notion that CLIL, EFL, and ELF are closely related and regarded as learner varieties of English within the broader WEs paradigm.

Theoretically speaking, this study also draws on Edwards' (2016) notion of "foundation-through-globalization," which aims to explore the relationship between the type of linguistic exposure and how it affects written performance, as the participants have been exposed to a mixed variety of English including both native-speaker and WEs forms (EFL, ESL, and ELF) and features in a non-postcolonial context. This reflects the variational dynamics of English in the broader European context, where English is now deeply entrenched due to the forces of globalization and used "primarily for international contacts and is necessarily exonormatively oriented" (Edwards 2014: 174).

2.4 ELF characteristics

We analyzed how typical linguistic features of ELF are employed in the written productions of CLIL and non-CLIL learners. We provide these characteristics to later refer to in our findings and discussion. Dewey (2007), for example, provided a data-driven list of characteristics, while Seidlhofer (2004) and Schneider (2012) presented a corpus-driven list by utilizing the Vienna-Oxford International Corpus of English (VOICE) (Seidlhofer et al. 2013). These can be summarized as:
- simplicity (omission of morphological markers verbal -s, plural -s, this + plural noun *this ideas*; omission of syntactic constituents),
- generalization (disregarding exceptionalities such as pluralizing words like *information* or *staff*),
- redundancy (repeated double marking of the same type of information as in *although he goes, but . . .*),
- rule regularization (avoiding exceptions as in using *goed* instead of *went*),
- analogy (transfer from a source domain to a target domain as in mapping information from one's L1 as in dropping plural -s for nouns modified by quantifiers by Turkish L1 speakers of L2 English),
- isomorphism (preference for finite clauses),
- grammaticalization,
- exaptation (functional reallocation),
- and complement reduction (replacing infinitival constructions with noun clauses) (Schneider 2012).

To extend our framework, we also draw on Dewey's (2007) work and include the ELF features he adapted from Seidlhofer (2004: 220). Therefore, in addition to what Schneider (2012) accentuates, insertion of redundant prepositions (e.g., he should tell *to* you) and overdoing explicitness (e.g., *small* pond) are also taken into our coding scheme. These all indeed underscore the need for communicative success rather than a native-like ultimate attainment perspective, typical of ELF. By the same token, ELF use is "an adaptive mode of speech behavior, a linguistic strategy, and a systematic type of performance supported and shaped by cognitive and communicative needs and considerations" (Schneider 2012: 87). Operationalizing the variety provided by CLIL in Turkey as ELF within the broader WEs paradigm, this study aims to investigate the above-mentioned characteristics of ELF in the current dataset along with word-level simplicity (lexical frequency profiles) as a lexical complexity feature.

To summarize, CLIL in Europe still needs to be explored in terms of its influence on written development by adopting a comparative design including quantitative and qualitative data analysis. More importantly, the variety of English provided in the underexplored Turkish CLIL context should be analyzed through students' written complexity and lexical profiles, drawing on it being an instance of ELF within the broader WEs paradigm (Schneider 2012) in a non-postcolonial setting (Edwards 2016). Motivated by such gaps in the literature, this study aims to comparatively investigate the written CAF development of two groups of Turkish L1 secondary school pupils learning English in a CLIL or EFL context. It also seeks to provide insights into the connection among CLIL, EFL, and ELF through the analysis of participants' written outputs in terms of ELF features, such as analogy (L1 transfer), rule regularization, simpler lexicality, and high-frequency vocabulary. The following research questions guide the study:

1. Does the type of instruction as CLIL or EFL affect secondary school students' written syntactic and lexical complexity gains after a semester of 16 weeks?
2. Does learners' written production display ELF characteristics in terms of syntactic and lexical complexity constructs along with their lexical frequency profiles?

3 Methods

3.1 Design

Following a quasi-experimental pretest-posttest design, the current study quantitatively investigated written syntactic and lexical complexity development over the course of a 16-week semester. The dependent variables were syntactic and lexical performance scores from the pretests and posttests. The independent variable was the type of instruction as CLIL and EFL in the quantitative analyses. Additionally, textual data were analyzed qualitatively for ELF characteristics, such as simplification, following a data (Dewey 2007) and corpus-driven coding scheme (Schneider 2012). Considering lexical profiling, a corpus-driven quantitative approach was taken (Dewey 2007; Schneider 2012).

3.2 Contexts (CLIL vs. EFL)

The study included 33 9th graders studying in two contexts: (1) a private CLIL high school (N = 31) and another private high school instructing EFL following an intensive integrated skills curriculum. The former context provided 24 hours a week of EMI instruction following a science and technology-enhanced curriculum (STEM) (Bybee 2013) along with 7 hours of EFL instruction. Thus, as part of the STEM-based CLIL curriculum, mathematics, biology, physics, and chemistry classes are taught in English in this setting. In the latter context, the participants had 9 hours of EFL instruction per week. All other content classes were taught in Turkish. Therefore, the major difference between the two contexts is the amount of exposure to the TL. In both contexts, the pupils were exposed to books written by native speaker experts and published for language classes by global EFL publishers, such as Pearson and Cambridge. In the CLIL setting, content classes were taught following books written in English by Turkish authors who are experts in the given content.

3.3 Participants

Two intact classes of participants (N = 33) who are Turkish L1 high school students (9th graders) aged 14–16 (M = 15) years old participated in the study. In Turkey, formal English instruction starts in the 4th grade. However, some of these participants started to learn the TL long before. The age of onset for the CLIL participants ranged from 3–10 years old (M = 7.42), EFL participants ranged from 2–10 (M = 5.32) years old. All the participants are learners of English as a foreign language in two contexts: CLIL (N = 15) and EFL (N = 18). None of the participants were enrolled in a third language (L3) class at the time of the study, but some of the participants had previously studied German (N = 22) and Italian (N = 5) as an L3 in middle school.

3.4 Instruments

The data analyzed in the current study were elicited using a variety of methods. To determine initial proficiencies of the participants, an elicited imitation test (EIT; Ortega et al. 1999) was implemented. EIT is a test of oral production in the form of sentence repetition. Test-takers listen to model TL sentences varying in syllable length (19–30 syllables) and then repeat these sentences as accurately as possible. One can score a maximum of 120 points as each item is worth 4 points. Following the original scoring rubric (Ortega et al. 1999), the data from the EIT were coded and analyzed by two fellow researchers to ensure inter-coder/inter-scorer reliability. Any incongruent scores were discussed and revised, reaching a final agreement for over 91% of repeated sentences. The data from the EITs were checked for any initial significant proficiency differences among participants at the onset of the study. Thus, EIT scores were used as covariants in the statistical tests.

To discern written development in two different contexts over an academic semester of 16 weeks, written performance data were elicited with a timed written production task. The participants were asked to write as much as possible about their past, present, and future expectations within 15 minutes (Llanes and Muñoz 2013). The rationale behind such a prompt was that students would not need any technical or subject-specific vocabulary and could provide a variety of structures to write about their lives. This task was administered twice: once as a pretest at the beginning of the semester and once as a posttest 16 weeks later. The data from this task were also analyzed in terms of the above-mentioned ELF characteristics and lexical profiling.

The written production data were analyzed quantitatively in terms of syntactic and lexical complexity dimensions using the web-based L2 Syntactic Complexity Analyzer (Lu and Ai 2015). There are a large number of indices available in second language acquisition (SLA) literature to measure syntactic and lexical complexity. We follow Ortega (2003) and operationalize sentence length and subordination (longer T-units or more dependent clauses) as indicators of a more complex syntactic sentence structure performed by more proficient learners. Syntactic complexity was thus determined by the total number of finite and nonfinite clauses divided by T-units (CL/TU) and mean length of T-units (MLTU). Lexical variation, richness, and diversity was measured through the ratio between types and tokens (TTR) to discern lexical variation, Guiraud's index (GUI) was used to detect lexical richness via the Lexical Complexity Analyzer (LCP) (Lu 2012), and D (also referred to as VOCD, McKee, Malvern, & Richards 2000) to tap lexical diversity via D_Tools (Meara and Miralpeix 2018). D is a measure for lexical diversity sensitive to text length and was confirmed to be a more robust measure for shorter texts.

3.5 Lexical profiling

The written performance data from the pretests and posttests were also analyzed using *VocabProfile* (Cobb 2020). This tool segments texts into word-frequency bands (Paul and Nation 1995), as the first 1000 or k1, the second 1000 or k2, and third 1000 or k3 most frequent words in English. It also reports on the use of academic words and a group of residuals called the *off-list*, words which cannot be categorized into the above-mentioned bands.

3.6 Data collection procedures

The data were collected by the researchers at the respective schools. First, the participants were shortly interviewed about their language learning experiences. After having been briefed about the scope of the study, the participants completed the EIT. Finally, at a separate meeting, they completed the timed written task.

3.7 Data analysis procedures

The written data were transcribed and prepared for analysis in compliance with the selected automated analyzers. In this pretest-posttest, between-within design, the independent variables were time and context (CLIL and EFL as different instructional methods), while the dependent variables were syntactic complexity (MLTU, CL/TU), lexical complexity in the form of lexical variation (TTR), richness (GUI), and diversity (D) scores of the participants. As for the quantitative analysis, the dataset from the written texts was first checked to see if it violated any assumptions of the parametric tests selected. The results of the Kolmogorov-Smirnov tests showed the data to be normally distributed. The homogeneity of variances, independence, and linearity assumptions were also met. The results of the EIT test and the pretest-posttest design were found to be significant ($t(31) = 3.396$, $p = .003$). This showed that the two groups had different levels of proficiencies at the onset of the study, as the EFL group ($M = 100.89$, $SD = 8.27$) significantly outperformed the CLIL group ($M = 85.80$, $SD = 15.46$). This result led the researchers to prefer a series of repeated measures analysis of variance (ANOVA) controlling for proficiency as a covariant. The written data were also analyzed to discern lexical vocabulary profiles and ELF features of the participants using *VocabProfile* (Cobb 2020) and AntConc (Anthony 2019). All the statistical analyses were computed using the Statistical Package for Social Sciences (SPSS) version 27.

Considering qualitative analyses, the dataset was manually coded for the selected syntactic and lexical ELF features. A fellow researcher proficient in Turkish and English checked the coded dataset to ensure reliability. All areas of incongruence were discussed and revised if necessary.

4 Results

4.1 The effects of type of instruction as CLIL and EFL on syntactic and lexical complexity gains

First, mean scores (*M*) and standard deviations (SD) were determined to be used in the statistical analyses. Table 6.1 summarizes the descriptive statistics for both context groups on syntactic and lexical measures. Controlling for proficiency, the results of the repeated measures ANOVAs indicated no significant main effects for time (F(1, 30) = .408, p = .528, η2 = .013) or interaction between time and context (F(1, 30) = .006, p = .941, η2 = .000) regarding MLTU. The results were also insignificant for syntactic complexity in the form of subordination (CL/TU) with no effects for time (F(1, 30) = .962, p = .334, η2 = .027) or interaction between time and context (F(1, 30) = .306, p = .584, η2 = .010). Similarly, no main effects were found for lexical variation (F(1, 30) = .005, p = .945, η2 = .000) measured by TTR and richness (F(1, 30) =

Table 6.1: Descriptive statistics for syntactic and lexical complexity measures.

Context group	Written dimension	Measure	Pretest-*M* (SD)	Posttest-*M* (SD)
CLIL (N = 15)	Syntactic complexity	MLTU	11.16 (2.33)	11.22 (1.85)
		CL/TU	1.42 (.237)	1.56 (.279)
	Lexical complexity (variation, richness, diversity)	TTR	.547 (.061)	.615 (.074)
		GUI	6.91 (1.18)	6.76 (1.10)
		D*	62.98 (19.68)	85.11 (28.28)
EFL (N = 18)	Syntactic complexity	MLTU	15.25 (3.41)	14.54 (3.16)
		CL/TU	1.67 (.400)	1.62 (.194)
	Lexical complexity (variation, richness, diversity)	TTR	.507 (.050)	.682 (.426)
		GUI	6.99 (.666)	6.44 (1.37)
		D*	66.87 (14.47)	75.29 (18.27)

*Significant gains were detected for this construct.

.738, p = .397, η2 = .024) measured by GUI. There were no interaction effects for these constructs either. Only in terms of lexical diversity did the results of the repeated measures ANOVA indicate a significant main effect of time on the D measure ($F(1, 30)$ = 5.687, p = .024, η2 = .159) with a large effect size. This result showed that all the participants developed their lexical diversity after a 16-week semester regardless of group membership. In other words, time was the only significant factor for their lexical diversity gains. No interaction effects were found regarding this measure ($F(1, 30)$ = .017, p = .897, η2 = .001). Thus, we cannot claim any effects of the type of instruction as CLIL or EFL on participants' gains in lexical diversity.

4.2 ELF characteristics in participants' written production

Participants' written production was analyzed in terms of their lexical profiles via *VocabProfile* (Cobb 2020). In both groups, words from the most frequent 1000- and 2000- bands comprise the largest proportion (91.1% for CLIL and 92.1% for EFL) of the participants' lexical profiles. Having a closer look at the off-list words, a high number of proper nouns in Turkish or English was found to be used in the dataset (e.g., the names of their schools, their names and surnames, names of cities and countries they expect to travel to, and higher education institutions they hope study at). Thus, no significant uses of off-list words were detected. As for the AWL proportion, it should be kept in mind that the task used to elicit written data is related to a non-academic topic. Hence, a smaller proportion of AWL in their lexical profiles is inevitable. Table 6.2 summarizes the results of the analysis.

Table 6.2: Lexical frequency profiles of the CLIL and EFL groups.

Frequency bands	CLIL			EFL		
	Pretest	Posttest	Mean	Pretest	Posttest	Mean
k1 words	88.05%	87.49%	87.76%	89.98%	87.87%	87.70%
k2 words	3.82%	2.86%	3.34%	3.27%	3.47%	3.30%
AWL words	2.95%	2.42%	2.69%	2.37%	2.37%	3.63%
off-list words	5.18%	7.23%	6.21%	4.58%	6.29%	5.37%
TOTAL	100%	100%	100%	100%	100%	100%

k1 = the first 1,000 most frequent words of English, k2 = 1,001–2,000 most frequent words of English, AWL = academic word list (Laufer and Nation 1995).

Considering the qualitative analyses to address the second research question, the dataset was manually coded over two rounds of coding for the predetermined

ELF features drawing on the two frameworks provided by Schneider (2012) and Dewey (2007). The results of the analysis indicate that both groups show traces of ELF in their written production. The most frequently encountered features of ELF in their texts are simplicity, analogy, insertion of redundant prepositions, and generalization and rule regularization. Table 6.3 summarizes the results of the analysis with examples from the dataset.

Table 6.3: ELF characteristics in participant production written data.

ELF Characteristics (Dewey 2007; Schneider 2012)		Example(s)
Simplicity	Omission or misuse of morphological markers (articles, third person -s, -ing, plural -s)	I studied there for *four year*. If I did not stop playing [the] piano . . . As [a] conclusion, in [the] future I want to work in a job . . . I had *an* happy childhood. I want to be *a* industry designer. . . . being *a* effective, good student . . . I will have *this* same *hobbies* probably. I was *get* on well. I am also *want*.
Analogy (morphological or syntactic)	Transfer from a source domain to a target domain as in mapping information from one's L1	We *came* to Izmir for my father's job six years ago (meaning *moved*). I *became* 7 years old (meaning *turned* 7). It would be the most *logical* job for me (meaning *reasonable*). I *ended up* playing badminton (meaning *stopped* playing). Like a *classic* child, I wanted to be a doctor (meaning *typical*). I began to *make* philosophy and literature (meaning to do something as a hobby) I am *expecting* to go to a good high school (Turkish progressive tense use).

Table 6.3 (continued)

ELF Characteristics (Dewey 2007; Schneider 2012)		Example(s)
Insertion of redundant prepositions	He should tell *to* you to go.	When I started *to* seventh grade . . . Now I am studying *to* my lessons. I will register *to* a university . . . I may choose *to* department of engineering . . . Nobody knows what will happen *at* now.
Generalization & rule regularization	Disregarding exceptionalities or avoiding exceptions	My expectations were [the] same as many other *childs*.
Grammaticalization		None
Exaptation		None
Complement reductions		None
Overdoing explicitness	Small pond	None
Isomorphism	Preference for finite clauses	None
Redundancy	Repeated double marking (e.g, although . . ., but . . .)	None

5 Discussion

To begin with, we detected that our participants had different proficiency levels at the beginning of the study. Thus, we preferred to control for proficiency as a covariant to ensure a robust statistical analysis. That being the case, the results of the quantitative analyses showed no significant main effects of time or interaction between time and CLIL or EFL instruction on general (MLTU) and subordination-level (CL/TU) syntactic complexity development of the participants over the course of a 16-week semester. This result suggests that there are no differences in L2 written complexity development after a semester of instruction received in either a CLIL or EFL setting. This result aligns with the literature in that written complexity as a performance construct might require a longer period of time to bring about any substantial linguistic changes (Ortega 2003). CLIL studies could detect significant changes in syntactic complexity after at least two semesters of instruction (Gené-Gil, Juan-Garau, and Salazar-Noguera 2015; Roquet and Pérez-Vidal 2017).

However, the lack of statistical significance is remarkable in the sense that the substantially higher amount of exposure in the CLIL setting (24 hours of English input, 7 of which is language instruction) has not led to statistically significant writing gains in terms of syntactic complexity. This result underscores the previous findings in the literature and the hypotheses that CLIL might have long been inflated as an effective language teaching methodology (Llinares and Whittaker 2006). But more importantly, the reason behind these syntactically less complex written performances of the participants might be caused by the type of instructional input they have been exposed to in both CLIL and EFL settings, which is characterized by the linguistic features of ELF. Although both groups were instructed in English via materials exposing native-speaker varieties (e.g., course books published by Cambridge or Pearson), all the teachers are Turkish L1 non-native speakers of English. By the same token, the CLIL group has studied STEM content through books written in English by Turkish L1 authors and instructed in the classroom by Turkish teachers with similar linguistic profiles (Gierlinger and Wagner 2016). We suggest that the type of exposure might be a factor on the L2 writing development in CLIL and non-CLIL contexts. The students' exposure to the ELF-oriented instruction might have primed their writing production.

As for lexical complexity dimensions, the results indicated only a significant effect of time on lexical diversity gains as measured by D. Again, no interaction effects were found. This result indicates that all the participants developed their lexical diversities over the course of a semester regardless of the method of instruction, which contradicts with the findings in the literature (Lasagabaster 2008). Therefore, we might not claim that the CLIL instruction has an advantage over EFL in this study, at least within a semester-long time frame (16 weeks). These results, which display significance for lexical diversity but statistical insignificance for lexical variation (TTR) and richness (GUI), might also suggest that these participants receive rich lexical input, but this is only comprised of repetitive high-frequency words (Gierlinger and Wagner 2016). By and large, we should keep in mind that it might take a longer time than a 16-week semester to detect significant gains in most aspects of syntactic and lexical complexity.

Considering the participants' lexical profiles (frequency, depth, and range), the results of the analysis remarkably pointed out that more than 90% of both CLIL and EFL students' written production comes from the first two most frequent bands, k1 and k2. This result highlights a typical characteristic of learner Englishes as EFL, ESL, and ELF within the WEs paradigm: simplified vocabulary made of a large proportion of high-frequency words. When taking the low TTR and GUI into the equation, we can claim that the lexical profiles of the participants from the CLIL and EFL groups hold ELF characteristics, such as a word choice of repetitive highly frequent items. Not only the type of task, but also the dominant type of input received from non-native speakers of English that these participants have been exposed to might be responsible for such a lexical profiling. More importantly, the Turkish EFL context truly represents a non-postcolonial country (Edwards 2016) within the expanding circle where English is mostly taught in formal instructional settings or used as a medium of instruction at secondary or higher education institutions. By the same token, these findings might exemplify Edwards' (2016) notion of "foundation-through-globalization" as the type of linguistic exposure might affect written performance and a mixed variety of English including both native-speaker (English language course books) and WEs forms and features in a non-postcolonial context.

Furthermore, the written data were also confirmed to include some of the morphosyntactic and lexical ELF features, such as simplicity, analogy, insertion of redundant prepositions, and generalization and rule regularization. A closer look at the data revealed that the systematic uses of these ELF features are also related to the participants' L1, Turkish. The participants in both groups might have tended to omit definite articles and ignore pluralization marking as their L1 has no such morphosyntactic features. Also, the odd collocations as instances of analogy (e.g., *classic child, make philosophy*) and redundant prepositional uses (e.g., register to a university = bir universiteye kayit yaptirmak marking the accusative case in Turkish) show direct mapping (or negative L1 transfer as an SLA term) from the participants' native languages. Thus, such systematic uses might confirm the link between EFL, ESL, and ELF, especially drawing on the notion of negative L1 transfer or analogy in ELF terms. Echoing Schneider (2012) and Seidlhofer (2009), the results resonate the need to classify ESL, EFL, and ELF as varieties of the same kind within the WEs paradigm (Buschfeld 2021) given the type of exposure, contact, and learner output representing a non-postcolonial context like Turkey. Such results stress the idea that ELF might very well function as the cross-section among ENL-ESL-EFL categorization as part of the WEs paradigm. Another justification for the abundance of ELF features in the CLIL learners' written production is that the CLIL pedagogy does not provide an explicit presentation of grammatical features and facilitates students' discovery of construction by processing the content-focused input. Similarly, the students in the EFL group also displayed a consistent use of grammatical features of ELF, which might be partly due to the marked differences between L1 and L2.

Finally, the chapter contributes to this current volume with its methodological innovation. We drew on verbal and written performances of CLIL and non-CLIL students to ensure that we accessed their productive skills. First, we used an elicited imitation test (Ortega et al. 1999) where students were to speak naturally and perform their lexicogrammatical knowledge in a limited time. Similarly, we elicited students' written productions through a timed written production task (Llanes and

Muñoz 2013) where the students were encouraged to write as much as they could. These data collection tools challenged them to use their authentic linguistic resources without having time to self-correct, which made their ELF-characterized language visible and traceable, thus leading to a valid linguistic analysis.

This study also contributes to the broader field of linguistic research by taking a joint approach to second/foreign language acquisition and adolescents in World Englishes through the inspection of a specific language teaching methodology, CLIL.

6 Conclusion

This study aimed to shed light on different areas of L2 written performance and to clarify how prominent ELF/WEs features are in the participants' written production by comparing two types of instruction, CLIL and EFL, in a non-postcolonial context. The results indicated that participants of both types of instruction showed ELF features in their written performances in terms of syntactic and lexical complexity and lexical profiling, which we associated with the ELF-features of the teachers interactional and instructional input.

We also acknowledge certain limitations in our research. Considering the linguistic performance constructs explored, a longitudinal design might have yielded different results in favor of one of the instructional styles. A longer exposure and practice period might bring about favorable outcomes, especially in terms of syntactic complexity (Ortega 2003). Hence, we are considering conducting follow-up research which would bring in a longitudinal perspective. In our analysis, we did not compare our written learner corpus with a corresponding native speaker corpus for lexical frequency profiling. That being the case, a corpus-based comparative design might accentuate different results as well.

Last but not least, the study has several pedagogical implications. Our results have shown no superiority of CLIL over EFL instruction in terms of gains in written syntactic and lexical complexity. The huge difference in the amount of exposure (17 hours of content instruction and 7 hours of focused English instruction in the CLIL setting) was not confirmed to have an advantage over a focused integrated-skills EFL curriculum (9 hours per week). It might take a longer time of exposure to CLIL to find significant gains in L2 writing proficiency, such as syntactic and lexical complexity. That being the case, language teaching practitioners and those making program related decisions might revisit the scopes of their programs and learning objectives in terms of TL instruction. Most importantly, the similarities between learner varieties (EFL and ESL) and ELF, as depicted in the current study, might help language practitioners to question the notion of native-like ultimate attainment in formal instruction settings and prioritize ELF-aware pedagogies (Yalçın, Bayyurt, and Alahdab 2020), such as effective communication skills and successful conveyance of meaning over native-like performances.

References

Anthony, Laurence. 2019. *AntConc* (Version 3.5.8) [Computer Software]. Tokyo, Japan: Waseda University.

Augustín Llach, María del Pilar. 2014. Exploring the lexical profile of young CLIL learners: Towards an improvement in lexical use. *Journal of Immersion and Content-Based Language Education* 2 (1). 53–73.

Buschfeld, Sarah. 2021. Grassroots English, learner English, second-language English, English as a lingua franca . . .: What's in a name?. In Christiane Meierkord & Edgar W. Schneider (eds.), *World Englishes at the grassroots*, 23–46. Edinburgh: Edinburgh University Press.

Bybee, Rodger W. 2013. *The case for STEM education: Challenges and opportunities*. Arlington, Virginia: National Science Teachers Association, NSTA Press.

Cobb, T. *VocabProfile v.3* [Computer program]. www.lextutor.ca/vp/eng/ (accessed 1 February 2020).

Dafouz, Emma & Abbie Hibler. 2013. 'Zip your lips' or 'Keep quiet': Main teachers' and language assistants' classroom discourse in CLIL settings. *The Modern Language Journal* 97 (3). 655–669.

Dalton-Puffer, Christiane. 2008. Outcomes and processes in Content and Language Integrated Learning (CLIL): Current research from Europe. In Werner Delanoy & Laurenz Volkmann (eds.), *Future perspectives for English language teaching*, 139–157. Heidelberg: Carl Winter.

Dalton-Puffer, Christiane. 2011. Content-and-language integrated learning: From practice to principles. *Annual Review of Applied Linguistics* 31. 182–204.

Dewey, Martin. 2007. *English as a lingua franca: An empirical study of innovation in lexis and grammar*. King's College London: Unpublished Doctoral dissertation.

Edwards, Alison. 2014. The progressive aspect in the Netherlands and the ESL/EFL continuum. *World Englishes* 33 (2). 173–194.

Edwards, Alison. 2016. *English in the Netherlands: Functions, forms and attitudes* (Varieties of English Around the World G56). Amsterdam: John Benjamins.

Gené-Gil, Maria, Maria Juan-Garau & Joana Salazar-Noguera. 2015. Development of EFL writing over three years in secondary education: CLIL and non-CLIL settings. *The Language Learning Journal* 43 (3). 286–303.

Gierlinger, Erwin Maria & Thomas Wagner. 2016. The more the merrier – Revisiting CLIL-based vocabulary growth in secondary education. *Latin American Journal of Content and Language Integrated Learning* 9 (1). 37–63.

Goris, José A., Eddie J. P. G. Denessen & Ludo T. W. Verhoeven. 2019. Effects of content and language integrated learning in Europe A systematic review of longitudinal experimental studies. *European Educational Research Journal* 18 (6). 675–698.

Hüttner, Julia. 2018. ELF and Content and Language Integrated Learning. In Jennifer Jenkins, Will Baker & Martin Dewey (eds.), *The Routledge handbook of English as a lingua franca*, 481–493. New York: Routledge.

Jiménez Catalán, Rosa M. & María del Pilar Augustín Llach. 2017. CLIL or time? Lexical profiles of CLIL and non-CLIL EFL learners. *System* 66. 87–99.

Kachru, Braj B. 1985. Standards, codification and sociolinguistic realism: The English language in the outer circle. In Randolph Quirk & Henry G. Widdowson (eds.), *English in the world: Teaching and learning the language and literatures*, 11–30. Cambridge: Cambridge University Press.

Kırkgöz, Yasemin & Kenan Dikilitaş. 2018. Recent developments in ESP/EAP/EMI contexts. In Yasemin Kırkgöz and Kenan Dikilitaş (eds.), *Key issues in English for specific purposes in higher education*, 1–10. Cham: Springer.

Lasagabaster, David. 2008. Foreign language competence in content and language integrated courses. *The Open Applied Linguistics Journal* 1 (1). 30–41.

Laufer, Batia &Paul Nation. 1995. Vocabulary size and use: Lexical richness in L2 production. *Applied Linguistics* 16 (3). 307–322.

Lightbown, Patsy M. 2014. *Focus on content-based language teaching – Oxford key concepts for the language classroom*. Oxford: Oxford University Press.

Llanes, Àngels & Carmen Muñoz. 2013. Age effects in a study abroad context: Children and adults studying abroad and at home. *Language Learning* 63 (1). 63–90.

Llinares, Ana & Rachel Whittaker. 2006. Linguistic analysis of secondary school students' oral and written production in CLIL contexts: Studying social science in English. *Current Research on CLIL, Vienna English Working Papers* 15 (3). 28–32.

Lu, Xiaofei. 2012. The relationship of lexical richness to the quality of ESL learners' oral narratives. *The Modern Language Journal* 96 (2). 190–208.

Lu, Xiaofei & Haiyang Ai. 2015. Syntactic complexity in college-level English writing: Differences among writers with diverse L1 backgrounds. *Journal of Second Language Writing* 29. 16–27.

McKee, Gerard, David Malvern & Brian Richards. 2000. Measuring vocabulary diversity using dedicated software. *Literary and linguistic computing* 15 (3). 323–338.

Meara, Paul & Imma Miralpeix. 2018. *D_Tools*. Swansea: Lognostics (Centre for Applied Language Studies, University of Wales, Swansea).

Mewald, Claudia, Monika Prenner & Jörg Spenger. 2004. *Englisch als Arbeitssprache (EAA) auf der Sekundarstufe 1*. BMUK: GZ 20.233/4-VI/A/3/01.

Ortega, Lourdes. 2003. Syntactic complexity measures and their relationship to L2 proficiency: A research synthesis of college-level L2 writing. *Applied Linguistics* 24 (4). 492–518.

Ortega, Lourdes, Noriko Iwashita, Sara Rabie & John M. Norris. 1999. *A multilanguage comparison of syntactic complexity measures and their relationship to foreign language oral proficiency* [Funded Project]. Honolulu, HI: University of Hawaii, National Foreign Language Resource Center.

Roquet, Helena & Carmen Pérez-Vidal. 2017. Do productive skills improve in content and language integrated learning contexts? The case of writing. *Applied Linguistics* 38 (4). 489–511.

Ruiz de Zarobe, Yolanda. 2010. Written production and CLIL: An empirical study. In Christiane Dalton-Puffer, Tarja Nikula & Ute Smit (eds.), *Language use and language learning in CLIL classrooms*, 191–212. Amsterdam/Philadelphia: John Benjamins Publishing Company.

Ruiz de Zarobe, Yolanda. 2011. Which language competencies benefit from CLIL? An insight into applied linguistics research. In Yolanda Ruiz de Zarobe, Juan Manuel Sierra & Francisco Gallardo del Puerto (eds.), *Content and foreign language integrated learning: Contributions to multilingualism in European contexts*, 129–154. Bern: Peter Lang.

Saladrigues Rosello, Gemma & Angels Llanes. 2014. Examining the impact of amount of exposure on L2 development with CLIL and non-CLIL teenage students. *Sintagma: revista de lingüística* 26. 133–147.

Schneider, Edgar W. 2012. Exploring the interface between World Englishes and second language acquisition – and implications for English as a lingua franca. *Journal of English as a Lingua Franca* 1 (1). 57–91.

Seidlhofer, Barbara. 2004. Research perspectives on teaching English as a Lingua Franca. *Annual Review of Applied Linguistics* 24. 209–239.

Seidlhofer, Barbara. 2009. Common ground and different realities: World Englishes and English as a lingua franca. *World Englishes* 28 (2). 236–245.

Seidlhofer, Barbara, Angelika Jezek-Breiteneder, Theresa Lehner Klimpfinger, Stephan Majewski, Ruth Osimk-Teasdale, Marie Luise Pitzl & Michael Radeka. 2013. *VOICE – The Vienna-Oxford international corpus of English* (version 2.0 XML).

Sylvén, Liss Kerstin. 2013. CLIL in Sweden – why does it not work? A metaperspective on CLIL across contexts in Europe. *International Journal of Bilingual Education and Bilingualism* 16 (3). 301–320.

Yalçın, Şebnem, Yasemin Bayyurt & Benan Rifaioğlu Alahdab. 2020. Triggering effect of CLIL practice on English as a lingua franca awareness. *ELT Journal* 74 (4). 387–397.

Whittaker, Rachel, Ana Llinares & Anne McCabe. 2011. Written discourse development in CLIL at secondary school. *Language Teaching Research* 15 (3). 343–362.

Sarah Buschfeld and Gerold Schneider

7 Investigating child language acquisition from a joint perspective: A comparison of traditional and new L1 speakers of English

Abstract: This chapter presents one of the first studies on the acquisition of English by young children that is informed by both corpus linguistics and World Englishes research. It compares the acquisition of past tense marking across different variety types and acquisitional settings based on data from the CHEsS corpus (Children's English in Singapore; Buschfeld 2020) and different corpora from the CHILDES database (https://childes.talkbank.org). Specifically, we compare two- to twelve-year-old simultaneous bilingual English-Chinese children in Singapore, Hong Kong, and the US, and monolingual English children in the US. Our results suggest that important differences exist between past tense marking in the different scenarios. It is shown that, different from the monolingual US children, missing past tense inflections are characteristic of the Chinese-English bilinguals' productions, even in later acquisitional stages. The degree to which the Chinese bilingual speakers retain them, however, depends on their acquisitional background and the linguistic input they receive.

Keywords: language acquisition, past tense marking, World Englishes, corpus linguistics, bilingualism, Singapore, Hong Kong, US

1 Introduction

Studies on the acquisition of English by young children that are informed by both corpus linguistics and World Englishes research are still rare. Similarly, the two relevant research paradigms, i.e. World Englishes and language acquisition research, have traditionally been two independent disciplines with only little information being shared, even though they clearly overlap in many of their objectives. Both

---

Note: We would like to thank two reviewers for their valuable comments and feedback. All remaining shortcomings are, of course, our own responsibility.

Sarah Buschfeld, TU Dortmund University, Germany
Gerold Schneider, University of Zurich, Switzerland

https://doi.org/10.1515/9783110733723-007

are concerned with the results and frameworks of language acquisition. The only difference lies in the particular contexts on which they focus, and the stage of the language acquisition process with which they are mainly concerned. While the language acquisition paradigm is mainly geared towards describing the language acquisition processes in individuals acquiring British or American English, the World Englishes paradigm focuses on the products of societal language acquisition such as Singaporean English (SingE) and other postcolonial varieties of English. The present paper is among the first to bridge the research gap between the two disciplines. We use corpus linguistic methods to address the following research questions: How are the acquisitional outcome and route taken by new native speakers of English (e.g. as emerging in former colonies of the British Empire such as Singapore and other Asian and African contexts) different from that of traditional native speakers? Which role do language input and the acquisitional background play? To answer these questions, we compare the acquisition of past tense marking across different variety types and acquisitional settings. In particular, the present study compares the acquisition of English past tense marking by simultaneous bilingual English-Chinese children in Singapore, Hong Kong, and the US, and monolingual children who acquire English in the US. The children are all between two and twelve years old. Omissions of past tense inflections have been reported as characteristic of early child language (see e.g. Brown 1973), but they are also a feature of new varieties of L1 English (e.g. Buschfeld 2020 on Singapore English) as well as learner Englishes (Lardiere 2004; Namtapi and Pongpairoj 2016; Salaberry and Shirai 2002). We therefore expect to find bare verbs for all groups of investigated children, and in particular for the Chinese-speaking bilinguals, since both Mandarin and Cantonese are highly analytic languages, in which verbs are not marked for tense (Li and Thompson 1981: 13). In addition, we will investigate the use of the past tense marker *finish*, which is a direct translation from Chinese *wán*, one of the common particles used to indicate completeness of an action ("finish," following the verb), as this realization also falls into the class of alternative ways to express past tense in SingE (e.g. Bao 2005: 248–249; Ross and Sheng Ma 2014: 244–252).

Section 2 presents traditional and new perspectives on the acquisition of past tense marking. We give an overview of the most relevant findings on the acquisition of past tense marking in British (BrE) and American English (AmE) (Section 2.1) as well as of the relatively rare studies of language acquisition in varieties of English other than BrE and AmE (Section 2.2). We introduce our comparative study of past tense marking in different variety types in Section 2.3. Section 3 gives an overview of our data and methods and Section 4 presents the results. Our findings suggest that important differences exist between past tense marking in the different scenarios. Whereas missing past tense inflections are characteristic of early child language, they decrease in frequency and ultimately disappear in the monolingual native speakers from the US. The bilingual Chinese-English speakers retain them to different degrees even at later acquisitional stages, depending on their acquisitional background and the input they receive. In Section 5, we discuss our findings in light of our research questions. We further address three related aspects, i.e. what our findings suggest 1) about the current state and nature of the English language, i.e. its heterogeneity worldwide and the new functions and roles it has started to assume, 2) about the concept of the native speaker, and 3) what the findings imply for the re-theorization of both the World Englishes and language acquisition paradigms. We conclude that only a combined approach, drawing on theories and findings from both linguistic fields involved, can provide an informed understanding of the heterogeneity and development of the English language and the emergence of new generations of native speakers in formerly non-native contexts.

2 The acquisition of past tense marking: Old and new perspectives

The language acquisition paradigm has traditionally focused on individuals who acquire BrE or AmE, either as a first (L1) or a second language (L2). This is why, in the following, we first outline earlier research findings on the acquisition of past tense marking in the two traditional standard varieties BrE and AmE. We do not differentiate between BrE and AmE since no major differences exist between the two for those aspects of past tense marking on which we focus in our study.

2.1 British and American English

In BrE/AmE, the verb is morphologically marked for past tense either by adding an *-ed* morpheme to the stem or irregularly via different marking strategies, i.e. either by suffixation of *-t* or *-d* (in contrast to *-ed*) or by stem allomorphy (e.g., *sang, bit, ate, flew, brought, went*) (Biber et al. 1999: 394–396, 453).

When children acquire English verbs, numerous studies have shown that they first produce bare forms that are unmarked for tense, even if they refer to past events (e.g., Marchman and Bates 1994; Paradis and Crago 2001; Wexler 1998). It has been reported that children first start marking their verbs for past tense around the age of two years (cf. Brown 1973; Philips 1995), but variably until approximately the end of their third year of life (e.g. Wexler 1992, 1994; Harris and Wexler 1996: 1–2).

The end of this phase, i.e. the point when children start using marked forms consistently, slightly varies from child to child and is not to be considered a sudden shift from bare verbs to marked verbs but a gradual development towards the BrE/AmE target norms (e.g., Nicoladis, Song, and Marentette 2012: 469–470).

In the acquisition of the BrE/AmE target, children correctly produce irregular verbs earlier than regular ones (Marcus et al. 1992), probably because of the high token frequencies of irregular verbs in child directed speech. This often results in the children acquiring these verb forms by entrenchment or rote memory (e.g. Bybee 1995: 433–434; Marchman 1997: 284; Pinker and Ullman 2002: 456). Regular past tense forms are high in type frequency, which ultimately leads to the children's productive use of regular past tense verb forms (e.g. Bybee 1995: 433–435; Marchman 1997: 291; Marchman and Bates 1994: 341). Their use of regular verbs increases, and with it the error rate since children have two competing strategies at their disposal (e.g. Kuczaj 1977: 593; Marcus et al. 1992: 1–2, 129). Some of these errors, for example overgeneralizations, might last until the age of six or even seven (cf. Kuczaj 1977: 600; Marcus et al. 1992: 44–45), but by then BrE-/AmE-speaking children seem to have fully acquired the traditional Modern English past tense paradigm.

For multilingual children, the acquisitional path is basically the same as the one outlined for monolingual children. However, since multilinguals on average experience less exposure to their languages than their monolingual peers to their one language, this might lead to slight delays in the acquisition process, so that even school-aged bilingual children may not have "reached ceiling in their accuracy of past tense marking" (Nicoladis, Song, and Marentette 2012: 460).

When it comes to cross-linguistic influence, which is often a source of differences between mono- and multilingual children, not much research exists on the bilingual acquisition of past-tense marking. Nicoladis, Song, and Marentette (2012) compare the production of past tense marking in 14 Chinese-English (aged 5 to 11) and 14 French-English (aged 5 to 12) bilinguals by means of a story retelling task. Their general results suggest that bilingual children acquire the past tense in English like monolinguals, just slightly later. Still, they also find some differences, "many of these likely due to transfer from their other language" (Nicoladis, Song, and Marentette 2012: 471). We report those that are relevant for the present study. First of all, the Chinese-English children were more accurate in their use of irregular verbs than with regular verbs, while the French-English children were more accurate with regular than with irregular verbs. Second, in their non-target production of verbs, the Chinese-English group mainly produced verb stems both for regular and irregular verbs. The few irregularization errors that occurred in the study were all made by the Chinese-English group. These findings make perfect sense from a language-typological perspective: the children clearly avoid the use of inflectional morphemes since they do not know this strategy from their highly analytic other language, Chinese (Nicoladis, Song, and Marentette 2012: 471). As would be expected from the above observations, Nicoladis, Song, and Marentette (2012: 469–470) found that the children's accuracy rates were generally very high when compared to adult L2 learners and that the older the children grew, the fewer bare verbs they produced.

2.2 Beyond the traditional paradigm

As outlined above, much of the research related to the mono- or multilingual acquisition of English as a first language involves one of the two standard varieties, BrE or AmE. To our best knowledge, only a handful of studies have investigated the acquisition of English in one of the L1 English-speaking settler communities; most of these focus on Australian children (e.g. James et al. 2008; McLeod, van Doorn, and Reed 2001; Yuen, Cox, and Demuth 2014). None of these focus on the L1 acquisition of past tense morphology, though, but are mainly concerned with the phonological domain.

Research into former L2 varieties that have started to develop towards English L1 status is still in its infancy, even though this development constitutes an important sociolinguistic reality of English today. We find "new" L1 speakers of English in many parts of the world, and in particular in several Asian and African countries. In Singapore, the development from L2 to L1 seems to be most advanced and most widely spread in the general population, when compared to other countries or contexts. Gupta's (1994) monograph on L1 child language acquisition in Singapore was a first groundbreaking contribution, since she raised some early awareness of an emerging L1 variety of English in Singapore and has clearly posited this development as a new topic for research. The few empirical contributions that followed suit mostly employ an educational perspective (e.g. Goh and Silver 2006; Silver and Bokhorst-Heng 2016; Silver, Goh, and Alsagoff 2009). However, to understand the complex sociolinguistic realities of L1 SingE, we also have to consider what children do and how they acquire the English language outside the school context. Furthermore, it is equally, if not even more important to dismiss the deficit perspective employed in some of these approaches, viz. that L1 SingE cannot be a legitimate L1 variety and that colloquial SingE forms are to be delimited from standard forms of English as "nonnative forms of English" (Liow and Lau 2006: 870); that Singaporeans do not have full proficiency in English, even though they learn it from birth; and that they speak an inferior variety of English, in particular when using features associated with more colloquial registers. Such attitudes are often still to be found not only in scientific discourse but also in governmental attitudes as well as in speakers' self-assessments (e.g. the study by Leimgruber, Siemund, and Terassa 2018). Tan's (2014) contribution adds a welcome new perspective in that her study reports findings from an investigation of the language use and perceptions of English as a marker of Singaporean identity based on 436 Singaporeans of different age and ethnic groups. On the basis of her empirically well-grounded findings, she convincingly argues "that English in Singapore has to be reconceptualized as a new mother tongue" (Tan 2014: 319).[1] Buschfeld (2020) is the first to investigate the acquisition of L1 SingE in some detail. A subpart of her study focuses on the acquisition of past tense marking. The results on the acquisition of past tense marking show that L1 SingE is characterized by an extended past tense paradigm that goes beyond what can be found in the traditional native speaker varieties of English. Next to the standard marking strategies outlined in Section 2.1, L1 child SingE makes use of bare verb forms in contexts where other contextual clues tie the action to a past event and a specific SingE marking strategy, i.e. the use of *finish* as a past tense marker. Examples (1) and (2) (from Buschfeld 2020: 147, 148) illustrate these extended strategies:

(1) Child (5;6, female, Chinese): *[. . .] he took some [. . .] sticks and then [. . .] he make a [/] a stick house.*

(2) Child (6;7, female, Chinese): *He eat finish everything.*

This past tense marker of SingE was apparently transferred from the Mandarin Chinese aspectual marker *wán* ("to finish") and was relexified in colloquial SingE.

2.3 Our study: L1 past tense marking across variety types

The present study compares English past tense marking strategies in bilingual English-Chinese (Mandarin or Cantonese) children who acquire English in different sociolinguistic settings, i.e. Singapore, Hong Kong, and the US. A group of monolingual American children serves as a control group. We aim to shed light on the impact that input and the sociolinguistic acquisitional setting have on the acquisition of past tense marking. Hong Kong and Singapore were both colonies of the British Empire and English has developed as L2 contact varieties in these contexts. Hong Kong English, however, is far less advanced than SingE. According to Edgar Schneider's (2003, 2007) Dynamic Model,[2] it has reached Phase 3 (nativization) only and English

---

[1] For a more detailed overview of these earlier approaches to L1 SingE, see Buschfeld (2020: 22–25).
[2] The model approaches the description and categorization of varieties of English along the lines of five developmental stages: 1) foundation; 2) exonormative stabilization; 3) nativization; 4) endonormative stabilization; 5) differentiation (for further details, see Schneider 2007: 29–56).

is not as prominently supported by the Hong Kong government as it is by the Singaporean. One of the important reasons is Singapore's language policy of "English-based bilingualism" (Tickoo 1996: 438). Singapore has at least reached Phase 4 (endonormative stabilization) (cf. the respective case studies in Schneider 2007), though more recent research points towards Phase 5 (differentiation) status, not least due to the growing numbers of L1 speakers. Even though acquiring the same language pairing, bilingual English-Chinese learners in the US constitute yet another group of language learners since they grow up in a traditional L1 English setting. Normally, the English they are exposed to in their surrounding would be more of the traditional standard type, AmE. However, as we will see in Section 3.1, the US-Chinese bilingual children grow up in a Chinese-dominant community and their proficiency in English is rather limited. Of course, the sociolinguistic, acquisitional setting is not the only factor potentially influencing language acquisition outcomes, here, the omission of past-tense marking. Several studies in the language acquisition paradigm have shown that language experience variables affect children's acquisition outcomes at an individual level (e.g. Carroll 2017; Chondrogianni and Marinis 2011; Torregrossa et al. 2021). Language acquisition outcomes may therefore also vary on the basis of individual language profiles. We cannot really attend to this in the discussion of our results, since the CHILDES corpora lack information on age of onset or amount of language exposure to English.

The mechanisms and procedures in bilingual language acquisition, here Chinese-English, are basically comparable across the different contexts. Still, Singapore is the most complex and thus a particularly interesting scenario. It is one of the very few cases in which an L1 variety has been developing from an L2 contact variety that evolved under the circumstances of second-language variety formation. These are all intricate developments in themselves (on the question of what makes a second-language variety a second-language variety, see, for example, Buschfeld 2013). Second-language variety formation involves a multitude of processes and mechanisms of language contact and second-language acquisition, most importantly L1 transfer, but also cultural adaptation, linguistic accommodation, simplification, overgeneralization, regularization, and language drift (e.g., Mollin 2007: 171; Schneider 2007: 88–90; Williams 1987). The case of Singapore (and other similar contexts) is of particular complexity because these processes and mechanisms have operated within a unique scenario: a highly multilingual country with complex sociolinguistic realities, rigidly controlled by governmental and educational policies yet fuelled by the conflicting forces of globalization and local identities.

3 Data and methods

The data for the present study come from bi-/multilingual Chinese-English children of Singaporean, Hong Kong, and Chinese ethnicity as well as a group of monolingual US American children. The Singapore data were extracted from the CHEsS corpus (Children's English in Singapore; Buschfeld 2020). The other data used in the present study are part of the CHILDES Database (childes.talkbank.org), which is the child language component of the TalkBank system (talkbank.org). We briefly describe the corpora in turn.

3.1 The corpora

The Singapore data

The Singapore data come from a corpus of spoken L1 child English (CHEsS; Buschfeld 2020) that contains data from bi-/multilingual children with either a Chinese or one of the Indian languages spoken in Singapore as their other language(s). The majority of the children is English dominant. None of the parents is a native speaker of one of the standard varieties BrE or AmE, but a number of parents themselves speak SingE as an L1 already. For the present study, we use the data from those 19 children in the corpus who are of Chinese ethnicity and speak a Chinese language as their other L1. The children are aged 2;6 (2 years; 6 months) to 8;6. The data were elicited in video-recorded task-directed dialogue between the researcher and the children by means of various data elicitation techniques, ranging from controlled linguistic experiments to free interaction: (1) a grammar elicitation task, viz. the past tense probe of the Rice/Wexler Test of Early Grammatical Impairment (Rice and Wexler 2001); (2) a story retelling task based on the story *The Three Little Pigs*; (3) data from elicited narratives; and (4) from free interaction, both between the children and the children and the researcher.

The Hong Kong data

The Hong Kong data come from two CHILDES corpora, the CUHK Bilingual Corpus, and the YipMatthews Bilingual Corpus. The CUHK Bilingual Corpus comprises seven children, aged 1 to 12. Most of them are bilingual English-Mandarin/Cantonese, some of them have English as their only language. The data are naturalistic and were collected by students in Brian MacWhinney's course at CUHK in 2007.

The YipMatthews Bilingual Corpus data (Yip and Matthews 2007) were collected for a longitudinal study. The corpus contains data from nine children aged 1;3 to 4;6 exposed to both Cantonese and English regularly from birth. For many of the children one parent is a native speaker of BrE. However, most children are more proficient in Cantonese.

The Chinese data

The Guthrie Bilingual Corpus (Guthrie 1983, 1984; Guthrie and Guthrie 1988) contains speech data from 14 bilingual Chinese-American first-graders, aged 6;4 to 8;0, in classroom interaction with their two teachers. The children live in the US, but their language proficiency is assessed as "Limited-English-Speaking". The school is a Chinese elementary school with a predominantly Chinese population located close to a large Chinatown community on the West Coast. Most of the Chinese students attending the school have very low proficiency in English: 28% are classified as Limited-English-Speaking (LES), 61% as non-English-speaking (NES). The two teachers have native(-like) proficiency in English.

The US monolingual data

The monolingual data come from the Gillam Corpus (Gillam and Pearson 2004), which contains 250 target and 520 control participants aged 5;0 to 11;11. The children are monolingual speakers of AmE. The data were collected by means of naturalistic storytelling.

We have manually annotated a large subset of these corpora, stratified by age as far as possible, as described in Section 3.2. Table 7.1 indicates the size of each corpus in words and the number of instances of past tense marking strategies.

Table 7.1: Size of the annotated material in terms of instances and words.

	Singapore (CHEsS)	Hong Kong (YipMatthews)	Hong Kong (CUHK)	Chinese (Guthrie)	US (Gillam)
Instances	1001	209	43	166	478
Words	48360	432000	36000	76000	19000

3.2 Data coding and analysis

All data are available in their orthographically transcribed form. The data sets were manually coded for the standard BrE/AmE past tense marking strategies outlined in Section 2.1 (*-ed*, *-t* or *-d*, or stem allomorphy) as well as for unmarked verbs and the VERB+*finish* structure identified for L1 child SingE (Section 2.2). Our annotation is restricted to positive lexical verbs, i.e. auxiliary verbs and negated structures were ignored to make the envelope of variation more homogeneous and the coding and analysis easier and more straightforward.

We statistically model the influence of the intralinguistic variable VERB TYPE and the extralinguistic variables AGE (in months) and CORPUS (Singapore, CUHK = Hong Kong 1, YipMatthews = Hong Kong 2, Guthrie = Chinese American first-graders, Gillam = monolingual US) by means of both conditional inference trees and regression models. The latter variable reflects the differences in acquisitional scenario and parental input we are interested in.

For the conditional inference tree analysis (ctree), we used the package "partykit" in R (Hothorn et al. 2006; R Development Core Team 2014). A conditional inference tree (ctree) analysis applies recursive partitioning algorithms to the data set in order to "classify / compute predicted outcomes / values on the basis of multiple binary splits of the data" (Bernaisch, Gries, and Mukherjee 2014: 14). In other words, a ctree analysis investigates a data set in a recursive fashion "to determine according to which (categorical or numeric) independent variable the data should be split up into two groups to classify / predict best the known outcomes of the dependent variable" (Bernaisch, Gries, and Mukherjee 2014: 14). As one of their major advantages, ctrees can handle small sets of data characterized by small numbers of observations but large numbers of predictors – a situation not uncommonly encountered in linguistic research. Another advantage of ctrees is that they are not overly sensitive to outliers (Levshina 2015: 292).

Logistic regression models are very well studied and widely used in any branch of model statistics (see e.g. Evert 2006; Gries 2010; Schneider and Lauber 2019). These methods predict the dependent variable, in our case absence or presence of past marking, by regressing to the independent variables in combination. Unlike in significance testing, the interaction between the variables is taken into consideration; this allows us to detect and exclude variables that are significant in isolation but not in combination with others. The effect sizes and significance levels of the combined features also permit an assessment of the importance of the features.

4 Results

When looking at the results, the following picture emerges. First of all, as Figure 7.1 through 7.3 illustrate, AGE has an important influence on the realization of past tense marking. The use of unmarked verb forms decreases with increasing age. Unfortunately, the monolingual AmE corpus (Figure 7.1) contains data from children aged 5 to 9 only so that we cannot show how the use of unmarked structures decreases in this child cohort. However, as discussed in Section 2.1, the use of unmarked verbs by young BrE or AmE children has repeatedly been reported in the literature (see also Buschfeld 2020: Chapter 7). The important point we see in Figure 7.1 is that, beyond the age of 5, monolingual American children indeed make close to no use of unmarked verb forms. This finding is in line with earlier results from language acquisition research as reported in Section 2.1. In the Singapore corpus (Figure 7.2), the decline of unmarked verb forms with increasing age is clear, but two interrelated aspects need to be pointed out: first of all, the decline is not as drastic and clear-cut as with monolingual BrE/AmE children (e.g. Buschfeld 2020: 192). Secondly, the use of unmarked verbs does not disappear completely, and even the 8-year olds still use bare verbs. Another interesting observation is that only the Singapore children make use of the VERB+*finish* structure, despite the fact that the bilingual children all have the same additional language, viz. Chinese. We will further discuss this finding in Section 5. In the Chinese-English comparison corpus, including the CUHK, Guthrie, and YipMatthews corpora, the realization of unmarked verbs according to age group seems rather erratic (Figure 7.3). No clear correlation between an increase in

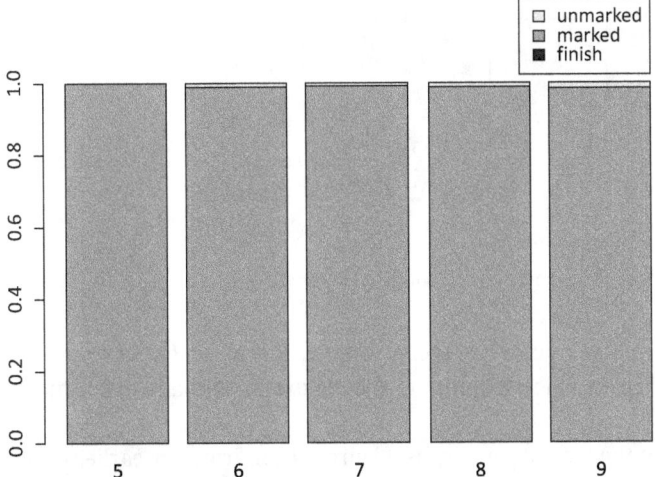

Figure 7.1: Realizations by age in Gillam Corpus (5 to 9 years).

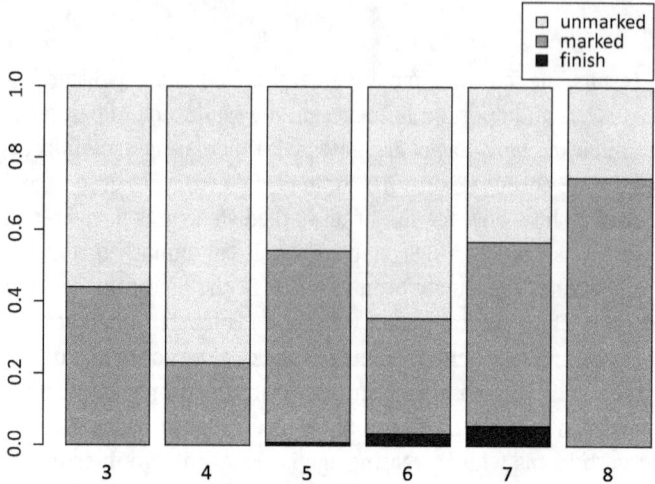

Figure 7.2: Realizations by age in Singapore Corpus (3 to 8 years).

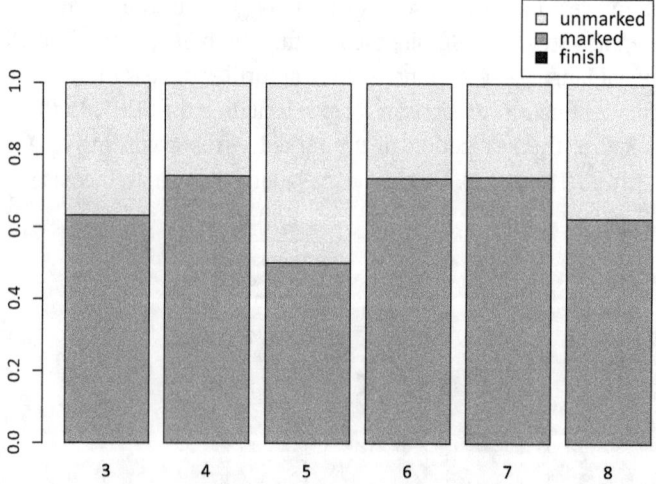

Figure 7.3: Realizations by age in Comparative Corpus (3 to 8 years).

age and a decrease in unmarked verbs seems to exist. This is due to the strong heterogeneity of the corpora when it comes to the children's ages and acquisitional backgrounds.

When looking at the results per corpus, Figure 7.4 confirms our earlier observation that almost no unmarked verbs are used by the monolingual American children in the Gillam corpus. The percentage of unmarked verbs is clearly highest in the Singapore corpus (≈ 50%). The frequency of the VERB+*finish* structure is rather low (≈ 4%) but it is interesting that the Singapore corpus is the only one in which this structure occurs, despite the shared linguistic backgrounds of the children. The results from the three comparison corpora, i.e. the CUHK, the Guthrie, and the YipMatthews, also come as a surprise. Despite the fact that the age ranges of the individual corpora are very different (see the histogram in Figure 7.5), they contain a strikingly similar percentage of unmarked verbs (≈ 35%). While the much younger age of the speakers in the YipMatthews corpus is the reason for the very low usage of past reference generally (see Table 7.1), the speakers' choices in the envelope of variation, i.e. the percentage of unmarked forms, is similar.

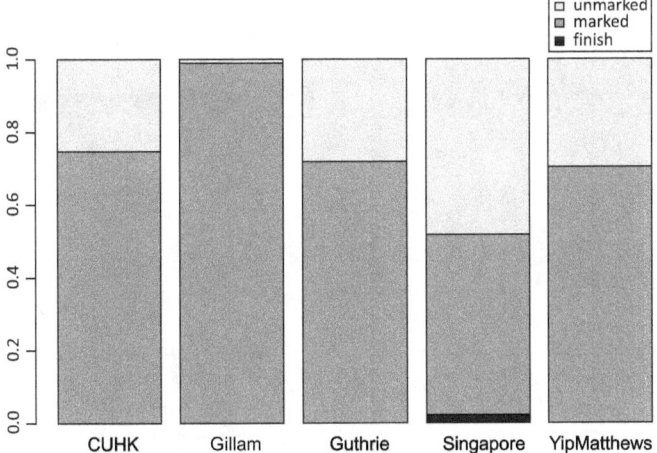

Figure 7.4: Realizations by corpus.

As Figure 7.5 illustrates, the Guthrie and YipMatthews corpora are complementary in age since the former contains data from children 6 to 8 years of age while the latter consists of data of 2- to 5-year-olds. Based on the assumption that older children make use of unmarked verb forms to a lesser extent than younger children, we would expect a much lower rate of unmarked verbs for the Guthrie corpus, which is not the case. Even though we cannot compare the children's utterances to child-directed speech as produced by the adults, this can be explained on the basis of the input the children receive. As stated in the corpus descriptions in Section 3.1, for most of the children in the YipMatthews corpus one of the parents is an L1 speaker of BrE. Even though the bilingual children in the Guthrie corpus live in the US, the corpus contains data from classroom interactions in a predominantly Chinese school between English-low-proficiency students and their teachers. The Chinese students attending this school are generally of rather low proficiency in English. It is therefore not surprising that, even though the children are much older, they produce more unmarked verb forms than the YipMatthews children.

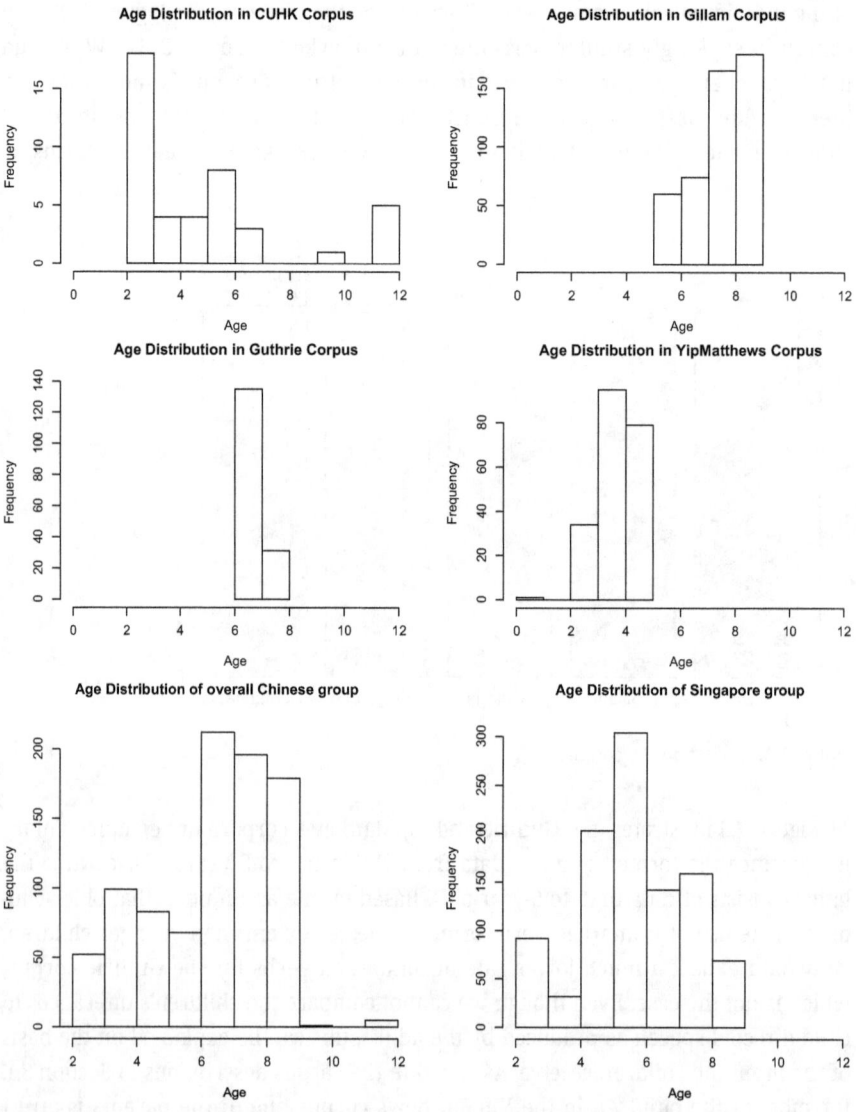

Figure 7.5: Distribution of age in the individual corpora and the resulting overall Chinese corpus, compared to the Singapore corpus (absolute frequencies).

The ctree analyses (Figures 7.6 and 7.7) summarize and strengthen these findings and show that the variables identified above do indeed have a significant influence on past tense marking strategies. The significance level is set to 0.1%. The balanced accuracies of 0.715 (for the model of Figure 7.6) and 0.687 (for the model of Figure 7.7) suggest that the models are quite strong.

As the ctree in Figure 7.6 illustrates, CORPUS has the strongest influence on the results in two successive nodes. In Node 1, the dataset is split into the Gillam corpus and all other corpora investigated, which reveals a significant difference between the monolingual children growing up in the US and all bilingual Chinese-English children. In a second split (Node 2), the Singapore data is split off from the other datasets. These findings lend themselves to an interesting conclusion about the status and type of L1 English as spoken in the contexts under observation (traditional monolingual L1 AmE, postcolonial emerging L1 English in Singapore, and family-based, situationally motivated bilingualism in Hong Kong and the US) to be discussed in detail in Section 5.

The Singapore dataset is further split by AGE (Node 8), with the older children (> 96 months; 8 years) producing no unmarked verbs while the younger children (≤ 96 months) use unmarked verb forms in more than half of all instances coded. The explanation is quite straightforward in that around the age of 7 (≈ 84 months), Singaporean children enter school and receive increasingly formal, BrE-oriented language instruction.

For the children from the CUHK, Guthrie, and YipMatthews corpora, the data are further split by VERB TYPE (Node 3). In general, irregular verbs are less frequently unmarked than regular verbs, which is in line with earlier research on Chinese-English bilinguals (Nicoladis, Song, and Marentette 2012; see Section 2.1). For the regular verbs, another interesting and at first sight surprising split occurs (Node 5). The data are again split by AGE but it is the older children (> 54 months; 4;6 years) who make significantly stronger use of unmarked verbs. This seems to contradict the general observation in language acquisition research that younger children make stronger use of unmarked verbs than older children. However, in our current example there must be a different reason. Looking at the number of participants and age-distributions in the three corpora again (Figure 7.5), it becomes obvious that most of the data of the older children come from the Guthrie corpus (≥ 6 years) whereas much of the data of the younger children are part of the YipMatthews corpus (≤ 5). It can be assumed that the Guthrie children had particular problems in the realization of regular past tense endings which is, once again, in line with earlier research (Nicoladis, Song, and Marentette 2012; cf. Section 2.1). Looking at the linguistic and acquisitional background of the children, the input they probably receive in their immediate speech community, their late age of onset, and their resulting proficiency in English, the finding is no

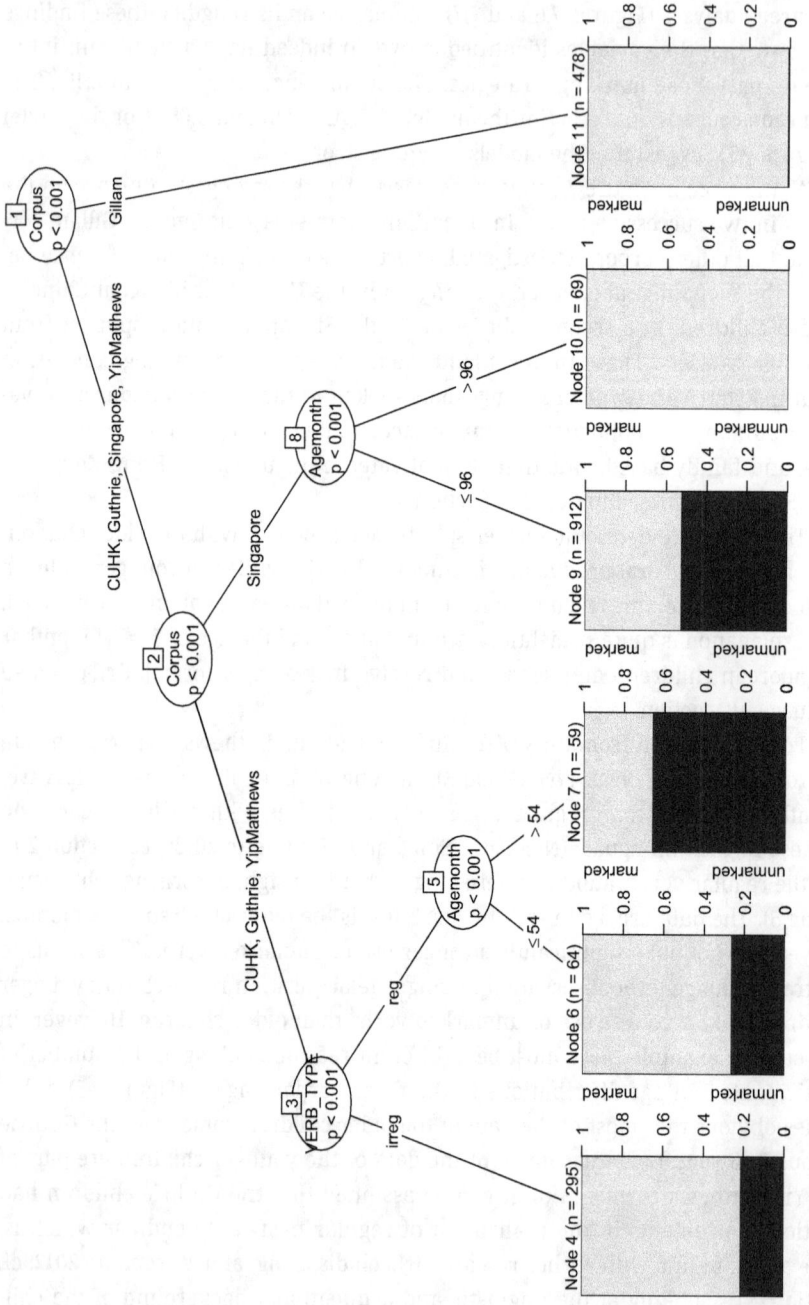

Figure 7.6: Ctree (full model) of the realization of past tense marking.

longer surprising. Most of the children in the YipMatthews corpus have at least one parent who is a native speaker of BrE and thus regularly receive BrE standard input. Even though the Guthrie children all grow up in the US, they all visit a Chinese-dominant school, close to a large Chinatown community, and are therefore surrounded by mainly Chinese and non-native speakers of English, who, if they use English, very likely produce unmarked verb forms themselves.

If we omit AGE as a factor in the model, the resulting ctree (Figure 7.7) confirms our assumption that the age split in Figure 7.6 (Node 5) is motivated by the differences between the Guthrie and YipMatthews corpora (Node 7). What is new, however, is the CORPUS split for the irregular verbs in Node 4. Here, two interesting observations can be made. First of all, the CUHK corpus now is in one group with the Guthrie corpus and not, as in Node 7, with the YipMatthews corpus. Second, the Guthrie corpus shows a lower rate of unmarked verbs for irregular verbs than the YipMatthews dataset. We therefore observe a reverse pattern here. The CUHK appears to pattern with the corpus that shows lower numbers of unmarked verbs with the respective verb types and is generally the more "neutral" corpus as it does not have an age bias or is influenced by an "extreme" input scenario. Once again, typological effects of Chinese on English can explain the observation that the Guthrie children produce statistically higher numbers of unmarked regular verbs when compared to the YipMatthews corpus but the reverse pattern for irregular verbs when compared with the YipMatthews data. Since Chinese is an analytic language without regular inflectional marking, problems with regular inflections have not only been reported for bilingual Chinese-English children (Nicoladis, Song, and Marentette 2012; cf Section 2.1) but also for L2 adult speakers. Irregular verbs are often favored for tense marking over regular verbs by adult Chinese learners of English (Goad, White, and Steele 2003; Hawkins and Liszka 2003). This very likely manifests in the input that the Guthrie children receive in their Chinese-dominant speech community and thus also affect the present data set. In the YipMatthews corpus, the frequencies of regular and irregular unmarked verbs are very similar. This suggests that the use of unmarked verb forms is largely age-related. The Guthrie children are quite young and as we have seen in Section 2.1, bare verb forms are also a feature of early child BrE and AmE.

5 Discussion

Returning to our research questions, what do these findings suggest when it comes to potential differences in the acquisitional outcome and route taken by new native speakers and traditional native speakers of English, and what role do the children's

150 — Sarah Buschfeld and Gerold Schneider

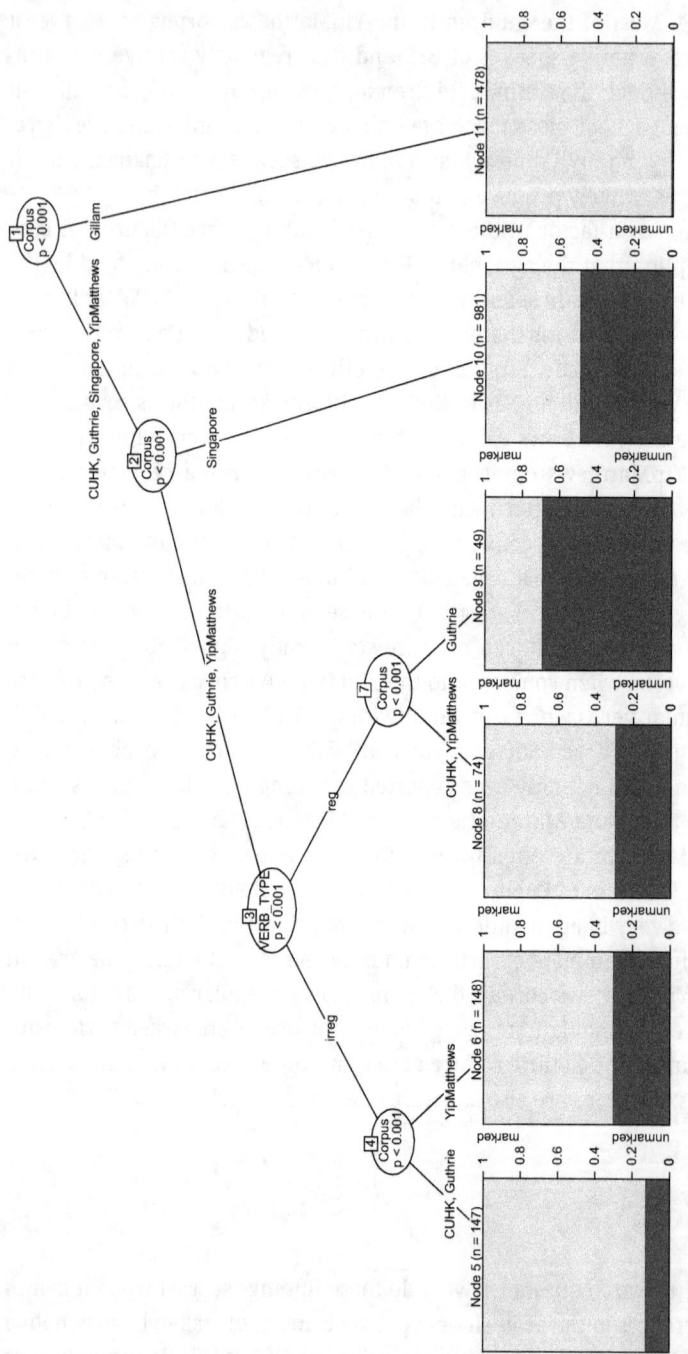

Figure 7.7: Ctree (excluding age) of the realization of past tense marking.

acquisitional background and the input they receive play? In general, we have seen that with an increase in age, the use of unmarked verb forms decreases for the Singapore children (Figure 7.2). This is in line with earlier findings on BrE and AmE children. The finding is not as clear for the Chinese comparative corpus (i.e. the CHUK, the YipMatthews, and the Guthrie corpora) but this is most likely due to the differences in the acquisitional background, input, and English-proficiency of the child data in the three corpora. Even though we could not trace such a decrease in unmarked verb forms for the monolingual American children since they were all older than five years (Figure 7.1), the finding that they produce hardly any unmarked verb forms is fully in line with the general observation. As our results have shown, significant differences exist between the monolingual children growing up in the US (the Gillam corpus) and the rest of the corpora (Figures 7.6 and 7.7). While the monolingual children hardly ever produce any bare verb forms, the Chinese-English children do, albeit to different extents.

The Singapore children stand out from the other Chinese-English bilingual children in that they produce significantly higher numbers of unmarked verb forms (Figures 7.6 and 7.7) than the other children. Furthermore, they are the only group using the Chinese-derived VERB+*finish* structure (Figure 7.4). This can be interpreted in light of the historico-political development and sociolinguistic context of Singapore. English has played an important role in the country from its foundation, due to a variety of interrelated reasons. First and foremost, these include Singapore's nearly 150 years as a British colony (see, for example, Lim 2007: 452; Schneider 2007: 153–155), its unique language policy of "English-based bilingualism" (Tickoo 1996: 438), and the ethnic neutrality of English within Singapore. More recently, the impact of general forces of globalization on the worldwide spread and entrenchment of the English language plays an important role in the Singaporean context, too. Some of these factors such as globalization and British colonization are, of course, also responsible for the spread and entrenchment of English in other regions such as Hong Kong and the fact that increasing numbers of children acquire English as an L1 worldwide. Still, Singapore's strong orientation towards English as the gateway to western economic success and modernity (Wee 2004: 1020–1021) has spurred its spread and entrenchment to a point where families are giving up their ancestral languages for the sake of English (as expressed in some of the interviews in Buschfeld's 2020 study). Even though the Singaporean government rejects English – and in particular Singlish – as an acceptable mother tongue (Wee 2004: 1020–1021) and vehemently tries to counteract the use of local forms of English, colloquial forms of SingE carry local prestige and are a carrier of linguistic and social identity for Singaporeans (Buschfeld 2020: 15–19). The original source of input for the L1 variety has been an L2 contact variety of English since most of the parents who initially passed on the English language to their children as an L1 are non-native speakers of the language. Thus, language contact and mechanisms of L2 language acquisition together with a high demand for and local prestige of English have led to this exceptional development and status the language has today. After independence in 1965, and therefore in less than 60 years, SingE has developed from an L2 variety into an L1 for around 70% of the primary-school-age population in all three major ethnic groups in Singapore, i.e. the Chinese, Indian, and Malay (Chan 2020). Due to the specific sociolinguistic development in post-independence Singapore and the status the English language has gained, the features observed as characteristics of the variety, such as the prominent use of unmarked verbs and the VERB +*finish* structure observed in the present paper, cannot be interpreted as performance errors or instances of incomplete acquisition.[3] We have to consider Singaporean speakers native speakers on a par with traditional native speakers of, say, BrE or AmE, even if this requires questioning and reconsidering our long-standing notion of the English native speaker (see Hackert 2012 for a critical reflection of the native speaker concept and Buschfeld 2020: 55–64 for the case of Singapore).

However, significant differences exist not only between the monolingual children, the Singaporeans, and the rest of the bilingual corpora. The influence of acquisitional background and differences in the input varieties the children are exposed to leads to an even more complex picture. As we have seen, significant differences in the realization of past tense marking exist between the three other bilingual corpora as well (Figure 7.7). These differences cannot be explained on the basis of age. In Section 4, we have argued that the differences between the Guthrie and the YipMattthews corpora must be related to the children's acquisitional background (e.g. their late onset) and the input they receive, in particular since the Guthrie children, who show slightly higher frequencies of unmarked verb forms (Figure 7.4), are older (≥ 6 years) than the YipMatthews children (2–5 years). Even though the Guthrie children grow up in the US and the YipMatthews children grow up in Hong Kong, the former appear to be strongly rooted in a Chinese community, are Chinese dominant, and attend a predominantly Chinese school. As a result, their English language proficiency is rather limited and if they receive English input from community members, it is very likely of strongly Chinese-influenced L2 nature. The Guthrie children can therefore be characterized as heritage speakers, while the children from Hong Kong are simultaneous bilinguals. This, too, may be responsible for the differences in the acquisition outcomes we have observed between the two groups.[4]

---

[3] This term is implicitly suggested by Meisel (2011: 121) to account for linguistic systems emerging in children who receive their major input from second-language speakers.
[4] We would like to thank one of the external reviewers for pointing this out to us.

For the CUHK, the Guthrie, and the YipMatthews children, we have further identified a significant split in VERB TYPE. In line with earlier research on both L1 and L2 acquisition of Chinese-English (Goad, White, and Steele 2003; Hawkins and Liszka 2003; Nicoladis, Song, and Marentette 2012; Section 2.1), the Chinese-English bilingual children in the three corpora produced unmarked verbs statistically more frequently with regular verbs than with irregular verbs. This is not surprising since Chinese is an analytic language that does not make use of inflectional marking. Therefore, the Chinese-English children avoid regular past tense inflections but acquire the respective past tense form in irregular verbs not as a past tense marking in the strict sense, i.e. as verb plus marking (even if in portmanteau form), but they very likely memorize these forms as one morpheme. Interestingly, this significant influence of verb type could not be observed for the Singaporean data, even if it has been identified as a significant predictor in Buschfeld's (2020: 210) study. Note, however, that it was one of the less influential predictors in Buschfeld's study. Furthermore, taking apart a data set and investigating only a part of it might lead to different dynamics and interactions in the data and, in turn, to slightly diverging statistical results.

6 Conclusion

The present chapter has offered three major insights. First of all, we have compared diverse acquisitional settings involving English, i.e. the monolingual acquisition of AmE in the US in comparison with bilingual Chinese-English acquisition in Singapore, Hong Kong (both former British colonies), and in a Chinese community in the US. We have shown that the acquisitional outcome and route taken by new native speakers of English are different from that of traditional native speakers of AmE and from each other, depending on the acquisitional background of the speakers and, in relation to that, the input they receive. Such a comparative approach combining traditional monolingual acquisition scenarios with the acquisition of English in postcolonial settings and the bilingual acquisition of English in a Chinese dominant community located in the US is, to our best knowledge, unprecedented. However, we have illustrated how it contributes to a deeper understanding of the relevant factors and mechanisms influencing language acquisition and their outcomes on the one hand. On the other hand, we have shown how such studies enhance our understanding of the emergence of new L1 varieties. Our study therefore contributes to both the language acquisition and World Englishes paradigms and shows how only an approach combining the two disciplines can shed conclusive light on the complex acquisitional realities most children are facing in today's globalizing world. Whatever the reasons may be for the long neglect of comparative studies of children with such various acquisitional backgrounds, when treating these developments as manifestations of first language acquisition processes embedded in a World Englishes sociolinguistic framework (which they indisputably are), our study has clearly shown that an in-depth understanding of these processes requires both an investigation and understanding of the sociolinguistic realities of such speech communities as well as of the acquisitional aspects involved. Such a perspective seems inevitable if we are aiming at a comprehensive understanding of current linguistic ecologies, not only in these contexts but also in what McArthur (2003: 56) and Mesthrie and Bhatt (2008) have labelled the "English Language Complex" in general, i.e. the many different manifestations of the English language worldwide, which all have their beginnings in language acquisition.

Since our study is one of the very first of its kind and based on one linguistic feature and on a limited set of corpora and speakers, much research remains to be done. We would like to encourage future study to continue using cross-paradigmatic approaches and explore the options that existing corpora provide as well as the potential of further data collection. In particular, this should involve countries and speech communities not traditionally associated with L1 speakers of English for which relevant corpora often do not exist.

References

Bao, Zhiming. 2005. The aspectual system of Singapore English and the systemic substratist explanation. *Journal of Linguistics* 41 (2). 237–267.

Bernaisch, Tobias, Stefan Th. Gries & Joybrato Mukherjee. 2014. The dative alternation in South Asian English(es): Modelling predictors and predicting prototypes. *English World-Wide* 35 (1). 7–31.

Biber, Douglas, Stig Johansson, Geoffrey Leech, Susan Conrad & Edward Finegan (eds.). 1999. *Longman grammar of spoken and written English*. Harlow: Pearson.

Brown, Roger. 1973. *A first language: The early stages*. London: Allen & Unwin.

Buschfeld, Sarah. 2013. *English in Cyprus or Cyprus English? An empirical investigation of variety status*. Amsterdam: John Benjamins.

Buschfeld, Sarah. 2020. *Children's English in Singapore: Acquisition, properties, and use*. London: Routledge.

Bybee, Joan. 1995. Regular morphology and the lexicon. *Language and Cognitive Processes* 10 (5). 425–455.

Carroll, Susanne. 2017. Explaining bilingual learning outcomes in terms of exposure and input. *Bilingualism: Language and Cognition* 20 (1). 37–41.

Chan, Margaret. 2020. English, mother tongue and the Singapore identity. *The Straits Times*. www.straitstimes.com/opinion/english-mother-tongue-and-the-spore-identity (accessed 14 June 2021).

Chondrogianni, Vasiliki & Theodoros Marinis. 2011. Differential effects of internal and external factors on the development of vocabulary, tense morphology and morpho-syntax in successive bilingual children. *Linguistic Approaches to Bilingualism* 1 (3). 318–345.

Evert, Stefan. 2006. How random is a corpus? The library metaphor. *Zeitschrift für Anglistik und Amerikanistik* 54 (2). 177–190.

Gillam, Ronald B. & Nils A. Pearson. 2004. *Test of Narrative Language*. Austin, TX: Pro-Ed Inc.

Goad, Heather, Lydia White & Jeffrey Steele. 2003. Missing inflection in L2 acquisition: Defective syntax or L1-constrained prosodic representations? *Canadian Journal of Linguistics* 48 (3). 243–263.

Goh, Christine Chuen Meng & Rita Elaine Silver. 2006. *Language learning: Home, school and society*. Singapore: Pearson/Longman.

Gries, Stefan Th. 2010. Methodological skills in corpus linguistics: A polemic and some pointers towards quantitative methods. In Tony Harris & María Moreno Jaén (eds.), *Corpus linguistics in language teaching*, 121–146. Frankfurt am Main: Peter Lang.

Gupta, Anthea Fraser. 1994. *The Step-tongue: Children's English in Singapore*. Clevedon: Multilingual Matters.

Guthrie, Larry F. 1983. *Learning to use a new language: Language functions and use by first grade Chinese-Americans*. Oakland, CA: ARC Associates.

Guthrie, Larry F. 1984. Contrasts in teachers' language use in a Chinese-English bilingual classroom. In Jean Hanscombe, Richard Orem & Barry Taylor (eds.), *On TESOL '83: The question of control*, 39–52. Washington, DC: TESOL.

Guthrie, Larry F. & Grace P. Guthrie. 1988. Teacher language use in a Chinese bilingual classroom. In Susan Goldman & Henry Trueba (eds.), *Becoming literate in English as a second language*, 205–234. Norwood, NJ: Ablex.

Hackert, Stefanie. 2012. *The emergence of the English native speaker. A chapter in nineteenth-century linguistic thought*. Berlin & Boston: De Gruyter Mouton.

Harris, Tony &Kenneth Wexler. 1996. The Optional-infinitive stage in Child English. In Harald Clahsen (ed.), *Generative perspectives in language acquisition: Empirical findings, theoretical considerations and crosslinguistic comparisons*, 1–42. Amsterdam: John Benjamins.

Hawkins, Roger &Sarah Ann Liszka. 2003. Locating the source of defective past tense marking in advanced L2 English speakers. In Roeland van Hout, Aafke Hulk, Folkert Kuiken & Richard J. Towell (eds.), *The lexicon-syntax interface in second language acquisition*, 21–44. Amsterdam: John Benjamins.

Hothorn, Torsten, Kurt Hornik & Achim Zeileis. 2006. Unbiased recursive partitioning: A conditional inference framework. *Journal of Computational and Graphical Statistics* 15 (3). 651–674.

James, Deborah G. H., Jan van Doorn, Sharynne McLeod & Adrian Esterman. 2008. Patterns of consonant deletion in typically developing children aged 3 to 7 years. *International Journal of Speech Lang Pathology* 10 (3). 179–192.

Kuczaj, Stan A. 1977. The acquisition of regular and irregular past tense forms. *Journal of Verbal Learning and Verbal Behavior* 16 (5). 589–600.

Lardiere, Donna. 2004. Knowledge of definiteness despite variable article omission in second language acquisition. In Alejna Brugos, Linnea Micciulla & Christine E. Smith (eds.), *Proceedings of the 28th Boston University Conference on Language Development (BUCLD 28)*, 328–339. Somerville, MA: Cascadilla Press.

Leimgruber, Jakob R.E., Peter Siemund & Laura Terassa. 2018. Singaporean students' language repertoires and attitudes revisited. *World Englishes* 37 (2). 282–306.

Levshina, Natalia. 2015. *How to do linguistics with R: Data exploration and statistical analysis*. Amsterdam: John Benjamins.

Li, Charles N. & Sandra A. Thompson. 1981. *Mandarin Chinese: A functional reference grammar*. Berkeley: University of California Press.

Lim, Lisa. 2007. Mergers and acquisitions: On the ages and origins of Singapore English particles. *World Englishes* 26 (4). 446–473.

Liow, Susan J. Rickard & Lily H.-S. Lau. 2006. The development of bilingual children's early spelling in English. *Journal of Educational Psychology* 98 (4). 868–878.

MacWhinney, Brian. 2000. *The CHILDES project: Tools for analyzing talk*, 3rd edn. Mahwah, NJ: Lawrence Erlbaum Associates.

Marchman, Virginia A. 1997. Children's productivity in the English past tense: The role of frequency, phonology and neighborhood structure. *Cognitive Science* 21 (3). 283–304.

Marchman, Virginia A. & Elizabeth Bates. 1994. Continuity in lexical and morphological development: A test of the critical mass hypothesis. *Journal of Child Language* 21 (2). 339–366.

Marcus, Gary F., Steven Pinker, Michael T. Ullman, Michelle Hollander, T. John Rosen, Fei Xu & Harald Clahsen (eds.). 1992. *Overregularization in language acquisition. Monographs of the society for research in child development 228*. Chicago: Society for Research in Child Development.

McArthur, Tom. 2003. World English, Euro English, Nordic English? *English Today 73* 19 (1). 54–58.

McLeod, Sharynne, Jan van Doorn & Vicki A. Reed. 2001. Consonant cluster development in two-year-olds: General trends and individual difference. *Journal of Speech, Hearing, and Language Research* 44 (5). 1144–1171.

Meisel, Jürgen. 2011. Bilingual language acquisition and theories of diachronic change: Bilingualism as cause and effect of grammatical change. *Bilingualism: Language and Cognition* 14 (2). 121–145.

Mesthrie, Rajend & Rakesh M. Bhatt. 2008. *World Englishes: The study of new linguistic varieties*. Cambridge: Cambridge University Press.

Mollin, Sandra. 2007. New variety or learner English? Criteria for variety status and the case of Euro-English. *English World-Wide* 28 (2). 167–185.

Namtapi, Itsara & Nattama Pongpairoj. 2016. The acquisition of L2 English non-null arguments by L1 Thai learners. *Kasetsart Journal of Social Sciences* 37 (3). 150–157.

Nicoladis, Elena, Jianhui Song & Paula Marentette. 2012. Do young bilinguals acquire past tense morphology like monolinguals, only later? Evidence from French-English and Chinese-English bilinguals. *Applied Psycholinguistics* 33 (3). 457–479.

Paradis, Johanne & Martha Crago. 2001. The morphosyntax of specific language impairment in French: Evidence for an extended optional default account. *Language Acquisition* 9 (4). 269–300.

Philips, Colin. 1995. Syntax at age two: Some cross-linguistic differences. *Papers on Language Processing and Acquisition. MIT Working Papers in Linguistics* 26. 325–382.

Pinker, Steven & Michael T. Ullman. 2002. The past and future of the past tense. *Trends in Cognitive Science* 6 (11). 456–463.

R Development Core Team. 2014. *R: A language and environment for statistical computing*. Vienna: R Foundation for Statistical Computing.

Rice, Mabel L. & Ken Wexler. 2001. *Rice/Wexler Test of Early Grammatical Impairment: Examiner's manual*. San Antonio, TX: The Psychological Corporation.

Ross, Claudia & Jin-Heng Sheng Ma. 2014. *Modern Mandarin Chinese grammar. A practical guide*, 2nd edn. London: Routledge.

Salaberry, M. Rafael & Yasuhiro Shirai. 2002. *The L2 acquisition of tense-aspect morphology*. Amsterdam: John Benjamins.

Schneider, Edgar W. 2003. The dynamics of New Englishes: From identity construction to dialect birth. *Language* 79 (2). 233–281.

Schneider, Edgar W. 2007. *Postcolonial English: Varieties around the world*. Cambridge: Cambridge University Press.

Schneider, Gerold & Max Lauber. 2019. *Statistics for Linguists: A patient, slow-paced introduction to statistics and to the programming language R*. Pressbooks. https://dlf.uzh.ch/openbooks/statisticsforlinguists/ (accessed 15 June 2021).

Silver, Rita Elaine & Wendy D. Bokhorst-Heng (eds.). 2016. *Quadrilingual education in Singapore: Pedagogical innovation in language education*. Singapore: Springer.

Silver, Rita Elaine, Christine Chuen Meng Goh & Lubna Alsagoff (eds.). 2009. *Language learning in New English contexts: Studies of acquisition and development*. London: Continuum.

Talk Bank System. 2003. https://talkbank.org/ (accessed 15 June 2021).

Tan, Ying Ying. 2014. English as a 'mother tongue' in Singapore. *World Englishes* 33 (3). 319–339.

Tickoo, Makhan L. 1996. Fifty years of English in Singapore: All gains, (a) few losses?. In Joshua A. Fishman, Andrew W. Conrad & Alma Rubal-Lopez (eds.), *Post-imperial English: Status change in former British and American colonies, 1940–1990*, 431–455. Berlin & Boston: De Gruyter Mouton.

Torregrossa, Jacopo, Maria Andreou, Christiane Bongartz & Ianthi Maria Tsimpli. 2021. Bilingual acquisition of reference: The role of language experience, executive functions and cross-linguistic effects. *Bilingualism: Language and Cognition* 24 (4). 694–706.

Wee, Lionel. 2004. Singapore English: Phonology. In Edgar W. Schneider Kate Burridge, Bernd Kortmann, Rajend Mesthrie & Clive Upton (eds.), *A handbook of varieties of English. Volume 1: Phonology*, 1017–1033. Berlin & Boston: De Gruyter Mouton.

Wexler, Ken. 1992. *Optional infinitives, head movement, and the economy of derivation in child grammar*. Cambridge, MA: MIT Center for Cognitive Science.

Wexler, Ken. 1994. Optional infinitives, head movement and the economy of derivations. In David Lightfoot & Norbert Hornstein (eds.), *Verb Movement*, 305–350. Cambridge: Cambridge University Press.

Wexler, Ken. 1998. Very early parameter setting and the unique checking constraint: A new explanation of the optional infinitive stage. *Lingua* 106 (1–4). 23–79.

Williams, Jessica. 1987. Non-native varieties of English: A special case of language acquisition. *English World-Wide* 8 (2). 161–199.

Yip, Virginia & Stephen Matthews. 2007. *The bilingual child: Early development and language contact*. Cambridge: Cambridge University Press.

Yuen, Ivan, Felicity Cox & Katherine Demuth. 2014. Three-year-olds' production of Australian English phonemic vowel length as a function of prosodic context. *Journal of the Acoustic Society of America* 135 (3). 1469–1479.

Giuliana Regnoli and Thorsten Brato
8 Speech rhythm in Cameroon English: A cross-generational study

Abstract: Recent years have seen an increase of sociolinguistic interest in World Englishes and second language acquisition (Buschfeld 2020; Lacoste 2012). However, little attention has been given to the language of children and adolescents as well as to suprasegmental variation in postcolonial contexts. This paper aims to contribute to this growing body of research by providing insights into patterns of rhythmic variation among pre-adolescents and their parents in Cameroon. Drawing on conversational data collected in a primary school in Yaoundé through sociolinguistic interviews, map drawing tasks, and memory games, the study investigates the speech rhythm of four children and five adults. Speech rhythm was calculated using duration-based metrics (%V, ΔC, nPVI-V, rPVIV-V). The reported results indicate that the children's rhythm is more syllable-timed than that of their parents and suggest insights into the process of accommodation to L2 speech rhythm.

Keywords: child-directed speech, speech rhythm, Cameroon English, World Englishes

1 Introduction

The term Cameroon English (CamE) refers to the English spoken by the Anglophone population in Cameroon. Due to its strategic position at the crossroads between West and Central Africa, the country is sometimes identified as West African, other times as Central African. However, Cameroon is subsumed under West Africa in linguistic terms (Gut 2017). Here, English has been in use for more than four centuries: first as the language of the Baptist missionaries, then as the language of the British colonial power in the then Western Cameroon, and finally, after independence in 1961, as the official language of the country in addition to French (Todd 1982).

Cameroon is divided into ten regions, of which two are Anglophone – the Northwest and the Southwest regions, which constitute 16% of the population – and eight are Francophone. While the majority of the population speak French

---

Giuliana Regnoli, Thorsten Brato, University of Regensburg, Germany

(57.6%), English is the first language of 25.2% of Cameroonians (Census Data – Cameroon Data Portal 2005). As is the case with many postcolonial contexts of the second diaspora, i.e., countries colonised by Great Britain in the eighteenth and nineteenth centuries in which English is generally spoken as a second language (Schneider 2007; e.g., on India, Kachru [1986] 1990), the linguistic diversity of the country is remarkable. Cameroon has 250 languages that co-exist along with English and French, the dominant languages. However, local languages are gradually losing their appeal among the youngsters who tend to be almost exclusively bilingual in English and French (Atechi 2015).

General Cameroon English is an umbrella term used to describe multiple varieties of English spoken in the country by speakers of varying ethnic, linguistic, and socio-cultural backgrounds (Simo Bobda 2008). Overall, there are three major sub-varieties: CamE, i.e., "the English of the educated Anglophone Cameroonian" (Simo Bobda 2008: 115), Cameroon French English (CamFE), i.e., the variety spoken by the Francophone part of the population (Atechi 2015), and Cameroon Pidgin English (CPE), a pidgin spoken throughout the country by most of Cameroonians irrespective of their educational or language backgrounds (Schröder 2003). Thus, Cameroonian varieties of English (CamEs) developed their nativised, hybrid nature in multilingual regions in which patterns of indigenous transmission and use progressively entered the superstrate languages, i.e., English and French. According to Simo Bobda (2008, 2012), CamEs represent a rather complex phenomenon as they pose a number of challenges for phonological models.

As far as scholarly treatments are concerned, the description of CamE structural properties is relatively under-researched and is restricted to the acrolectal variety (Gut 2017; Polzenhagen 2007; Simo Bobda 2008). Moreover, acoustic studies of CamE phonology are rare and face issues of generalisability. Recent investigations of CamE phonology have increased the need for further investigation, as they either documented a "particular" (Simo Bobda 2008: 132) and "variable" (Brato and Atechi 2021) vowel system or intonation patterns "analogous" to other Englishes (Kouega 2000: 150). One of the aspects that has so far been neglected in empirical research on CamE is speech rhythm. CamE has traditionally been described as syllable-timed (Kouega 1991; Simo Bobda and Mbangwana 1993). Yet, none of these studies investigated the acoustic phonology of the language of children, which is a neglected area of research in World Englishes (WEs).

The present study is an analysis of the rhythmic patterns of English as spoken by L1 speakers of English and French attending an English-medium primary school in Yaoundé and by their parents. In order to determine whether there is variability in the rhythm of CamE, the paper will investigate the question whether the children's speech rhythm is more syllable-timed than that of their parents. After an outline of the current state of research on the speech rhythm of CamE (Section 2), and the social and linguistic background of the participants (Section 3), the paper will describe how the data were gathered and analysed (Section 4). We will finally present and interpret the results, i.e., the differences between the two groups in the production of speech rhythm (Sections 5–6). Conclusions and an outlook will be given in Section 7.

2 Conceptualising speech rhythm

2.1 Approaches to speech rhythm

Speech rhythm is considered the most distinctive characteristic of a language (Wiltshire 2020). As a matter of fact, languages have long been distinguished in terms of their rhythmic properties. Romance languages, e.g., French and Italian, have been described as "syllable-timed" and Germanic languages, e g., English and German, as "stress-timed" (Abercrombie 1967; Pike 1945). While syllable-timed languages exhibit isochrony at the syllable level, i.e., syllables tend to have the same duration, stress-timed languages exhibit isochrony at the foot level, i.e., inter-stress intervals tend to have the same duration.[1] However, empirical studies have challenged the original formulation of syllable- versus stress-based isochrony (Roach 1982), claiming that the idea of stress-/syllable-timing may be derived from the presence/absence of specific phonological properties in a language, i.e., syllable structure, vowel reduction, complex consonantal clusters, and phonetic realisations of stress (Dauer 1983). This new approach to speech rhythm implies a shift from a categorical notion of rhythm to a gradient one, such that languages are said to be more stress-/syllable timed than others. Hence, current research explores a continuum of rhythmic realisations, based on different acoustic measurements characterising different rhythmic properties (Ramus, Nespor, and Mehler 1999).

Among the different metrics that have been proposed to account for rhythmic differences between languages (cf. e.g., Fuchs 2016: 39–86), the most commonly used ones are duration-based. They aim to account for the variability in duration of consonantal, vocalic, and syllabic intervals. In this respect, Ramus, Nespor, and Mehler (1999) proposed the %V/deltaC model, which measures global properties of utterances. %V accounts for the proportion of vocalic intervals in an utterance, deltaC is the standard deviation of consonantal intervals (Ramus, Nespor, and

---

[1] A third type, mora-timing, has been suggested to account for languages such as Japanese, in which isochrony is maintained at the level of the mora, i.e., a sub-syllabic constituent that includes either onset and nucleus or a coda (Murty, Otake, and Cutler 2007).

Mehler 1999). %V values are higher in languages perceived as syllable-timed presumably due to their lack of vowel reduction and complex consonant clusters. Conversely, deltaC values are lower since duration of consonantal intervals is more variable in stress-timed languages. Other rhythmic metrics focus on the degree of durational contrast between neighbouring events. A common model is the Pairwise Variability Index (PVI) (Grabe and Low 2002), which takes into account the temporal succession of the vocalic and consonantal intervals instead of joining all the values and calculating the standard deviation. The two parameters in question are the normalised Pairwise Variability Index (nPVI) and the raw Pairwise Variability Index (rPVI). Respectively, they calculate the variability of durations of vocalic intervals – which are more prone to undergo the influence of speech rate – and consonantal ones. The values of both parameters are lower in syllable-timed languages.

Though both the terminology "syllable-/stress-timing" and individual measures of rhythm have limitations as well (e.g., Arvaniti 2009; Gut 2012), the reported results are discussed using the terminology and metrics provided by each study.

2.2 World Englishes, children, and adolescents

Varieties of English have also been described as differing in rhythm. Overall, it has been observed that British English and varieties that have reached stage 5 in Schneider's (2003, 2007) Dynamic Model of Postcolonial Englishes are more stress-timed than L2 varieties of English (Crystal 1995; Fuchs 2016; Gut 2005; Nishihara and van de Weijer 2011). Furthermore, a considerable number of studies have provided acoustic evidence that learner varieties of English such as German (Ordin, Polyanskaya, and Ulbrick 2011) and Spanish (Dellwo, Diez, and Galves 2009) are syllable-timed as well. Overall, it seems that in cases of language contact between English and a syllable-timed language, the emerging variety of English is more syllable-timed than British English or American English (which are generally used as points of comparison). Moreover, it has also been observed that L2 and learner varieties of English tend to share features associated with stress timing, e.g., syllable reduction in unstressed positions and vowel lengthening in stressed syllables (Fought 2003). This is due to a combination of prosodic elements from (stress-timed) British English or American English and (syllable- or mora-timed) substrate languages (see e.g., for Indian English, Sirsa and Redford 2013; Wiltshire and Harnsberger 2006; for Nigerian English, Gut 2005).

CamE has traditionally been described as a syllable-timed variety (Kouega 1991; Simo Bobda and Mbangwana 1993). However, empirical studies are rare and the only recent one that has investigated the speech rhythm of CamE mainly provides a descriptive approach. Nankep Kouanang (2018) examines rhythmic convergence between 20 speakers of CamE and 20 speakers of CamFE. Using a contrastive analysis framework, which is rarely employed in empirical speech rhythm research, Nankep Kouanang compares the total number of stressed and unstressed syllables in monosyllabic and polysyllabic words. The study provides some evidence of convergence between the two varieties. However, due to the methodology applied, these results are hardly comparable. Thus, in order to achieve a more reliable description of the rhythm of CamE, different ways of quantifying speech rhythm need to be considered (see Section 4).

Moreover, notwithstanding the new approach to the description of speech rhythm in degrees of stress and syllable timing, a closer look at the literature on WEs speech rhythm reveals a number of gaps and shortcomings. These include a focus on read speech over spontaneous speech and the selection of participants being restricted to adults. Very few studies have taken into account spontaneous speech. Despite Arvaniti's (2012) work addressing this issue by pointing to potential rhythmic contrasts between the two speech styles, a great number of varieties of English have been studied using read speech. Work by Coggshall (2008) on Cherokee English and Lumbee English and Ordin, Polyanskaya, and Ulbrick (2011) on German English are notable exceptions. Many studies also relied only on adult participants. As a result, child-directed speech has been hardly considered in research on speech rhythm in WEs. This is likely due to the broader separation of WEs and the field of second language acquisition.

Traditional sociolinguistic research has emphasised that children and adolescents play a fundamental role in the diffusion of innovative linguistic variants and are influential transmitters of language change (Brato 2016; Kerswill and Williams 2000; Tagliamonte 2016). As facilitators of language change, children tend to acquire the vernacular(s) of the area (Labov 1970) mainly from their caregivers (Trudgill 1986) and peer group (Chambers 2009). Moreover, they learn a second dialect easily by the age of nine (Chambers 1992; Payne 1980) and L2 prosodic systems by the age of 12–15 (Kerswill 1996). In high-contact situations, children tend to distinguish between innovative and conservative features and are more likely to pick innovative forms (e.g., Brato 2016). Yet, studies on children and adolescents are still far and few in WEs. Variationist work by Buschfeld (2020) in Singapore, Lacoste (2012) in Jamaica and ongoing work in other Caribbean varieties (e.g., Schmalz 2019) are notable exceptions. Moreover, most work in sociolinguistic theorising on the role of children has mainly focussed on Western (white) societies (Labov 2007). The assumption that children acquire the sociolinguistic norms of their community from their parents only to dissociate themselves from them due to peer influence may not necessarily hold true for children growing up in different contexts (Alam and Stuart-Smith 2011; Sharma 2011, 2017), e.g., African societies in which fluidity is the linguistic norm.

In light of these considerations, a study of Cameroonian pre-adolescents with different language backgrounds might provide first insights into the patterns of acquisition of L2 speech rhythm as well as on the role of children as pacemakers of linguistic change.

3 The case study

Located at the interface of sociolinguistics and WEs, the present study is part of a wider project on language variation and change in Cameroon English. The project aims to investigate the interplay of English, French, and the local languages in the multilingual and multi-ethnic Cameroonian society and to provide a first glimpse into the role of children as facilitators of linguistic change in the country.

The data were gathered in 2018 in an English-medium primary school located in Francophone Yaoundé from 32 children (17 boys and 15 girls) and 10 adults (5 males and 5 females). The children were between 9 and 11 years old at the time of the fieldwork and most of them were born in Yaoundé. 18 were Anglophone, 11 francophone and 3 were bilingual. The adults, aged 31–53, had all migrated from other parts of the country. Nine of them were Anglophone and one was Francophone.

The focus of the project lies on sociophonetics, thus speech data covering all vowels and consonants in different phonological contexts and sociolinguistic styles were collected by means of different tasks. The recordings were made using a Zoom H4N Pro digital recorder and two Audio-Technica AT 831 lavaliere microphones. The children's tasks included a "spot the difference" game, a memory game with typical market items, and a map task. In the "spot the difference" game, the participants had to identify the differences between two similar photos; in the memory game they had to pair the same images on the cards. The aim of both tasks was to collect as much unmonitored speech as possible. The map task – a well-tested technique in language acquisition (e.g., McCarthy and Stuart-Smith 2013), consisted of the children moving around a track and discussing the items they found along the way. It allowed for almost complete control over the items and facilitated data elicitation. The adults' data were gathered through the same map task presented to the children, the reading passage "The boy who cried wolf" (Deterding 2006), and a word list of 100 items containing at least two tokens of all lexical sets as well selected consonant variables. Additional sociolinguistic material included a short informal sociolinguistic interview for both groups.

Some of our intended methods for gathering data from the children were not successful. Specifically, the "spot the difference" task and the memory game with market items proved to be confusing for the children who, in turn, felt overwhelmed and struggled to complete the tasks. We tried to adapt them on the spot to largely maintain the comparability to the data collected from the adult speakers, and included a short interview. Each session lasted roughly 10 minutes for the children and 30 minutes for the adults, for a total of approximately 23 hours of speech.

A first look at the sociolinguistic mark-up of the sample showed that 31 children reported speaking French, four reported speaking a Cameroonian/local language, and 15 reported understanding their local language, but not speaking it. One adult reported speaking a local language, one Cameroon Pidgin English, five could understand but not speak French and two could understand a local language different from their home language. Finally, one out of nine Anglophone adults claimed to speak French. These findings emphasise a rapid decline in the knowledge and use of the local languages among children. As a matter of fact, they all reported speaking French, which is almost a prerequisite for everyday life in Yaoundé. This could be indicative of an emerging type of French-English bilingualism at the expense of the local languages, whose linguistic consequences may affect the language ecology of Cameroon in the long run. The predominant use of French among the children may also denote a possible French influence in their CamE L2 rhythmic patterns, which may be comparably more syllable-timed than their parents'.

In light of these observations, the paper endeavours to contribute to the growing body of research on CamE speech rhythm by investigating rhythmic contrast across generations. In doing so, the following hypotheses have been formulated:

H1: The rhythm of CamE is variable.
H2: The children's speech rhythm is more syllable-timed than the speech rhythm of their parents due to a possible French influence.

4 Data and methodology

The data set consists of the semi-spontaneous speech of nine respondents: four children and five adults. The children are 10 and 11 years old, they come from similar L1 backgrounds, and they all attend English-medium schools. The adults are between 31 and 42 years old and most of them have English as their L1. Since most adults are elementary school teachers, it is plausible to assume that they speak an acrolectal variety of CamE (cf. Table 8.1). The L1 of the speakers and their Anglophone/Francophone background was determined on the basis of their answers to a sociolinguistic questionnaire focusing on the participants' linguistic background and language use.

Table 8.1: Social characteristics of the speakers.

Speaker	Age	Gender	L1	L2	Grow up region	Anglophone/ Francophone	Education/ profession
1f01	10	female	French	N/A	Central	Anglophone	English-medium
1f04	11	female	French	N/A	Central	Francophone	English-medium
1m15	11	male	French	N/A	North-West	Anglophone	English-medium
1m16	10	male	French	N/A	Central	Anglophone	English-medium
2f01	39	female	English	N/A	South-West	Anglophone	GCE Advanced/ Teacher
2f02	31	female	French	English	South-West	Anglophone	CAPIEMP/Teacher
2f03	40	female	English	N/A	South-West	Anglophone	GCE Ordinary/Teacher
2f04	35	female	English	French	Central	Francophone	BFS/Hairdresser
2f05	42	female	English	N/A	West	Anglophone	GCE Advanced/Teacher

The speakers were recorded performing the tasks discussed in Section 3. The children's data, however, have some shortcomings: a high number of short replies and syntactic pauses were registered. Thus, the comparison of an equal number of tokens resulted in the segmentation of five minutes of the children's speech and of two minutes of the adults' speech.

The choice of semi-spontaneous material also deserves a note. We are aware that the choice of naturalistic data has long been considered inappropriate in speech rhythm research (see section 2.2). However, our choice is justified by two main reasons: (i) it is difficult to engage in reading tasks with children – even more so in L2 contexts, and (ii) the endeavour to model speech rhythm should include spontaneous speech.

The recordings were transcribed in ELAN (version 6.0; Sloetjes and Wittenburg 2008). Utterances were segmented using the BAS web service (Schiel 1999) and the resulting textgrids as well as the sound files were concatenated using a Praat script. Acoustic measurements were carried out with Praat (version 6.1.35; Boersma and Weenink 2017). Measurements were first corrected manually on the phonetic tier and then an additional tier of CV (consonant and vowel) segments was included. CV boundaries were identified by visual inspection of the spectrogram and waveform. The data were segmented according to the recommendations provided by Ramus, Nespor, and Mehler (1999):

1. [w] and [j] were treated as consonants and the boundary was placed between the approximant and the vowel;
2. vowels on either side of a pause counted as one interval;

3. in vowel + nasal consonant sequences, the nasalised portion of the vowel was included in the vowel;
4. in case of initial voiced stop consonants, the first boundary corresponded to the onset of glottal pulses.

Respiratory and syntactic pauses were marked as silent. Other disfluencies, e.g., laryngealisations, nasalisations, and vocalisations, were treated as filled pauses. Speech rhythm was calculated using duration-based metrics (%V, deltaC, nPVI, rPVI; see Section 2.1). The correlates were computed with Correlatore (version 2.3.4; Mairano and Romano 2010) on all consonantal/vocalic intervals in the textgrids. A descriptive-oriented approach based on the rhythmic contrast between the adults' and the children's groups will be adopted.

5 Results

Figures 8.1 and 8.2 show individual variances according to the rhythmic correlates described in Section 2.1. Children are represented by triangles and adults by circles. Mean and standard deviation values are visualised in black and error bars. Their calculations are displayed in Table 8.2.

Figure 8.1 shows the results for %V and deltaC for both groups. The model suggests a visible stress- vs. syllable-timed trend in line with Ramus, Nespor, and Mehler's (1999) predictions in relation to the proportion of vocalic intervals, i.e., syllable-timed languages tend to occupy the right side of the graphic, corresponding to higher %V values. Average %V values for the adults' group (45.3) are 5.7% lower than those for the children's group (48), revealing a gradual shift towards syllable-timing for the children. Moreover, %V values are more uniform in the adults' group (st.dev. 0.63) as compared to that of the children (1.7). According to previously observed trends (Ramus, Nespor, and Mehler 1999), deltaC values should be lower in syllable-timed patterns. Yet, the deltaC values of the adults' group (62.7) are 12.9% lower than those for the children's group (71.4). They are also subject to more variability (st.dev. 3.7). This finding supports H1, according to which there is considerable variability in the rhythmic patterns of CamE.

Furthermore, a closer look at Figure 8.1 reveals that both groups include two outliers: 1f04 and 2f02. 1f04 is an 11-year-old girl whose L1, i.e., French, is in line with her self-reported Francophone background. She is the only one in the sample to display such behaviour. Interestingly enough, 1f04 exhibits more syllable-timing than the other group members for both parameters (%V: 52.5; deltaC: 65.1). This could be indicative of an alleged French influence on her CamE. The second

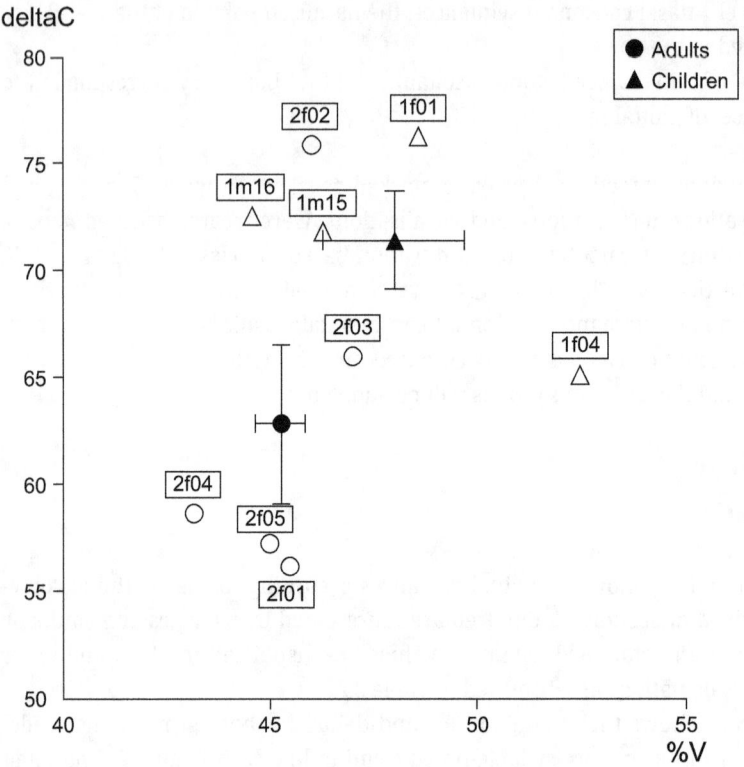

Figure 8.1: Individual differences according to the %V/deltaC model (Ramus, Nespor, and Mehler 1999).

outlier, 2f02, is a 31-year-old female teacher. Again, she is the only one in her group who reported speaking French as her L1. Her rhythmic behaviour is similar to that of the children's group with respects to both parameters, and mainly to C segments (%V: 46; deltaC: 75.8). In other words, her high %V and deltaC values are analogous to the children's values, which indicate more syllable-timing in relation to V segments. Moreover, her (syllable-timed) Francophone background may be responsible for her high %V values due to lack of vowel reduction. Overall, these findings may corroborate H2, which posits that the children's speech rhythm is more syllable-timed than the speech rhythm of their parents due to a possible syllable-timed French influence.

Figure 8.2 shows the rhythmic behaviour of both groups according to the PVI model. As in Figure 8.1, the separation between the two groups is rather clear-cut. According to Grabe and Low (2002), syllable-timed languages should exhibit lower values of rPVI and nPVI than stress-timed ones. Thus, syllable-timed lan-

Table 8.2: Mean and standard derivative values of rhythmic correlates.

Metrics	Children		Adults	
	Mean	St.dev.	Mean	St.dev.
%V	48	1.7	45.3	0.6
deltaC	71.4	2.3	62.7	3.7
n-PVI	47.9	1	52.2	4.9
r-PVI	78	2.1	63.8	3.5

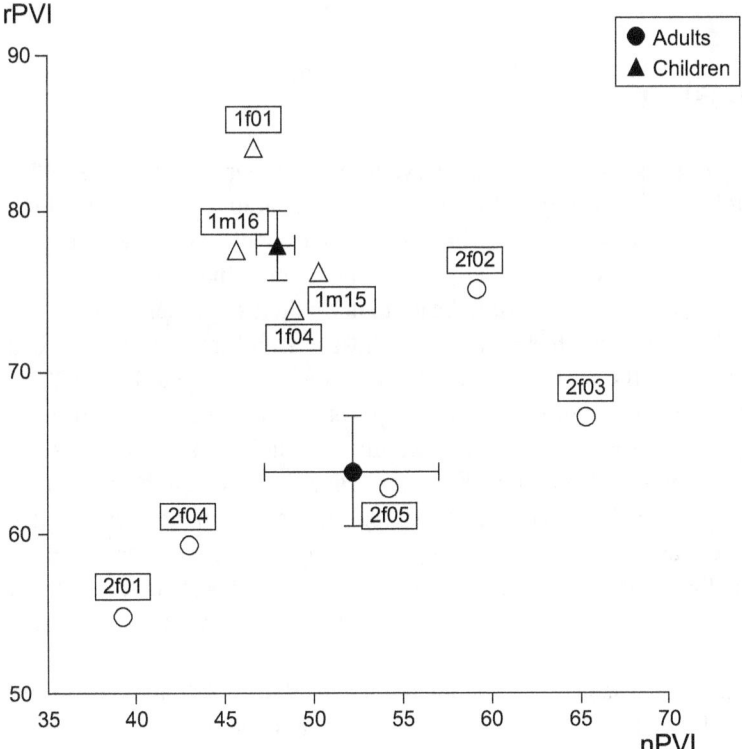

Figure 8.2: Individual differences according to the PVI model (Grabe and Low 2002).

guages should be situated in the lower left corner of the chart. As can be seen, nPVI values for the adults' group (52.2) are 8.5% higher than those for the children (47.9). This indicates more syllable-timing for the children's group. The adults' group also exhibits more variation (st.dev. 4.9). In keeping with previous results (Grabe and Low 2002), rPVI values should be lower in syllable-timed languages.

Yet, similarly to the previous model in relation to deltaC, the rPVi values of the adults' group (63.8) are 20.02% lower than those for the children's group (78). rPVI values are also more uniform in the children's group (st.dev. 2.1).

The PVI model identifies the same outliers detected in the %V/deltaC model, and shows a similar trend: 1f04 has the lowest PVI values (nPVI: 49.1; rPVI: 73.9), indexing more syllable-timing and 2f02 shows a rhythmic behaviour similar to that of the children's group with respects to C segments (rPVI: 75.1). Once again, these findings support H1 and H2, as they shed light on they variability of CamE speech rhythm as well as on a possible (syllable-timed) French influence on the children's speech productions.

6 Discussion

The findings of this study concur with previous descriptions of L2 varieties of English as more syllable-timed than L1 varieties (e.g., Fuchs 2016; Nishihara and van de Weijer 2011) and of CamE as a syllable-timed variety of West African English (Kouega 1991; Nankep Kouanang 2008; Simo Bobda and Mbangwana 1993). The duration-based metrics used here indicate that, qualitatively, there is considerable variability in the speech rhythm of CamE. This result is in line with previous trends observed in the phonological system of the variety (Simo Bobda 2008). While more data and a more quantitative approach are needed to confirm this trend, it is nonetheless interesting to note that the findings show fine-grained rhythmic differences between the children's group and the adults' group. Both the %V/deltaC and the PVI models capture important aspects in the rhythmic classification of CamE as they were able to provide a qualitative assessment of the variability of the variety across generations. This corroborates the first hypothesis formulated in Section 3 according to which the speech rhythm system of CamE is variable (H1). As a matter of fact, the models suggest that the rhythm of the children's group is more syllable-timed than that of the adults in relation to V segments (%V, nPVI) and that it exhibits little variation as shown in the standard deviation of most parameters (deltaC, nPVI, rPVI). Bearing in mind the sociolinguistic mark-up of the sample, i.e., the children attending private schools and the adults being highly educated, these findings provide a first glimpse into the rhythmic patterns of near-standard speakers of CamE.

The results have revealed one outlier in each sample. In the children's group, the outlier in question is 1f04, an 11-year-old female whose speech rhythm values are more syllable-timed compared to that of her group members. Since the present study focused on children attending English-medium schools, it is unlikely that the differences between 1f04 and her peers could be attributed to divergent proficiency levels. The only social attribute that seems to distinguish 1f04 from her peers is her self-reported Francophone background. While more research is needed to dig into a possible French influence, it is nevertheless interesting to note that the rhythmic values of 1f04 show considerable syllable-timing for the metrics applied (%V, n-PVI). The outlier of the adults' group exhibits a similar behaviour: 2f05 is a 31-year-old female teacher whose rhythmic values are similar to those of the children with respect to C segments for both metrics (deltaC; r-PVI). Her L1, i.e., French, is the only variable that seemingly differentiates her from her group members. Even in this case, it is possible to assume that a French influence plays a role in her rhythmic behaviour. This finding reinforces the interpretation of the nature of the outliers in the sample: since French has traditionally been described as more syllable-timed than English (e.g., Abercrombie 1967; Pike 1945), it is plausible to speculate that the rhythmic patterns of 1f04 and 2f02 are rooted in this social attribute. This result would corroborate the second hypothesis formulated in Section 3, i.e., the speech rhythm of the children's group is more syllable-timed than that of the adults' group due to an alleged French influence (H2). Whether this may be due to consonantal lengthening and/or nasalisation is yet to be investigated. Nevertheless, the findings supported by H2 are in line with current research on L2 speech rhythm, according to which, in cases of language contact between English and a syllable-timed language (in this case, French), the emerging variety of English tends to be more syllable-timed (e.g., Dellwo, Diez, and Galves 2009; Gut 2009).

The reported results emphasise the importance of adopting an integrative approach to both language acquisition and WEs research (e.g., Buschfeld 2020) and WEs and variationist sociolinguistics (e.g., Sharma 2011, 2017). With respect to the former areas of investigation, the sociolinguistic mark-up of the sample supports previous claims that local languages are losing their appeal among the youngsters (Atechi 2015). The children in our sample are exclusively bilingual in (Cameroon) English and French. While this could be indicative of an emerging bilingualism at the expense of the local languages – whose linguistic consequences may affect the ecolinguistic diversity of Cameroon – it also emphasises that more investigation is needed in high-contact postcolonial contexts for a full understanding of L1 acquisition of an L2 variety of English by a new generation of speakers (see e.g., Buschfeld 2020).

Current work in WEs variationist sociolinguistics has indicated that some of the basic assumptions regarding sociolinguistic norms and mechanisms of language change may not necessarily hold true for non-western communities (e.g., Alam and Stuart-Smith 2011; Sharma 2011, 2017). Besides, what is considered "common knowledge" and "common fieldwork practice" in predominantly monolingual, Western societies may not be applicable to non-western multilingual communities. Our study showed that the adoption of data collection methods tested in Western contexts was problematic. Some of our intended methods for gathering data from the children did not work out and had to be adapted to maintain the comparability to the data collected from the adult speakers. This reinforces the idea that data collection methods other than the Labovian approach should be taken into consideration in WEs research and should be informed by the language acquisition paradigm. We argue that more in-depth, context-oriented fieldwork is necessary to allow for future developments of new data collection techniques. Using an ethnographic approach may also allow for further implementations of sociolinguistic material to suit the specific needs of the postcolonial societies under investigation.

7 Conclusion

The present paper set out to provide the first description of the rhythm of CamE in a small group of children in a primary school in Yaoundé and compare it to that of a group of adult speakers. Rhythm was calculated using duration-based metrics (%V, deltaC, nPVI, rPVI). The reported results concur with earlier descriptions of CamE as syllable-timed (Kouega 1991; Nankep Kouanang 2008; Simo Bobda and Mbangwana 1993) and show that the metrics applied capture important aspects in the rhythmic classification of English varieties. In particular, the findings indicate fine-grained differences between the two groups and confirmed the hypotheses that the rhythm of CamE is variable and the children's rhythm is more syllable-timed than that of the adult speakers due to a possible syllable-timed influence of French. Moreover, the reported results emphasise that new data collection methods ought to be developed in multilingual, non-western communities for a full understanding of L1 acquisition of L2 varieties of English by a new generation of speakers. To do so, more in-depth fieldwork research is needed to suit the needs of the specific contexts at issue.

Future research in the project will expand on a possible French influence and compare the speakers' productions in English and French in different speech styles using quantitative approaches. Moreover, it will take into account more integrated models for the analysis of rhythm that include parameters other than duration, i.e., intensity, loudness and sonority (Fuchs 2016; Galves et al. 2002; Low 1998) and extend the analysis to pitch, F0, and other stress correlates (Cumming 2010; He 2012). Finally, the project will consider the challenges of adopting a Labovian approach to data collection in the Cameroonian context and develop/implement new data elicitation methods and sociolinguistic material.

References

Abercrombie, David. 1967. *Elements of general phonetics*. Edinburgh: Edinburgh University Press.
Alam, Farhana & Jane Stuart-Smith. 2011. Identity and ethnicity in /t/ in Glasgow-Pakistani high-school girls. In *Proceedings of the 17th International Congress of Phonetics Sciences (ICPhS)*, 216–219. Hong Kong.
Arvaniti, Amalia. 2009. Rhythm, timing and the timing of rhythm. *Phonetica* 66 (1–2). 46–63.
Arvaniti, Amalia. 2012. The usefulness of metrics in the quantification of speech rhythm. *Journal of Phonetics* 40. 351–373.
Atechi, Samuel. 2015. The emergence of Cameroon Francophone English and the future of English in Cameroon. *British Journal of English Linguistics* 3 (3). 23–55.
Boersma, Paul & David Weenink. 2017. *Praat: Doing phonetics by computer* [Computer Programme].
Brato, Thorsten. 2016. *Variation and change in Aberdeen English: A sociophonetic study*. Frankfurt: Peter Lang.
Brato, Thorsten & Samuel Atechi. 2021. The sociolinguistics of a class of primary school children in Yaoundé: Background, variation and change. Paper presented at the ISLE6 Conference on Evolving English and the Digital Era, University of Eastern Finland, 2–5 June.
Buschfeld, Sarah. 2020. *Children's English in Singapore: Acquisition, properties, and use*. London: Routledge.
Census Data – Cameroon Data Portal. 2005. https://cameroon.opendataforafrica.org/rfdefze/census-data (accessed 22 September 2021).
Chambers, Jack K. 1992. Dialect acquisition. *Language* 68 (4). 673–705.
Chambers, Jack K. 2009. *Sociolinguistic theory. Linguistic variation and its social significance*. Oxford: Blackwell.
Coggshall, Elizabeth L. 2008. The prosodic rhythm of two varieties of native American English. *University of Pennsylvania Working Papers in Linguistics* 14 (2). 1–9.
Crystal, David. 1995. Documenting rhythmical change. In Jack Windsor Lewis (ed.), *Studies in general and English phonetics: Essays in honour of Professor J. D. O'Connor*, 174–179. London: Routledge.
Cumming, Ruth E. 2010. *The language-specific integration of pitch and duration*. Cambridge: University of Cambridge PhD dissertation.
Dauer, R.M. 1983. Stress-timing and syllable-timing reanalized. *Journal of Phonetics* 11. 51–62.
Dellwo, Volker, Francisco Gutiérrez Diez & Nuria Gavalda. 2009. The development of measurable speech rhythm in Spanish speakers of English. In Eloína Miyares Bermúdez (ed.), *Actas de XI Simposio Internacional de Comunicacion Social*, 594–597. Santiago de Cuba.
Deterding, David. 2006. The north wind versus a wolf: Short texts for the description and measurement of English pronunciation. *Journal of the International Phonetic Association* 36 (2). 187–196.
Fought, Carme. 2003. *Chicano English in context*. Houndmills & New York: Palgrave Macmillan.
Fuchs, Robert. 2016. *Speech rhythm in varieties of English*. Singapore: Springer.
Galves, Antonio, Jesus Garcia, Denise Duarte & Charlotte Galves. 2002. Sonority as a basis for rhythmic class discrimination. In Bernard Bel & Isabelle Marlien (eds.), *Proceedings of Speech Prosody 2002*, 323–326. Aix-en-Provence.
Grabe, Esther & Ee Ling Low. 2002. Durational variability in speech and the rhythm class hypothesis. In Carlos Gussenhoven & Natasha Warner (eds.), *Papers in Laboratory Phonology 7*, 515–546. Berlin & New York: De Gruyter Mouton.
Gut, Ulrike. 2005. Nigerian English prosody. *English World-Wide* 26 (2). 153–177.

Gut, Ulrike. 2009. *Non-native speech. A corpus-based analysis of phonological and phonetic properties of L2 English and German*. Frankfurt: Peter Lang.

Gut, Ulrike. 2012. Rhythm in L2 speech. In Gibbon Dafydd, Hirst Daniel & Campbell Nick (eds.), *Rhythm, melody and harmony in speech: studies in honour of Wiktor Jasse*. [Special issue]. *Speech and Language Technology* 14/15. 83–94. Poznań: Polish Phonetic Association.

Gut, Ulrike. 2017. English in West Africa. In Markku Filppula, Juhani Klemola & Devyani Sharma (eds.), *The Oxford handbook of World Englishes*, 491–507. Oxford: Oxford University Press.

He, Lei. 2012. Syllabic intensity variation as a quantification of speech rhythm: Evidence from both L1 and L2. In *Speech Prosody*, 6th International Conference, 466–469. Shanghai.

Kachru, Braj B. 1990 [1986]. *The alchemy of English. The spread, functions and models of non-native Englishes*. Urbana, IL: University of Illinois Press.

Kerswill, Paul. 1996. Children, adolescents and language change. *Language Variation and Change* 8. 177–202.

Kerswill, Paul & Ann Williams. 2000. Mobility and social class in dialect levelling: Evidence from new and old towns in England. In Klaus Mattheier (ed.), *Dialect and migration in a changing Europe*, 1–13. Frankfurt: Peter Lang.

Kouega, Jean-Paul. 1991. *Some speech characteristics of Cameroon media news texts*. Yaoundé: University of Yaoundé PhD dissertation.

Kouega, Jean-Paul. 2000. Some aspects of Cameroon English prosody. *Alizés: Revue Angliciste de La Réunion*. 137–153.

Labov, William. 1970. Stages in the acquisition of Standard English. In Harold Hungerford, Jay Robinson & James Sledd (eds.), *English Linguistics*, 275–302. Glenview: Scott Foreman.

Labov, William. 2007. Transmission and diffusion. *Language* 83 (2). 344–387.

Lacoste, Véronique. 2012. *Phonological variation in rural Jamaican schools*. Amsterdam: John Benjamins.

Low, EE Ling. 1998. *Prosodic prominence in Singapore English*. Cambridge: University of Cambridge PhD dissertation.

Mairano, Paolo &Antonio Romano. 2010. Un confronto tra diverse metriche ritmiche usando Correlatore. In Stephan Schmid, Michael Schwarzenbach & Dieter Studer (eds.), *La dimensione temporale del parlato. Proceedings of the V National AISV Congress, Zurich* 2009, 79–100. Torriana: EDK.

McCarthy, Owen & Jane Stuart-Smith. 2013. Ejectives in Scottish English: A social perspective. *Journal of the International Phonetic Association* 43 (3). 273–298.

Murty, Lalita, Takashi Otake & Anne Cutler. 2007. Perceptual tests of rhythmic similarity: I. Mora rhythm. *Language and Speech* 50 (1). 77–99.

Nankep Kouanang, William. 2018. *Rhythm in Cameroon English and Cameroon Francophone English: A descriptive and a comparative analysis*. Yaoundé: University of Yaoundé BA dissertation.

Nishihara, Tetsuo & Jeroen van de Weijer. 2011. On syllable-timed rhythm and stress-timed rhythm in World Englishes: Revisited. *Bulletin of Miyagi University of Education* 46. 155–163.

Ordin, Mikhail, Leona Polyanskaya & Christiane Ulbrick. 2011. Acquisition of timing patterns in second language. In Piero Cosi, Renato De Mori, Giuseppe Di Fabbrizio & Roberto Pieraccini (eds.), *Proceedings of Interspeech 2011*, 1129–1132. Florence.

Payne, Arvilla. 1980. Factors controlling the acquisition of the Philadelphia dialect by out of state children. In William Labov (ed.), *Locating language in time and space*, 143–158. New York: Academic Press.

Pike, Kenneth L. 1945. *The intonation of American English*. Ann Arbor: University of Michigan Press.

Polzenhagen, Frank. 2007. *Cultural conceptualisations in West African English*. Bern: Peter Lang.

Ramus, Franck, Marina Nespor & Jacques Mehler. 1999. Correlates of linguistic rhythm in the speech signal. *Cognitorium* 73 (3). 265–292.

Roach, Peter. 1982. On the distinction between 'stress-timed' and 'syllable-timed' languages. In David Crystal (ed.), *Linguistic controversies*, 73–79. London: Edward Arnold.

Schiel, Florian. 1999. Automatic phonetic transcription of non-prompted speech. In John J. Ohala (ed.), *Proceedings of the 14th International Congress of Phonetic Sciences (ICPhS-14) 1999*, 607–610. San Francisco.

Schmalz, Mirjam. 2019. *The interplay of language perceptions and education in St. Kitts*. Paper presented at the 24th Conference of the International Association for World Englishes (IAWE). Limerick, 20 June.

Schneider, Edgar W. 2003. The dynamics of new Englishes: From identity construction to dialect birth. *Language* 79 (2). 233–281.

Schneider, Edgar W. 2007. *Postcolonial English: Varieties around the world*. Cambridge: Cambridge University Press.

Schröder, Anne. 2003. Cameroon Pidgin English: A means of bridging the Anglophone-Francophone division in Cameroon? *AAA: Arbeiten aus Anglistik und Amerikanistik* 28 (2). 305–327.

Sharma, Devyani. 2011. Style repertoire and social change in British Asian English. *Journal of Sociolinguistics* 15 (4). 464–492.

Sharma, Devyani. 2017. World Englishes and sociolinguistic theory. In Markku Filppula, Juhani Klemola & Devyani Sharma (eds.), *The Oxford handbook of World Englishes*, 232–251. Oxford: Oxford University Press.

Simo Bobda, Augustin. 2008. Cameroon English: Phonology. In Rajend Mesthrie, Bernd Kortmann & Edgar W. Schneider (eds.), *4 Africa, South and Southeast Asia*, 115–132. Berlin & New York: De Gruyter Mouton.

Simo Bobda, Augustin. 2012. Reading the phonology Cameroon English through the trilateral process. In Eric A. Anchimbe (ed.), *Language contact in a postcolonial setting: The linguistic and social context of English and pidgin in Cameroon*, 77–98. Berlin & Boston: De Gruyter Mouton.

Simo Bobda, Augustin & Paul Mbangwana. 1993. *An introduction to English speech*. Lagos: University Press.

Sirsa, Hema & Melissa A. Redford. 2013. The effects of native language on Indian English sounds and timing patterns. *Journal of Phonetics* 41 (6). 393–406.

Sloetjes, Han & Peter Wittenburg. 2008. Annotation by category: ELAN and ISO DCR. In Nicoletta Calzolari, Khalid Choukri, Bente Maegaard, Joseph Mariani, Jan Odijk, Stelios Piperidis & Daniel Tapias (eds.), *Proceedings of the sixth International Conference on Language Resources and Evaluation (LREC 2008)*, 1–5. Marrakesh.

Tagliamonte, Sali. 2016. *Teen talk: The language of adolescents*. Cambridge: Cambridge University Press.

Todd, Loreto. 1982. *Cameroon*. Heidelberg: Groos.

Trudgill, Peter. 1986. *Dialects in contact*. Oxford: Blackwell.

Wiltshire, Caroline. 2020. *Uniformity and variability in the Indian English accent*. Cambridge: Cambridge University Press.

Wiltshire, Caroline & James D. Harnsberger. 2006. The influence of Gujarati and Tamil L1s on Indian English: A preliminary study. *World Englishes* 25 (1). 91–104.

Patricia Ronan and Sarah Buschfeld

9 From second to first language: Language shift in Singapore and Ireland

Abstract: This chapter investigates development patterns of English from an L2 to an L1 in Singapore and Ireland in order to find out how previous developments in a language shift variety of English may help to predict developments in a contemporary variety of English. To this end, we investigate specific salient morphosyntactic features of the respective varieties, namely Singapore English zero-subject pronouns and Irish English *after*-perfects. The investigations are based on a comparison of corpus-based evidence from young speakers as well as adult speakers to trace potential processes of language shift.

The results of the study show that the use of the variety-specific morphosyntactic features in the emerging L1 varieties is rule governed and has evolved from language contacts. The Irish English data sets illustrate results of language change processes while the Singapore data show grammatical change in progress in the language use of young and very young speakers. The study thus showcases the important role that children and adolescents have in language change and shift.

Keywords: L2 to L1 change, zero subject pronouns, after-perfect, Singapore English, Irish English, first language acquisition, second language acquisition, World Englishes

1 Introduction

In recent times, a wave of language shifts towards English as an L1 has reached many of the third diaspora L2 English-speaking former colonies of the British Empire (e.g. Kachru, Kachru, and Nelson 2006 for the diaspora-based classification of Englishes). Singapore is one of the pioneers in this development with more than half of the younger generation acquiring and speaking English as their first and often dominant home language (Buschfeld 2020). This trend has also been observed in a variety of other Asian and African contexts (e.g. Anchimbe 2012 on Cameroon). With English mainly being acquired on the basis of contact-induced L2 language input, this development may, at first sight, appear unprecedented. However, this type of large-scale language shift also formed the basis for the ear-

---

Patricia Ronan, TU Dortmund University, Germany
Sarah Buschfeld, TU Dortmund University, Germany

https://doi.org/10.1515/9783110733723-009

lier emergence of shift-induced L1 English varieties in first diaspora contexts such as Ireland, Scotland, and Wales.

The present chapter is the first of its kind to shed light on the parallels and differences between first and third diasporic contexts in their shift from L2 to L1 English-speaking nations. It sets out to unveil the differences and similarities in the development of English from L2 to L1 in Singapore and Ireland. Due to its socio-political situation, Ireland has experienced a large-scale shift from a mainly L1 Irish-speaking to a mainly L1 English-speaking country due to the Famine from the mid-19th century (Foster 1989: 201–204). Singapore seems to have been undergoing a rapid process of language shift in recent times (cf. Schneider 2007: 157), and it has even been proposed that this might ultimately result in English monolingualism for major parts of the population (Mesthrie and Bhatt 2008: 221–222). The motives and driving forces for these developments, however, differ substantially in these two countries. We will delve into these differences but also discuss an important parallel and potentially strong factor in the process of language shift and structural change, that is the role of language acquisition in general (both first and second, and both guided and unguided) and the role of children in particular. To that end, our chapter consists of two independent studies, each of which discusses a salient characteristic of the variety in question. For Singapore English, we report on the results of a comparison of subject-pronoun realization in spoken adult and child data. We further compare the evidence of language contact and untutored acquisition of English in Ireland in the Early and Late Modern period to evidence of tutored L2 acquisition from the early 20th century. The Singaporean data come from the spoken component of the Singapore component of the International Corpus of English (an early 1990s component of the International Corpus of English, ICE-Singapore) and the CHEsS corpus (Children's English in Singapore; Buschfeld 2020). The data for Ireland come from different sources, the majority of which are represented in The Corpus of Irish English (Hickey 2003), and the Schools' Collection,[1] dating back to 1937 and 1938. Choosing one salient morphosyntactic feature in each variety, we investigate the data sets for the realization of local characteristics and compare frequencies between the adult and the child data to trace potential changes initiated by bilingual children in language contact and change scenarios.

The questions we ask in this respect are:
1. What are the mechanisms and processes behind such language change and, in the case of Ireland, language shift towards English?

---

[1] www.duchas.ie/en/cbes, accessed 6 December 2021.

2. How will the linguistic future of Singapore develop? Will the country also turn into a largely monolingual English society?

Both analyses show differences in frequency between the child and adult data and suggest that children have indeed played an important role in further rooting the contact language characteristics as widely used characteristics of Irish and Singapore English. We ultimately discuss what the Irish case can tell us about potential future developments in Singapore. The chapter therefore highlights the importance of an integrated approach to child language and the study of World Englishes to fully understand the current (and older) developments of the English language. In Section 2 we will introduce the context of Singapore English (SingE), the method used in the SingE study, and its results. Section 3 presents the case of Irish English, the method used, and its results. Section 4 provides a comparative analysis which discusses the findings against the background of earlier research on language change, and in particular, potential sources for and mechanisms at work in language change scenarios. Finally, we draw our findings together in the Conclusion section.

2 Language change and shift in new varieties of English

In the last three decades, an interesting sociolinguistic trend has emerged in a number of third diaspora L2-English countries which are former colonies of the British Empire (e.g. Kachru, Kachru, and Nelson 2006: 13–14 for the diaspora-based classification of Englishes), in particular in Southeast Asia and Africa. Rising numbers of L1 speakers of English have repeatedly been noted for countries such as Singapore (e.g., Bolton and Ng 2014; Gupta 1994; Kwan-Terry 1986; Tan 2014, among many others) and Cameroon (e.g. Anchimbe 2012). Singapore pioneers this development and is the only context for which the newly emerging L1 variety has been empirically and systematically investigated in some detail (Buschfeld 2020). As part of a large-scale study, Buschfeld (2020: Chapter 6) investigates the use of zero subject pronouns by Singaporean children of different ethnicities (Chinese, Indian, and mixed). She investigates the rates of zero subjects of four different subject pronoun types, i.e. referential subjects (*I, you, he, she, we, you, they*), and referential, contextual referential, and expletive *it*. The type "referential *it*" (also called "referring *it*") includes those uses of *it* which refer to a noun phrase. Contextual referential *it* corresponds to what Halliday and Hasan (1976: 52–53) call "extended reference" or "text reference," as some uses of it show "a greater degree of referentiality" than others. This might be, for example, someone talking about a past event that is not expressed by a single NP but by some larger entity of preceding discourse and referring back to it by *it*: *It was just perfect*. Expletive *it* (also "prop *it*") "is used as an 'empty' or 'prop' subject, especially in expressions denoting time, distance, or atmospheric conditions" (Quirk et al. 1985: 348). Buschfeld's (2020) results show that all pronouns can be realized as zero but that the use of the zero variants strongly depends on the type of pronoun type. Examples (1)–(3) illustrate some zero uses as found in the corpus.

(1) Researcher: *[. . .] And this guy is picking some flowers for his mummy and . . .*
    Child: *Now Ø [HE] is done picking the flower.*

(2) Child: *I have one friend toy. Ø [IT] Is a dog and has sparklings all over.*

(3) Researcher: *[. . .] what do you do with your friends? Do you play with them?*
    Child: *[Ø I] Play with them. Sometimes drawing. [. . .] Sometimes [Ø WE] play some fun things.*

The following study draws on the findings from Buschfeld's subject study but extends the analysis in an important way to track potential evidence of language change in SingE. As outlined in Section 2.2.1 in more detail, it compares the results from the child study to an analysis of adult data from the ICE-Singapore of the early 1990s.

2.1 Singapore English: From L2 to L1

SingE is one of the most comprehensively studied L2 varieties in the World Englishes paradigm. Singapore was under British rule for nearly 150 years (for a historical overview see, e.g. Turnbull 2017), which initially paved the way for the emergence of a contact-induced L2 variety of English. The postcolonial years, however, were responsible for the rather rapid development of SingE towards L1 status. As in other contexts around the globe, the ethnic neutrality of English and, more recently, the impact of the general forces of globalization have promoted its spread and entrenchment in Singapore. Singapore's unique language policy of "English-based bilingualism" (Tickoo 1996: 438), however, is what makes it stand out. In the perception of many Singaporeans, English is the only language directed towards the future. Some families have even given up on their ethnic languages and raise their children monolingually in English. The Straits Times, one of the leading newspapers in Singapore, lately reported that the number of Primary One students who speak mostly English at home has risen to around 70% in all three major ethnic groups, i.e. Chinese, Malay, and Indian, in Singapore (Chan 2020). This development appears unprecedented at first sight. However, when looking further back in history, a comparably spontaneous language shift from L2 to L1 English can also be observed for the case of Ireland, which is why we compare the two cases in the present chapter.

Section 2.2 presents the data and methodology of the Singapore study (Section 2.2.1) and some selected results on the realization of subject pronouns (zero vs. realized) in the two corpora under analysis (Section 2.2.2).

2.2 Language change in Singapore English

2.2.1 Data and methods

The Singapore study aims to investigate language change in SingE from both an apparent-time and real-time perspective. Presenting parts of the results from an earlier study (Weihs and Buschfeld 2021b), we look into subject pronoun realization in SingE and compare spoken data from Singaporean adults (1990s) and Singaporean children (2014). We discuss what our findings suggest about current linguistic developments in SingE (Section 2.3) and what they might predict for the linguistic future of Singapore when compared to the findings from Ireland (Section 5)[2].

The data come from the spoken part of the ICE-Singapore and the CHEsS Corpus. The CHEsS data were collected by means of different elicitation methods, namely from free interaction / spontaneous speech, a story retelling task (*The Three Little Pigs*), and the past tense probe of the Rice/Wexler Test of Early Grammatical Impairment (TEGI) (Rice and Wexler 2001). All in all, it contains data from 29 children, aged 2;5 (2 years, 5 months) to 12;1. 20 children are of Chinese origin (age median: 5;2) and 9 are of Indian ethnicity (age median: 6;3). For the present study, only the data from those 21 children older than 3;7 were considered (MLU groups 2 and 3) to avoid acquisition effects, i.e. the production of zero subjects in early phases of child language acquisition (e.g. Roeper and Rohrbacher 2000). MLU refers to Mean Length of Utterance, which is a long-established method in research on child language development to determining a child's gross language development (Brown 1973). The overall study contained two further MLU groups, i.e. group 1, which consists of children younger than 3;8, and an outlier group, both of which are not relevant for the study at hand (for further details, see Buschfeld 2020: 102–110, 156–161).

---

[2] We are grateful to Claus Weihs for his support in conducting the statistical analysis and his comments on the interpretation of the results.

MLU group 2 comprises those children aged 3;8 to 6;11, and MLU group 3 includes all children age seven and older. The sub-corpus used for this study amounts to approximately 36,000 words.

The ICE-data come from 90 transcripts of approximately 2,000 words each in the spoken component of face-to-face-conversations, all in all comprising approximately 202,000 words from 254 adults (ages 18 and over). The data from both sets were manually coded for the realization of subject pronouns (*I, you, he, she, we, you, they*, and expletive, referential, and contextual referential *it*). In total, 3,225 tokens were extracted from the child corpus, 2,899 realized and 326 zero tokens. In the adult corpus, 17,325 tokens were coded, 16,543 as realized and 782 as zero. To adjust for the high imbalance between the large and the small classes, undersampling was applied (Weihs and Buschfeld 2021b). The larger class was randomly undersampled to 6% with 999 repetitions. To adjust for the high imbalance between the child and adult data, the latter were also randomly undersampled to match the size of the child corpus with 10 repetitions (for further details, see Weihs and Buschfeld 2021b). To statistically model the influence of a number of predictor variables, the PrInTD approach (Weihs and Buschfeld 2021a), which is based on decision trees (ctrees, Hothorn, Hornik, and Zeileis 2006), was applied. Table 9.1 summarizes the variables, their levels, and the abbreviations used in the decision trees.

Table 9.1: Overview of variables modelled in PrInDT.

Variable type	Variable	Levels	Abbreviation	Explanations
dependent	class	realized, zero	PRN_TYPE	
independent	pronoun type	referential (refer), demonstrative (dem), expletive *it* (*it*_ex), referential *it* (*it*_ref), contextual referential *it* (*it*_con)		
	mean length of utterance	2, 3, adult	MLU	the levels for the adult speakers (from the 1990s ICE-Sing) are one-way manifestations since the corpus lacks the kind of sociolinguistic information available for CHEsS
	(ethnic) group	Chinese children (C), Indian children (I), adults (n_a)	ETHN_GROUP	
	age	in months of the individual child; for all adults 216 months (numeric)	AGE	

All results (ctrees) were generated by means of the R-function PrInDT (Weihs and Buschfeld 2021a) in R (R Core Team 2019) using the R-package 'party'. In the following, we report the best tree from nested undersampling (Weihs and Buschfeld 2021b), which has a balanced accuracy of 0.6635. The significance level was set to 0.05.

2.2.2 Results

Let us now turn to the results of the study in order to determine how language change may be proceeding in SingE. As Figure 9.1 illustrates, the strongest predictor for subject pronoun realization in the child and adult corpora is pronoun type. In Node 1, the data are split into the three types of *it* on the one hand and referential pronouns and demonstratives on the other. For *it*, the realization further depends on the group of speakers (Node 2). As a comparison of Nodes 3 and 4 reveals, the rate of zero realizations is much higher for both groups of children (≤ 145 months = Indian and Chinese children) than for the adults (>145). In general, Figure 9.1 shows that zero subject pronouns are most frequently used for *it* (all three types) by the Chinese and Indian children.

For referential and demonstrative pronouns, the data are further split by MLU (Node 5). Interestingly, the older children (MLU 3), i.e. those 7 years and older, are grouped with the adults (for a discussion why, see Section 2.3). MLU group 2 is further split by AGE at 66 months (Node 13). The fact that the older children are the ones that realize zero pronouns significantly more frequently than the younger ones might seem surprising against the background of the theoretical finding that normally the younger children go through a zero-subject phase in language acquisition. However, this finding can be explained on the basis of the data set since the MLU group 2 children older than 66 months all speak Chinese, and thus a null subject language, as their other L1.

The group of adults and MLU 3 children is then split by pronoun type again (Node 6). For demonstrative pronouns, the rate of zero subjects is extremely low so that the group 3 children and adults hardly ever use zero pronouns of this type (Node 7). Whether the group 3 children and adults realize referential pronouns or make use of the zero variant further depends on the speaker group again (Node 8). Here, the Chinese children perform significantly differently from the Indian children, and the adults in that the former have a stronger inclination towards zero subjects than the two other groups;[3] this does not necessarily contradict the

---

[3] We deliberately leave out an interpretation of node 10 since this split represents individual children only and does not contribute to our general discussion.

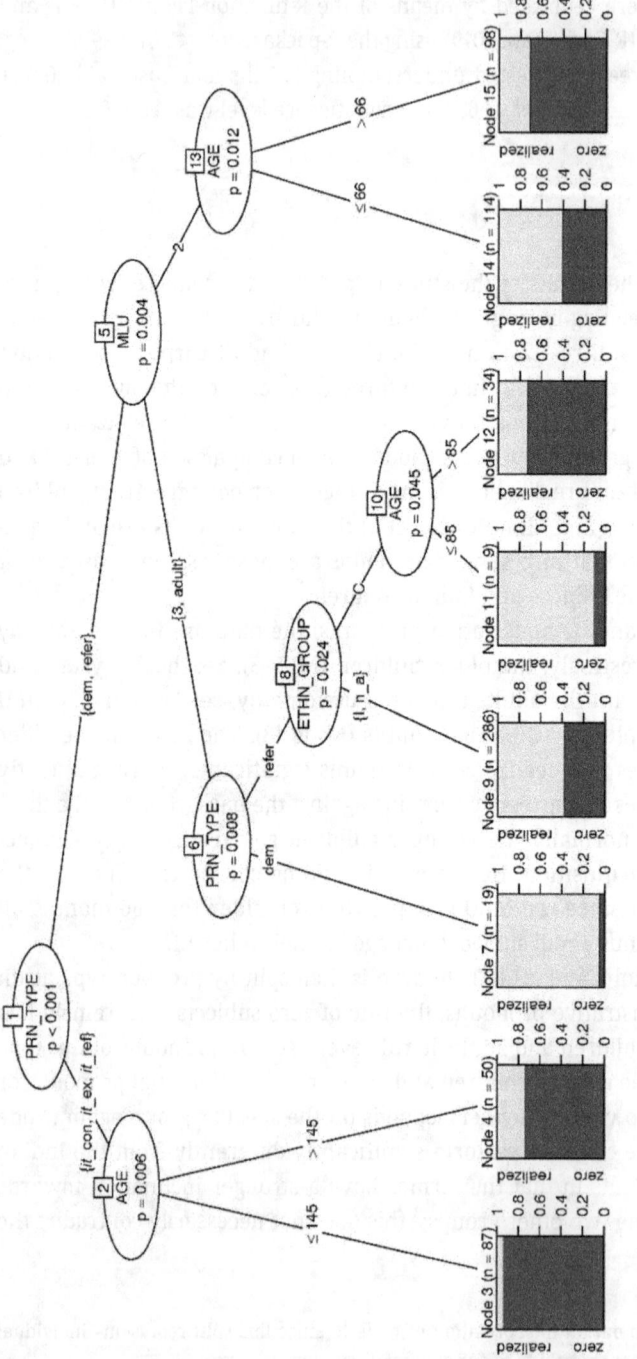

Figure 9.1: Zero vs. realized expletive *it* in the child and adult corpora.

finding that important differences in zero realization exist between the child and 1990s adult data as is discussed in the following section (2.3).

2.3 Discussion of results: Language change in Singapore English

In the following, we discuss what the findings presented in Section 2.2.2, and in particular the statistically significant differences between the children and adults, suggest about language change in Singapore. However, before jumping to overly strong conclusions, one potential caveat has to be taken into consideration, namely possible task/corpus effects. The ICE data are well known to be situated on the standard end of the lectal cline. They might therefore be more acrolectal than our child data. Still, we argue that the differences are too strong to be due to a corpus or task effect only, and that the fact that younger speakers use considerably more zero subjects than older speakers can be interpreted as first evidence for ongoing language change in Singapore (cf. Fuchs and Gut 2015 for a similar line of argumentation with respect to Nigerian English).

The type of linguistic discontinuity between generations as observed in the data at hand has been reported as characterizing contact scenarios (cf. Kerswill et al. 2013: 266) and age has been identified as an important factor in initiating and advancing language change (e.g. Fuchs and Gut 2015; Labov 1994; Tagliamonte and Hudson 1999). The questions that arise from these observations are the following:
1. Do the differences between the adults and children occur as the result of an age-graded difference which will level out again?
2. Who initiates internally motivated language change? Is it young children during first language acquisition, or adults, or both? (for a detailed discussion see, e.g. Thomason 2013)
3. Can children be considered the driving forces of language change?

All three questions are of a somewhat speculative nature. We still try to assess them in turn, on the basis of the findings from our study as well as earlier findings and theoretical considerations.

Concerning question 1, age-grading has been prominently reported in the sociolinguistic literature (e.g. Wagner 2012). It is generally not unlikely to be a factor in Singapore, especially since the government strongly propagates the use of standard SingE. The Speak Good English Movement, for example, generally "prohibits" the use of vernacular features such as zero subjects. Adults are certainly more strongly affected by governmental norm regulations. Such conscious orientation towards linguistic norms, which are quite prominent for Singaporean adults (cf.

Vida-Mannl, this volume), are less pronounced in children. Still, it has been shown that even young children are not free of attitudes towards language (e.g. Carroll 2017: 12). The question whether age-grading will play a role in the case of Singapore cannot be answered conclusively as it will depend on the children's linguistic development and future norm orientation. However, our results provide some first evidence in this respect if we take a closer look at Nodes 2 and 5 in our ctree (Figure 9.1). As briefly described in the preceding section, a significant split can be observed between the adults and children for the pronouns *it*. This points towards language change in terms of the use of zero subjects for these types of pronouns. The percentages of zero expletive *it* vs. realized expletive *it*, for example, reinforce this assumption, since the difference between the adults and children is immense, namely 45.8% zero for the child group vs. 7.8% for the adults (measured on the basis of the overall token frequencies). We argue that this difference is too prominent to be due to age-grading only. Still, the ctree also reveals evidence in favor of age-grading in Node 5 (Figure 9.1). With referential and demonstrative pronouns, the oldest child cohort (7+ years = MLU 3) behaves similarly to the adults and together they show a significant difference towards the younger children. This suggests that language change occurs for the referential, expletive, and contextual referential pronouns *it* (see Footnote 3 for further explanation) but not for the rest of the pronouns, for which an age-grading effect can be observed. The reasons why this change can be observed for *it* seem to be only intralinguistic in nature. It comes as no surprise that the rate of zero subject pronoun realization is highest for the semantically empty "dummy *it*" (expletive *it*) since these forms have no reference. Their only function is to occupy the subject position in a language that traditionally requires a subject pronoun for full grammaticality (cf. Valian 2016: 387). What is remarkable, though, is that the differences between expletive *it* and the other two types are rather marginal and that referential *it* behaves so differently from the other referential pronouns. This observation is interesting because the three types of *it* are so different in terms of their degree of anaphoric reference and semantic meaning. The similarities in behavior must therefore be due to the phonological similarities between the three types (see also Buschfeld 2020: 182) and phonological assimilation/elision in forms such as *it's*, which are frequent in spoken discourse.

Questions 2 and 3 have been the at the core of some dispute. Still, a number of approaches have attributed an important role to children in language change scenarios. As Roberts (2013: 264) points out "[t]he foundations for adolescent, and adult, speech patterns are laid down in childhood, during the early language acquisition process, and it would appear useful to look to the dialects of children for answers to some of the questions of linguistic variation and change". In general, younger speakers are considered to represent a more advanced stage in ongoing language change, older speakers represent an earlier stage (e.g. Boberg 2004; Fuchs and Gut 2015:

383). Furthermore, Meisel (2011) assumes that if L2 speakers constitute the only or strongly predominant input for children acquiring the same language as an L1, the input they receive can contain the triggers for language change. In our case, the input Singaporean children receive provides competing forms (beyond what is found in the traditional L1 varieties of English) and therefore holds the potential for language change to take place. Of course, whether language change ultimately takes place depends on what the children choose from the input and which variants ultimately win. This, in turn, depends on extra- as well as intra-linguistic mechanisms such as cross-linguistic influence, homogenization tendencies, norm orientations, attitudes and use, and modes of acquisition, in particular the question whether the languages are acquired in tutored or untutored ways.

In our concrete example, zero subjects originate in adult L2 SingE and are the results of language contact and (mostly) untutored language acquisition (here, L2 acquisition). In Section 2.2, we observed differences in the realization of zero *it* (referential, expletive, contextual referential) between the adult and child data sets, which suggest that these characteristics have become even more deeply entrenched in the child generation. This is due to the fact that they not only emerge as the result of contact effects but are available in the input the children receive via zero subjects in the adult language; this input is ultimately reinforced by mechanisms of language contact and language acquisition. In the bilingual first language acquisition scenario of English in Singapore, many of the characteristics found in the parents' input (resulting from transfer and other mechanisms of L2 acquisition) correspond to the typical characteristics of early language acquisition (here: zero subjects). The children therefore receive positive evidence for these early productions in the input they receive. This might prolong, if not stabilize, the use of these characteristics. What is more, cross-linguistic influence from the other languages the children speak, which once constituted the sources for transfer in the evolution of L2 SingE, further reinforces the particular characteristics the children find in their input. More precisely, if the input the children receive, for example, contains the information that both zero and realized subject pronouns are potential options and the other language the child speaks allows for either the same options or just the zero option, this can have another amplifying effect on the use of zero subjects (cf. Hulk and Müller's 2000 structural overlap/ ambiguity hypothesis). L1 SingE therefore seems to have emerged as the product of the peculiar sociolinguistic ecologies of Singapore, language contact, and an unprecedented "acquisition chain," including effects of mainly untutored second language acquisition (as transmitted through the adult input) and first language acquisition. Both processes are, in turn, influenced by particular mechanisms of language contact, transfer/cross-linguistic influence, and other effects of language acquisition.

We thus agree that Meisel (2011: 121) brings forward an important point when he states that "[i]f [. . .] children receive sustained input from second language learners," this input can contain the triggers for grammatical change. The data at hand clearly point in that direction. However, to our knowledge, so far not much further evidence exists to empirically corroborate this assumption. Let us therefore look into the case of Irish English, a much older L1 variety of English, which experienced a language shift from an L2 to L1 status when L2 SingE was still in its infancy.

3 Irish English

Like Scotland and Wales, Ireland belongs to the first countries to have experienced an influx of colonizers and settlers from England. When these colonizers first reached Ireland in the late twelfth century, they were led by Anglo-Norman nobles, who spoke French rather than English. These French speakers were mainly accompanied by English speakers from lower social classes. The Anglo-Norman nobles largely integrated into the Irish-speaking society of their social peers in Ireland. English was a language used by members of lower and professional classes, while Irish remained an upper-class and prestige language. This changed from the 14th century onwards, when the British crown put increasing pressure on the nobles to denounce Irish customs, Irish names, and the Irish language, which many of the English settlers had adopted. During the 17th century, British efforts in this were redoubled when large-scale colonialization went under way in Ireland, starting in the northern provinces, where settlers mainly from northern England and Scotland were settled, and continuing in the southern provinces in the latter part of the century with the settlement of British colonizers predominantly from more southerly parts of Britain. Given the growing English-speaking population groups, military exploits, and political pressure from Britain, the use of English increased during the next centuries, particularly in urban areas in the east of the country, while Irish was increasingly relegated to rural, especially western areas. As social advancement was tied to competences in the English language, especially the 18th and 19th centuries saw large scale language shifts from Irish to English. Before the introduction of the National School system, English language acquisition was often from other second-language speakers and often in what is known as *hedge schools*, which were non-established, locally run schools, for non-Anglicans, who were excluded from formal education. The acquisition of English from other L1 Irish speaking teachers led to a strong influence of the Irish language during this foundation phase of Irish English. In the middle of the 19th century, the rural areas, particularly in the west of the country, were especially badly hit by the potato blight, which lead to a severe famine and massive depopulation, particularly in these Irish speaking areas, resulting in a drop of the overall numbers of Irish speakers from a half to a little more than a quarter of the population. Political changes from the late 19th century caused a surge in interest in the Irish language and from the foundation of the Irish Free State in 1921 onwards, the state has been giving strong financial and ideological support to Irish language teaching and the preservation of Irish-language culture. In spite of these efforts, in recent years the number of Irish speakers has been declining and Irish as a community language is endangered. English, officially the second language of the state, predominates (cf. Hickey 2007: 30–76; Kallen 2013: 2–38; Ronan 2017, 2020).

Typical features of Irish English partly derive from language contact with the Irish language. Similar to the situation in contemporary Singapore, the English language in Ireland was acquired in a language shift context, where linguistic influences from Irish were replicated repeatedly (Filppula 1999; Hickey 2007). This facilitated the inclusion of language contact features in Irish English. However, other features that are typical of Irish English are also, at least partly, derivable from the input variety of English in Ireland: 17th century varieties of English provided models of English language use which have been retained in Irish English. A good example of this can be found in the constituent order of auxiliary verbs, object, and past participle in what is often referred to as the Medial Object Perfect (MOP; Filppula 1999), as in *I have my dinner eaten*. In Irish English, this is typically considered a result-state perfect. Other features, however, seem to derive clearly from Irish language models. One of these features is not only highly salient, but also frequent. This is known as the *after*-perfect, which is typically considered a hot-news perfect, a perfect of recency (Filppula 1999), which is clearly based on the analogy of similar expressions of recency in Irish (Example 4):

(4) *Tá sé tréis marú* [Is-he-after-dying] 'He is after dying (i.e. *he just died*)'.

The Irish and Irish English *after*-perfect does not denote intentionality, but recently completed events. Some speakers of contemporary Irish English even extend the use of the *after*-perfect to completed events (*I'm after paying 12 pounds for a pram for Tony forty-seven years ago . . .*; Ronan 2005: 263). *The after-* perfect and the MOP are used to express specific semantics within the meaning range of the English perfect. By contrast, the Standard English (StE) perfect is often used to express the current relevance of a situation, for example *'tis come bourying you are de corp, . . ., of a verie good woman, . . ., fwom cruel deat hate devoure* ('you have come here to bury the corpse of a very good woman whom cruel death has devoured,' Report of a Sermon), i.e. "you are here because she has died". Thus generally, the *after*-perfect more specifically denotes "hot news," while the MOP expresses a result-state deriving from a preceding event (Filppula 1999).

In the current case study, we will investigate the usage patterns of these highly emblematic perfect structures in the early Irish English shift variety and compare them to their use in 20th century bilingual varieties in order to illustrate how this feature has developed in the stabilization of the variety.

3.1 Investigating language shift in Ireland: Data and method

3.1.1 Data sources

The Irish English data used for this study predominantly stems from two different types of sources. Data from the language-shift period of Irish English is represented by literary representations of Irish English. Such data has been collected in Bliss (1979). The data is not unproblematic as the literary representation of the variety is typically found in works of British English authors, whose aim may be to create a comical effect rather than a faithful representation of the variety. Particularly in literary representations of Irish English, we have to be aware of the danger that salient features of the variety may be overrepresented, and less salient features may not be transmitted. However, the representation of salient features, particularly if they are cross-validated by their representation in different sources, has the advantage of showing unambiguously what is perceived as typical of a given variety. Thus, even potentially biased literary data can give us a good insight into typical features of a variety of a language. The texts used here represent a subsection of texts of which 7 can also be found in Hickey's (2003) Corpus of Irish English. In addition to representations of Irish English by English authors, 2 literary representations by Irish authors (Banim; Boucicault) have been added. In each of these instances, only representations of Irish English are taken into consideration and representations of British English are not considered. The texts, their provenance, and their word count are given in Table 9.2. The word total is 10,562 words.

The data set displays typical Irish English features. These are in particular a large amount of Irish pragmatic markers, which are found as code-switches in the data. Features of Irish pronunciation are very clearly displayed in the shape of eye-dialect: here we find, in particular, the representation of the voiced bilabial fricative /w/ as <v> or <f>, voiced and voiceless dental fricatives being represented as corresponding stops <t, d>, and occasional representation of /s/ as /ʃ/ by using the spelling (cf. Hickey 2007), for example *tauke a pot of drenk vid him, [. . .], vile he did mauke request to shom Skrivishner to vrite a Letter* (Bog Witticims). Beyond these, morphosyntactic features expressing the tense- and aspect system of Irish

Table 9.2: Sources of literary representation of early Irish English data.

Text	Date	Number of words	Source
Bog Witticisms	1687	611	Bliss 1979
The Irish Hudibras	1689	842	Bliss 1979
The Irishmen's Prayers	1689	605	Bliss 1979
Report of a Sermon, John Dunton	1689	1479 (some in Latin)	Bliss 1979
The Twin Rivals, George Farquhar	1702/1703	757 (vernacular data only)	Bliss 1979
Ireland Preserved, John Michelburne	1705	1443	Bliss 1979
A Dialogue between Teigue and Dermot	1713	740	Bliss 1979
The Rival Dreamers, John Banim	1865	1969 (vernacular data only)	The Bit o' Writin, Dublin 1865
Shaughraun, Act 1, Sc. 1, Dion Boucicault	1874	2116 (vernacular data only)	The Shaughraun. 1885.

English are prominently displayed, including the *after*-perfect, whose use is investigated here. As the complete envelope of variation (Labov 1969) between *after*-perfect and StE *have* and *is* perfects has been manually annotated and considered, the data set had to be short to allow workability of the data.

The second main data set stems from a collection of oral folklore, which took place in Ireland in the 1930s, the so-called Schools' Collection. Here, school pupils collected oral folklore in their area of residence. Collections are both in Irish and in English. Materials from completely Irish-speaking areas are in Irish throughout, those from monolingually English-speaking areas are in English. For our purposes the most interesting are those materials that stem from bilingual or recent language shift areas. In areas which are considered English speaking, schooling will be through English, but a proximity of Irish speaking areas, as well as potential bilingualism in parts of the community will result in pupils having competencies in both English and Irish that go beyond school knowledge. The area that has been selected for investigation here, Roundstone, is in County Galway, close to some of the strongest Irish-speaking areas in the country. Recent bilingualism in the investigated community is evidenced by various factors. One factor is that one of the 45 texts is in fact in Irish and included in the collection. Two texts have Irish titles but are in English, suggesting both the availability of the same text in

Irish within the community and recent translation into English. The other factor is that a number of code-switches into Irish can be observed in the texts.

Unfortunately, the age of the school pupils who wrote down the tales is not given, nor is it known whether the original sources of the data were quoted verbatim or whether summaries were recorded in the students' own words. In any event, the language recorded by the pupils will represent language use in the community which the pupils were exposed to at the time. The materials of the Schools' Collection have recently been digitized and are available online at www.duchas.ie/en/cbes. The Roundstone materials consist of 45 short oral narratives, recorded in the years 1937 and 1938, and run to a total of 13,588 words. They represent language use in a predominantly English-speaking community, where Irish still has a presence, so Irish will not only be a school subject, but will also be familiar to the pupils as a community language.

3.1.2 Methods used

In this study, only one of the most salient features of Irish English deriving from language shift from Irish is discussed. This is the use of the most salient dialectal alternatives to the StE perfect, namely the *after*-perfect and the Medial Object Perfect (MOP).

Examples of the *after*-perfect and the MOP were manually identified and recorded in the data sources. Instances where alternatives to the dialectal perfects could have been used, in particular the Standard English *have* perfect, and the relative variation between these variants is determined. In this study, specific Irish English forms of perfect formation that do not contain perfect marking, like experiential *did you ever see* or *I am living there twenty-four years*, have not been considered in the envelope of variation. The factors that are used in the analysis of the perfects have previously been found to have an influence on the use of Irish English (IrE) perfect selection (Ronan 2005). In particular these are the semantic value that is expressed (recency/result-state/present relevance) and the morphological complexity of the verb phrase. Morphological complexity results when the verbal group includes modal verbs, such as *she could have filled it just as easy*, Sch0007_074, or a past tense marker, for example *[w]hen they had gone the man got a bottle of the water*, Sch0007_052. In preparation for the analysis, the data have been coded for the century of their attestation, the type of perfect used, apparent core semantic features of current relevance, recency / "hot news" or focus on result of the action. The data were also marked for the social status of the speaker, but this proved not to play a statistically significant role. The statistical approach used here predicts whether a dialectal or a StE perfect form will be used. As in the investigation of the Singapore data, ctrees were also created for this task using the R-package 'party'. Table 9.3 summarizes the variables used in the decision trees.

Table 9.3: Variables used in the Irish English perfect decision trees.

Variable type	Variable	Levels	Abbreviation	Explanations
dependent	class	StE perfect, dialectal perfect (*after*-perfect, Medial Object perfect)		
independent	semantic value	recency (Rec), result (Result), present relevance (*PresRel*)	SemValue (Rec, Result, PresRel)	
	Present Day Irish English	Present Day Irish English (20th century), non-PDIrE (17th, 18th, 19th century)	PDIrE	nodes marked *1* for PDIrE and *0* for non-PDIrE
	complexity	modal auxiliary, past auxiliary, no further tense, mood, aspect modification	(Mod, Past, Simple)	

3.2 Results

In the Irish English data in general, we find StE perfect and non-StE perfect formations. In the early, literary data, in line with the English standards of the period, StE perfects either use the auxiliary *have* for transitive verbs (*Y have geeven de Vaaterman Shixpensh*, Bog Witticisms) or the auxiliary *be* for intransitive verbs (*he will soon run away Ven he hears dat Duke Scomberg and his Army is come*, Irishman's Prayer). As a non-standard form in the early Irish data we find the *after*-perfect. In particular, the *after*-perfect is used in the early data to express the result of an event (*you shee here de cause dat is after bringing you to dis plaace*, i.e. 'the cause that has resulted in you being here,' Report of a Sermon). The use of *after*-perfects is statistically significantly conditioned by denoting recency throughout the data (X-squared = 7.3502, df = 1, p-value = 0.006705). However, a number of these *after*-perfect markers are used in a way that is puzzling from a contemporary perspective, especially where used together with the StE present perfect marker (*his Graash Tir-cannel fill not let de Officer go in Brogue, he has been after wearing dem himself*, Ireland Preserved) or with future- or volition marker *will* (*de Priest fill not be after give us de Absolushon widout dem*, Ireland Preserved).

In the present-day Irish English data, we find both StE *have* perfects, and *after*-perfects. These are joined by a further form, the MOP (Filppula 1999), which denotes a state resulting from a previous action (*When they had enough of them picked they went into a graveyard and began counting them*, Sch0007_062). The expression of result-states is significantly frequently carried out by MOP rather than StE perfects (X-squared = 8.8896, df = 1, p-value = 0.002868). However, the MOP is not found in the literary Early Irish English data. This may be due to the fact that similar structures were previously used in British English as well, and they might thus not have been considered worthy of stereotyping literary representation. In Figure 9.2, we present a ctree modelling the significant factors predicting the choice of either a StE perfect form or one of the dialectal variants. The significance level of the model is set at 0.05.

The ctree in Figure 9.2 shows that throughout the data, we find a statistically highly significant difference in the expression of StE Perfect versus non-StE Perfects: Node 1 shows that for the expression of present relevance, the StE (*have*) perfect is used exclusively (Node 7, p < 0.001). For meanings of recency or result, Node 2 shows that usages in Irish English pattern significantly differently in Present Day Irish English and earlier Irish English (p = 0.004). While Present Day Irish English (PDIrE) uses *after*-, MOP and StE perfects (Node 6), the MOP is not found in the early IrE data. This earlier data set does show significant preferences according to complexity of the verbal group (Node 3; p = 0.03). *After*-perfects are mainly used with a modal verb (Node 4) and StE perfects without modal verbs and with past tense auxiliaries (Node 5). With a balanced accuracy of 0.834, this model offers a good fit of the decisions taken.

At this point, let us take a look at the individual factors that may be responsible for the distribution of StE perfects shown in Nodes 4 and 6. When doing so, we find that in early IrE, present relevance is mainly expressed by StE perfect forms, but that the expression of recency and result allow for both StE and non-StE forms. In the PDIrE data, by contrast, present relevance is consistently expressed by the StE form, and recency and result are quite consistently expressed by non-StE forms. StE perfect forms are used where past perfects and modal perfects are used, even where recency or result is expressed (Examples (5) and (6)). By contrast, in the early IrE data, a StE perfect may also express current relevance or recency (Examples (7) and (8))

(5) *After a while the robbers came and when they saw some one had eaten the food they thought it was the peelers so they were on the watch* (Sch0007_007)

(6) [. . .] *but then he said to himself, if only I had a bigger pail she could have filled it just as easy* (Sch0007_074).

9 From second to first language: Language shift in Singapore and Ireland — 195

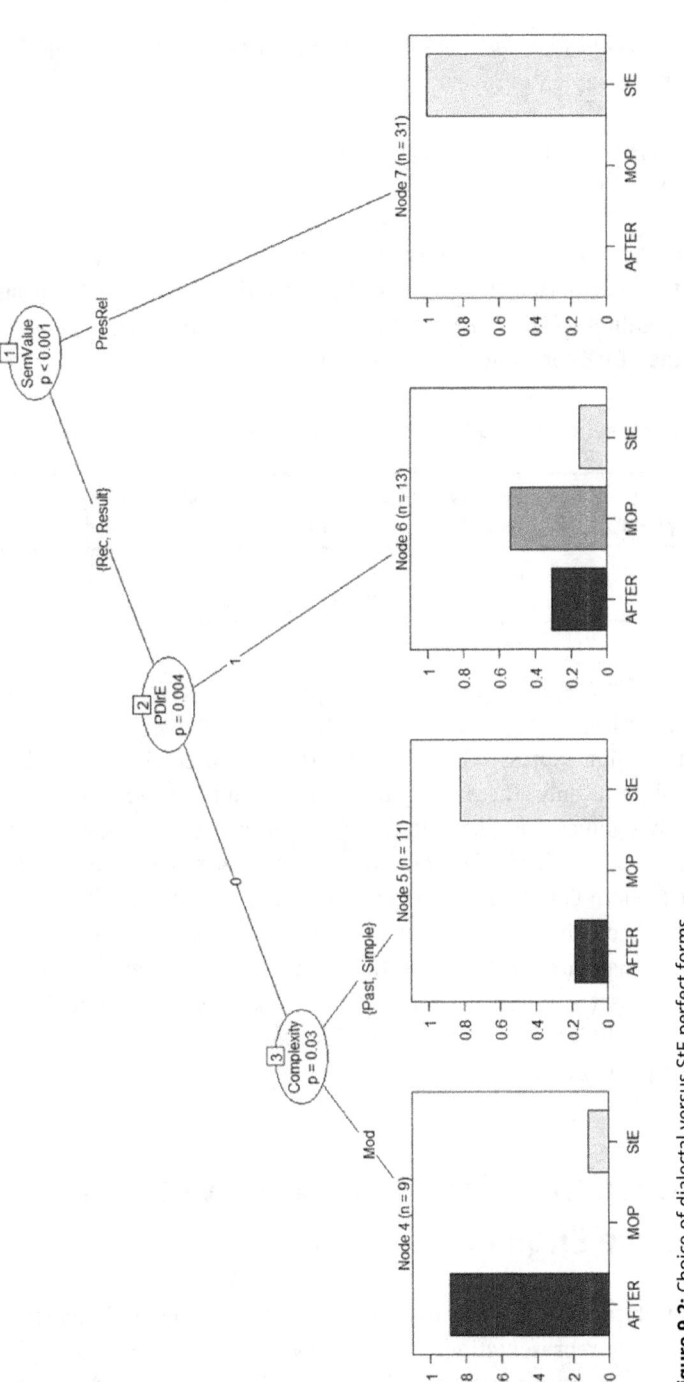

Figure 9.2: Choice of dialectal versus StE perfect forms.

(7) *King Yeamus he will soon run away Ven he hears dat Duke Scomberg and his Army is come* (Irishmen's Prayer)

(8) *I'm sure the Croon pieceish are awake, for I have been taaking with dem dish half hour* (Twin Rivals)

These examples illustrate that parameters in the choice of forms vary between the earlier and the later period. Table 9.4 shows attestation figures of the forms in the corpus depending on their semantic value and on whether they belong to the early IrE or the PDIrE component of the data.

Table 9.4: Distribution of raw frequencies StE versus non-StE perfects in the early IrE and PDIrE data.

	Present relevance early data	Recency or result early data	Present relevance PDIrE data	Recency or result PDIrE data
StE form	18	9	14	2
NonStE form	1	9	0	11

Table 9.4 shows a difference in frequencies of StE and non-StE perfect forms. We see that while presence relevance is fairly consistently expressed by the StE perfect, recency or result are at first expressed by both standard and dialectal forms and then largely by dialectal forms only. These differences, albeit with low token frequencies are also statistically significant in line with the results of the ctree and suggest that the PDIrE use the non-Standard *after-* and Medial Object perfects is rule based, whereas the Late Modern English (LModE) use may not be fully rule based yet.

Overall, this section shows us that for meanings of recency or result in the Present Day Irish English data, the dialectal variant of the perfect, the *after-*perfect or Medial Object Perfect are likely to be chosen, whereas Early Irish English shows more variation and aspectual modification of the verbal group by modal verbs is frequently found.

4 Discussion: Can Ireland help predict the future of Singapore English?

The Irish data on perfect use is not entirely unproblematic as the early material derives from a literary representation of the variety. It is nevertheless useful in showing us what was perceived as salient about the dialect. Moreover, the dialectal uses of the early IrE perfect broadly resemble those in the PDIrE data: dialectal perfects are used for the specific semantic expression of recency and resultatives; StE perfects predominate for present relevance of an action. This observation provides additional evidence for the broad authenticity of the earlier data. The evidence of the earlier and the PD varieties indicates more variation in the earlier data than in the latter. This may be partly due to the variability of the language use of the speakers of the early dialect, who speak a shift variety which represents language change in progress. But the fact that the chroniclers of the dialect were not speakers of the variety themselves may also play a role as the writers may not be presenting the variety faithfully. By contrast, the clearly distributed post-language shift data of 20th century adolescent language users from a bilingual community suggests rule-governed language use, which follows a variety-internal grammar that has been set due to prolonged language contact with the Irish language. As a result, this contact variety of PDIrE retains salient features of the variety, which are paralleled by structural features in the contact language, Irish.

The role of children in this process may be two-fold: on the one hand, the school-aged English language users, who are the source of the 20th century data, build their own grammar of English on the basis of the input of adult language users. On the other hand, the pupils themselves are also exposed to the Irish language and its grammatical features both in school and evidently partly in the community as well. That the Irish language still was a community language is suggested by the Irish language materials which form part of the corpus. The adolescents thus possess bilingual repertoires and their language use shows the effects of both bilingual language acquisition and of their resulting bilingual repertoire on the use of their variety of English.

Despite the fact that much of what has been discussed above remains speculative in nature, the results lend further support to the position that children play a role in language change. Their role is certainly neither exclusive nor sufficient. Still, the data and results of the studies at hand leave no doubt as to their potential involvement. Some further assumptions and observations, coming from different linguistic fields, corroborate the general observation that children are strongly involved in language change and therefore further support our interpretation. From the perspective of new dialect formation, Schreier (2013: 155), for example, notes that "[d]ialects mix and interact as speakers accommodate to each other, which is why new-dialect formation (or koinéization) is particularly strong when children grow up in a multi-dialectal environment" (see also Kerswill et al. 2013). From a broader sociolinguistic perspective, linguistic variability within and between generations has been argued and shown to be indicative of language change ever since the early publications of Labov. We therefore suggest we may be observing language change in the making – change that is actually at its peak – in Singapore, with the child generation currently in the process of negotiating the structures of the emerging L1 variety, potentially involving major typological changes in SingE (when compared to the traditional L1 Englishes). Age-grading has been identified as an important variable in this process and for the interpretation of our results, but some of the differences found for the child and adult language productions appear to be too strong to be simply the result of age-grading.

The future development of SingE will, at least to some extent, also depend on whether and to what extent the government upholds the clear-cut distinction between Colloquial Singapore English (CSE) / Singlish on the one hand and Standard Singapore English (SSE) on the other and continues propagating the use of the latter. At some point, the children will enter the school system and become active members of the overall society. As such, they might be more and more frequently confronted with the more standard realizations of the language and the strong governmental opposition to the non-standard realizations of SingE. This clearly shows that predicting the future of SingE is indeed an intricate issue, depending on many linguistic as well as sociopolitical factors and developments. Still, the leveling of SSE and CSE contrasts has been observed before. Ansaldo (2004: 147), for example, observes that young Singaporeans, even of medium- to well-educated status, tend to use less acrolectal versions of SingE than speakers of previous generations and of a similar background (see also Buschfeld 2020). He claims that "for these students, the contrast between StdE and SE [referring to a mesolectal variety] is often blurred" and he also aptly points out: "Languages go their own ways, whether we like it or not" (Ansaldo 2004: 147). Or, as Carroll (2017: 13) states with reference to the example of Hebrew: language cannot be frozen in time, preserved as "spoken by the last of the original native speakers. Exposure makes it possible but learners themselves decide what input they will make use of". It will be interesting to see which way SingE will go in that respect. If it follows the example of the development of Irish English, it may happen that SingE focuses on select, salient features, which have parallel structures in its contact languages.

Finally, we briefly address another issue related to the future of SingE, one that has arisen and has been discussed against the backdrop of the sociolinguistic developments observed in Singapore. Might Singapore ultimately develop into a mainly monolingual English country? Of course, this is again hard to predict, but similar large-scale language shift towards English has occurred as in the example of Ireland; such a development therefore cannot be excluded in principle. As Romaine (2013: 455) points out, "[l]anguage shift generally involves bilingualism (often with diglossia) as a stage on the way to eventual monolingualism in a new language. Typically a community which was once monolingual becomes bilingual as a result of contact with another (usually socially more powerful) group and becomes transitionally bilingual in the new language until their own language is given up altogether".

For the time being, bilingualism – especially Mandarin-English bilingualism – seems to be increasing in Singapore as the result of governmental campaigns and the country is far away from monolingualism. Still, some of the parents in the Singapore study clearly expressed the opinion that they believe it is much more important to put emphasis on the acquisition of English, as individual future success and national competitiveness depend on proficiency in English. This attitude is clearly also confirmed by the questionnaire study in Buschfeld's (2020) study which shows that the majority of the children acquire and speak English as their dominant language. However, this does not necessarily lead to strict monolingualism. Once more, the development of this issue will strongly depend on the future linguistic courses taken by the government and the influence this will have on the language attitudes and linguistic practices of the population as a whole.

On the basis of what we see in the comparison of the earlier Irish English language shift data and the 20th century data from a community that was still bilingual at that time, we would assume that in the earlier phases of bilingualism strong language contact features will be visible which, when language shift is completed, may end up leading to a clearly defined grammar of the new L1 variety of English. As we have seen in the example of Ireland and, even if at a far earlier stage in L1 SingE, these local characteristics are amalgamated both from StE and from the grammars of the contact languages. A variety like Irish English, where a large-scale language shift has taken place, may show us a possible endpoint of such a language shift, while a variety where language change – and maybe ultimately shift – is in progress, like Singapore, can illustrate some of the mechanisms at work.

5 Conclusion

This study has set out to illustrate differences and similarities in the patterns of two language contact varieties of English, one of which has experienced large-scale language shift towards English and the other one may be on its way towards such shift. The Irish English data, with due consideration of the shortcomings of the early parts of the data set, indicate that the grammar of this variety has been stabilizing during the language shift phase and the 20th century data illustrate this endpoint of language shift. The data from the still bilingual community show that features are rule governed on the basis of a grammar that is an amalgamation of the grammars of the contact varieties. The Singapore data illustrate clearly how grammatical change is taking place in young and very young speakers of Singapore English. From a more general perspective, our comparative study illustrates the role children and adolescents play in language change and shift.

Of course, the above elaborations can only offer sketches of a complex and important matter that clearly deserves more detailed attention, not only in the context of Singapore and Ireland but in general. We hope that future research pays some further attention to the empirical investigation of such issues in the Singaporean context and wherever else new L1 varieties of English are emerging since these emerging L1 contexts offer the rare opportunity to investigate language change in progress. Furthermore, understanding such contexts will help us foresee the complex future development of the English language in general, caught between tendencies of globalization (and thus homogenization) and, probably even more importantly, localization and thus linguistic fragmentation.

We have further shown how a joint approach between World Englishes, sociolinguistics, and language acquisition research as well as diachronic and synchronic investigation can contribute to a better and deeper understanding of the intricate processes and mechanisms involved in the study of language change in English. We have presented ways to methodologically meet the intricate task of sketching these changes and developments by drawing on a number of very different data sources. For the Singapore study, adult and child data collected at different points in times (across roughly two generations) were compared. By doing so, we have combined apparent-time and real-time perspectives. For the IrE study, we have drawn on historical written data, as no spoken data were available. This was born out of necessity, but we have demonstrated how and why these data are still fruitful sources for studying language change.

References

Anchimbe, Eric A. 2012. Language contact in a postcolonial setting: Research approaches to Cameroon English and Cameroon Pidgin English. In Eric A. Anchimbe (ed.), *Language contact in a postcolonial setting: The linguistic and social context of English and pidgin in Cameroon*, 3–26. Berlin & Boston: De Gruyter Mouton.

Ansaldo, Umberto. 2004. The evolution of Singapore English. Finding the matrix. In Lisa Lim (ed.), *Singapore English: A grammatical description*, 127–149. Amsterdam, Philadelphia, PA: John Benjamins.

Banim, John. 1865 [1838]. The Rival Dreamers. *The bit o' writin*. Dublin: Duffy & Co.

Bliss, Alan. 1979. *Spoken English in Ireland, 1600–1740: Twenty-seven representative texts*. London: Prometheus Books.

Boberg, Charles. 2004. Real and apparent time in language change: Late adoption of changes in Montreal English. *American Speech* 79 (3). 250–269.

Bolton, Kingsley & Bee Chin Ng. 2014. The dynamics of multilingualism in contemporary Singapore. *World Englishes* 33 (3). 307–318.

Boucicault, Dion. 1885. *The Shaughraun*. New York: Samuel French & Son.

Brown, Roger. 1973. *A first language: The early stages*. London: George Allen & Unwin.
Buschfeld, Sarah. 2020. *Children's English in Singapore: Acquisition, properties, and use*. London: Routledge.
Carroll, Susanne E. 2017. Exposure and input in bilingual development. *Bilingualism: Language and Cognition* 20 (1). 3–16.
Chan, Margaret. 2020. English, mother tongue and the Singapore identity. *The Straits Times*. www.straitstimes.com/opinion/english-mother-tongue-and-the-spore-identity (accessed 27 February 2021).
Filppula, Markku. 1999. *The grammar of Irish English. Language in Hibernian style*. London: Routledge.
Foster, Robert Fitzroy. 1989. Ascendancy and union. In Robert Fitzroy Foster (ed.), *The Oxford illustrated history of Ireland*, 161–213. Oxford: Oxford University Press.
Fuchs, Robert & Ulrike Gut. 2015. An apparent time study of the progressive in Nigerian English. In Peter Collins (ed.), *Grammatical change in English world-wide*, 373–387. Amsterdam: John Benjamins.
Gupta, Anthea Fraser. 1994. *The step-tongue. Children's English in Singapore*. Clevedon: Multilingual Matters.
Halliday, Michael A.K. & Ruqaiya Hasan. 1976. *Cohesion in English*. London: Longman.
Hickey, Raymond. 2003. *Corpus Presenter. Software for language analysis with a corpus of Irish English*. John Benjamins.
Hickey, Raymond. 2007. *Irish English: History and present-day forms*. Cambridge: Cambridge University Press.
Hothorn, Torsten, Kurt Hornik & Achim Zeileis. 2006. Unbiased recursive partitioning: A conditional inference framework. *Journal of Computational and Graphical Statistics* 15 (3). 651–674.
Hulk, Aafke & Natascha Müller. 2000. Bilingual first language acquisition at the interface between syntax and pragmatics. *Bilingualism: Language and Cognition* 3 (3). 227–224.
Kachru, Braj B., Yamuna Kachru & Cecil L. Nelson. 2006. Introduction: The world of World Englishes. In Braj B. Kachru, Yamuna Kachru & Cecil L. Nelson (eds.), *The handbook of World Englishes*, 1–14. Malden, MA: Blackwell.
Kallen, Jeffrey L. 2013. *Irish English volume 2: The Republic of Ireland*. Berlin & Boston: De Gruyter Mouton.
Kerswill, Paul, Jenny Cheshire, Sue Fox & Eivind Torgersen. 2013. English as a contact language: The role of children and adolescents. In Daniel Schreier & Marianne Hundt (eds.), *English as a contact language*, 258–282. Cambridge: Cambridge University Press.
Kwan-Terry, Anna. 1986. The acquisition of word order in English and Cantonese interrogative sentences: a Singapore case study. *Regional Language Centre (RELC) Journal* 17 (1). 14–39.
Labov, William. 1969. Contraction, deletion, and inherent variability of the English copula. *Language* 45 (4). 715–759.
Labov, William. 1994. *Principles of linguistic change: Internal factors*. Oxford Blackwell.
Meisel, Jürgen M. 2011. Bilingual language acquisition and theories of diachronic change: Bilingualism as cause and effect of grammatical change. *Bilingualism: Language and Cognition* 14 (2). 121–145.
Mesthrie, Rajend & Rakesh M. Bhatt. 2008. *World Englishes. The study of new linguistic varieties*. Cambridge: Cambridge University Press.
Quirk, Randolph, Sidney Greenbaum, Geoffrey Leech & Jan Svartvik. 1985. *A comprehensive grammar of the English Language*. London: Longman.
R Core Team. 2019. R: A language and environment for statistical computing. *R Foundation for Statistical Computing*. www.R-project.org/ (accessed 27 February 2021).

Rice, Mabel L. & Kenneth Wexler. 2001. *Rice/Wexler Test of Early Grammatical Impairment: Examiner's manual*. San Antonio, TX: The Psychological Corporation.

Roberts, Julie. 2013. Child language variation. In J.K. Chambers & Natalie Schilling (eds.), *The handbook of language variation and change*, 2nd edn., 263–276. New Jersey: John Wiley & Sons, Inc.

Roeper, Tom &Bernhard Rohrbacher. 2000. Null subjects in early child English and the theory of economy of projection. In Susan M. Powers & Cornelia Hamann (eds.), *The acquisition of scrambling and cliticization*, 345–396. Dordrecht: Kluwer Academic Publishers.

Romaine, Suzanne. 2013. The bilingual and multilingual community. In Tej K. Bhatia & William C. Ritchie (eds.), *The handbook of bilingualism and multilingualism*. 2nd edn., 445–465. Malden, MA: Wiley Blackwell.

Ronan, Patricia. 2005. The *after*-perfect in Irish English. In Markku Filppula, Juhani Klemola, Marjatta Palander & Esa Pentillä (eds.), *Dialects across borders: Selected papers from the 11th International Conference on Methods in Dialectology (Methods XI), Joensuu, August 2002*, Current Issues in Linguistic Theory 273, 253–270. Amsterdam: John Benjamins.

Ronan, Patricia. 2017. Language relations in early Ireland. In Raymond Hickey (ed.), *Sociolinguistics in Ireland*, 133–153. London: Palgrave.

Ronan, Patricia. 2020. English in Ireland: Intra-territorial perspectives on language contact. In Sarah Buschfeld & Alexander Kautzsch (eds.), *Modelling World Englishes: A joint approach to postcolonial and non-postcolonial varieties*, 322–346. Edinburgh: Edinburgh University Press.

Schneider, Edgar W. 2007. *Postcolonial English. Varieties around the world*. Cambridge: Cambridge University Press.

Schools' Collection. www.duchas.ie/en/cbes (accessed 24 May 2020).

Schreier, Daniel. 2013. English as a contact language: Lesser-known varieties. In Daniel Schreier & Marianne Hundt (eds.), *English as a contact language*, 149–164. Cambridge: Cambridge University Press.

Tagliamonte, Sali & Rachel Hudson. 1999. Be like et al. beyond America: The quotative system in British and Canadian youth. *Journal of Sociolinguistics* 3 (2). 147–172.

Tan, Ying-Ying. 2014. English as a 'mother tongue' in Singapore. *World Englishes* 33 (3). 319–339.

Thomason, Sarah G. 2013. Innovation and contact: The role of adults (and children). In Daniel Schreier & Marianne Hundt (eds.), *English as a contact language*, 283–297. Cambridge: Cambridge University Press.

Tickoo, Makhan L. 1996. Fifty years of English in Singapore: All gains, (a) few losses?. In Joshua A, Fishman, Andrew W. Conrad & Alma Rubal-Lopez (eds.), *Post-imperial English: Status change in former British and American colonies, 1940–1990*, 431–455. Berlin & Boston: De Gruyter Mouton.

Turnbull, C.M. 2017. *A history of modern Singapore: 1819–2005*. 3rd edn. Singapore: National University of Singapore Press.

Valian, Virginia. 2016. Null subjects. In Jeffrey Lidz, William Snyder & Joe Pater (eds.), *The Oxford handbook of developmental linguistics*, 386–413. Oxford: Oxford University Press.

Wagner, Suzanne. 2012. Real-time evidence for age grad(ing) in late adolescence. *Language Variation and Change* 24 (2). 179–202.

Weihs, Claus & Sarah Buschfeld. 2021a. *Combining prediction and interpretation in decision trees (PrInDT) – a linguistic example*. https://arxiv.org/abs/2103.02336 (accessed 21 December 2021).

Weihs, Claus & Sarah Buschfeld. 2021b. *NesPrInDT: Nested undersampling in PrInDT*. arXiv:2103.14931 (accessed 21 December 2021).

Part III: **Attitudes and identity**

Mirjam Schmalz
10 Children's language attitudes in a World Englishes community: A focus on St. Kitts

Abstract: This chapter presents the results of a verbal guise study conducted with 62 ten- to fourteen-year-old children in St. Kitts in the Eastern Caribbean. Even though it is widely acknowledged that children and adolescents play a prominent role in language change, research in World Englishes and language attitudes studies only rarely feature them. The present study attempts to start filling this gap by analysing the language attitudes of Kittitian children towards different exocentric and endocentric varieties of English. While the results show a rather strong exonormative orientation in the status dimension, they also outline an attitudinal change in process towards more pronounced levels of endonormativity or multinormativity. This study thus outlines the importance of working with data from children for the understanding of current changes in norm orientation in World Englishes communities.

Keywords: language attitudes, attitude acquisition, children, St. Kitts, Caribbean, World Englishes

1 Introduction

Within the field of attitudinal research in the Caribbean, a focus on the education sector is regularly present. However, these studies mostly research language attitudes of teachers (Deuber 2009; Mühleisen 2001; Winford 1976) or students in secondary or tertiary education (e.g. Deuber 2013; Meer et al. 2019). A focus on younger students, on the other hand, is mostly lacking. Nevertheless, special attention should be paid to children, as language attitudes start developing from an early age as part of the acquisition of the "sociolinguistic competence" (Tagliamonte and Molfenter 2007: 653). At the age of eleven to twelve years, speakers "realize that there is a correlation between language variation and societal prestige" (De Vogelaer and Toye 2017: 117). Thus, studying perceptions and attitudes at this young age is a valid endeavour and potentially proves important in order to understand the bigger linguistic picture present within a community. As language attitudes potentially have an impact on

Mirjam Schmalz, University of Zurich, Switzerland

https://doi.org/10.1515/9783110733723-010

language change in general (Coupland 2014) and as the important role of children in language change is unquestioned, a focus on language attitudes of children is vital in order to provide insights into attitudinal change over time. In a World Englishes context of the Caribbean, this is of particular importance as norm re-orientation and re-negotiation processes are currently underway (Hackert 2016). To understand these changes in norm orientation better, language attitudes of speakers of all age groups need to be taken into consideration (Sand 2011).

Drawing on data collected in St. Kitts in 2019 in the form of attitudinal experiments with 62 students (mean age = 12), this paper looks at younger informants' language attitudes towards several local and non-local varieties of English. St. Kitts itself is located in the Eastern Caribbean and belongs to the smaller islands of the area. The students taking part in the experiment listened to recordings of speakers from Jamaica, St. Kitts, Trinidad, and Grenada, as well as from Southern England, Northern England and the USA and rated them according to different criteria associated with the dimensions of status and solidarity. The experiment thus includes both endonormative as well as exonormative varieties. Based on these data, this paper suggests that children in St. Kitts are currently (still) strongly favouring exonormatively oriented standards in formal contexts over endonormative varieties. Nevertheless, based on the experiment, a change towards more positive attitudes towards local Caribbean varieties seems to be in progress, in line with the supposed re-evaluation of non-local and possible local standards already present in other locations (Hackert 2016).

First, an overview of the main steps in the acquisition of attitudes and previous findings from attitudinal research with children will be outlined, followed by a brief description of St. Kitts, the participants of the current study, and the methodology employed. The analysis of the data will then outline attitudinal patterns of the children taking part in the current study before turning to a more detailed discussion of the results and conclusions that can be drawn on their basis in connection with the wider field of language attitudes and language variation in the Caribbean.

2 Previous research

2.1 Acquisition of attitudes

As mentioned above, the acquisition of sociolinguistic competence, which entails the acquisition of the "social meaning of variants in their full complexity" (De Vogelaer and Toye 2017: 117), starts very early on in life, illustrated by the fact that familiar accents are preferred over non-familiar ones in children at five months (Butler et al. 2011). In older children, aged five to six years old, it was furthermore found that the content of the recordings played to the children also had an effect on which accents they preferred (Kinzler and DeJesus 2013). Kinzler and DeJesus (2013) found that the children only favoured the local accent if the content was positive or neutral but disfavoured the local accent if the content was negative. This implies a "negativity bias" to be present (Kinzler and DeJesus 2013: 658), hinting at a pronounced moral compass to be present amongst children on top of a general preference for familiar accents.

While a distinction between "sufficiently different" languages is possible from birth on (Nazzi, Bertocini, and Mehler 1998; as paraphrased in Kinzler, Shutts, and Spelke 2012: 217), "phonological constancy" needs to be acquired to differentiate between more similar language varieties. Phonological constancy describes the ability to recognise different linguistic realisations of one word as still referring to the same referent, "despite phonetic variations that leave phonological structure intact, for example, across speech registers or regional accents" (Best et al. 2009: 539). The acquisition of phonological constancy has been shown to be complete amongst children at 19 months (Best et al. 2009: 539). This constitutes a major milestone for acquisition of language attitudes, as a speaker first needs to realise that different possible pronunciations of the same word exist without changing its meaning before linking these different pronunciations with certain social information. Another important step is the ability to group different speakers together based on the language variety of a speaker. Jeffries (2019) found in an experiment carried out in York in the north of England that children between three to four years of age are already able to group speakers with a Yorkshire accent and a Southern Standard British English accent correctly. She furthermore found a positive effect of input varieties on the ability to group speakers, namely that children who have different input varieties from their caregivers fared better in grouping the recordings of the experiment than children who solely received Yorkshire input from their caregivers.

A considerable change in language attitudes can be found around pre-school and early school years, as the development of social networks is often initiated or accelerated around that time (Jeffries 2019: 329). Even though a causal development should not be assumed too straight forwardly (De Vogelaer and Toye 2017: 144), studies have repeatedly recorded a certain effect setting in around that time (see e.g. Day 1980; Giles et al. 1983; Kasberger and Kaiser 2019). In Austria for example, Kasberger and Kaiser (2019) found that while children between four and six years old did not show any preference for the standard or the nonstandard variety; however, after the age of six, a preference for the standard variety could slowly be detected (321), which further increased at the age of seven to eight (321) but started decreasing again after the children had left school (330). These results are especially insightful, as a standardised form of language is the main variety used in education in these areas, while a non-standard variety is spoken as a first language (L1) or a first dialect (D1) by the majority of children. This is also generally the case in St. Kitts, where Standard English is the main language of instruction in the education system, while Kittitian Creole (KC), an English-based Creole, is the variety natively spoken by the majority of the population.

Studies that focus on multilingual children have furthermore revealed insights into the acquisition of sociolinguistic competence. Children as young as two years old in a French English bilingual context in Canada have shown "sensitivity to their language choice of their interlocutor" (Paradis and Nicoladis 2007: 277). Even though they could not fully differentiate between the two languages yet, they nevertheless showed "some understanding of language choice patterns and levels of bilingualism in their community" (Paradis and Nicoladis 2007: 294). Similarly, high levels of language awareness could also be detected in research focusing on Trinidad (Youssef 1993, 2005), a community exhibiting a similar language situation to St. Kitts. In her longitudinal study with children from two to four years and nine months old, Youssef found that the children were style shifting depending on various factors, such as the addressee, topics (e.g. school), or the level of excitement (Youssef 1993: 272–273). Similar results on the ability to style shift by young children could also be reported, for example, from Scotland (Smith, Durham, and Fortune 2007; Smith, Durham, and Richards 2013) or England (Snell 2008). The ability to use different varieties present within the community depending, for example, on context again illustrates the high level of awareness present from an early age on. The input the children receive affects their acquisition of the sociolinguistic competence in the process of socialisation within a given community (Garrett 2010: 22). This input can come from various sources, such as from parents, teachers, advertisements, media (Garrett 2010: 22–23), or movies (Lippi-Green 2012). A large-scale study with different age groups from eight to eighteen years old carried out in the Netherlands found that children at the age of eleven to twelve years old "perceive[d] a correlation between the use of certain varieties and social prestige and success" (De Vogelaer and Toye 2017: 146). This shows that at this age, children start exhibiting more stable language attitudes and should not be discarded as unsuitable participants for attitudes studies. The children between ten to fourteen years of age who took part in the current study are therefore an ideal participant group for the study of language attitudes on the island.

2.2 Attitudes research in the Caribbean

In the Caribbean, research on attitudes, which can be broadly defined as "a disposition to respond favorably or unfavorably to an object, person, institution, or event" (Ajzen 1988: 4), goes back to the early 1970s (Haynes 1973 in Barbados and Guyana; Reisman 1970 in Antigua; Winford 1976 in Trinidad). Winford (1976) researched attitudes of teachers in Trinidad, which established a focus on the education sector. This was followed up upon in later attitudinal research that also focused heavily on teachers or students in secondary and tertiary education (e.g. Deuber 2013; Meer et al. 2019; Mühleisen 2001). Winford's (1976) participants mainly saw the local varieties of English and Creoles as one language with Trinidad Creole English as being "bad English" or "not correct English," rather than as seeing them as separate varieties. This has changed in the meantime as Mühleisen (2001) suggests, who compared her data gathered in Trinidad in the 90s with Winford's initial results. Mühleisen (2002: 38) found that even though English and Trinidad Creole English were still strongly associated with different language domains (cf. Fishman 1972), overall "the uses and functions of Creole within certain domains have changed considerably". Furthermore, her participants saw the two language varieties as two separate systems, rather than the Creole variety being just a "corruption" of English (Mühleisen 2001: 75). This change in language attitudes is especially important to keep in mind for the present study, as teachers present a role model to their students, both when it comes to language production and perception (cf. Deuber and Youssef 2007).

Following scattered initial studies, the last two decades saw a considerable rise in language attitudes research in the Caribbean which focused on different geographical territories as well as different language domains. The overall picture that emerges from the present research is that of a complex attitudinal situation; the complexity applies to both the attitudes towards the locally spoken Creole varieties and the different varieties of English. Even though, as mentioned above, the locally spoken Creole varieties are now more frequently used in language domains formerly only reserved for English, the language attitudes towards Creoles are still ambivalent to a certain degree, ranging between a "symbol of solidarity and truth" and a "symbol of powerlessness and degeneracy" (Rickford and Traugott 1985: 31; also cf. Mair 2002).

Studies that focus on attitudes towards English and the norm development thereof have gained ground recently, bringing ongoing attitudinal changes to the surface (e.g. Deuber and Leung 2013; Meer and Deuber 2020; Meer et al. 2019; Westphal 2017; see Hackert 2016 for an overview). However, while more positive evaluations of local varieties of English were found in different domains and geographical locations, different exonormative varieties remain strong as well (e.g. Deuber and

Leung 2013; Westphal 2017). This has led Meer and Deuber (2020) to argue for an inclusion of what they call "multinormativity" into the Exta- and Intra-territorial Forces (EIF) Model (cf. Buschfeld and Kautzsch 2017). Meer and Deuber (2020: 288) define it as "a stable and systematic multidimensional orientation involving several coexisting norms" in which no single "standard emerged as a superordinate norm" (281). This multinormativity, they argue, could be an alternative outcome to the endonormative stabilisation suggested by Schneider (2007).

When it comes to the geographical coverage of the current attitudinal research of the area, most research focuses on more populous and bigger locations, such as Trinidad or Jamaica. Smaller locations, on the other hand, are less well represented in the academic discourse. This, however, would be of great importance to gain more holistic insights into the linguistic developments across the area. While tendencies towards a higher level of endonormatively oriented standard language development can be seen in certain language domains of bigger communities of the English-speaking Caribbean, such as Jamaica or Trinidad (e.g. Westphal 2017), the situation might be somewhat different in smaller locations of the Caribbean (cf. Schmalz 2021). Thus, in addition to adding more data from different age groups, especially from children to the current discourse, data from lesser studied varieties also is greatly needed. This paper combines both of these research gaps by working with children from St. Kitts, a lesser studied variety of the Caribbean.

3 St. Kitts

St. Kitts is part of the island state of St. Kitts and Nevis in the Eastern Caribbean (see Figure 10.1). Even though it is larger and more populous than its sister island Nevis, St. Kitts belongs to the smaller locations of the Caribbean with approximately 35,000 inhabitants (St. Kitts and Nevis Statistics Department 2011) and an area of about 168 km^2. St. Kitts was the first English island colony in the Caribbean, with an English settlement starting in 1623 (Baker 1999: 338). Even though parts of the island were also settled by the French in 1625, the island ultimately ended up in British possession and English has remained the only official language of the island ever since. Similar to other Caribbean locations, a local variety of English, Kittitian English (KE), as well as a local English-based Creole, Kittitian Creole, is spoken on the island. Even though KC does not enjoy the status of an official language, it is the first language of the majority of the community. The two language varieties are distributed according to different languages domains, with English taking over more formal domains, such as education.

KC can be divided into three main dialect areas, one each around the capital of Basseterre, Sandy Point in the north-west, and Cayon on the eastern side of St. Kitts (Martin 1983: 6). While some initial attempts were made at documenting KC, including some anecdotal comments on language attitudes (Baker and Pederson 2013; Cooper 1979; Martin 1983), first systematic attitudinal research has only recently started to be carried out (see Perez and Schmalz 2021; Schmalz 2021, 2023). The high levels of mobility of the Kittitian population for work or tertiary education in combination with the strong tourist industry on the island leads to a lot of interaction with people from around the world. This in turn consolidates the importance of Standard English for the island's population and arguably also influences their language attitudes.

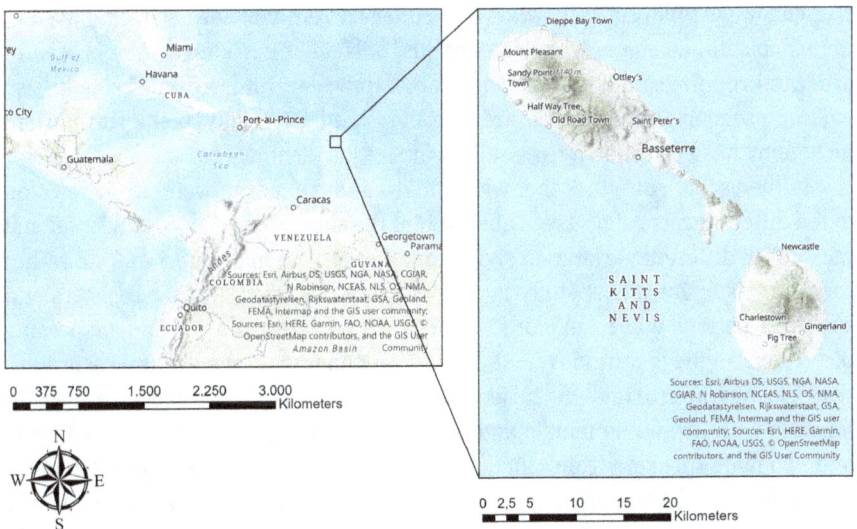

Figure 10.1: Map of St. Kitts and Nevis in the Caribbean.

4 Methodology and participants

The perceptual task carried out for this study was conducted in 2019. Out of the 62 children who participated in it, there were 39 girls and 23 boys, who were aged between ten and fourteen years old (mean age = 12). In the background questionnaire, I asked them for their L1. 27 indicated to have KC as their L1, 25 ticked English, and three have both KC and English as their L1s. Two children indicated to have English and Spanish as their L1, two indicated Spanish as their L1 (but have grown up in St. Kitts), one indicated to have KC, English, and Papiamento, one to have KC, English, and one to have Chinese, Hindi, Sindhi, and English as their L1s. However, the information provided by the children on their L1 needs to be taken with a grain of salt, as I cannot be entirely sure if the students perceive English and Kittitian Creole to be two separate language systems or as belonging to a broad category of English. This is especially so as several children who indicated to have English as their L1 provided certain answers to the questionnaire in KC. Even though it would be very interesting to look into this in more detail and find out more about when/if speakers start perceiving the two varieties as separate entities, this is not the focus of the current study and will thus not be followed up in more detail here.

The children were recruited via four different schools, three of which were located in Basseterre and one at the outskirts of the capital. The schools were recruited via personal contacts who were either currently or formerly employed at the schools in questions. Schools in and just outside of Basseterre were chosen in order to keep the sample more comparable. However, future studies should also look into schools in more rural areas of the island, especially as the rural/urban dichotomy has been shown to be salient in St. Kitts (Schmalz 2023).

In the verbal guise task that was employed, the children were asked to listen to ten different recordings (see Table 10.1) of the short story "The North Wind and the Sun" in different varieties. A short story was chosen in order to go for a rather formal register for a first study in St. Kitts. In a next step, further registers and speech situations will be explored in order to receive a more all-encompassing picture of language attitudes in St. Kitts. The students listened to the recordings twice, lasting approximately 20 seconds each. The different recordings they listened to were from one female and one male speaker from St. Kitts, one female and two male speakers from Jamaica, and one male speaker each from Grenada, Trinidad, the US, Southern England and Northern England, respectively. All the recordings from the US, England, and St. Kitts, and one of the male Jamaican recordings were recorded specifically for this experiment by personal contacts, while the recordings from Trinidad, Grenada, and the remaining recordings from Jamaica were taken from The International Dialects of English Archive (IDEA 2018). All speakers were speakers of the respective varieties of English, and the female Kittitian speaker had a Creole-influenced variety in the recording. The speaker from the US speaks with a General American accent (GenAm) and the speaker from southern England speaks with Standard Southern British English accent (SSBE). The northern English recording from Newcastle upon Tyne (henceforth Newcastle) was chosen in order to add a non-standard recording from an inner-circle country. This was added as I am interested to see how a supposedly non-stereotypical speaker from the UK will be perceived in contrast to the more stereotypical speaker of Southern Standard British English.

Table 10.1: Recordings used for the perceptual task in 2019.

Location recording	Code recording
Saint Kitts female	SK_F
Saint Kitts male	SK_M
Jamaica female	JAM_F
Jamaica male 1	JAM_M1
Jamaican male 2	JAM_M2
Grenada male	GREN_M
Trinidad male	TRIN_M
USA male	US_M
Southern England male	SE_M
Northern England male	NE_M

The children were then asked to first place the different recordings, whenever possible, in the area, country, or region they believed the speakers to come from. If they were not sure they could indicate that they did not know or simply leave it blank, as I did not want to exert unnecessary pressure on them. The results of the placement task will, however, not be analysed in detail in the present paper. Even though previous research from the US suggests that children are able to connect accents with geographical affiliation at the age of five to seven, the recognition rates are generally rather low for children (Beck 2014). Moreover, for the Caribbean, very low recognition rates are also frequently recorded in studies working with adult participant groups (e.g. Hänsel and Deuber 2019). Similarly, the present participants also achieved low recognition rates. An exception to the low rates was the creole-influenced Kittitian variety with an approximately 79% recognition rate, which is arguably because that is the variety the children are likely to be the most familiar with. Nevertheless, due to the low overall recognition rates, this will not be focused on in the analysis in any more detail.

Second, I asked the children to rate each recording on different dimensions on a 5-point Likert scale, ranging from "strongly agree" = 5 to "strongly disagree" = 1. The scale was further illustrated through emojis to make it more intuitive for the children to rate the recordings. The dimensions on which the children were asked to rate the recordings were whether they perceived the speakers of the recordings to be polite, easy to understand, arrogant, trustworthy, friendly, proper, fun, educated, and to sound foreign, like an English teacher, like a news broadcaster, and whether the accent sounds standard. The instructions were all given orally, and all the different dimensions were first looked at in class in order to make sure that all children understood what the dimensions were about in order to rule out any potential language problems. Moreover, students could ask questions throughout the experiment, which lasted for about 30 to 40 minutes, if they were unsure about anything. Due to time constraints, the students listened to the recordings as a group, rather than individually. After the task, there was a question-and-answer session in which the children asked me about the experiment and the project in general and in which I was able to ask them more qualitative questions on top of the questionnaire.

In the following, the results of the Likert scale task will be presented and analysed. First, the focus will be on the status dimension before turning to the solidarity dimension.

5 Data and analysis

The results of the listening task are presented in Figures 10.2–10.5. To facilitate readability, the attitudinal dimensions included in the experiment are visualised separately, with the different items aiming at the status dimensions visualised in Figures 10.2 and 10.3 and the items aiming at the solidarity dimension visualised in Figures 10.4 and 10.5. The item of perceived easiness of understanding was added to Figure 10.2. The different shades represent the different recordings that were played to the participants and are grouped according to the different individual items of the questionnaire. On the x-axis, the different items and recordings are visible, and the y-axis represents the mean values of all responses.

5.1 Status dimensions

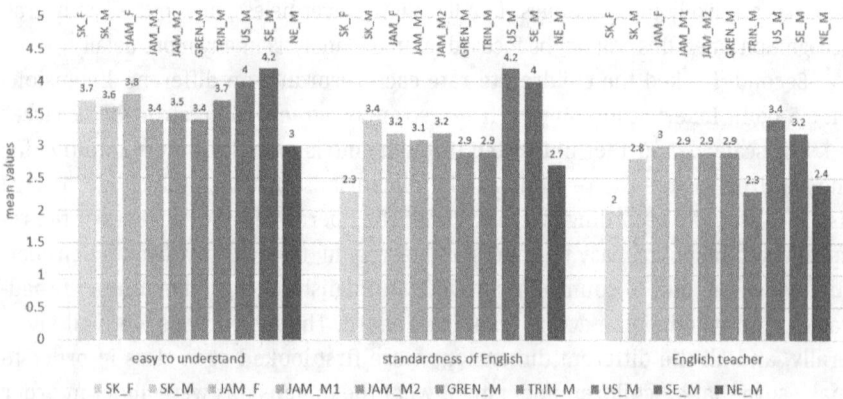

Figure 10.2: Mean values of the Likert scale ratings for the status dimension (n = 62).

10 Children's language attitudes in a World Englishes community: A focus on St. Kitts — 215

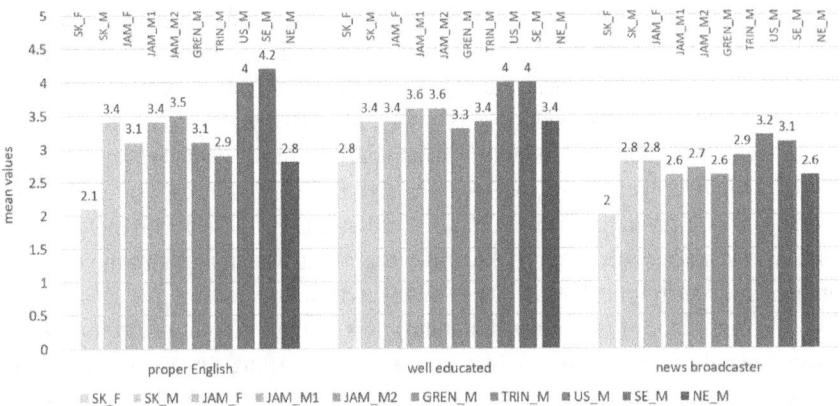

Figure 10.3: Mean values of the Likert scale ratings for the status dimension (n = 62).

A first glance at the data shows that the female Kittitian recording, the Creole-influenced recording, was generally ranked lowest, apart from the item of the perceived easiness of understanding. The two exonormative standard varieties of US_M and SE_M ranked highest on all of the dimensions illustrated above. Between those two extremes, the other Caribbean varieties (apart from SK_F) clustered together rather clearly, with the male Kittitian recording ranking reasonably high amongst the other recordings. This indicates a dissociation of Creole-influenced speech with status. Status seems to be rather associated with the two exonormative varieties. For the item of the perceived easiness of understanding, SK_F ranked rather high, especially compared to the low overall rankings of the Creole-influenced recording. While US_M (4.2) and SE_M (4.2) still rank highest for this item, SK_F (3.7) was placed close to the other Caribbean recordings, and the NE_M (3), the non-normative file from England ranked lowest. This is not surprising, as the children are most likely not familiar with a Newcastle accent, resulting in them ranking the recording lower on the scale of understandability. They are more likely to be familiar with all Caribbean accents, as well as a General American accent and a Southern Standard British English accent.

In order to look at the results in more detail, an analysis of variance (ANOVA) and a post-hoc Scheffé test were performed on the data. The ANOVA test showed significant differences in perception on all levels outlined above: the perceived ease of understanding (F = 3.66, p = 0.0002), standardness of English (F = 13.04, p<0.00001), sounding like an English teacher (F = 7.43, p<0.00001), proper English (F = 12.08, p<0.00001), the perceived level of education (F = 5.57, p<0.00001), and whether the recording sounds like a news broadcaster (F = 4.82, p<0.00001).

For the perceived easiness of understanding, the initial suspicion can be confirmed, namely that the main difference is between the exonormative recordings US_M and SE_M, and the recording from Newcastle, NE_M. More precisely, both US_M (T = 4.51, p = 0.017) and SE_M (T = 4.29, p = 0.033) were perceived as significantly easier to understand than the non-standard recording from the north of England. For all other recordings, however, no significant differences were found. The fact that the Creole-influenced Kittitian recording clusters closely with the other Caribbean recordings furthermore illustrates that these are all varieties the children are generally surrounded by and find equally easy to understand.

The question of the perceived standardness of the different recordings led to various significantly different ratings. Overall, the recordings US_M and SE_M were perceived to be the closest depictions of a standard of English. The Scheffé test showed that the GenAm accent was perceived to sound significantly more standard than all other varieties, apart from the SE_M and the SK_M recording. The US_M recording sounded more standard than SK_F (T = 8.58, p<0.00001), JAM_F (T = 4.59, p = 0.014), JAM_M1 (T = 4.95, p = 0.0041), JAM_M2 (T = 4.59, p = 0.014), GREN_M (T = 5.64, p = 0.0003), TRIN_M (T = 5.88, p<0.00001), and NE_M (T = 6.81, p<0.0001). Furthermore, the second exonormative recording (SE_M) was perceived to sound significantly more standard than SK_F (T = 7.61, p<0.0001), GREN_M (T = 4.67, p = 0.011), TRIN_M (T = 4.89, p = 0.005), and NE_M (T = 5.83, p = 0.0001). Last but not least, the Kittitian English recording was perceived to sound significantly more standard than the Creole-influenced Kittitian recording (T = 4.91, p = 0.005).

This shows that the children seem to clearly distinguish between the two local varieties, namely KE and KC, with the latter not being associated with sounding like "standard" English. Thus, the awareness of the difference in overt prestige and usage of the two language varieties present in St. Kitts seems to be in place at this young age already. Moreover, there also seems to be a clear general exonormative orientation, with both GenAm and SSBE ranking significantly higher than many of the Caribbean varieties. Furthermore, the fact that the children rate the KE recording as the most standard like recording amongst the Caribbean files potentially suggests a strengthening of endonormativity amongst this generation and a move towards multinormativity (cf. Meer and Deuber 2020). Further support of an attitudinal change in progress can be found in the individual ratings. In line with the statistical results outlined above, the SE_M and US_M recordings exhibited a cluster of 4- and 5-point ratings, while the Creole-influenced Kittitian recording exhibited a cluster of 1- and 2-point ratings, which indicates that most participants agreed on it being a non-standard variety. The Caribbean English recordings, on the other hand, did not exhibit such a clear clustering towards either exclusively low or exclusively high ratings, which is an indication for a change towards a stronger endocentric norm orientation. In order to look into this claim further, longitudinal data is needed.

The dimension of sounding like an English teacher again shows an orientation towards the two exonormative recordings US_M and SE_M. The US_M recording was perceived to sound significantly more like an English teacher than SK_F (T = 6.11, p<0.00001), TRIN_M (T = 4.95, p = 0.004), and NE_M (T = 4.37, p = 0.026). The SE_M recordings was perceived to sound significantly more like an English teacher than SK_F (T = 5.59, p = 0.0004), and TRIN_M (T = 4.41, p = 0.023). Moreover, JAM_F, which was the most highly ranked of the Caribbean English recordings, was rated significantly higher than the Creole-influenced Kittitian recording (T = 4.47, p = 0.0196). This, on the one hand, implies a strong exonormative orientation and disfavour of Creole-influenced varieties in education, but, on the other hand, also shows that the Caribbean varieties of English are not generally disfavoured but rather seen as an accepted part of the reality in education.

Connected with this is the item of "proper English," for which both the Creole-influenced Kittitian and the northern English recording were rated rather low. The SK_F recording was rated significantly lower than SK_M (T = 5.88, p<0.00001), JAM_F (T = 4.22, p = 0.0395), JAM_M1 (T = 5.6, p = 0.0003), JAM_M2 (T = 6.09, p<0.00001), GREN_M (T = 4.53, p = 0.016), US_M (T = 8.21, p<0.0001), and SE_M (T = 8.29, p<0.00001). In addition to that, the two exonormative recordings were again perceived as being "more proper" than the other varieties. The US_M recording was perceived as significantly more "proper" than TRIN_M (T = 4.73, p = 0.0085) and NE_M (T = 4.93, p = 0.0043). The SE_M recording was perceived as significantly more "proper" than the TRIN_M recording (T = 4.74, p = 0.0082) and the NE_M recording (T = 4.95, p = 0.0041). This again illustrates that the children who took part in this study differentiate between the Creole-influenced recording and the recordings of varieties of Caribbean Englishes, as well as the exonormative varieties of English, which they generally associate with a higher status. In addition to that, the non-standard northern English recording adds another interesting layer, indicating that the children differentiate between SSBE and regional varieties of the British Isles that do not fall into a SSBE category.

The final dimensions presented in Figure 10.3, the perceived level of education of the speakers and the perceived likeliness of the speakers sounding like news broadcasters, again show a certain exonormative orientation. The US_M recording was perceived to be significantly more educated than the SK_F recording (T = 5.95, p<0.00001), and also as sounding significantly more like a news broadcaster than SK_F (T = 5.76, p = 0.0002). The same goes for the SE_M recording, which was also considered to sound more educated (T = 5.63, p = 0.0003) and more like a news broadcaster than SK_F (T = 5.097, p = 0.0024). This again illustrates that the two exonormative varieties of GenAm and SSBE comprise higher levels of overt prestige on status dimensions than the local, Creole-influenced variety. Nevertheless, the fact that the exonormative varieties were not ranked significantly higher than the recordings of different Caribbean Englishes also implies a growing level of endonormative orientation on items associated with status and overt prestige.

5.2 Solidarity dimensions

The items associated with the solidarity dimension are illustrated in Figures 10.4 and 10.5.

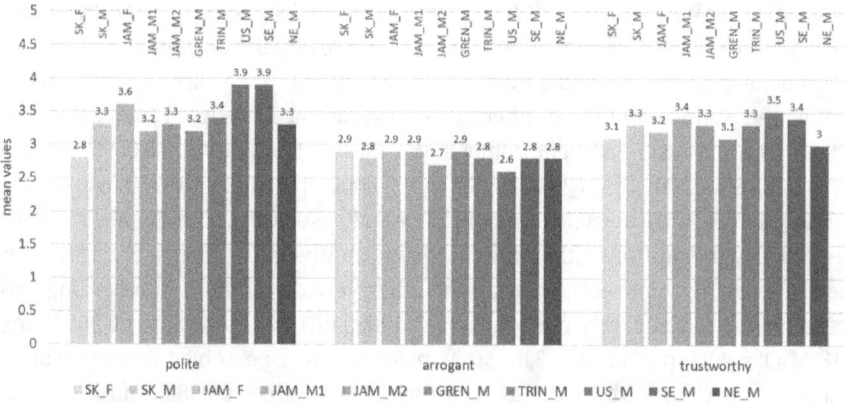

Figure 10.4: Mean values of the Likert scale ratings for the solidarity dimensions (n = 62).

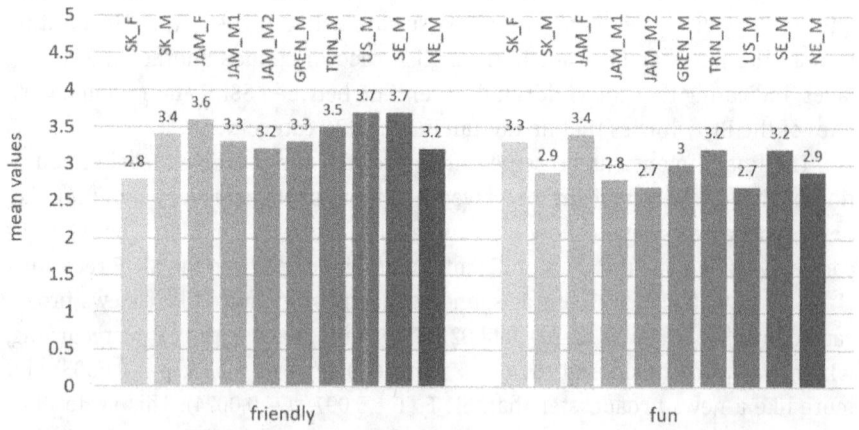

Figure 10.5: Mean values of the Likert scale ratings for the solidarity dimensions (n = 62).

An initial glance at Figures 10.4 and 10.5 again shows that the two recordings SE_M and US_M tend to score high; however, the picture that evolves is more complex than the one for the status dimension. SE_M and US_M do indeed score highest for the items of friendliness and politeness but not considerably higher than the other varieties for trustworthiness, and they blend in with the other varieties for the perceived level of fun and arrogance. Furthermore, unlike for the status dimension, for the solidarity dimension, the Creole-influenced Kittitian recording does not consistently score considerably lower than other varieties but even receives the second highest rating (3.3) for the perceived level of fun of the speaker. This represents the social reality of St. Kitts in which KC is the community language with attached cultural and social value, but not the language of overt prestige and economic mobility.

The ANOVA test showed that only the dimensions of perceived levels of politeness ($F = 6.30$, $p < 0.00001$) and friendliness ($F = 3.76$, $p = 0.0001$) exhibited significant differences. For the other three dimensions, the perceived levels of arrogance, fun, and trustworthiness, no significant differences could be detected. The more detailed statistical analysis with the post-hoc Scheffé showed clear patterns for the perceived levels of friendliness and politeness. The SK_F recording was perceived as significantly less friendly than US_M ($T = 4.53$, $p = 0.016$) and SE_M ($T = 4.75$, $p = 0.0082$). Similarly, the SK_F recording was perceived as significantly less polite than US_M ($T = 4.23$, $p = 0.039$), SE_M ($T = 5.83$, $p = 0.0001$), and JAM_F ($T = 5.86$, $p = 0.0001$). This seems to indicate that within the solidarity dimension, the two items of politeness and friendliness carry further associations which lead the children to differentiate between the local Creole-influenced speaker and the prestigious exonormative recordings.

However, it can also be seen that the Creole-influenced recording does not attract overall negative attitudes, as it did for the status dimension. For the solidarity dimension, SK_F shows higher mean values overall, as can be seen when looking at all mean values of all status dimension and all solidarity dimensions, respectively. A "classical pattern" (Bayard et al. 2001: 23) can be found in the ratings of several recordings, namely for SK_F, JAM_F, TRIN_M, NE_M, US_M, and SE_M. On the one hand, the US_M (status = 3.76, solidarity = 3.28) and the SE_M (status = 3.7, solidarity = 3.4) exhibit higher mean values for the status dimension, while exhibiting lower mean values for the solidarity dimension. On the other hand, SK_F (status = 2.24, solidarity = 2.98), JAM_F (status = 3.10, solidarity = 3.34), TRIN_M (status = 2.88, solidarity = 3.24), and NE_M (status = 2.78, solidarity = 3.04) exhibit the reverse pattern. The other differences were not considered, as they are below a difference of 0.2.

The fact that the two prestigious exonormative varieties score higher for the status dimension than the solidarity dimension, while the Caribbean varieties as well as the non-standard English variety score higher on the solidarity dimension than the status dimension aligns with the classical pattern, predicting higher ratings on the status dimension for standard varieties and higher ratings on the solidarity dimension for non-standard varieties. Especially interesting is the fact that the Creole-influenced recording exhibited the largest difference between the average mean value of the status dimension and the solidarity dimension (+0.74). This again points at a high level of awareness of the children that KC is the community language associated with covert prestige and solidarity, but not a language of international status and overt prestige.

6 Discussion and conclusion

The results provided by the 62 Kittitian children who took part in the attitudinal study in 2019 presented in the present chapter provide valuable insights into the attitudinal picture of the island's inhabitants. While children were traditionally seen as "'acquirers' of the vernacular of a speech community and not necessarily as contributors to its maintenance and change" (Roberts 2013: 263), the present chapter has outlined possible ongoing attitudinal changes present amongst, if not led by, the children of the community.

The participants were asked to listen to ten different recordings and rate them on several items belonging to the status or solidarity dimension. This verbal guise test consisted of recordings from St. Kitts, Jamaica, Grenada, Trinidad, the US, and England. The general pattern found that the GenAm recording and the SSBE recording tended to score high on the status dimension, while the Creole-influenced Kittitian recording tended to score low. For the dimensions of perceived level of education, standardness of English, and whether the speaker sounds like an English teacher, the GenAm and the SSBE recording received significantly higher ratings than the Creole-influenced Kittitian recording. For the question of whether the recording sounds like "proper English," the SK_F recording was even rated significantly lower than most of the other recordings. This resonates with the frequent definition of standardness in the Caribbean "in terms of distance from Creole" (Hackert 2016: 85).

The Creole-influenced recording generally scored higher on items connected to the solidarity dimension than on the status dimension. This is in line with De Vogelaer and Toye (2017: 144) who state that "non-standard varieties get increasingly associated with forms of covert prestige". Furthermore, Giles et al. (1983:

141) argue that non-standard varieties could have "increasingly more positive attitudes [. . .] when the variety is perceived as a valued symbol of ingroup identity and pride". This is arguably the case with my participants as well, as they rated the Creole-influenced local recording lower on the status dimension, but higher on the solidarity dimension, which implies that higher levels of covert prestige are associated with KC influenced accents. This points to the fact that the children who participated in this study have already largely acquired the societal attitudes towards the two varieties of KE and KC. This is in line with other research which found that children acquire societal norms of overt prestige once schooling has begun (e.g. Day 1980; Giles et al. 1983; Kinzler, Shutts, and Spelke 2012).

As mentioned above, while the US_M, SE_M, and SK_F recordings led to rather pronounced attitudes, the recordings of Caribbean varieties of English were perceived as the middle ground between the two extremes. Especially striking amongst the Caribbean English recordings were the ratings received by the Kittitian English recording, SK_M, which received rather positive ratings. These ratings were generally more positive than the ratings the same recording received in an experiment conducted with adult Kittitian participants in 2018 (cf. Perez and Schmalz 2021). This points at a potential attitudinal change in progress towards a stronger endonormative orientation. However, in order to detect whether these results are actually identifying change in progress or are simply a case of age grading, further longitudinal research is needed.

A second striking point outlined in the present study is the attitudes towards the NE_M recording from Newcastle upon Tyne in England. The NE_M recording was the only one rated to be significantly harder to understand than both the SE_M ($T = 4.29$, $p = 0.03$) and the US_M ($T = 4.51$, $p = 0.02$). This indicates that the participants were not familiar with the Newcastle accent and found it difficult to understand. Even though Kinzler, Shutts, and Spelke (2012: 219) found in their study conducted in South Africa that "preferences were not due exclusively to the intelligibility of the speech," the ratings for the Newcastle speaker were rather low across the board, including the perceived levels of standardness, "proper English," and sounding like an English teacher. Giles et al. (1983) also found that their primary school participants rated a non-familiar non-standard variety lower on the status dimension than Received Pronunciation after having started schooling, which seems to also be the case in my Kittitian data. However, in order to find out whether the non-standard recording would receive higher ratings before schooling of the children started, further studies with younger children would be needed. Nevertheless, the fact that an unfamiliar sounding variety, which was categorised as non-standard, was rated low on the status dimension but not on the solidarity dimension provides interesting insights into possible attitudinal dynamics present amongst speakers of non-standard varieties towards other non-standard varieties; this calls for further investigation.

This study has provided first insights into language attitudes of Kittitian children. However, the present chapter can by no means be seen as an all-encompassing view on language attitudes of this age group in St. Kitts. Further studies need to focus on more fine-grained subdivisions of this age group, including pre-school children, in order to determine the effect of schooling on language attitudes more closely. In addition, while the present results provide valuable data for a quantitative analysis, material obtained via conversations, narrative tasks, or white-canvas tasks should be used for further qualitative analyses, focusing both on implicit and explicit attitudes. Moreover, language attitudes do not exist in a vacuum in individual subgroups of a community but should always be looked at in relation to the language attitudes of other subgroups as the individual groups have a reciprocal influence on one another. Thus, in the case of children, a look at the educational sector as well as their parents is vital as well.

Despite the abovementioned shortcomings, this chapter has outlined the importance of working with data from children and adolescents for the understanding and tracking of language change in progress. In the larger context of World Englishes, this is even more important as the re-negotiation of the status of exonormative and endonormative varieties is constantly underway (cf. Hackert 2016). By showing that said re-negotiations have now arguably been initiated in St. Kitts as well, this chapter could start filling in important gaps in the research on smaller Caribbean communities, by working with one of the driving forces of language change, with children.

References

Ajzen, Icek. 1988. *Attitudes, personality and behaviour*. Milton Keynes: Open University Press.

Baker, Philip. 1999. Investigating the origin and diffusion of shared features among the Atlantic English Creoles. In Philip Baker & Adrienne Bruyn (eds.), *St. Kitts and the Atlantic Creoles*, 315–364. London: Westminster Press.

Baker, Philip & Lee Pederson. 2013. *Talk of St Kitts and Nevis*. London: Battlebridge.

Bayard, Donn, Ann Weatherall, Cynthia Gallois & Jeffery Pittman. 2001. Pax Americana? Accent attitudinal evaluations in New Zealand, Australia and America. *Journal of Sociolinguistics* 5 (1). 22–49.

Beck, Erica L. 2014. *The role of socio-indexical information in regional accent perception by five to seven year old children*. Ann Arbor, MI: University of Michigan PhD dissertation.

Best, Catherine T., Michael D. Tyler, Tiffany N. Gooding, Corey B. Orlando & Chelsea A. Quann. 2009. Development of phonological constancy: Toddlers' perceptions of native- and Jamaican accented words. *Psychological Science* 20 (5). 539–542.

Buschfeld, Sarah & Alexander Kautzsch. 2017. Towards an integrated approach to postcolonial and non-postcolonial Englishes. *World Englishes* 36 (1). 104–126.

Butler, Joseph, Caroline Floccia, Jeremy Goslin & Robin Panneton. 2011. Infants' discrimination of familiar and unfamiliar accents in speech. *Infancy* 16 (4). 392–417.

Cooper, Vincent O. 1979. *Basilectal creole, decreolization, and autonomous language change in St. Kitts-Nevis*. Princeton, NJ: Princeton University PhD dissertation.

Coupland, Nikolas. 2014. Language change, social change, sociolinguistic change: A meta-commentary. *Journal of Sociolinguistics* 18 (2). 277–286.

Day, Richard R. 1980. The development of linguistic attitudes and preferences. *TESOL Quarterly* 14 (1). 27–37.

De Vogelaer, Gunther & Jolien Toye. 2017. Acquiring attitudes towards varieties of Dutch: A quantitative perspective. In Gunther De Vogelaer & Matthias Katerbow (eds.), *Acquiring sociolinguistic variation*, 117–154. Amsterdam: John Benjamins.

Deuber, Dagmar. 2009. Standard English in the secondary school in Trinidad: Problems – properties – prospects. In Thomas Hoffmann & Lucia Siebers (eds.), *Varieties of English around the world: G40. World Englishes – problems, properties and prospects: Selected papers from the 13th IAWE conference*, 83–104. Amsterdam: John Benjamins.

Deuber, Dagmar. 2013. Towards endonormative standards of English in the Caribbean: A study of students' beliefs and school curricula. *Language, Culture and Curriculum* 26 (2). 109–127.

Deuber, Dagmar & Glenda-Alicia Leung. 2013. Investigating attitudes towards an emerging standard of English: Evaluations of newscasters' accents in Trinidad. *Multilingua* 32 (3). 289–319.

Deuber, Dagmar & Valerie Youssef. 2007. Teacher language in Trinidad: A pilot corpus study of direct and indirect creolisms in the verb phrase. *Proceedings from the Corpus Linguistics 2007 Conference*. Birmingham. www.birmingham.ac.uk/documents/college-artslaw/corpus/conference-archives/2007/31Paper.pdf (accessed 4 March 2022).

Fishman, Joshua A. 1972. Domains and the relationship between micro- and macrosociolinguistics. In John J. Gumperz & Dell Hymes (eds.), *Directions in sociolinguistics: The ethnography of communication*, 435–453. New York: Holt, Rinehart and Winston.

Garrett, Peter. 2010. *Attitudes to language*. Cambridge: Cambridge University Press.

Giles, Howard, Chris Harrison, Clare Creber, Philip M. Smith & Norman H. Freeman. 1983. Developmental and contextual aspects of children's language attitudes. *Language & Communication* 3 (2). 141–146.

Hackert, Stephanie. 2016. Standards of English in the Caribbean: History, attitudes, functions, features. In Elena Seoane & Cristina Suárez-Gómez (eds.), *World Englishes: New theoretical and methodological considerations*, 85–112. Amsterdam: John Benjamins.

Hänsel, Eva Canan & Dagmar Deuber. 2019. The interplay of the national, regional, and global in standards of English. A recognition survey of newscaster accents in the Caribbean. *English World-Wide* 40 (3). 241–268.

Haynes, Lilith M. 1973. *Language in Barbados and Guyana: Attitudes, behaviours, and comparisons*. Stanford, CA: Stanford University PhD dissertation.

International Dialects of English Archive. 2018. www.dialectsarchive.com (accessed 31 January 2022).

Jeffries, Ella. 2019. Pre-school children's categorisation of speakers by regional accent. *Language Variation and Change* 31 (3). 329–352.

Kasberger, Gudrun & Irmtraud Kaiser. 2019. 'I red normal' – eine Untersuchung der varietätenspezifischen Sprachbewusstheit und -bewertung von österreichischen Kindern. In Lars Bülow, Ann K. Fischer & Kristina Herbert (eds.), *Dimensions of Linguistic Space: Variation –*

multilingualism – conceptualisations. *Dimensionen des sprachlichen Raums: Variation – Mehrsprachigkeit – Konzeptualisierung*, 319–340. Berlin: Peter Lang.

Kinzler, Katherine D. & Jasmine M. DeJesus. 2013. Children's sociolinguistic evaluations of nice foreigners and mean Americans. *Developmental Psychology* 49 (4). 655–664.

Kinzler, Katherine D, Kristin Shutts & Elizabeth S. Spelke. 2012. Language-based social preferences among children in South Africa. *Language Learning and Development* 8 (3). 215–232.

Lippi-Green, Rosina. 2012. *English with an accent: Language, ideology and discrimination in the United States.* Oxon & New York: Routledge.

Mair, Christian. 2002. Creolisms in an emerging standard: Written English in Jamaica. *English World-Wide* 23 (1). 31–58.

Martin, Julie. 1983. *A description of the dialect spoken in St. Kitts*. Kingston: University of the West Indies unpublished Bachelor's thesis.

Meer, Philipp & Dagmar Deuber. 2020. Standard English in Trinidad: Multinormativity, translocality, and implications for the dynamic model and the EIF Model. In Sarah Buschfeld & Alexander Kautzsch (eds.), *Modelling World Englishes: A joint approach to postcolonial and non-postcolonial varieties*, 274–297. Edinburgh: Edinburgh University Press.

Meer, Philipp, Michael Westphal, Eva Canan Hänsel & Dagmar Deuber. 2019. Trinidadian secondary school students' attitudes toward accents of Standard English. *Journal of Pidgin and Creole Languages* 34 (1). 83–125.

Mühleisen, Susanne. 2001. Is "bad English" dying out? A diachronic comparative study of attitudes towards Creole versus Standard English in Trinidad. *Philologie im Netz* 15. 43–78.

Mühleisen, Susanne. 2002. *Creole Discourse: Exploring prestige formation and change across Caribbean English-lexicon Creoles.* Amsterdam: John Benjamins.

Nazzi, Thierry, Josiane Bertocini & Jacques Mehler. 1998. Language discrimination by newborns: Towards an understanding of the role of rhythm. *Journal of Experimental Psychology: Human Perception and Performance* 24 (3). 756–766.

Paradis, Johanne & Elena Nicoladis. 2007. The Influence of dominance and sociolinguistic context on bilingual preschoolers' language choice. *The International Journal of Bilingual Education and Bilingualism* 10 (3). 277–297.

Perez, Danae & Mirjam Schmalz. 2021. Complex patterns of variety perception in the Eastern Caribbean. In Danae Perez & Eeva Sippola (eds.), *Postcolonial Varieties in the Americas*, 271–292. Berlin & Boston: De Gruyter.

Reisman, Karl. 1970. Cultural and linguistic ambiguity in a West Indian village. In Norman E. Whitten & John F. Szwed (eds.), *Afro-American anthropology*, 129–144. New York: The Free Press.

Rickford, John & Elizabeth Closs Traugott. 1985. Symbol of powerlessness and degeneracy, or symbol of solidarity and truth? Paradoxical attitudes towards pidgins and creoles. In Sidney Greenbaum (ed.), *The English language today*, 31–47. Oxford: Pergamon.

Roberts, Julie. 2013. Child language variation. In Jack K. Chambers & Natalie Schilling (eds.), *The handbook of language variation and change*, 263–276. Hoboken: John Wiley and Sons.

Sand, Andrea. 2011. Language attitudes and linguistic awareness in Jamaican English. In Lars Hinrichs & Joseph T. Faquharson (eds.), *Variation in the Caribbean: From creole continua to individual agency* (Creole Language Library 37), 164–187. Amsterdam: John Benjamins.

Schmalz, Mirjam. 2021. *Language attitudes in St. Kitts: Changing norms of English and creole in a Caribbean community.* Zurich: University of Zurich PhD dissertation.

Schmalz, Mirjam. 2023. Mapping perceptions in New Englishes: A case study from St. Kitts. In Guyanne Wilson and Michael Westphal (eds.), *New Englishes new methods*, 201–220. Amsterdam: John Benjamins.

Schneider, Edgar W. 2007. *Postcolonial English. Varieties around the world*. Cambridge: Cambridge University Press.
Smith, Jennifer, Mercedes Durham & Hazel Richards. 2013. The social and linguistic in the acquisition of sociolinguistics norms: Caregivers, children and variation. *Linguistics* 51 (2). 285–324.
Smith, Jennifer, Mercedes Durham & Liane Fortune. 2007. 'Mam, my trousers is fa'in doon!': Community, caregiver, and child in the acquisition of variation in a Scottish dialect. *Language Variation and Change* 19 (1). 63–99.
Snell, Julia. 2008. *Pronouns, dialect and discourse: A socio-pragmatic account of children's language in Teeside*. Leeds: University of Leeds PhD dissertation.
St. Kitts & Nevis Statistics Department. 2011. St. Kitts and Nevis statistics population and housing census.
Tagliamonte, Sali A. & Sonja Molfenter. 2007. How'd you get that accent?: Acquiring a second dialect of the same language. *Language in Society* 36 (5). 649–675.
Westphal, Michael. 2017. *Language variation on Jamaican radio*. Amsterdam: John Benjamins.
Winford, Donald. 1976. Teacher attitudes toward language varieties in a creole community. *International Journal of the Sociology of Language* 1976 (8). 45–75.
Youssef, Valerie. 1993. Children's linguistic choices: Audience design and societal norms. *Language in Society* 22 (2). 257–274.
Youssef, Valerie. 2005. 'May I have the bilna?': The development of face-saving in young Trinidadian children. In Susanne Mühleisen & Bettina Migge (eds.), *Politeness and face in Caribbean Creoles*, 227–254. Amsterdam: John Benjamins.

Jette G. Hansen Edwards
11 Youth identity as linguistic identity: Political engagement and language acquisition and use in Hong Kong

Abstract: Drawing on data from a longitudinal mixed-methods study, this chapter examines the impact of social movements on youth language acquisition and use in Hong Kong, where language is highly politicized and language acquisition, resistance, and use are Acts of Identity (Le Page and Tabouret-Keller 1985). Specifically, the chapter examines the acquisition and use of Hong Kong's three official spoken languages – English, Cantonese, and Putonghua. It also examines the acquisition and use of varieties of English, and in particular, Hong Kong English, a postcolonial variety of English that is gradually gaining acceptance in Hong Kong. The chapter argues that acquisition and use of these languages and varieties cannot be understood without an examination of the socio-political forces impacting the language ecology of Hong Kong.

Keywords: identity, Hong Kong English, language acquisition, political engagement, World Englishes, language attitudes

1 Introduction

This chapter examines the impact of social movements on youth language acquisition and use in Hong Kong and how Cantonese, English, and Putonghua are viewed as identity markers in Hong Kong. The chapter argues that any research on second language acquisition (SLA) within a World Englishes and/or multilingual context needs to examine the status of English vis-à-vis other languages in the language ecology to understand the status and use of a local variety in that given context. In Hong Kong, for example, it is critical to examine the status of English vis-à-vis Cantonese and Putonghua in order to fully understand why the local variety of English, Hong Kong English (HKE), is targeted for acquisition and use. In addition, the status of any L2 in a World Englishes and/or multilingual setting is also impacted by social and political movements. In Hong Kong, the rise of English in the language ecology, and the targeting and use of HKE as the local identity marker, has been largely led

Jette G. Hansen Edwards, The Chinese University of Hong Kong, Hong Kong

https://doi.org/10.1515/9783110733723-011

by adolescents in resistance to the increasing political and linguistic mainlandization of Hong Kong (Ho and Hung 2020); mainland here refers to Mainland China, the geopolitical area for the territories directly under administration of the People's Republic China (PRC). It excludes both Macau and Hong Kong, which are both Special Administrative Regions of the PRC with higher degrees of autonomy than other regions of the PRC. The main argument of this chapter is that there is a need to incorporate sociocultural, sociolinguistic, and socio-political theory into any framework of SLA to account for language acquisition and use within World Englishes and/or multilingual contexts. Data to support this argument are drawn from a longitudinal mixed-methods study on language attitudes in Hong Kong, consisting of over 2000 surveys and 60 interviews conducted since the eve of the Umbrella Movement in 2014 through the political unrest in 2019 and 2020. The paper also draws upon a number of theoretical frameworks to discuss language acquisition and use in Hong Kong, including Le Page and Tabouret-Keller's (1985) Acts of Identity, Bourdieu's (1980) Theory of Capital, Brewer's (1991) Optimal Distinctiveness Theory, Gal and Woolard's (2001) concept of Linguistic Authority, and Schneider's (2007) Dynamic Model of the evolution of Postcolonial Englishes. The paper argues that each theoretical framework on its own cannot capture the complexity of language development and change in multilingual societies, and that a new theoretical framework is required that incorporates an analysis of the impact of social movements on youth language acquisition and use in multilingual societies.

2 The sociopolitical context and language ecology of Hong Kong

The Hong Kong Special Administrative Region (SAR) was a British colony for over 150 years; in 1997, it was returned to the People's Republic of China (PRC). Hong Kong is governed under the 'One Country, Two Systems' rule for a period of 50 years after the handover; as such, Hong Kong, as a SAR, has a different economic and administrative system from Mainland China although it is part of the 'One Country' of the PRC. In the past decade, there has been increasing tension in Hong Kong, particularly between individuals who advocate for greater autonomy for Hong Kong versus those who view integration into the PRC as beneficial. In the first decade after the handover, Hong Kong held a special status as the economic and financial hub of the PRC; the spread of SARS in 2003, the Asian financial crisis in 2009, as well as the rapid economic development of the PRC have shifted the power balance, and Hong Kong has become increasingly economically dependent upon and integrated into the PRC. The Hong Kong and PRC governments are also promoting greater assimilation of Hong Kong into the PRC (see Shen 2021). Prior to COVID-19, Hong Kong saw increased tourism from the mainland, with over 51 million visitors in 2018, an increase of 14.8% from 2017 (Siu 2019). Approximately 1.5 million mainland Chinese have migrated to Hong Kong since the handover, amounting to approximately 20% of Hong Kong's population (O'Neill 2017).

Language has always been a site of struggle as well as an identity marker in Hong Kong, both during Hong Kong's more than 150 years of British colonial rule as well as in the present day. Hong Kong has three official spoken languages – Cantonese, English, and Putonghua – and two official written languages, English and traditional written Chinese. English was Hong Kong's first official language and the sole de facto official language from 1883 until 1974 when, facing increasing public pressure to make Cantonese an official language in Hong Kong, the colonial government enacted the Official Languages Ordinance, which declared both English and Chinese to be the official languages of Hong Kong. While not explicitly named in the Ordinance, the Chinese in the Official Language Ordinance has widely been interpreted to be Cantonese, which is spoken by 88.1% of Hong Kong's population of 7.5 million (see Poon 2000). The pressure to give Cantonese official status in Hong Kong, called the Chinese Language Movement, was one of the first youth-led social movements in Hong Kong as the pressure came both from local counsellors in the legislature as well as from student unions of several local universities in Hong Kong, including Hong Kong University, and Chung Chi College, which is now part of the Chinese University of Hong Kong (Chen 2001). During the colonial period, English and Cantonese were in a diglossic language situation, with English serving as the "high" language of the judiciary and government while Cantonese was the "low" language of the home and social sphere. Cantonese is now the main language of government.

High English proficiency is required for university admission in Hong Kong, with most of Hong Kong's eight public universities having an English-only medium of instruction policy. This has led to a washdown effect on local primary and secondary schools due to parental demands for English language instruction to provide their children with an important edge in university admissions (Poon 2009). As such, English is widely viewed as having a pragmatic function in Hong Kong as an instrumental language providing educational and economic opportunities to proficient users.

Putonghua is the national language of the PRC and an official language in Hong Kong since the handover in 1997. It is the mother tongue of 3.9% of Hong Kong's population. Putonghua was introduced into the Hong Kong education system prior to the handover; it is a required language in both primary and secondary schools and has increasingly been adopted as the "Chinese" medium of instruction, replacing Cantonese. Recent research suggests that 72% of local primary and 37% of secondary schools now teach Chinese through Putonghua rather than Cantonese (Varsity 2017), leading to fears that Cantonese is under threat in Hong Kong (Hansen Edwards 2021).

The increasing tourism and residency of mainland Chinese, as well as replacement of Cantonese with Putonghua, have exacerbated existing political tensions in Hong Kong. These tensions – linguistic, demographic, and political – have led to a number of large-scale protests against the Hong Kong Special Administrative Region (HKSAR) government. One such protest was the 79-day Umbrella Movement that occurred in 2014; it sought universal suffrage[1] to establish greater autonomy in Hong Kong. From June 2019 until the COVID-19 crisis starting in January of 2020 in Hong Kong, millions of Hong Kong people took to the streets to protest a proposed fugitive extradition bill between Hong Kong and the PRC (called the anti-ELAB movement). Hong Kong has since implemented a National Security Law, creating further divisions within Hong Kong society. The impact of these divisions on language acquisition and use is discussed below.

3 Methodology

Since 2014, I have been collecting survey and interview data on the Hong Kong identity and language attitudes. The survey comprised both open and closed ended questions about language and identity in Hong Kong; follow up interviews probing survey responses were held with sixty participants who were selected to represent a wider demographic based on gender, identity, and age; all interviews were individual between the participant and a trained research assistant who was also fluent in Cantonese, Putonghua, and English, and could clarify any of the questions. The interview questions were all open-ended and semi-structured to probe survey responses and to gain further information based on the interviewees' answers to the open-ended question. Photographs from the protests in 2019 were also collected and analyzed for language use and linguistic features.

Table 11.1 gives an overview of the demographics of the survey respondents. Aside from 2017, when the survey was conducted at all of Hong Kong's eight publicly funded institutions as well as private universities and colleges (see Hansen Edwards 2018), the survey was conducted at my university, The Chinese University of Hong Kong (CUHK). The survey was conducting using SurveyMonkey, through which Z-tests were conducted on the data. Table 11.1 indicates the majority of the respondents were

---

[1] Universal suffrage refers to the right of the public to elect their own chief executive, or prime minister. The chief executive is currently elected by a panel of legislators appointed by the government and approved by the PRC.

young, with most aged 18–20, followed by 21–25. The majority of the respondents are women, which is not unusual in applied linguistics research. I also collected data on cultural identification, and from 2017–2020, on political engagement.

Table 11.1: Survey respondents.

2015–2020	2014 N = 307	2015 N = 292	2016 N = 240	2017 N = 568	2019 N =290	2020 N = 342
Age						
15–17	–	–	–	<1%	1%	–
18–20	61%	64%	67%	53%	64%	74%
21–25	34%	34%	29%	45%	28%	19%
26–30	3%	2%	4%	1%	5%	5%
31–35	2%	–	<1%	<1%	<1%	2%
36+	–	–	–	–	2%	1%
Gender						
Women	72%	74%	73%	57%	71%	73%
Men	28%	26%	27%	43%	29%	27%
Cultural Identification						
Hong Konger	61%	74%	73%	72%	77%	87%
Hong Kong Chinese	35%	24%	25%	6%	18%	11%
Chinese	4%	2%	2%	2%	2%	1%
Politically Engaged						
Yes	NA	NA	NA	28%*	50%*	56%
No				72%*	50%*	44%

*Statistical significance within each cell at p < 0.05.

There are three main cultural identifications in Hong Kong: Hong Konger, Hong Kong (HK) Chinese, and Chinese. Hong Konger can be defined as any inhabitant of Hong Kong regardless of ethnic group affiliation; it is most commonly seen as a local identity marker geographically restricted to Hong Kong. It is also viewed as a localist identity; localism is a grassroots political movement to preserve Hong Kong's unique cultural, historical, and linguistic heritage (Kaeding 2017). HK Chinese, in contrast, reflects a bi-cultural identity, someone who is a Hong Konger but part of larger China – a bridge between Hong Kong and the rest of the PRC. Chinese is a pan-ethnic identity; within Hong Kong, it also refers to someone from Mainland China and/or as a national PRC identity. The localist Hong Konger identity has risen from 61% in 2014 to 87% in 2020 while the bi-cultural HK Chinese identity has fallen from 35% in 2014 to 11% in 2020, indicating that the majority of respondents not only have a localist identity but that the proportion of respondents who claim this identity is increasing across time. The increase in the Hong Konger identity from 61% in 2014 to 74% in 2015 and from 77% in 2017 and 2019 to 87% in 2020 were significant ($p < 0.001$). Conversely, the decrease in the HK Chinese identity from 35% in 2014 to 24% in 2015 was significant ($p < 0.01$) while decreases from 25% in 2016 to 19% in 2017 and from 18% in 2019 to 11% in 2020 were both significant at $p < 0.05$. In sum, there has been a significant increase in participants' indexing of their cultural identity as a localist Hong Konger from 2014 to 2020; conversely, there has been a significant decrease in the number of participants who index a bi-cultural HK Chinese identity. Very few individuals indicate they have a Chinese identity. Similar findings have been found in other large-scale surveys of ethnic identity in Hong Kong, indicating that this is a widespread change across the population of Hong Kong (see HKPORI 2021).

In 2017, I also began asking about the participants' level of engagement. The participants were asked to indicate "Yes" or "No" to the question: *Are you interested in or actively involved in Hong Kong politics?* In 2017, a minority (28%) of the participants indicated that they were interested or involved in politics; in 2019, 50% of the participants stated they were interested or actively involved in politics, a significant increase ($p < 0.0001$). In 2020, 56% of the participants stated they were interested or engaged in politics, a slight increase from 2019.

Participants were also asked which political parties they were interested or engaged in: In 2017, 58% named parties that were pro-democratic or localist while 42% stated that there was no particular party in which they were interested. In 2017, the number of participants who named localist/pro-democratic parties rose to 92%, with 8% noting that there was no particular party of interest; in 2020, 83% named localist/pro-democratic parties while 17% stated there was no particular party of interest.

The study also examined whether levels of interest and/or active involvement in Hong Kong politics differed by gender and cultural identification; this is shown in Table 11.2. Gender differences were found for political engagement in 2017, with significantly more men than women indicating that they were interested in Hong Kong politics ($p < 0.05$). Political engagement differed significantly by cultural identification across all three years, with significantly more Hong Kongers engaged or interested in politics than HK Chinese or Chinese ($p < 0.05$).

In sum, I found that while political engagement and/or interest in politics was not widespread among the participants in 2017, it increased significantly to 50% in 2019, likely due to the significant civil unrest in 2019. Cultural identification was connected with political interest and engagement, with levels higher among Hong Kongers than HK Chinese and Chinese. The study also found that the politically engaged or interested respondents had a strong affiliation with democratic and/or localist political parties.

Table 11.2: Political engagement by gender and cultural identification 2017–2020.

	Gender		Cultural Identification		
	Women	Men	Hong Konger	HK Chinese	Chinese
2017	24%*	33%*	32%*	15%*	14%
2019	51%	48%	58%*+	25%*	20%+
2020	58%	49%	60%*+	29%*	0%+

*,+ indicates each set of statistically significant percentages at p < 0.05.

4 Language and identity in Hong Kong

As I have argued elsewhere (Hansen Edwards 2018), to understand attitudes towards Hong Kong English (HKE), it is important to examine how Hong Kong's linguistic identity has shifted against an increasingly divisive political landscape – to take a multilingual and sociopolitical approach to the study of World Englishes. My research has, therefore, examined how Cantonese, English, and Putonghua are viewed as identity markers in Hong Kong. From 2017–2020, I asked participants to indicate the language(s) of their self-identity as well as the language(s) of Hong Kong's identity. A range of options were available, including Putonghua only and "Other". Of these options, Cantonese only, Cantonese/English, and Cantonese/English/Putonghua, were the three most commonly selected; these results are presented in Figure 11.1. Figure 11.1 shows that aside from 2017, the majority of respondents indexed a bilingual Cantonese/English self-identity. While many respondents also indexed a monolingual Cantonese identity, very few individuals indexed a trilingual identity. Some changes across time were significant: The decrease from 41% in 2017 to 32% in 2019 for a monolingual self-identity and increase from 35% in 2017 to 46% in 2019 for a bilingual self-identity were both significant at p < 0.01. In 2017, the monolingual self-identity was significantly higher than both the bilingual (p < 0.05) and the monolingual identity (p < 0.0001). However, in 2019, at a time of significant civil unrest, the number of participants who indexed a bilingual self-identity was significantly higher than the number who indexed a trilingual or monolingual identity (both at p < 0.001); the possible reasons for this will be explored below. In 2020, the bilingual self-identity stayed significantly higher than the trilingual (p <0.01) or monolingual (p < 0.0001) identity.

The indexing of Hong Kong's linguistic identity is shown in Figure 11.2; the majority of the respondents view Hong Kong as bilingual – as having a Cantonese/English identity. Surprisingly, fewer respondents view Hong Kong having a monolingual Cantonese identity and very few respondents view Hong Kong as trilingual. There were no significant changes across time. Within time, however, the indexing of Hong Kong

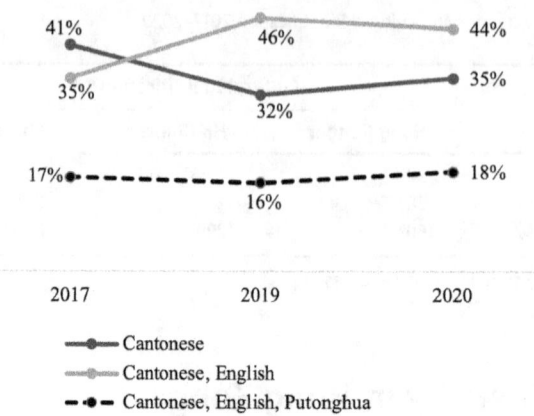

Figure 11.1: Language of self-identity.

as bilingual was significantly higher than the trilingual or monolingual identity at all three data collection points (2017: bilingual over monolingual at $p < 0.05$; bilingual over trilingual at $p < 0.0001$; 2019 and 2020: bilingual over monolingual and trilingual at $p < 0.0001$).

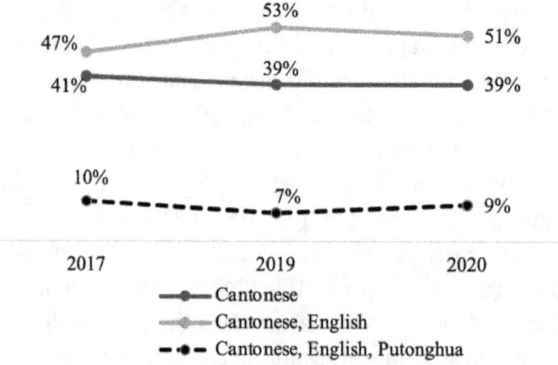

Figure 11.2: Language of Hong Kong's identity.

These results are interesting, given that much of the prior research on the status of English in Hong Kong (see for example Lai 2011, 2012) suggests that English has a pragmatic role in Hong Kong's language ecology, yielding economic capital to proficient users. This research has also found that Cantonese, as the local vernacular, expresses the Hong Kong identity. In contrast, my findings show that English has become like Cantonese for many individuals in Hong Kong – an authentic language of Hong Kong. Bilingualism in Cantonese and English is part of Hong Kong's identity for many respondents and is becoming part of a self-identity as well.

A further analysis by gender, cultural identification, and political engagement (see Tables 11.3 and 11.4), indicates that differences in language of self-identity in Hong Kong exist on the basis of gender, as men are more likely to index a bilingual language identity. A robust body of research (see Coates 2007) has established that women have more positive attitudes towards languages that are viewed to have more economic/pragmatic utility and bestow prestige on the speaker whereas men have more positive attitudes to languages that confer local value. While significantly more women than men indexed a trilingual identity in 2017 and 2020, men are more likely to index a Cantonese/English identity than women, suggesting that English – along with Cantonese – is viewed as a local language (and Putonghua as a pragmatic/economic language). Perhaps not surprisingly, the language of self-identity also differs by cultural identification, as those with a local Hong Konger identity are more likely to identify as bilingual in Cantonese/English while HK Chinese are more likely identify as trilingual. Those that are politically engaged are also more likely to self-identify as bilingual. These findings further illustrate that English has joined Cantonese to become an authentic local language, particularly for men, and for those who have a localist Hong Konger identity and/or are engaged in politics.

Table 11.3: Language of self-identity 2017–2020.

	2017			2019			2020		
	C	CE	CEP	C	CE	CEP	C	CE	CEP
Gender									
Men	39%	42%*	13%*	32%	45%	17%	22%*	55%*	0%*
Women	43%	30%*	20%*	31%	49%	15%	40%*	40%*	3%*
Cultural Identity									
HKER	42%*	41%*	0%*	36%	51%*	12%*	36%	48%*	14%*
HKC	44%	23%*	6%*	21%	34%*	36%*	34%	16%*	42%*
Chinese	20%*	17%*	17%*	40%	20%	20%	0%	40%	60%
Political Engagement									
Yes	35%	47%*	13%	30%	56%*	10%*	37%	50%*	11%*
No	43%	31%*	18%	31%	36%*	25%*	33%	37%*	27%*

*Statistical significance within each cell at p < 0.05.
C = Cantonese
CE = Cantonese/English
CEP = Cantonese/English/Putonghua

In contrast, as Table 11.4 shows, the indexing of a bilingual language identity for Hong Kong is consistent across time and by gender, cultural identification, and political engagement, with the exception of 2019 with political engagement. In other words, while the linguistic representation of self is related to the participant's gender, cultural identification, and political engagement, the linguistic representation of Hong Kong is consistent regardless of these factors. This suggests a more uniform view of Hong Kong exists – participants may feel they have a monolingual Cantonese identity and still view Hong Kong as bilingual in Cantonese/English.

Table 11.4: Language of national identity 2017–2020.

	2017			2019			2020		
	C	CE	CEP	C	CE	CEP	C	CE	CEP
Gender									
Men	41%	48%	8%	34%	57%	7%	30%*	60%	0%
Women	41%	46%	11%	41%	52%	7%	42%*	48%	0%
Cultural Identity									
HKER	40%	50%	8%	40%	53%	6%	40%	52%	0%*
HKC	44%	41%	13%	36%	53%	11%	37%	45%	3%*
Chinese	49%	37%	9%	20%	40%	20%	20%	60%	0%
Political Engagement									
Yes	38%	52%	9%	36%	61%*	3%*	40%	51%	8%
No	43%	45%	10%	42%	36%*	12%*	38%	52%	10%

*Statistical significance within each cell at p < 0.05.
C = Cantonese
CE = Cantonese/English
CEP = Cantonese/English/Putonghua

There is no data prior to 2017 on language of identity in Hong Kong, possibly because English has largely been perceived to hold an instrumental value in Hong Kong, as evidenced by the questions posed in previous research. This research has focused on comparing the integrative vs. instrumental value of Hong Kong's spoken languages (Lai 2011, 2012). My research (see also Hansen Edwards 2018, 2020) in contrast, focuses on examining how participants view the languages that form part of the language ecology of Hong Kong as representative of their own or Hong Kong's identity. This approach has yielded important insight on the status of English, which appears to have a much more integrative and symbolic role in Hong Kong and among people in Hong Kong than previous research has found. Also interesting is the lower rate of acceptance of Putonghua as a language of Hong Kong's identity in contrast to a language of self-identity. Acceptance of Putonghua as a language of self-identity is low as well, particularly for Hong Kongers, men, and those that are politically engaged. All participants are likely to have similar levels of proficiency in Putonghua; they also have similar levels of proficiency in English (Census and Statistics Department HKSAR 2019). What these findings suggest is that there is an active resistance to Putonghua among the participants, with greater resistance among men, Hong Kongers, and those that are politically engaged.

English and Cantonese (and written traditional Chinese) have both been used as visible markers of the Hong Kong identity during the protests, particularly during the 2014 Umbrella Movement and in 2019 during the anti-ELAB protests. Both written English and traditional written Chinese, the latter also an in-group marker of a Hong Kong identity,[2] have been used in posters, graffiti, and on social media, including at CUHK, where a stand-off between protesters and police shut down the campus for five days in November 2019. Spoken English and Cantonese have also both been used in interviews and news conferences.

Figure 11.3: Protests at CUHK (Wong 2019).

As a language of the protests, English may be viewed as a powerful mechanism for engagement with an international audience via social media and online news. It may also publicly mark a Hong Konger identity in contrast to a Chinese identity. As one

---

2 Simplified written Chinese is used in other regions of the PRC and Asia, with the exception of Macau, Taiwan, and Hong Kong.

participant stated, *"The bilingual ability is what distinguish Hong Konger from other Chinese"* while another stated, *"I am not a Chinese but I am a Hong Konger and a global citizen"*. This is also supported by my previous research (Hansen Edwards 2020), in which I found that English symbolized linguistic and political differentiation from the PRC; as an interviewee noted, *"Hong Kongers are bilingual"*. In contrast, both in the current research and my previous study, I found that some Hong Kongers resisted the use of Putonghua, which they viewed as an imposed language, representing a contested national (PRC) identity *"Hong Kong is NOT China"* (Hansen Edwards 2020).

As Figures 11.3 and 11.4 both show, protesters used traditional written Chinese and English to fill public spaces as the languages of Hong Kong. The visible use of English (including at my own university, as seen in Figures 11.3 and 11.4) may also serve as a reminder of Hong Kong's colonial history and of the UK's responsibility to enforce the Sino-British Joint Declaration, which guaranteed Hong Kong "One Country, Two Systems" from 1997 until 2047, a guarantee that is being eroded, as evidenced by the attempted introduction of the extradition legislation and the implementation of the National Security Law. This view is illustrated by quotes by some of the participants: *"English represents western countries which emphasize democracy and freedom;" "I admire Great Britain. I don't want to be considered as a Chinese"*.

Figure 11.4: Graffiti at CUHK (Hansen Edwards 2019).

Interestingly, written Chinese has also become part of the political battle ground; one sign circulated on social media has the slogan *Ng dai sou kau yat bat hor* 'Five demands, not one less' as well as the place and time of an upcoming protest written in Cantonese using pinyin (romanization of Chinese characters). This technique is aimed at "deterring online trolls and people accused of being spies from mainland China" (Chen 2019). The use of pinyin, rather than traditional Chinese characters, makes the message more difficult to understand to non-Cantonese speakers, thus functioning as a gate-keeper and in-group communication within the Cantonese speaking community. In sum, political conflicts may serve as an accelerant for some participants, in particular those that have a localist Hong Konger identity and/or are politically engaged and for men over women to embrace and use English and/or Cantonese/English bilingualism to assert a Hong Konger identity both locally and internationally.

5 Acceptance and use of Hong Kong English

This brings me to Hong Kong English (HKE), a local variety of English that has emerged as a result of British colonization. HKE has often been researched in opposition to British English and American English, the other widely used varieties of English in Hong Kong, with HKE often cast in a more negative light in comparison to British and American English. Previous studies show that American and British English norms are held in prestige in Hong Kong, with HKE stigmatized and viewed as "inferior" and "erroneous" (Groves 2011; Zhang 2013). My own research is showing that HKE acceptance and use is rising among the younger generation as a symbolic marker of the Hong Konger identity *in English*.

Evidence of this can be found in the responses to in a series of questions I have asked survey respondents since 2014, including *Is HKE a 'real' variety of English*? As Figure 11.5 shows, there has been a significant increase in the acceptance and, therefore, legitimacy of HKE in Hong Kong. "No" responses significantly decreased from 40% in 2014 to 33% in 2015 ($p < 0.05$), and from 37% in 2017 to 18% in 2019 ($p < 0.0001$). The increases in "Yes" responses were significant from 31% in 2014 to 40% in 2015 ($p < 0.01$) and from 39% in 2017 to 55% in 2019 ($p < 0.0001$).

An analysis of the relationship between gender, political engagement, and cultural identification and acceptance of HKE was also conducted as shown in Table 11.5. Although not entirely comparative, this is similar to the question about the language of Hong Kong's identity as it focuses on the acceptance of HKE within Hong Kong, and therefore, as a language of Hong Kong. While some significant differences exist by gender in 2015 and 2019, with men leading the acceptance of HKE; by cultural engagement, with significantly more HK Chinese than Hong Kongers not accepting HKE in 2015; and by political engagement, with sig-

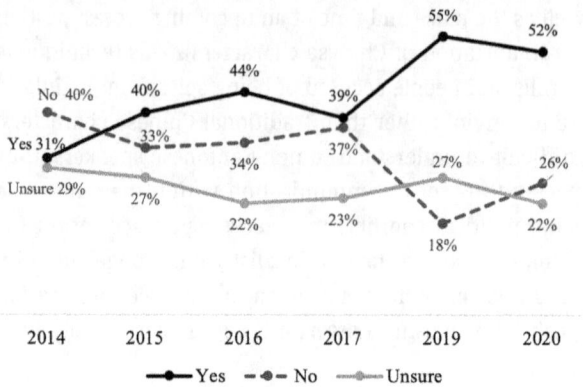

Figure 11.5: Is HKE a real variety of English?

Table 11.5: Acceptance of HKE and gender, cultural identity, and political engagement.

	Gender		Political Engagement		Cultural Identity	
	Women	Men	Pol Engaged	Not Pol Engaged	Hong Konger	HK Chinese
2014			NA	NA		
Yes	28%	37%			33%	25%
No	43%	33%			38%	45%
Unsure	29%	30%			29%	30%
2015			NA	NA		
Yes	33%*	58%*		NA	40%	42%
No	38%*	18%*	NA		28%*	46%*
Unsure	29%	23%			32%*	12%*
2016			NA	NA		
Yes	43%	47%			41%	52%
No	36%	30%			34%	37%
Unsure	21%	23%			25%*	12%*
2017						
Yes	36%	40%	43%	36%	39%	33%
No	41%	34%	34%	39%	38%	42%
Unsure	23%	26%	23%	25%	23%	26%

Table 11.5 (continued)

	Gender		Political Engagement		Cultural Identity	
	Women	Men	Pol Engaged	Not Pol Engaged	Hong Konger	HK Chinese
2019						
Yes	51%*	66%*	68%*	42%*	57%	48%
No	20%	11%	13%	23%	17%	20%
Unsure	29%	23%	20%*	35%*	26%	32%
2020						
Yes	51%	55%	57%*	46%*	53%	42%
No	27%	23%	24%	28%	25%	34%
Unsure	22%	21%	19%	26%	22%	24%

*Statistical significance at $p < 0.05$.

nificantly more politically engaged participants accepting HKE in 2019 and 2020, there is an increased acceptance of HKE across all participants across time.

The participants were also asked both whether they spoke HKE and whether they wanted to speak HKE. In answer to the question of *Do you speak Hong Kong English?*, as Figure 11.6 shows, across all six data collection points, the majority of the participants acknowledged they spoke HKE; this rose significantly from 60% in 2014 to 85% in 2020. Conversely, the number of participants who were either unsure or stated they did not speak HKE fell from 25% to 9% ("Unsure") and 16% to 6% ("No"). The rise in "Yes" responses from 60% in 2014 to 74% in 2015 was significant ($p < 0.001$), as was the rise from 72% in 2017 to 80% in 2019 ($p < 0.01$). Conversely, the decrease in "No" from 16% in 2014 to 9% in 2015 was significant ($p < 0.01$). It is possible that as acknowledgement of HKE as its own variety grew among the participants, as shown in Figure 11.5, participants' understanding and identification as their own speech as HKE shifted; this may help explain the decrease in "Unsure" responses across time.

Interestingly, across time, the only significant difference in gender was "not" speaking HKE in 2014; in 2017, significantly more politically engaged persons stated they spoke HKE while in 2014, 2015, and 2020, more HK Chinese stated they did not speak HKE compared with Hong Kongers (and significantly more Hong Kongers stated they spoke HKE in 2015 than HK Chinese). It is likely that few differences exist because of high rates of acknowledgement of speaking HKE within the survey population, with the lowest at 57% (women in 2014), and the highest at 87% (men in 2020).

As Figure 11.7 shows, there has been a sharp and significant decrease in "No" responses to the question of *Do you want to speak HKE?* across time, from 71% in 2014 to 33% in 2020, with a corresponding significant increase in "Yes" responses from 16% in 2014 to 47%, in 2020. If these responses are compared with those for the question of *Do you speak HKE?*, it is clear that while significantly more people indicate a desire for speaking HKE in 2020 than in 2014, there is still a gap between actually speaking HKE and wanting to speak HKE. In other words, while the vast majority of participants indicate they speak HKE, from 60% in 2014 to 85% in 2020, and while interest in speaking is also increasing across time, the number of participants who wish to speak HKE in 2020 is still under 50%.

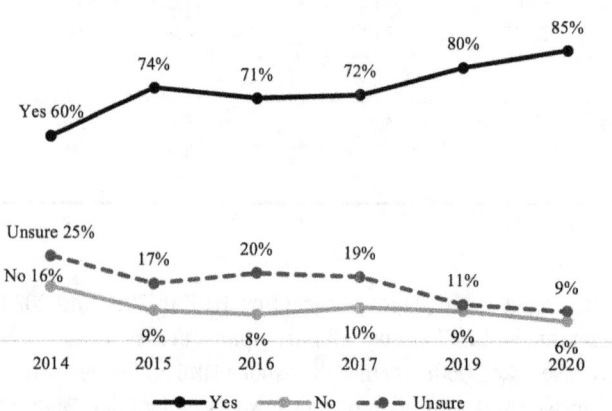

Figure 11.6: Do you speak HKE?

Table 11.6: Do you speak HKE?

	Gender		Political Engagement		Cultural Identity	
	Women	Men	Political Engaged	Not Political Engaged	Hong Konger	HK Chinese
2014			NA	NA		
Yes	57%	65%			64%	53%
No	19%*	9%*			10%*	23%*
Unsure	25%	26%			26%	23%
2015			NA	NA		
Yes	71%	80%			79%*	59%*
No	10%	5%			6%*	15%*
Unsure	18%	15%			15%	26%
2016			NA	NA		
Yes	70%	75%			73%	68%

Table 11.6 (continued)

	Gender		Political Engagement		Cultural Identity	
	Women	Men	Political Engaged	Not Political Engaged	Hong Konger	HK Chinese
No	9%	6%			8%	8%
Unsure	21%	19%			19%	24%
2017						
Yes	67%	73%	76%*	68%*	72%	69%
No	12%	11%	7%*	13%*	10%	7%
Unsure	21%	16%	17%	19%	18%	24%
2019						
Yes	81%	78%	82%	78%	84%	75%
No	9%	8%	5%	12%	5%*	18%*
Unsure	10%	14%	13%	10%	11%	7%
2020						
Yes	83%	87%	85%	84%	86%	74%
No	6%	6%	4%	9%	5%	11%
Unsure	10%	6%	11%	8%	9%	16%

*Statistically significant at $p < 0.05$.

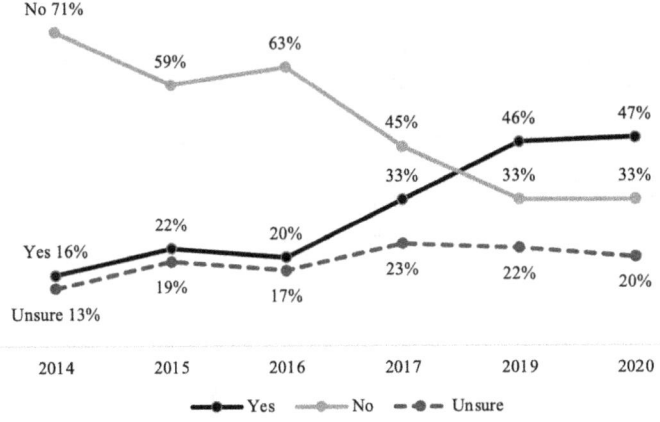

Figure 11.7: Do you want to speak HKE?

These responses were also analyzed by gender and cultural identification, and in 2017–2020, by political engagement, as shown in Table 11.7. Gender was a significant predictor from 2014–2017. In addition, in a similar pattern to the indexing of

Table 11.7: Do you want to speak HKE by gender, identity, and political engagement.

	Gender		Political Engagement		Cultural Identity	
	Women	Men	Political Engaged	Not Political Engaged	Hong Konger	HK Chinese
2014			NA	NA		
Yes	12%*	24%*			15%	17%
No	77%*	58%*			70%	74%
Unsure	11%	18%			14%	10%
2015			NA	NA		
Yes	15%*	36%*			21%	24%
No	67%*	41%*			58%	62%
Unsure	18%	22%			21%	13%
2016			NA	NA		
Yes	17%*	29%*			23%*	7%*
No	67%*	52%*			62%	70%
Unsure	16%	19%			15%	23%
2017						
Yes	28%*	36%*	38%*	29%*	35%*	25%*
No	51%*	38%*	38%*	48%*	43%	51%
Unsure	21%	26%	24%	22%	23%	24%
2019						
Yes	44%	51%	57%*	35%*	51%*	28%*
No	33%	32%	23%*	42%*	30%	42%
Unsure	23%	17%	20%	23%	19%	30%
2020						
Yes	45%	53%	52%	42%	49%*	32%*
No	33%	31%	29%	38%	30%*	50%*
Unsure	21%	16%	19%	20%	20%	18%

*Statistical significance at p < 0.05.

bilingualism in Cantonese/English to express a self-identity, significantly more men than women, Hong Kongers over HK Chinese, and those who were politically engaged vs. those who were not, wanted to speak HKE.

As these analyses show, HKE is increasingly viewed as acceptable and legitimate. A pattern of language use emerges: Men, Hong Kongers, and those that are politically engaged are more likely to index a bilingual Cantonese/English identity; they are also more likely to accept and want to speak HKE. As participants note, "It *is like our own language apart from Cantonese;*" "*It is our culture, a unique culture to stand out from the world*". The data shows that the rise of HKE in Hong Kong is parallel to a rise in the Hong Konger identity, political engagement, and the view of the self and Hong Kong as bilingual – in other words, we cannot separate HKE from the political situation or the other languages of Hong Kong. HKE, like Cantonese and English, offers a bilingual representation of Hong Kong to the world; as participants stated about why they spoke HKE, "*It represents that I am a real Hong Konger;*" "*To show others that I come from Hong Kong;*" "*. . . this can prove myself a Hong Kong people*". In sum, HKE has become the linguistic manifestation of a Hong Konger identity in English.

The increasing visibility of HKE as an identity marker in Hong Kong can also be seen in the use of HKE in the public space during protests. For example, Figure 11.8 from the protests in Hong Kong in 2019 shows a sign with the phrase *add oil*, a HKE phrase of encouragement that has entered the Oxford English Dictionary.

Figure 11.8: Displays during protests in November 2019 (James 2019).

6 Discussion: World Englishes and SLA

Figure 11.9 is a composite illustration of the linguistic and identity changes that have occurred in Hong Kong from 2014 until 2020. The changes seen for the indexing of a Hong Konger identity; Cantonese/English bilingual identity; and acceptance and use of HKE are rising in parallel. Of note is the significant increase from 2014 to 2015 in the Hong Konger identity and speaking, acceptance of, and

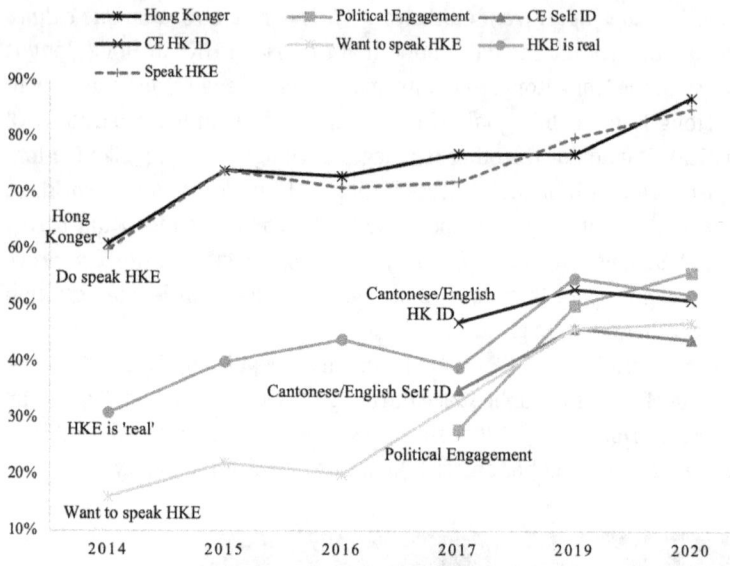

Figure 11.9: Linguistic and identity changes across time.

wanting to speak HKE. Data for the 2014 data set were collected on the eve of the Umbrella Movement, at a time of rising tensions before the movement unfolded. The 2015 data set was collected nine months after the Umbrella Movement ended and is likely reflective of the heightened political tensions occurring during and after the movement; it is also likely reflective of the increased awareness of a more localist meaning of the term "Hong Konger," and recognition of HKE as a variety of English. There is also a significant increase from 2017 to 2019 in political engagement; Cantonese/English self-identity; and speaking, wanting to speak, and acceptance of HKE; the 2019 data set was collected in May of 2019. The extradition treaty, which would allow the transfer of fugitives from Hong Kong to Taiwan, Macau, and Mainland China, was introduced in late March 2019. The treaty led to protests from March until COVID-19 led to social restrictions in Hong Kong. The 2019 data set was thus also collected at a time of protests, similar to the 2015 set. It is, therefore, not surprising that we see the largest and most significant increases of the Hong Konger identity, Cantonese/English as an identity-marker, and acceptance and use of HKE in both 2015 and 2019 – the most significant increases in local linguistic and identity markers occurred as political tensions rise.

As the above discussion has shown, the linguistic situation in Hong Kong is complex due to both historical and geopolitical factors. A key argument of this paper is that no one theory can capture the interplay between language, identity, and politics in Hong Kong. Instead, I draw on several theoretical frameworks to analyze Hong Kong's languages against a divisive political landscape. Bourdieu's (1980) Theory of Capital conceptualizes differential levels of symbolic power as capital: cultural, social, and economic. Cultural capital includes educational qualifications as well as linguistic resources; social capital refers to social obligations and/or connections whereas economic capital consists of the assets which particular elements of social and cultural capital can confer on individuals and groups. In previous research (see Lai 2011, 2012), English has been viewed as having cultural and economic capital in Hong Kong; I would argue that given the political conflicts over the past six years, English has moved from only giving its users cultural capital to becoming what Gal and Woolard (2001) describe as an "authentic language" of Hong Kong and of the self. Gal and Woolard's (2001: 7) theory of Linguistic Authority refers to the authenticity and/or anonymity a language or languages have in the eyes of members of a particular multilingual community; as they note, the ideology of authenticity exists when a language or variety is "rooted in and directly expresses the essential nature of a community or speaker" whereas the ideology of anonymity is when a language or variety is "a neutral vehicle of communication, belonging to no one in particular and thus equally available to all". Bilingualism in Cantonese and English, and HKE as a marker of that bilingualism, is increasingly used to express both Hong Kong's identity as well as the participants' self-identity, as the data as well as images of banners and posters from the protests show. As such, English has moved beyond having a pragmatic role in Hong Kong as economic capital, emerging as an identity marker of Hong Kong as a region and of the self as a Hong Konger. In contrast, Putonghua may be viewed as contested anonymous language (Gal and Woolard 2001), a language imposed by local and PRC governments through the replacement of Cantonese with Putonghua in local government schools. The long-term status of Putonghua is unclear; it is viewed to confer economic capital for some participants, as noted above; as more schools use Putonghua rather than Cantonese as the Chinese medium of instruction, it is possible that more participants will identify as trilingual and view Hong Kong as having a trilingual identity.

The rise of Cantonese/English bilingualism, and HKE as the manifestation of this bilingualism in English to represent the Hong Kong identity, can also be interpreted through Brewer's (1991) Optimal Distinctiveness Theory. Brewer argues that the selection of a social identity is derived from a need to balance in-group inclusion and in-group vs. out-group differentiation and that social identity is related to shared in-group distinctiveness from the out-group. Hong Kong as a region is linguistically distinctive from Mainland China because both English and Cantonese are official languages. The PRC, in contrast, has Putonghua as the sole official language. This creates a perception that a linguistic division exists been Hong Kong and Mainland China, even though Cantonese is widely spoken in other parts of the PRC; this division has grown for some participants due to the political conflicts in Hong Kong. Le Page and Tabouret-Keller's (1985) Acts of Identity theory is also useful to interpret language behavior in Hong Kong. As Le Page and Tabouret-Keller (1985) argue, individuals index their ethnic or social solidarity or difference through Acts of Identity. Based on the data shown above, I argue that the participants in the study use Cantonese/English bilingualism as well as HKE, and resisted Putonghua usage, as politicized by their Acts of Identity; this is evidenced in the use of language in physical space on banners and posters during the protests as well as the rise of bilingualism and HKE to mark a Hong Kong identity.

While these frameworks provide a useful lens to interpret the linguistic identification and use illustrated by the data and the images from the protests, none of these frameworks on their own capture the complex interplay between identities, language, and varieties that is unfolding in Hong Kong as the political landscape changes. Clear patterns emerge within this interplay: Greater identification with bilingualism and a Cantonese/English identity, identification as a speaker of HKE, and rejection of and resistance to usage of Putonghua among individuals who, as Hong Kongers, politically engaged, and men, to a lesser extent, wish to project a local identity in both Cantonese and English. For some participants, language use is not only an Act of Identity but an act of a political identity, and the rise of HKE is related to rise of the Hong Konger identity and political engagement, driven by political divisions and a need to create an optimal distinctiveness to protect Hong Kong's political, geographic and linguistic space.

Another model that has been widely used to interpret the development of HKE is Schneider's (2007) Dynamic Model of the evolution of Postcolonial Englishes (PCEs). Schneider's model presents the evolution of PCEs in five stages, with Stage 3 occurring after independence from colonialism, when "new" national building occurs. This model has been widely adopted to analyze HKE (Groves 2011; Zhang 2013), with researchers, including Schneider himself, arguing that HKE is somewhere between Stages 2, Exonormative Stabilization and 3, Nativization. Elsewhere, I have argued (Hansen Edwards 2018) that the model does not capture the multilithic nature of language in Hong Kong. Schneider (2007) himself argues that Hong Kong is an interesting test of the model as it is not truly a postcolonial society, unlike India and Singapore, as example.

Schneider's (2007) model is a model of language contact based on a particular (and static) language ecology. But what if the language ecology shifts due to sociopolitical changes? In the model, the evolution of HKE is disconnected to the status of Cantonese, English, and Putonghua in Hong Kong's sociopolitical climate. There has been a period of rapid change in acceptance of HKE in Hong Kong; as discussed above, this cannot be explained without looking at the status of Cantonese,

English, and Putonghua within Hong Kong's sociopolitical context. English has increased in value in Hong Kong as a marker of the self and Hong Kong's identity. The introduction of Putonghua into the language ecology of Hong Kong, and the increasing perception that Hong Kong's linguistic space is becoming mainlandized due to the promotion of Putonghua over Cantonese, has unsettled and shifted the language ecology. This, in turn, has impacted attitudes towards and use of English as well as HKE.

As examples, Stages 4 and 5 of Schneider's (2007) Dynamic Model do not reflect Hong Kong's situation, as Stage 4 represents Endonormative Stabilization during post-independence and/or self-dependence, and Stage 5 represents Differentiation in a stable young nation. Unlike other postcolonial societies discussed in relation to the model, including Singapore, Hong Kong did not become independent in 1997, but became part of the PRC, a process of re-colonization instead of self-dependence: Re-colonization by another power, with a different history, culture, language(s), and governance. Schneider's model sees the evolution of PCEs as part of nation building, with the development of a pan-ethnic national identity. In Hong Kong, HKE and Cantonese/English bilingualism as well as Cantonese monolingualism are part of the development of a pan-ethnic linguistic identity, but this identity is restricted to Hong Kong, a Special Administrative Region within the PRC, in resistance to larger PRC pan-ethnic nationhood and a national language identity. The use of English, and the HKE variety of English, along with Cantonese, is part of nation building but as a separate linguistic, geographic, and political space in a region within (and in contrast to) the "new" nation, which is the PRC. As Schneider (2007: 26) explains, "[c]entral to the model which I am advocating is the notion of social identity and its construction and reconstruction by symbolic linguistic means". This is what is happening in Hong Kong, but not within a national framework, but rather as acts of resistance, Acts of Identity against imposed national identity and imposed anonymous languages. Language is never de-politicized, as Hong Kong's example illustrates. This is the case in other politically tenuous places like the use of Euskera in the Basque region of Spain – where language space is contested and a site of struggle.

A new theoretical framework is required that incorporates an analysis of the impact of social movements on youth language acquisition and use in multilingual and multidialectal societies – a multilingual and socio-political theory of the acquisition and use of World Englishes. Buschfeld and Kautzsch's (2017) Extra- and Intra-Territorial Forces (EIF) Model offers one such approach; Buschfeld and Kautzsch expand on Schneider's (2007) Dynamic Model to account for the development of both PCEs and non-PCEs as well as the heterogeniety found in many contexts. The model has five major subcategories: (1) colonization (extra) / attitudes towards colonization (intra); (2) language policies (both intra and extra), (3) globalization (extra) / "acceptance" of globalization (intra), (4) foreign policies (both intra and extra), (5) the sociodemographic background of a country (Buschfeld and Kautzsch 2017: 113). Of particular relevance to the Hong Kong situation is the addition of language policies, attitudes towards the colonizing power, and sociodemographic background. This model provides a more nuanced approach to the study of World Englishes and SLA, allowing for a deeper analysis and understanding of language learning, use, and resistance in geopolitically complex contexts such as Hong Kong.

7 Conclusion: HKE, World Englishes, and SLA

This chapter has taken a multilingual and sociopolitical approach to examine the changing status of HKE, arguing that the acceptance and use of HKE, or any World English, needs to be examined in light of the status of English as well as all other languages in the language ecology and that this may change if there are shifts in the sociopolitical context. The chapter further argues that political events are driving acceptance of HKE. As a result of the increasing shift towards Putonghua in Hong Kong's language ecology by the HKSAR government, the status and role of English has shifted, particularly among those who have a localist identity as a Hong Konger or are engaged in politics; HKE is the linguistic manifestation of a Hong Konger identity in English. The status of HKE is one illustration of the nexus of SLA and World Englishes: What learners are acquiring and using (and resisting) in Hong Kong. Any theory that attempts to account for SLA within World Englishes contexts needs to examine the complex interplay among the various languages/varieties in a given language ecology against the (often changing) linguistic and political landscape. As the data from Hong Kong illustrates, learners' political stance impacts their use of language as an identity marker and their desire (and resistance) to using the various languages and varieties of English of Hong Kong. In sum, language learning, use, and resistance have become political acts for some learners in Hong Kong.

In attempting to describe and understand the shifting language ecology in Hong Kong, and the rising acceptance of English and Hong Kong English, multiple frameworks were adopted, in acknowledgement that no single framework can model the linguistic changes that are occurring in Hong Kong. Schneider's (2007) Dynamic Model of Postcolonial Englishes also does not explain the rise of HKE within Hong Kong's language ecology, as the model does not account for sociopolitical changes and/or status of the other languages in Hong Kong.

A more promising framework is Buschfeld and Kautzsch's (2017) EIF Model, which expands the Dynamic Model to including language attitudes and language polities. This model may be more appropriate for postcolonial societies that are undergoing political instability or change. As I have argued in this paper, the status of HKE cannot be analyzed in isolation from the other languages in Hong Kong's language ecology. The language policies of 1974, giving Chinese (widely interpreted to mean Cantonese) and English official language status, and 1997, giving Putonghua official status as well, have led to Hong Kong becoming a unique linguistic area within the PRC. This, in turn, has impacted not only the development of HKE as a unique variety in this region, but also the use of bilingualism in English and Cantonese as a regional Hong Kong as well as an individual Hong Konger identity marker with HKE expressing this identity in English. Buschfeld and Kautzsch's subcategory of attitudes towards the colonizing power can in Hong Kong be interpreted to mean both the British as well as the PRC; resistance to Putonghua, and therefore adoption of Cantonese/English bilingualism and HKE, demonstrate the linguistic manifestations of the attitudes towards both the British and PRC. Finally, Buschfeld and Kautzsch's subcategory of the role of sociodemographic factors is also integral to the Hong Kong situation as illustrated by the youth movements helping to lead language resistance and change in Hong Kong from the 1974 Chinese Language Movement, led in part by student unions from different universities in Hong Kong, to the use of English and Cantonese, and HKE, as symbolic markers during the 2019 protests in Hong Kong.

The chapter concludes by offering a number of questions that need to be addressed in any SLA and World Englishes theory. These questions have emerged from the analysis of the data in this chapter; many of these questions can be addressed in the EIF Model, as discussed above, indicating that this model provides a significant shift towards interpreting the development of PCEs (and non-PCEs) in complex multilingual settings like Hong Kong.

1. What happens in postcolonial countries/territories when they are re-colonized by a different power with a different language(s), history, and culture?
2. What happens when you are required to learn a language that you do not want to use?
3. Do theories need to incorporate resistance? Do you resist when the L2 (or L3) symbolizes a sociopolitical identity that you do not want to adopt?
4. What are the roles of different varieties of English in a multilingual, multidialectal society?
5. What role do different sociodemographic groups play in language preservation, resistance, and change? Are some groups, defined by age, ethnicity, language, or gender, among others, more likely to be engaged in language preservation, resistance, and change?

References

傑出男公關. 2019. *Ng dai sou kau yat bat hor* [Five demands, not one less] [Facebook Post]. www.facebook.com/1648246202123798/posts/ng-dai-sou-kau-kyut-yat-bat-horgum-lo-hai-littai-duc-ming-born-ngo-sharehong-kon/2398015757146835/ (accessed 31 August 2020).

Bourdieu, Pierre. 1980. *The logic of practice*. Stanford: Stanford University Press.

Brewer, Marilynn. 1991. The social self: On being the same and different at the same time. *Personality and Social Psychology Bulletin* 17 (5). 475–482.

Buschfeld, Sarah & Alexander Kautzsch. 2017. Towards an integrated approach to postcolonial and non-postcolonial Englishes. *World Englishes* 36 (1). 104–126.

Census and Statistics Department, HKSAR. 2019. *Thematic household survey report number 66*. HKSAR Government.

Chen, Kris. 2019. Si doi gak ming: Hong Kong protesters 'spell out' their message in effort to foil mainland Chinese trolls and 'spies'. *Hong Kong Free Press*. https://hongkongfp.com/2019/08/18/si-doi-gak-ming-hong-kong-protesters-spell-message-effort-foil-mainland-chinese-trolls-spies/ (accessed 31 August 2020).

Chen, Ping. 2001. Language policy in Hong Kong during the colonial period before July 1, 1997. In Ping Chen & Nanette Gottlieb (eds.), *Language planning and language policy: East Asian pespectives*, 111–128. Cornwall: Curzon Press.

Coates, Jennifer. 2007. Gender. In Carmen Llamas, Louise Mullany & Peter Stockwell (eds.), *The Routledge companion to sociolinguistics*, 62–68. New York: Routledge.

Gal, Susan & Kathryn Woolard. 2001. *Languages and publics: The making of authority*. Abingdon, UK: Routledge.

Groves, Julie M. 2011. 'Linguistic schizophrenia' in Hong Kong. *English Today* 27 (4). 33–42.

Hansen Edwards, Jette G. 2018. *The politics of English in Hong Kong: Attitudes, identity, and use*. Singapore: Routledge.

Hansen Edwards, Jette G. 2019. *Freedom is not free* [Photograph].

Hansen Edwards, Jette G. 2020. Borders and bridges: The politics of language and identity in Hong Kong. *Journal of Asian Pacific Communication Special 30th Anniversary Edition* 30 (1/2). 115–138.

Hansen Edwards, Jette G. 2021. 'I have to save this language, it's on the edge like an endangered animal': Perceptions of language threat and linguistic mainlandisation in Hong Kong. *Journal of Multilingual and Multicultural Development* 42 (4). 307–326.

HKPORI. 2021. *Categorical ethnic identity*. HKPORI. www.pori.hk/pop-poll/ethnic-identity-en/q001.html?lang=en (accessed 5 October 2021).

Ho, Wing Chung & Choi Man Hung. 2020. Youth political agency in Hong Kong's 2019 antiauthoritarian protests. *Hau: Journal of Ethnographic Theory* 10 (2). 303–307.

James, May. 2019. Hong Kong Add Oil [Photograph]. *Hong Kong Free Press*. https://hongkongfp.com/2019/11/02/hkfp-lens-frontline-shots-may-james-hong-kong-enters-22nd-weekend-protest-unrest/ (accessed 31 August 2020).

Kaeding, Malte P. 2017. The rise of 'localism' in Hong Kong. *Journal of Democracy* 28 (1). 157–171.

Lai, Mee Ling. 2011. Cultural identity and language attitudes – into the second decade of postcolonial Hong Kong. *Journal of Multilingual and Multicultural Development* 32 (3). 249–264.

Lai, Mee Ling. 2012. Tracking language attitudes in postcolonial Hong Kong: An interplay of localization, mainlandization, and internationalization. *Multilingua* 31 (1). 83–111.

Le Page, Robert B. & Andrée Tabouret-Keller. 1985. *Acts of identity: Creole-based approaches to language and ethnicity*. Cambridge: Cambridge University Press.

O'Neill, Mark. 2017. 1.5 million mainland migrants change Hong Kong. *EJ Insight*. www.ejinsight.com/ 20170619-1-5-million-mainland-migrants-change-hong-kong/ (accessed 20 March 2018).

Poon, Anita Y. K. 2000. *Medium of instruction in Hong Kong: Policy and practice*. New York: University Press of America.

Poon, Anita Y. K. 2009. A review of research in English language education in Hong Kong in the past 25 years: Reflections and the way forward. *Educational Research Journal* 24 (1). 7–40.

Schneider, Edgar W. 2007. *Postcolonial English: Varieties around the world*. Cambridge: Cambridge University Press.

Shen, Simon. 2021. *Beijing's tried and test plan to hollow out Hong Kong's legislature*. https://thediplomat.com/2021/06/beijings-tried-and-tested-plan-to-hollow-out-hong-kongs-legislature/ (accessed 4 October 2021).

Siu, Phila. 2019. *Chinese day-trippers to Hong Kong up 20 per cent as tourist figures soar*. www.scmp. com/news/hong-kong/hong-kong-economy/article/2184378/tourist-figures-hong-kong-reached-new-high-2018-651 (accessed 2 May 2019).

Varsity. 2017. *Cantonese, Putonghua or English? The language politics of Hong Kong's school system*. https://hongkongfp.com/2017/04/09/cantonese-putonghua-english-language-politics-hong-kongs-school-system/ (accessed 20 March 2018).

Wong, Winson. 2019. Chinese university students wear masks [Photograph]. *South China Morning Post*. www.scmp.com/news/hong-kong/education/article/3036693/chinese-university-students-wear-masks-and-chant-hong-kong (accessed 21 June 2021).

Zhang, Qi. 2013. The attitudes of Hong Kong students towards Hong Kong English and Mandarin-accented English. *English Today* 29 (2). 9–16.

Bianca Vowell
12 Varieties of English and Third Culture Kids in Hong Kong

Abstract: Third Culture Kids (TCKs) are temporary migrants who grow up outside of their parents' culture and outside of the host country's culture in an interstitial Third Culture (Useem and Downie 1976). This chapter focuses on seven such TCKs who had at least one parent from New Zealand and were living in Hong Kong. Their lexical, phonetic and phonological features are presented and discussed in the context of the fields of TCK research, second dialect acquisition, new dialect formation, and World Englishes.

The chapter will show that the TCKs selected features from the linguistic feature pool in highly individualised ways. They were influenced by the local community, the age at which they moved to Hong Kong, their parents' varieties, the curricula of their schools, and the globalised use of General American English features. These influences were mitigated by ideologies such as *international* versus *local* and showed that theoretical research paradigms must continue to evolve and remain flexible in order to account for mobile populations.

Keywords: Third Culture Kids, dialect, superdiversity

1 Introduction

As the field of World Englishes has evolved from Kachru's (1985) Circles Model to more dynamic (Schneider 2007) and broader perspectives (e.g. Buschfeld and Kautzsch 2017, 2020), it has become more inclusive of groups of English speakers who fall outside of traditional classifications. While there has been an increase in research focusing on the Englishes used by migrant populations (e.g. Cheshire et al. 2011; Meyerhoff and Schleef 2012), there is a population of temporary migrants who have received very little attention, and this group is known as Third Culture Kids (TCKs, Pollock and Van Reken 2001). They are children and adolescents living temporarily outside the country of their nationality because of their parents' work. Their communities are characterised by constant change as the TCKs' parents are typically employed in careers which require frequent migration and the linguistic environments of TCKs are superdiverse (Vertovec 2006).

Bianca Vowell, Massey University, New Zealand

https://doi.org/10.1515/9783110733723-012

This chapter presents the speech features taken from individually recorded sociolinguistic interviews with seven children and adolescents aged five to eighteen years, who have grown up as TCKs in Hong Kong. From a World Englishes perspective, they can be considered to be part of a bubble of Inner Circle varieties within the Outer Circle context of Hong Kong. Furthermore, they are both part of, and subject to, the extra- and intra-territorial forces (Buschfeld and Kautzsch 2017) on Hong Kong English (HKE). From a sociolinguistic perspective, their speech situation shares similarities with multiethnolects (e.g. Cheshire et al. 2011) and koines in the early stages of new dialect formation (Trudgill et al. 2000); however, the Third Culture environment is uniquely dynamic due to the constant in- and out-migration of community members. Thus, a joint approach across these paradigms was essential in order to interpret the data.

The central aim of this study was to investigate the ways in which TCKs reconciled a superdiverse feature pool and to understand how this relates to World Englishes. The specific research questions were:

1. Which features were used by the TCKs taking part in this study?
2. What were the likely sources of these features?
3. How do these results relate to the theories from the fields of TCK research, second dialect acquisition, new dialect formation and World Englishes?
4. Why are these insights important for the field of World Englishes?

The present chapter will outline theoretical approaches to TCK dialect formation followed by an analysis of the lexical variants, monophthong mergers, NEAR/SQUARE overlap, BATH/TRAP pattern and rhoticity used by these TCKs.

2 Third Culture Kids

The children and adolescents in this study belong to a group referred to in the literature as "Third-Culture Kids" (among other labels, such as "expatriates" [e.g. Starr 2019] or "Global Nomads" [e.g. Schaetti 2000]). According to the original definition, TCKs grow up outside of their parents' home culture (the first culture) and outside of the host culture (the second culture). The third culture is the *"interstitial culture* or culture between cultures" (Pollock and Van Reken 2001: 20). Children who grow up in this Third Culture typically assume that they will leave the host country one day, and therefore, there is no expectation for them to assimilate into the local culture. A distinctive feature of the Third Culture social environment is constant change. Parents of TCKs often have careers which lead to multiple international moves. Although some TCKs do not move often, the members of their community do, and as a consequence their childhoods are characterised by change as their peers, teachers and family friends move in and out of their social circles.

TCKs typically attend international schools, which tend to be globally oriented and foreground the multinational backgrounds of their students in their marketing. For example, some of the international schools in Hong Kong highlight "a culturally diverse community," "values of global mindedness," and "75 different nationalities" on the "About" pages of their websites (French International School 2020; The English Schools Foundation n.d.). This is a common feature of international schools around the world and Tanu (2016: 431) observed that this construct of the *international* is created through distancing from the *local*. She argued that dualities of "home" vs. "away," "temporary" vs. "permanent," "migrant" vs. "native," and "international" vs. "national" are constructed by international schools. In reality, the distinction between these labels is blurred and TCKs do not live entirely outside of the local culture. So-called local children attend international schools and the parents of the TCKs mix with locals in workplaces and social groups, such as through sports teams. Furthermore, some adaptations to the host country's customs and social behaviour are inevitable for TCKs when they move to a new place. Although TCKs may live outside of the physical country associated with their parents' cultures, the cultural influences undoubtedly persist in the family lives of these children and adolescents. Therefore, the labels of first culture, second culture, and third culture are simplifications of the concept of culture and of the reality of the lives of these TCKs and of TCKs in general. The label of TCK is an abstraction but is useful for understanding the sense of otherness that is implicit in TCK environments.

Much of the TCK literature has focused on two areas. The first is the impact of constant change on the mental wellbeing of TCKs (e.g. Hoersting and Jenkins 2011). Negative impacts on a TCK childhood have been reported, such as the experiencing of culture shock and rootlessness. However, positive impacts have also been outlined, such as open-mindedness and diplomacy (Langford 1998). The second focus present in previous research is on identity formation in the absence of being *from* somewhere (e.g. Reyal 2015). As TCKs negotiate feelings of cultural homelessness, they may form positive identities which are complex and reflect multiple cultural inputs about where they are from and where they belong. Hoersting and Jenkins (2011: 28) termed these "cross-cultural identities".

To my knowledge, the only studies to have considered the implications of the TCK environment on dialect have been undertaken by Starr and her colleagues (2016; 2017) in Singapore, a comparable setting to Hong Kong. The first of these studies found that children who have experienced multiple moves had a wider pool of lexical labels for the same item (such as being able to provide the labels *elevator* and *lift* in response to a picture) in comparison with more sedentary children. The other study found that children in international schools were able to identify accents at a younger age than children in local schools, but the children in local schools were more accurate with tasks requiring local knowledge. Starr et al. (2017: 513) found that children in international schools were likely to encounter people who spoke inner-, outer- and expanding-circle varieties of English and they used "a diverse set of Englishes".

In order to understand the linguistic processes involved in dialect formation for TCKs, it is helpful to consider the literature of the related fields of (second) dialect acquisition and new dialect formation. Second dialect acquisition (SDA) is relevant in this context as TCKs are a mobile population and bring linguistic features with them from the places they have lived before. The literature on first dialect acquisition has shown that children's vowel systems are mostly formed by 3 years of age (Donegan 2012: 66). Children who move to a new dialect area under the age of 7 years are likely to acquire the features of the new dialect, while those who move between 7 and 13 years are likely to show variability in their acquisition of these features (Chambers 1992).

In the field of new dialect formation, there are two scenarios that are comparable to the TCK environment. The first is the formation of multiethnolects in superdiverse communities and the second is koineisation. Vertovec (2006) coined the term *superdiversity* to describe the unprecedented scale of diversity in British cities from the turn of the century. In Blommaert's (2013: 10) discussion of this term, he argued that "it is driven by three keywords: mobility, complexity and unpredictability". These terms are all relevant descriptors of the TCK world. What makes TCKs even more interesting is that the in- and out-flow of individuals in the community creates a constantly changing mixture of linguistic features from these varieties. Sociolinguistic studies have identified new varieties and changes to existing varieties in these superdiverse communities, often termed multiethnolects. There has been an increase in these studies over recent years as global immigration has risen which has led to new patterns of variation and, in some cases, new dialect formation. In Cheshire et al.'s (2013: 74) multiethnolect research, they argue that "immense linguistic variation in the English spoken by different individuals [. . .] is accompanied by great flexibility in linguistic norms".

Third Culture environments are also similar to the early stages of koine formation. Siegel's (2001: 175) definition of a koine is "a stabilised contact variety which results from the mixing and subsequent leveling of features of varieties which are similar enough to be mutually intelligible, such as regional or social dialects". He (2001: 175) added, "[t]his occurs in the context of increased interaction or integration among speakers of these varieties". In Third Culture communities there is certainly mixing of mutually intelligible varieties. The key difference is that there is not an expectation that a stabilised variety will result from the contact, since the input is changeable over time. Nevertheless, there are steps in the process of koine formation and the situation of TCKs that resemble the second generation of migrants as described by Trudgill and colleagues (2000). The variety spoken by these children as they grow up is characterised by extreme variability and leveling.

In his discussion of koineisation, Mufwene (2001: 4) introduced the concept of a "feature pool" provided by the pre-existing dialects from which new dialect(s) emerge with their own unique combination of these features. Trudgill et al. (2000: 305) observed that "as a result of having many different adult linguistic models to aim at [. . .] in the second stage of the new-dialect formation process, children will have considerable freedom to select variants from different dialects at will and to form them into new combinations". Interestingly, they (2000: 305) added that "unlike in stable situations where children normally acquire the dialect of their peers, in a dialect-mixture situation there is no single peer-dialect for children to acquire, and the role of adults, especially perhaps of parents and other caretakers, will therefore be more significant than is usually the case".

With so much variability of input, there is varying prestige associated with different varieties in the TCK environment. For all children, General American English (GenAm) is gaining influence globally (Meyerhoff and Niedzielski 2003). For each child, prestige is arguably associated with the parents' variety(-ies). There are also different prestige varieties associated with the children's schools. Some schools follow a curriculum from a particular country, for example the Australian curriculum at the Australian International School Hong Kong (Australian International School Hong Kong n.d.) and the English National Curriculum in the International Stream of the French International School Hong Kong (French International School 2020). These schools, therefore, attract children with Australian or English backgrounds, respectively. The staff members recruited by these schools also tend to have teaching experience from said countries and are most often nationals of them. In this way, the overt prestige variety in these schools is clearly defined, although there are still multiple inputs from the other children and staff members who are part of the school community but do not speak varieties associated with those countries.

3 Modelling TCKs in Hong Kong

In order to describe the background of English in Hong Kong, it is appropriate to draw on models that have been developed in the World Englishes paradigm. Kachru's (1985) Circles Model was foundational in the field of World Englishes. In this model, Hong Kong English has been described as part of the Outer Circle (e.g.

Evans 2014: 596). However, it is difficult to define the English of the TCKs in this study using this model and it could best be described as a bubble of Inner Circle varieties, within the wider, Outer Circle context of HKE.

Schneider's (2007) Dynamic Model of new post-colonial varieties of English describes a five-phase process. Hong Kong English was considered to be in the third phase (nativisation), in which the settler (STL) and indigenous (IDG) populations are increasingly intertwined linguistically, culturally, and politically (2007: 155). This assessment was challenged by Evans (2014: 596), who observed that these two strands have remained quite separate ever since the arrival of English in Hong Kong through British annexation during the Opium Wars due in part to members of the STL strand being more like sojourners than settlers. The TCKs in this study would be most aptly considered to be sojourners. The Dynamic Model is more relevant to TCKs than the Circles Model, but it is still not completely satisfactory.

The Extra- and Intra-territorial Forces (EIF) Model proposed by Buschfeld and Kautzsch (2017) takes a more flexible approach and broadens the scope of consideration to be relevant to TCKs. This model not only includes TCKs in their role as an influence on HKE but also gives an account of the factors that are relevant to the English spoken by TCKs. According to the EIF Model, the role of English as spoken by expatriates (including TCKs) on HKE is an extra-territorial force: they provide the English that is heard in face-to-face situations by the local population. The impact of TCK English is mitigated by the intra-territorial force of the attitudes towards expatriates. There are some extra-territorial forces which are experienced by everyone in Hong Kong, such as the influence of globalisation. According to Buschfeld and Kautzsch's (2017: 114) definition, this includes the "linguistic and also cultural influences coming from the Internet, US popular culture, and modern media as well as trading relations between countries". There are intra-territorial forces which are likely to be more specific to TCKs. As monolingual English-speakers in international schools, the TCKs in this study would have exposure to the varieties of English spoken by their parents and to the great diversity of varieties in their TCK communities. Intra-territorial forces also include the attitudes of these individuals towards, for example, colonisation, HKE, globalisation and the varieties of English heard around them including the varieties spoken by their parents. The relevance of each of these research paradigms to the TCKs in the current study will be discussed further in Section 7.

4 Methodology

4.1 Participants

The participants were all aged between five and nineteen years (mean = 11;10, sd = 5;4) at the time of recording in 2015–2016. They all fit the definition of TCKs as they were all living in Hong Kong due to their parents' jobs, and they were all living there temporarily with the expectation that they would move (back) to New Zealand one day. The children had all lived in Hong Kong (HK) for at least five years and were all monolingual English speakers. They were recruited through my circle of friends and word of mouth.

Table 12.1: Details of participants and recordings.

Name	Sex	Date of birth	Age at move to HK	Date of recording	Age at recording date (years; months)	Recording duration
Poppy	F	28.05.2010	Birth	29.5.15	5;0	01:00:13
Jess	F	28.12.2008	Birth	21.5.15	6;4	00:59:22
Freddy *	M	29.4.2007	1	6.9.16	9;5	00:49:50
Josh *	M	7.4.2005	3	6.9.16	11;5	00:58:08
Timothy	M	2.8.2000	1	3.12.16	16;4	00:57:12
Katie §	F	14.2.2000	4	2.6.15	15;3	01:02:14
Lena §	F	10.3.1996	7	2.6.15	19;2	00:44:39

*brothers § sisters

The participants' pseudonyms are (in order of age from youngest to oldest) Poppy, Jess, Freddy, Josh, Timothy, Katie and Lena. Freddy and Josh are brothers and Katie and Lena are sisters. The biographical and recording details of these TCKs are listed in Table 12.1.

Recordings were made using a Zoom H5 and were conducted in the TCKs' homes in order for them to feel as relaxed as possible. Each child was recorded individually, and the recordings lasted approximately one hour. The actual durations of each recording are listed in Table 12.1. The interview structure was adapted from sociolinguistic interviews (Tagliamonte 2006) and included questions about where the TCK felt they were from and where felt like home in addition to conversations on topics of interest. For the younger participants, time was also spent discussing books, playing games, or engaging in pretend play.

Like the participants, I am a TCK who grew up in Hong Kong with New Zealand English (NZE)-speaking parents. My variety includes features from NZE and from the varieties I encountered as a TCK; therefore, the participants would not necessarily be accommodating towards or away from either of these varieties.

4.2 Variables

Broadly speaking, the input varieties contributing features to the feature pools for the TCKs of this study include:
1. Hong Kong English; as a variety present in the community
2. New Zealand English; as the variety spoken by at least one parent of all of the TCKs
3. Standard Southern British English; as the variety spoken by one parent of Freddy and Josh and as the prestige variety of many of the international schools attended by the TCKs in this study
4. Australian English; as the prestige variety at the international school attended by Timothy
5. General American English; as a variety contributing features globally and as a prestige variety at some of the international schools

Highly salient features from each of these varieties were selected as variables for analysis in the current study. Each feature was chosen to distinguish the five varieties listed above.
1. Lexical variants: the use of lexical items specific to HKE
2. Monophthong mergers: the distinctive HKE vowel system involving a merger of four pairs of vowels; FLEECE and KIT, TRAP and DRESS, GOOSE and FOOT, and LOT and THOUGHT (Hung 2000: 343)
3. Short front vowels: the use of the characteristic NZE chain shift pattern (Bauer and Warren 2004) and the distinctive Australian English (AusE) KIT raising and fronting (Horvath 2004)
4. NEAR/SQUARE merger: the distinctive NZE pattern (Bauer and Warren 2004)
5. BATH/TRAP pattern: the use of BATH realisations in selected words (e.g. *ask, chance, dancing*) as an indicator of influence from SSBE or NZE, or the use of TRAP realisations as an indicator of influence from GenAm or AusE (Collins and Mees 2003)
6. Rhoticity: the use of rhotic vowels in non-pre-vocalic contexts as an indicator of GenAm (Kretzschmar 2004) as distinct from SSBE (Hughes, Trudgill, and Watt [1979] 2012) and NZE (Bauer and Warren 2004)

Of course, these features are not entirely independent of each other. A merging of FLEECE and KIT or TRAP and DRESS would not only suggest the adoption of HKE features but would also rule out the expression of the NZE short front vowel pattern. The combinations of features are also important. For example, the use of BATH rather than TRAP realisations might be interpreted as indicating SSBE influence when the TCK also has an unmarked short front vowel pattern, separated NEAR and SQUARE vowels and categorical non-rhoticity. However, this same use of BATH realisations might be interpreted as being consistent with NZE influence if the TCK also has the NZE short front vowel pattern and a NEAR/SQUARE merger. This BATH versus TRAP variable is more relevant when identifying the influence of GenAm/AusE in contrast to SSBE/NZE.

4.3 Data extraction and measurements

Four main steps were undertaken to prepare the raw recordings for phonetic measurement. The recordings were orthographically transcribed using ELAN (2019) and anonymised using Audacity (Audacity Team 2019). Automatic phonemic boundary alignment was completed using MAUS (Kisler, Reichel, and Schiel 2017), and then these phonemic boundaries were hand corrected in Praat (Boersma 2001).

Examples of HKE lexical items were manually extracted from the orthographic transcripts of each recording. The F1, F2, and F3 formant values were extracted using Praat. Following the approach of Warren (2017), the formant values of the monophthongs were averaged over the middle 40% of each vowel's duration. The values in the first 30% and last 30% of each vowel's duration were not measured as these values are most affected by in- and out-transitions. Average values were used in order to avoid the fluctuations that may be present when measuring specific points. For NEAR and SQUARE, only the first targets were measured in order to capture the most different part of these diphthongs, as both are centering diphthongs and are likely to move towards more similar values towards the end of their durations (Warren 2019). For these vowels, the values between 20% and 50% of the duration of the vowel were averaged.

BATH and TRAP realisations and the use of non-pre-vocalic /r/ were coded based on auditory analysis during the hand correction stage of the data preparation. For rhoticity, tokens from the NEAR, NURSE, SQUARE, START, and THOUGHT vowels were counted as these are the stressed vowels from Wells' lexical sets that are potentially rhotic. The counts were only taken from situations in which any rhoticity unequivocally reflected a post-vocalic /r/. That is, contexts in which the following phoneme was a vowel or silence were excluded because even non-rhotic participants would likely have linking /r/ in contexts where a vowel was immediately following or anticipated. The plots in the results section were created using ggplot2 and the tidyverse suite of packages in R (Wickham 2017).

4.4 Hypotheses

It was anticipated that the children and adolescents in this study would not use features exclusively from their parents' varieties, i.e. NZE or SSBE, or from their host country's variety, i.e. HKE. Instead, they were predicted to use a new combination of features drawn from the changing feature pool in their Third Culture community. Based on findings from SDA research, the children who moved to Hong Kong when they were older were more likely to maintain some features of NZE, whereas the younger children were more likely to have acquired features from the varieties they were exposed to in Hong Kong (Siegel 2010).

According to the EIF model (Buschfeld and Kautzsch 2017), the TCKs were likely to use features from the varieties they were exposed to, including HKE, NZE, SSBE, AusE, and GenAm, and the relative influence of each of these varieties would be shaped by intra-territorial forces such as international schools' policies about curricula. The influence of these varieties on the English spoken by the TCKs would have also been mediated by their attitudes towards those varieties. An examination of these attitudes is beyond the scope of this study, but it can be assumed that each individual's ideas about the status of the varieties of English they were exposed to would have influenced their adoption of those features into their own dialects. In summary, the TCKs were likely to present linguistic features drawn from a superdiverse feature pool, which were realised in heterogeneous, even idiosyncratic, combinations for each of the TCKs in this study.

5 Results

5.1 Hong Kong English lexical items

In these recordings, there was minimal use of HKE lexical items. Poppy and Jess used no words that could be considered features of Hong Kong English. Freddy used only *dim sum*, a borrowing from Cantonese, and Josh used the localised term *junk* to refer to a type of boat. The three older children used a greater range of acronyms and localised terms, such as *band four*, relating to the local school classifications and *MTR* as the name of the local underground transportation system. While these examples do not strongly index HKE, the greater use of localised terms by the older TCKs mirror the results of Starr et al. (2016) who found that younger TCKs knew fewer local labels than older children.

5.2 Monophthong mergers

According to Hung's (2000: 342) study of 15 adult speakers of HKE, there are no distinctions in the following pairs of vowels: FLEECE/KIT, GOOSE/FOOT, TRAP/DRESS and THOUGHT/LOT.

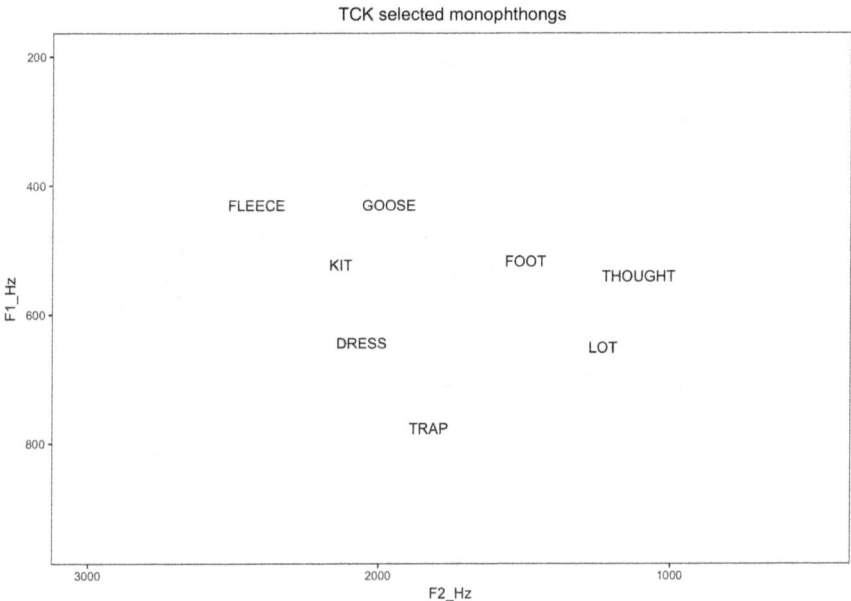

Figure 12.1: Vowel plot showing mean formant values from selected monophthongs for comparison with Hong Kong English speakers (n = 12,397).

Figure 12.1 shows a vowel plot of the same pairs of vowels for the participants in the current study. This plot shows clear separation of the F1 and F2 means for these pairs of vowels for the TCKs in this study.

Bhattacharyya's Affinity (BA, Calenge 2006) was used to measure the degree of overlap between the four pairs of vowels for each individual speaker. This method compares the cloud of tokens from each vowel and calculates the overlap, where 1 represents complete overlap and 0 represents complete separation (Johnson 2015). These scores were calculated for each participant and for each pair of vowels (Table 12.2). Most pairs had relatively low BA scores, indicating a quality difference, i.e. the F1 and F2 values were different enough for the vowels to be distinguished. Values marked with asterisks show an overlap of 0.85 or higher. These pairs were investigated further to establish whether a merger existed for that TCK.

Table 12.2: Bhattacharyya's Affinity scores for pairs of vowels for TCKs (n = 12,397).

Name	KIT FLEECE	TRAP DRESS	FOOT GOOSE	THOUGHT LOT
Poppy	0.79	0.81	0.74	0.85*
Jess	0.86*	0.59	0.89*	0.90*
Freddy	0.68	0.47	0.81	0.73
Josh	0.63	0.83	0.48	0.75
Timothy	0.84	0.73	0.57	0.76
Katie	0.69	0.84	0.64	0.87*
Lena	0.75	0.37	0.72	0.69
Mean TCK	**0.75**	**0.66**	**0.69**	**0.79**

In HKE, there is no durational difference between vowels that are classified as long or short in other varieties of English (Hung 2000). This long/short distinction would apply to all pairs in the current study except TRAP and DRESS. Table 12.3 lists the pairs of vowels that had BA scores of 0.85 or above together with their durational differences. According to Labov and Baranowski (2006), a difference of 50ms duration or higher is sufficient to distinguish two vowels. For comparison, the average durational differences for each vowel pair in Hung's data are listed in the fourth column.

Table 12.3: Durational differences for pairs of vowels with high overlap of formants (n = 1,407).

Name	Vowel pair	Duration difference (ms)	HKE duration difference (ms)
Poppy	THOUGHT/LOT	112	12
Jess	KIT/FLEECE	89	17
Jess	FOOT/GOOSE	80	12
Jess	THOUGHT/LOT	59	12
Katie	THOUGHT/LOT	8	12

A durational difference was evident in Poppy and Jess's vowel pairs, however, Katie's THOUGHT and LOT vowels were merged. This THOUGHT/LOT merger is also a salient feature of GenAm and, as will be shown in Sections 5.5 and 5.6, Katie had several other GenAm features. She did not exhibit any of the other mergers to resemble the HKE pattern; therefore, it is more likely that this THOUGHT/LOT merger came from GenAm influence rather than HKE influence. In summary, none of the TCKs had the HKE pattern of mergers for the four pairs of vowels.

5.3 Short front vowels

Figure 12.2 shows the mean formant values for each participant's short front vowels, namely KIT, DRESS, and TRAP. The mean formant values for FLEECE vowels are also shown for context as FLEECE is typically the highest and most fronted monophthong in the vowel space.

For the first six participants, the patterns of these vowels were comparable. They formed a more-or-less diagonal line from TRAP to FLEECE. Timothy's KIT vowel was raised slightly closer to FLEECE in comparison with the other speakers, indicative of the AusE influence from his school, although most AusE speakers in Australia would have more extreme KIT vowel raising (Cox 2020).

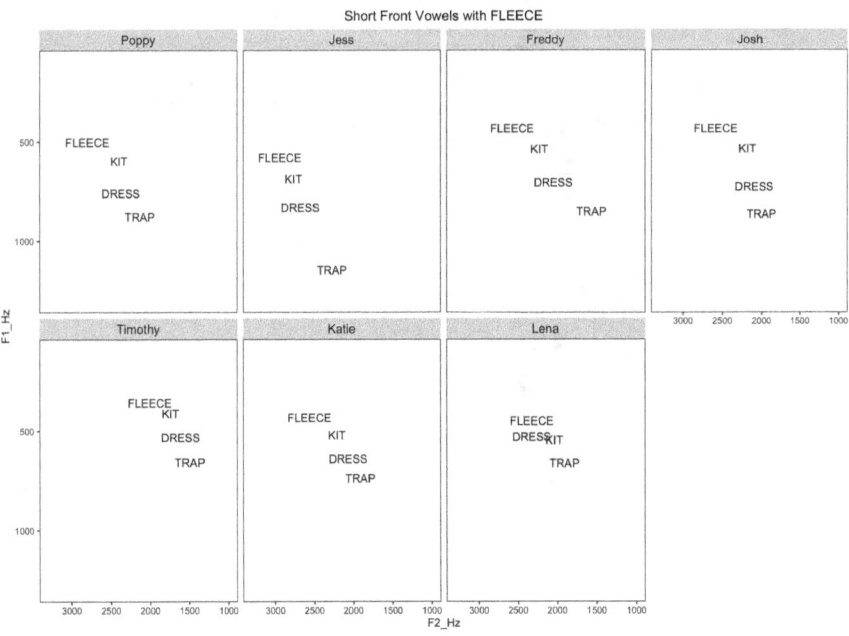

Figure 12.2: Plot of mean formant values from selected vowels showing the means of the fleece, kit, dress, and trap vowels (n = 8,931).

The most notably different vowel plot is Lena's. Her TRAP and DRESS vowels formed a diagonal line with FLEECE, but these two vowels were raised in comparison with those of the other speakers. Importantly, her KIT vowel was slightly retracted relative to DRESS and this constellation of TRAP, DRESS, and KIT is a salient feature of NZE. Typically, NZE-speakers her age who are living in New Zealand would have more extreme differences with DRESS vowels which are higher than FLEECE and KIT vowels that are more centralised (Warren 2017).

Both Lena and Timothy showed influences of salient features that were present in their phonological systems but, due to the mitigating influences from other varieties, these features were realised to a less extreme extent than would commonly be shown by adolescents of a similar age who were living in Australia or New Zealand.

5.4 NEAR/SQUARE merger

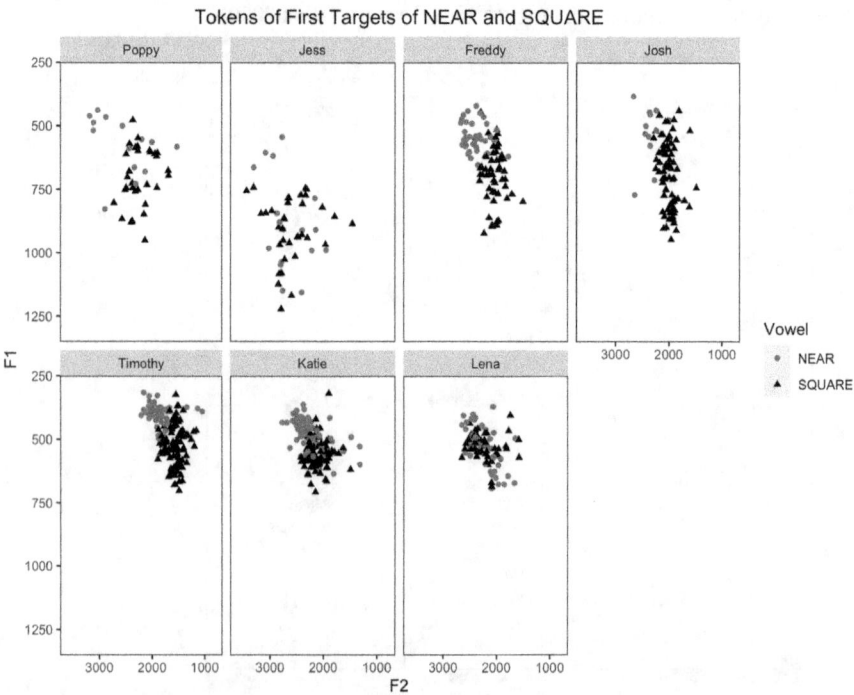

Figure 12.3: F1 and F2 values of the first targets for tokens of near and square for each participant (n = 715).

The plots in Figure 12.3 and the values in Table 12.4 show that Timothy and the brothers Freddy and Josh had the least overlap of their NEAR and SQUARE vowels and that Poppy and Katie also had reasonably separate realisations of these vowels. Jess and Lena both had a notably higher degree of overlap than the other TCKs (BA>0.90 compared with BA<0.80). The distribution of tokens was quite different for these two TCKs, because Jess was younger and younger children are known to have

Table 12.4: Bhattacharyya's Affinity scores for overlap of NEAR and SQUARE vowels, for each participant (n = 715).

Name	Bhattacharyya's Affinity score
Poppy	0.71
Jess	0.94
Freddy	0.52
Josh	0.44
Timothy	0.51
Katie	0.76
Lena	0.97

greater variability in their speech production than older children (Vorperian and Kent 2007: 1514). However, the degree of overlap suggests NZE influence for both.

5.5 BATH/TRAP patterns

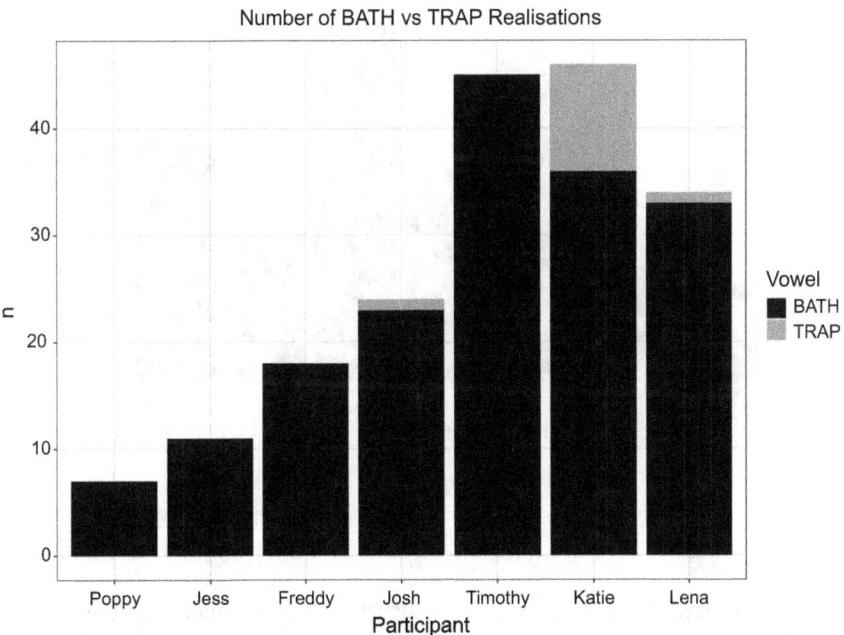

Figure 12.4: Counts of bath tokens versus trap tokens in optional contexts for each participant (n = 383).

Figure 12.4 shows the tokens of BATH and TRAP used by the participants in this study in contexts in which BATH realisations indicate SSBE or NZE influence, whereas TRAP realisations indicate GenAm or possibly AusE influence.

Most of the participants in this study categorically used BATH tokens in these optional contexts. These participants were Poppy, Jess, Freddy and Timothy. Both Josh and Lena had a single token of TRAP in their recordings. For Josh this was in the word *answer*, which could indicate AusE or GenAm influence. For Lena it was in the word *aunt*, which likely suggests GenAm influence. Katie used a notably higher percentage of TRAP tokens (22%) than the other participants (0–3%), which suggests greater influence of GenAm on her speech.

5.6 Rhoticity

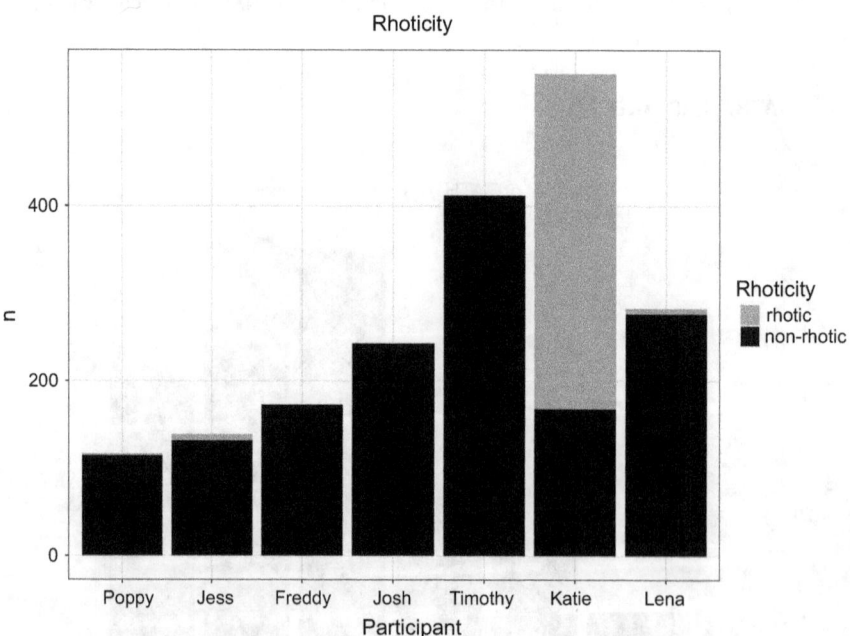

Figure 12.5: Rhoticity for each participant in the near, north, nurse, square, and start vowels in non-pre-vocalic contexts (n = 1,938).

Figure 12.5 shows the use of non-pre-vocalic /r/ by the participants in their recordings. The plot shows that Katie is the most rhotic of the seven TCKs in this study. Lena is Katie's sister; however, Lena is only sporadically rhotic, with rhoticity on only 5 out of 181 tokens. These were tokens of the words *university, terms, learning, early*, *there*, and *four*. Poppy had one rhotic token in the word *there*. Jess had three rhotic tokens in the words *or* and *her*.

The breakdown of Katie's rhoticity counts by vowel is shown in Figure 12.6. This plot shows that she was categorically rhotic with her NURSE vowels, almost categorical with NEAR and SQUARE vowels and was more than 50% rhotic with START (52 out of 95 tokens). Her NORTH vowels were comparatively less rhotic than her other potentially rhotic vowels with only 86 out of 206 tokens rhoticised. However, this still represented a notably higher degree of rhoticity than any of the other participants showed.

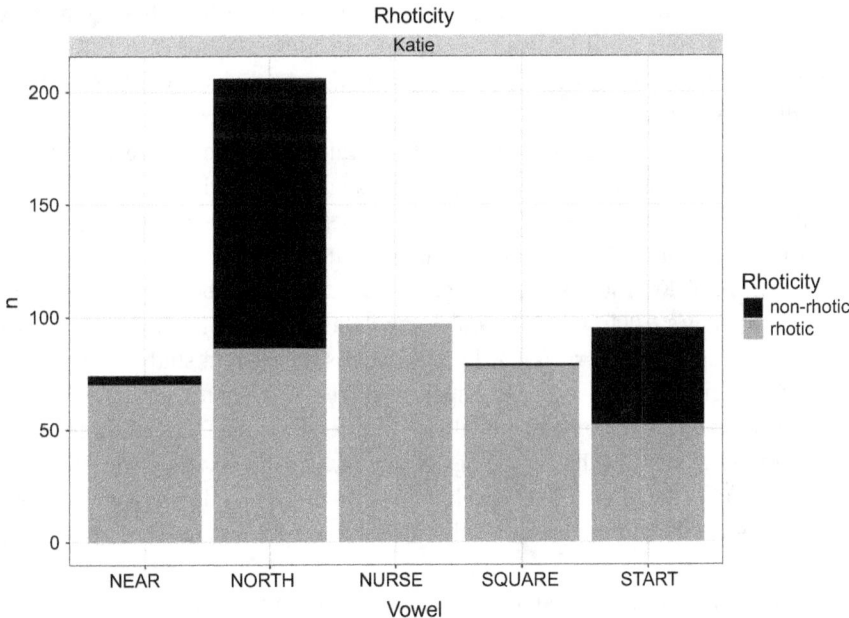

Figure 12.6: Rhoticity for Katie in the near, north, nurse, square, and start vowels in non-pre-vocalic contexts (n = 551).

6 Summary and discussion

In Section 1, the following research questions were asked:
1. Which features were used by the TCKs taking part in this study?
2. What were the likely sources of these features?

3. How do these results relate to the theories from the fields of TCK research, second dialect acquisition, new dialect formation and World Englishes?
4. Why are these insights important for the field of World Englishes?

Across the results for these TCKs, there was evidence of varying influence of HKE, NZE, SSBE, AusE, and GenAm varieties. There was great individuality in the specific features used by each TCK, reflecting the differences in input they each received and their idiosyncratic ways of combining features from the feature pool. As noted in Section 2, the sources of the features are assumed to be the local community, parents, exposure to and use of other varieties before moving to Hong Kong, school, and the globalised use of GenAm features. Evidence for each of these sources is found in the results. Further details on the specific influences for each TCK will be discussed in this section. They will be discussed individually, as the children exhibit very different patterns.

However, before discussing each TCK individually, the influence of HKE can be addressed across all of the TCKs. There was only weak evidence of local community influence in the use of some localised lexical items, particularly by the older children. Interestingly, there was no evidence of HKE influence in the phonology of the TCKs. There were methodological differences between the current study and Hung's (2000) study, to which my data were compared. Hung's results came from recordings of read word lists, whereas the current study used recordings of conversational speech. Read speech is likely to be more careful and have more distinctions than conversational speech; therefore, the fact that these mergers were not evident in the recordings of the participants in the current study is not likely to be due to methodological differences between this study and Hung's. Rather, the results of the current study suggest that HKE was not a target variety for these TCKs.

Poppy's pattern suggested a dominant influence of SSBE with the addition of one rhotic token. She categorically used BATH in contexts where BATH rather than TRAP indicates SSBE/NZE influence. Furthermore, she showed neither the NZE pattern of short front vowels nor a NEAR/SQUARE merger. It is assumed that the SSBE influence came from her teachers and peers as her school followed the English National Curriculum, which raised the presence and overt prestige of this variety.

Jess showed a more mixed profile. Her SSBE-like features included categorical use of BATH rather than TRAP in optional contexts and the absence of the NZE short front vowel pattern. She had a merger of NEAR and SQUARE vowels, which suggests NZE influence, likely from her NZE-speaking parents. She also showed evidence of globalised GenAm influence in her occasional use of rhotic tokens.

The brothers, Freddy and Josh, had quite similar patterns. Like Poppy, their patterns suggested a greater influence of SSBE. They did not show NZE patterns of short front vowels, nor did they show a NEAR/SQUARE merger. They were categorically non-rhotic and categorically used BATH in optional BATH/TRAP contexts. Parental influence is a likely factor in the SSBE-like pattern of Freddy and Josh's speech, as their mother is a SSBE-speaker; however, this was not the only source of SSBE for these brothers. The prestige variety at the school they attended was also SSBE.

Timothy's pattern of NEAR/SQUARE, BATH/TRAP and rhoticity suggested possible SSBE influence, which his family attributed to his peers at preschool who were mainly speakers of SSBE. These features would also be found in the speech of many AusE speakers and Timothy showed a slight indication of the influence of AusE in his use of a slightly more raised KIT vowel in comparison with the other TCKs in this study. At Timothy's school, the curriculum is Australian which explains this pattern.

Katie's dialect showed the strongest influence of GenAm in comparison with the other participants. This was evident in her notably higher degree of rhoticity and her greater use of TRAP in optional BATH/TRAP contexts. It should be noted that GenAm speakers would typically have categorical rhoticity and use of TRAP, so Katie also showed a mixture of influences. The non-rhotic tokens, the BATH realisations in optional contexts and the proximity of NEAR and SQUARE, all suggest NZE influence. In terms of sources, Katie's school falls along the continuum of international to local as her schoolmates studied towards both international and local Hong Kong qualifications. The overt school prestige variety was not as clearly defined for Katie's school as it was for other schools, but Katie reported that her accent and that of her friends was "American". The use of GenAm features is believed to be part of a broader influence of the US on cultures globally. It is suggested here that the use of these features is associated with the ideology of being international, particularly for TCKs in international schools. Therefore, it is likely that this more globally widespread use of GenAm features has influenced the prestige of this variety of Katie and her peers. The other TCKs' use of some rhotic tokens and TRAP tokens in optional BATH/TRAP contexts was also likely to be related to this phenomenon.

Lena's pattern of results across variables showed the strongest influence of NZE. She was the only one of the participants to approximate the NZE short front vowel pattern and she had the characteristic NZE NEAR/SQUARE merger. She showed occasional rhoticity and had a single TRAP realisation in optional contexts, which suggested additional influence from non-NZE varieties. Lena had NZE influence both from her parents and from her own previous use of the dialect. Lena was seven years old when she moved to Hong Kong, and Chambers (1992) found that children who moved at an age of seven years or older were likely to have variable acquisition of new dialect features. Lena's results are consistent with this finding as she predominantly had features of NZE mixed with some features of GenAm.

It is relatively easy to identify the sources which influenced the features found in the dialects of these TCKs. However, it is important to remember that even the TCKs who showed a dominance of features from one particular variety still had features from at least one other variety. In fact, no TCK in this study used features from one variety exclusively. All showed multiple influences to varying degrees. Furthermore, some of the more salient features that these TCKs used were realised in a less extreme form than in the source variety. For example, Timothy's KIT raising was slight, relative to AusE speakers in Australia and Lena's DRESS raising and KIT centralisation was slight relative to NZE speakers in NZ. Ideologies such as being international and being in an interstitial culture are expressed by these TCKs through their unique combinations of features selected from multiple sources.

7 Relevance of theoretical models

According to Pollock and Van Reken (2001: 19), TCKs assimilate elements of home and host cultures to create their own Third Culture. The prediction in the current study was that the TCKs would assimilate elements of home and host country dialects to create their own dialect. Linguistically, the TCKs exhibited minimal use of characteristic HKE features which can be explained by Tanu's (2016) observation that expatriate communities emphasize their international culture by distancing themselves from the local culture. However, there was evidence of orienting towards their home countries through the influence of parents' varieties in the speech of Freddy, Josh, Jess, Katie, and Lena. This was not universal, though, as there was no evidence of NZE influence for Poppy or Timothy. As noted in Section 6, the TCKs in this study all used features from a mixture of sources, and therefore, it can be concluded that the cultural homelessness experienced by TCKs is reflected in their linguistic homelessness.

The relevance of the field of second dialect acquisition was also evident for the TCKs in the current study. Only Poppy and Jess were born in Hong Kong – the other five TCKs were born in New Zealand. Freddy and Timothy moved to Hong Kong at around one-year of age, so they were not yet talking; however, all of the TCKs in the current study had NZE influence in their dialect acquisition from their parents. Josh, Katie, and Lena were all three years or older at the time of their move and would have been using some features of NZE at that age (Donegan 2012). Therefore, they would have experienced the process of second dialect acquisition after their move to Hong Kong, even if the target dialect was not clear. Lena's age at the time of her move is particularly important in the field of SDA research. She was seven years old at the time of her move to Hong Kong, and therefore, she was more likely to retain phonetic and phonological features of NZE (Chambers 1992). In contrast, the younger children were more likely to acquire new phonetic and phonological features from the varieties they were exposed to in Hong Kong. Interestingly, research has found that older age provides an advantage for acquisition of localised lexical features (Starr et al. 2017), and this was evident in the current study in which older children acquired more localised lexical items. SDA research helps to understand the factors, such as age, that are relevant to TCKs who bring features of their home dialect with them. What SDA does not account for in the TCK context is that the TCKs are not acquiring the local, HKE variety, but rather exhibit features drawn from a wide feature pool (Mufwene 2001).

The formation of new dialects, such as multiethnolects and koines, typically occurs in stable linguistic contexts; however, there are several relevant findings from research in these areas which apply to TCKs. Findings from multiethnolect research suggests that contact in superdiverse linguistic environments is likely to result in "flexibility in linguistic norms" (Cheshire et al. 2013: 74), which accounts for the variability between TCKs. Findings from koineisation research accounted for the TCKs using different strategies for reconciling the feature pool, including drawing greater influence from their parents than other children would in more stable contexts (Trudgill et al. 2000). New dialect formation research helps understand what happens in superdiverse linguistic environments. The difference with TCKs is that there is ever changing diversity due to the mobile nature of expatriate communities.

In the World Englishes paradigm, TCKs pose a challenge to existing models. They do not fit well within the Circles Model and they also differ from the typical communities who form the settler strand in the Dynamic Model as TCKs are more like sojourners than settlers. The most relevant World Englishes model which accounts for the use of English by TCKs is the EIF Model (Buschfeld and Kautzsch 2017) as it is sufficiently flexible to incorporate influences such as family, school curricula, globalised use of GenAm and the attitudes held by TCKs towards these influences.

8 Conclusion

TCKs are a niche, superdiverse, mobile population and have been largely overlooked in linguistic studies. Because of the diversity and lack of stability in TCK communities, it is difficult to apply many of the traditional theories to this population, as has been shown in the current study. However, different aspects from each paradigm have been helpful; the context of cultural homelessness from TCK research which links to linguistic homelessness; the understanding of how the age of a move is relevant in the acquisition of features in the TCK environment as a second dialect; the implications of superdiverse feature pools on dialect formation; and the need for flexibility in accounting for how these forces shape the combination of features used by an individual. Overall, more flexible theories are thus better equipped to account for varieties in this and other globally mobile populations. The current study has shown that it is important not to make assumptions that children living in a particular geographical location, such as Hong Kong, will assimilate to local dialectal norms or even that they will have a single variety as a target. Rather, linguistic features from parents' varieties, host country varieties, and school prestige varieties contribute to a dynamic, superdiverse feature pool, which the TCKs draw from in order to create their idiosyncratic, interstitial varieties.

To the best of my knowledge, there is no previous documentation or discussion of TCK varieties of English. This study is a first step in this direction. As globally mobile populations increase, superdiverse communities become more common. Thus, research must continue with mobile children and adolescents in other countries in order to test the broad applicability of the relevant paradigms, which include second dialect acquisition, new dialect formation and World Englishes. These paradigms must continue to evolve to account for this dynamic population and must be capable of flexibility and openness to these under-documented groups.

References

Audacity Team. 2019. *Audacity (R): Free audio editor and recorder* [Computer Programme]. https://audacityteam.org/ (accessed 10 March 2022).
Australian International School Hong Kong. n.d. *A short history of the school*. www.aishk.edu.hk/a-short-history-of-the-school/ (accessed 14 June 2020).
Bauer, Laurie & Paul Warren. 2004. New Zealand English: Phonology. In Bernd Kortmann, Edgar W. Schneider, Kate Burridge, Rajend Mesthrie & Clive Upton (eds.), *A handbook of varieties of English*, 580–602. Berlin & Boston: De Gruyter Mouton.
Blommaert, Jan. 2013. *Chronicles of complexity: Ethnography, superdiversity and linguistic landscapes* (Critical Language and Literacy Studies 18). Bristol: Multilingual Matters.
Boersma, Paul. 2001. Praat, a system for doing phonetics by computer. *Glot International* 5 (9–10). 341–345.
Buschfeld, Sarah & Alexander Kautzsch. 2017. Towards an integrated approach to postcolonial and non-postcolonial Englishes. *World Englishes* 36 (1). 104–126.
Buschfeld, Sarah & Alexander Kautzsch (eds.). 2020. Modelling world Englishes: A joint approach to postcolonial and non-postcolonial varieties. Edinburgh: Edinburgh University Press.
Calenge, Clément. 2006. The package adehabitat for the R software: A tool for the analysis of space and habitat use by animals. *Ecological Modelling* 197 (3–4). 516–519.
Chambers, Jack K. 1992. Dialect acquisition. *Language* 68 (4). 673–705.
Cheshire, Jenny, Paul Kerswill, Sue Fox & Eivind Torgersen. 2011. Contact, the feature pool and the speech community: The emergence of Multicultural London English. *Journal of Sociolinguistics* 15 (2). 151–196.

Cheshire, Jenny, Susan Fox, Paul Kerswill & Eivind Torgersen. 2013. Language contact and language change in the multicultural metropolis. *Review française de linguistique appliquée* XVIII (2). 63–76.
Collins, Beverley & Inger Mees. 2003. *Phonetics of English and Dutch*. Leiden: Brill.
Cox, Felicity. 2020. Phonetics and phonology of Australian English. In Louisa Willoughby & Howard Manns (eds.), *Australian English reimagined: Structure, features and developments* (Routledge Studies in World Englishes), 1st edn., 15–33. Milton: Routledge.
Donegan, Patricia. 2012. Normal vowel development. In Martin J. Ball & Fiona E. Gibbon (eds.), *Handbook of vowels and vowel disorders*, 63–129. New York: Taylor and Francis.
ELAN. 2019. Nijmegen: Max Planck Institute for Psycholinguistics, The Language Archive. https://archive.mpi.nl/tla/elan (accessed 20 May 2019).
Evans, Stephen. 2014. The evolutionary dynamics of postcolonial Englishes: A Hong Kong case study. *Journal of Sociolinguistics* 18 (5). 571–603.
French International School. 2020. *An excellent education for everyone*. www.fis.edu.hk/en/excellent-education-everyone-0 (accessed 23 May 2020).
Hoersting, Raquel C. & Sharon Rae Jenkins. 2011. No place to call home: Cultural homelessness, self-esteem and cross-cultural identities. *International Journal of Intercultural Relations* 35 (1). 17–30.
Horvath, Barbara M. 2004. Australian English: Phonology. In Edgar W. Schneider, Kate Burridge, Bernd Kortmann, Rajend Mesthrie & Clive Upton (eds.), *A handbook of varieties of English: A multimedia reference tool, Vol. 1: Phonology, Vol. 2: Morphology and syntax*, 625–644. Berlin & Boston: De Gruyter Mouton.
Hughes, Arthur, Peter Trudgill & Dominic Watt. 2012 [1979]. *English accents and dialects: An introduction to social and regional varieties of English in the British Isles*, 5th edn. Oxon: Taylor & Francis Group.
Hung, Tony T. N. 2000. Towards a phonology of Hong Kong English. *World Englishes* 19 (3). 337–356.
Johnson, Daniel Ezra. 2015. Quantifying vowel overlap with Bhattacharyya's Affinity. Paper presented at New Ways of Analyzing Variation (NWAV) 44, University of Oregon, 10–12 October. https://danielezrajohnson.shinyapps.io/nwav_44/ (accessed 11 March 2021).
Kachru, Braj B. 1985. Standards, codification and sociolinguistic realism: English language in the outer circle. In Randolph Quirk & Henry Widowson (eds.), *English in the world: Teaching and learning the language and literatures*, 11–36. Cambridge: Cambridge University Press.
Kisler, Thomas, Uwe Reichel & Florian Schiel. 2017. Multilingual processing of speech via web services. *Computer Speech & Language* 45. 326–347.
Kretzschmar, William A., Jr. 2004. Standard American English pronunciation. In Edgar W. Schneider, Kate Burridge, Bernd Kortmann, Rajend Mesthrie & Clive Upton (eds.), *A handbook of varieties of English: A multimedia reference tool, Vol. 1: Phonology, Vol. 2: Morphology and syntax*, 257–269. Berlin & Boston: De Gruyter Mouton.
Labov, William & Maciej Baranowski. 2006. 50 msec. *Language Variation and Change* 18 (3). 223–240.
Langford, Mary. 1998. Global nomads, third culture kids and international schools. In Mary Hayden & Jeff Thompson (eds.), *International education: Principles and practice*, 28–43, 1st edn. London: Kogan Page.
Meyerhoff, Miriam & Erik Schleef. 2012. Variation, contact and social indexicality in the acquisition of (ing) by teenage migrants. *Journal of Sociolinguistics* 16 (3). 398–416.
Meyerhoff, Miriam & Nancy Niedzielski. 2003. The globalisation of vernacular variation. *Journal of Sociolinguistics* 7 (4). 534–555.
Mufwene, Salikoko S. 2001. *The ecology of language evolution* (Cambridge Approaches to Language Contact). Cambridge: Cambridge University Press.
Pollock, David C. & Ruth E. Van Reken. 2001. *Third Culture Kids: The experience of growing up among worlds*. Boston: Nicholas Brealey.

Reyal, Gizem Meliha. 2015. *Global identity formation and current life choices: Adult Third Culture Kids*. ProQuest Dissertations Publishing.

Schaetti, Barbara F. 2000. *Global nomad identity: Hypothesizing a developmental model*. Cincinnati, OH: Union Institute PhD thesis.

Schneider, Edgar W. 2007. *Postcolonial English : Varieties around the World*. Cambridge: Cambridge University Press. https://ebookcentral.proquest.com/lib/vuw/detail.action?docID=295706 (accessed 28 February 2021).

Siegel, Jeff. 2001. Koine formation and creole genesis. In Norval Smith & Tonjes Veenstra (eds.), *Creolisation and contact*, 175–197. Amsterdam: John Benjamins.

Siegel, Jeff. 2010. *Second dialect acquisition*. Cambridge: Cambridge University Press.

Starr, Rebecca Lurie. 2019. Attitudes and exposure as predictors of -t/d deletion among local and expatriate children in Singapore. *Language variation and change* 31 (3). 251–274.

Starr, Rebecca Lurie, Andre Joseph Theng, Kevin Martens Wong, Natalie Jing Yi Tong, Nurul Afiqah Bte Ibrahim, Alicia Mei Yin Chua, Clarice Hui Min Yong, Frances Wei Loke, Helen Dominic, Keith Jayden Fernandez & Matthew Tian Jing Peh. 2017. Third culture kids in the Outer Circle: The development of sociolinguistic knowledge among local and expatriate children in Singapore. *Language in Society* 46 (4). 507–546.

Starr, Rebecca Lurie, Kevin Martens Wong, Nurul Afiqah Bte Ibrahim, Andre Joseph Theng, Alicia Mei Yin Chua & Natalie Jing Yi Tong. 2016. *Flip-flops, slippers, thongs and jandals: Cross-dialectal lexical awareness among children in Singapore*. Paper presented at the 90th Annual Meeting of the Linguistic Society of America. 7–10 January, Washington, D.C.

Tagliamonte, Sali A. 2006. *Analysing sociolinguistic variation* (Key Topics in Sociolinguistics). Cambridge: Cambridge University Press.

Tanu, Danau. 2016. Going to school in 'Disneyland': Imagining an international school community in Indonesia. *Asian and Pacific Migration Journal APMJ* 25 (4). 429–450.

The English Schools Foundation. n.d. About ESF. www.esf.edu.hk/about-esf/ (accessed 23 May 2020).

Trudgill, Peter, Elizabeth Gordon, Gillian Lewis & Margaret M. Maclagan. 2000. Determinism in new-dialect formation and the genesis of New Zealand English. *Journal of Linguistics* 36 (2). 299–318.

Useem, Ruth Hill & Richard D. Downie. 1976. Third-Culture Kids. *Today's Education* 65 (3). 103–105.

Vertovec, Steven. 2006. The emergence of super-diversity in Britain. *Centre on Migration, Policy and Society* (Working Paper No. 25).

Vorperian, Houri K. & Ray D. Kent. 2007. Vowel acoustic space development in children: A synthesis of acoustic and anatomic data. *Journal of Speech, Language, and Hearing Research* 50 (6). 1510–1545.

Warren, Paul. 2017. Quality and quantity in New Zealand English vowel contrasts. *Journal of the International Phonetics Association* 48 (3). 305–330.

Warren, Paul. 2019. Non-linear analysis of a diphthong merger. In Sasha Calhoun, Paola Escudero, Marija Tabain & Paul Warren (eds.), *Proceedings of the 19th International Congress of Phonetic Sciences, Melbourne, Australia 2019*, 1883–1887. Canberra: Australasian Speech Science and Technology Association Inc.

Wickham, Hadley. 2017. *Tidyverse: Easily install and load the 'Tidyverse'*. R package [Computer Programme]. https://CRAN.R-project.org/package=tidyverse (accessed 21 February 2022).

Philipp Meer
13 Variation and change in the NURSE vowel in Trinidadian English: An apparent-time analysis of adolescent and adult speakers

Abstract: US American English (AmE) influence has been identified as a potential force in variation and change in postcolonial Englishes. Adolescents are typically not examined in this context despite their crucial role in language variation and change and possibly greater exposure to AmE via digital media. Drawing on sociophonetic data from 65 secondary students and 35 teachers, the present study investigates rhotacization of the NURSE vowel in Trinidadian English (TrinE), an incipient sound change that has previously been linked to younger speakers and AmE influence. The results show that NURSE-rhotacization is led by male and female speakers associated with prestige schools – not necessarily adolescents per se but younger Trinidadians. Additionally, speakers do not draw on rhotacization to approximate an AmE vowel target but integrate this feature into their speech. Bearing in mind related findings on speech perception, the findings suggest that AmE influence is unlikely to be the only reason for increasing levels of rhotacization. More generally, the findings highlight the importance of adolescents and younger adults in variation and change in Caribbean and other postcolonial Englishes.

Keywords: variation and change, adolescents, Trinidadian English, rhotacization, US American English

Acknowledgements: This study was conducted in the framework of the project "Translocality in the Anglophone Caribbean II: Sociophonetic variation and perception" (PI: Dagmar Deuber) funded by the Deutsche Forschungsgemeinschaft (DFG, German Research Foundation) – 259827343. It is part of the PhD project of the author at the Faculty of Philology at the University of Münster, Germany. I would like to thank Dagmar Deuber, Ulrike Gut, and Romana Kopečková for their comments on (sections of) this work. I am also grateful for the suggestions from the anonymous reviewers.

Philipp Meer, University of Münster, Germany

1 Introduction

Linked to the post-World War II rise of the United States (US) to global supremacy in terms of economic, political, cultural, and military power, standard US American English (AmE) has gained prestige and established itself as one of the possible forces to be reckoned with in the development of present-day Englishes (Mair 2013: 264). Possible influences from AmE have been discussed with regard to many postcolonial varieties and across different levels of linguistic structure. Research in this context has focused on written language and mostly relied on corpus-linguistic approaches (e.g. Gonçalves et al. 2018). Most of this research has focused on a macro level; the question of whether and to what degree potential AmE influences might manifest homogenously within postcolonial speech communities or heterogeneously across different social groups has been rarely investigated. Phonetic studies in different postcolonial contexts have also raised the possibility of AmE influence regarding certain changes. A change that is frequently discussed as possibly being linked to American influence, at least inter alia, is increasing rhotacization across some Englishes traditionally described as non-rhotic (Hansen Edwards 2016; Tan 2012).

One group of speakers that is typically not examined in these studies is adolescents. Adolescents, however, have been frequently argued to be a crucial group to consider in variation and change (Labov 2001; Tagliamonte and D'Arcy 2009). They are usually identified as both the leaders and most influential transmitters of language change (Labov 2001: 455). At the same time, sociolinguistic insights on adolescents to date are primarily based on studies conducted in countries like the US, Canada, or the United Kingdom (e.g. Tagliamonte and D'Arcy 2009); less is generally known about the role of adolescents in variation and change in other English-speaking contexts. Besides, it is adolescents that often show a relatively high usage of digital media and are possibly more exposed to AmE via these channels and, in turn, potentially more susceptible to these influences (Lenhart et al. 2010).

In linguistic research on the Anglophone Caribbean, AmE is frequently discussed as one of the potential exonormative forces on language production and perception – not only as a result of direct language contact but also in conjunction with American influences via social and digital media (Deuber, Hänsel, and Westphal 2021: 450; Hackert 2022: 366–367; Meer et al. 2019: 111). These influences have occasionally been claimed to manifest particularly among adolescents (Youssef and James 2008: 326 for Trinidad). However, little systematic empirical research exists on whether adolescents in the Caribbean may lead variation and change that can potentially be linked, at least in part, to AmE influence.

The present study addresses these research gaps from the viewpoint of speech production and investigates sociophonetic variation and change in adolescent and adult speakers of Trinidadian English (TrinE), the English spoken on the Caribbean island of Trinidad. Drawing on auditory and acoustic data from 100 speakers (65 secondary students and 35 teachers), the study analyzes rhotacization of the NURSE lexical set (Wells 1982), an incipient sound change in a traditionally non-rhotic variety. The change seems to be particularly linked with adolescents and younger adults on the island (Ferreira and Drayton fc.: 8–13; Wilson 2014: 231, 238) and has been argued to be related to AmE influence via transnational contact and US media (Ferreira and Drayton fc.: 11). At the same time, preliminary evidence indicates Trinidad-specific patterns of variation, including variation depending on gender or type of school, and associations with both foreign and local social meanings (see Section 2.4 for details). While the current study scrutinizes variation in NURSE-rhotacization in production, it bears in mind related findings in perception (following Hackert 2022; Meyerhoff and Niedzielski 2003: 550). In so doing, the study not only contributes to the question of whether adolescents may be leading this change in Trinidad but also sets out to see to what degree it might be related to AmE influence or rather indicates local social meanings (e.g. Meer et al. 2019: 113). The study further complements the analysis with an investigation of acoustic variation in the NURSE vowel proper to see whether speakers may be approximating an AmE vowel target or whether rhotacization may co-occur with TrinE-specific realizations of NURSE.

2 Background and previous research

2.1 Adolescents and language variation and change

A common sociolinguistic finding is that the frequency of incoming variants in language variation and change is typically highest among adolescents (or younger adults) compared to other speakers (Labov 2001; Tagliamonte and D'Arcy 2009). From an apparent-time perspective, this pattern is referred to as "adolescent peak". The peak is typically associated with an approximate age of 17 years old (Labov 2001: 448; Tagliamonte and D'Arcy 2009: 59). However, empirical research suggests that some degree of variation may be expected. While most peaks may occur between the ages 13 and 16 years old, some may also be found in older age groups (17–19 or even 20–29 years old; Labov 2001; Tagliamonte and D'Arcy 2009: 98).

Variationist studies have further revealed that adolescent peaks may show gender-based differences. In Labov (2001), only a few variables showed an adolescent peak among male speakers; most changes were led by female adolescent speakers with well-pronounced peaks. Other research observed peaks in speakers of both genders but to different degrees (Tagliamonte and D'Arcy 2009): Female adolescents often showed sharper peaks, i.e. higher rates of change, while male speakers had peaks less consistently and often spanning a larger period of years into younger adulthood.

2.2 The Trinidadian sociolinguistic context

Trinidad is the most southern island of the Caribbean, located off the coast of Venezuela. Together with its much smaller sister island, it forms the twin-island country Trinidad and Tobago, a former British colony, which became independent in 1962. Trinidad is the second most populous island in the Anglophone Caribbean with a population of approximately 1.3 million (Republic of Trinidad and Tobago 2021).

As in other Anglophone Caribbean islands, TrinE coexists with an English-derived Creole, Trinidadian English Creole (TEC), along a continuum of sociolinguistic variation (Deuber 2014: 11). Functionally, their distribution resembles a diglossic situation in that TEC is mostly associated with informal domains and TrinE with formal domains, such as news media, politics, or education (Deuber 2014: 244). While some direct influence of TEC on TrinE may be observed, in very formal contexts, this influence is often indirect: As speakers typically define standard English in opposition to Creole, they may produce features that are explicitly not Creole or perceived as such (Deuber and Leung 2013; Meer and Fuchs 2022: 949; Wilson 2014: 302).

2.3 Possible American English influence in Trinidad

As with the wider Anglophone Caribbean, Trinidad has been assumed to be particularly prone to AmE influence due to geographical proximity, strong economic ties, and sociohistorical relations with the US (Hackert 2022: 373). Transnational US-Trinidadian mobility is common in the educated population and highly-skilled workforce from the island (UNESCO 2018). The US is by far the country with the highest number of Trinidadians in the diaspora, currently about 276,000 (Orozco 2020), an approximate equivalent to 20 percent of the population residing in Trinidad. At the same time, it is not uncommon for these Trinidadians to maintain close relationships and networks with people located in Trinidad itself (Meer and Deuber 2020: 290–292).

Previous research indicates that certain patterns of variation (and change) in TrinE – including some frequently found in younger (female) speakers, both adolescents and younger adults – might be linked to AmE influence, or this aspect of variation is at least discussed as a likely possibility amongst others. Corpus-linguistic evidence shows the spread of an AmE-led global linguistic pattern, quotative *(be) like*, into standard Trinidadian speech, especially among younger and female speakers (Deuber, Hänsel, and Westphal 2021). The authors (2021: 450) suggest that "direct US influence through diasporic movements, media, and other channels can be seen as a major path through which *(be) like* has been integrated into language use in Trinidad". Similarly, Wilson (2023) observes that while Trinidadians may generally prefer AmE lexical variants over British ones, younger speakers show a relative increase in this preference compared to older ones – at least for some lexical items. Both studies also show that the use of AmE-originated linguistic features may be spearheaded by transnationally mobile speakers, especially those who live or have lived or extensively traveled to the US (Deuber, Hänsel, and Westphal 2021; Wilson 2023). More generally, folklinguistic evidence suggests that standard English in Trinidad, apart from the assumed opposition of English and Creole, is often perceived in relation to AmE influences, which are frequently associated with younger and female speakers (Stell 2018). Attitudinal findings further indicate that AmE plays an important role in secondary school students' norm orientation (Meer et al. 2019).

However, recent research also indicates that a nuanced view of potential AmE influence is required. Putative Americanization may be both feature-specific and not necessarily always due to AmE influence but governed by local (socio-)linguistic forces. Sociophonetic research indicates, for instance, that the retraction of /s(tr)/ toward [ʃ], a supralocal sound change particularly common in the US, may be more advanced in TrinE and possibly primarily phonetically conditioned (Ahlers and Meer 2019). Apparent AmE features may also be combined with local ones and incorporated in local standard varieties (Kraus 2017: 278). Findings on the perception of *(be) like* further indicate that the feature may be enregistered and associated with local social meanings in addition to American influence, including educatedness, middle to upper-class speech, and prestige schools (Deuber, Hänsel, and Westphal 2021: 447–448; see also Stell 2018: 128–130).

2.4 Variation in NURSE(-rhotacization) in Trinidad and related contexts

TrinE has been described as a non-rhotic variety in several studies conducted since the 1970s, the majority impressionistic in nature (Wells 1982: 58; Winer 1993: 16; Winford 1978; Youssef and James 2008: 330). More recently, however, studies have observed a tendency toward rhotacization in selected contexts (Deuber and Leung 2013; Ferreira and Drayton fc.; Wilson 2014). As Ferreira and Drayton (fc.: 11) argue, (NURSE-)rhotacization is a recent phenomenon in TrinE and may be seen as an incipient sound change, likely brought about, as they suggest, by transnational US-Trinidadian contact and influence of US media. On a regional level, these tendencies coincide with an apparently parallel change toward rhotacization in educated Bahamian English in the last 20–30 years (Hackert 2022; Kraus 2017), possibly due to AmE influence (Kraus 2017: 260–261), at least in part (Hackert 2022: 372).

While previous empirical research on rhotacization in TrinE is limited, there are indications that variation in this feature is foremost dependent on language-internal factors. Ferreira and Drayton (fc.: 11–13) suggest that rhotacization is conditioned by both vowel class and syllable stress, such that rhotacization, to date, is largely restricted to the "close-mid central vowel" in the stressed position – i.e. vowel tokens belonging to the NURSE class. These observations find parallels in empirical research on TrinE. In her study on accent variation in choral singing, Wilson (2014: 295) also identifies NURSE as the only variably rhotacized vowel. Similarly, among the local Trinidadian newscaster accents described in Deuber and Leung (2013: 301–302, 312–316), NURSE was the only variably rhotacized stressed vowel. Parallel tendencies concerning the favoring role of NURSE and syllable stress in rhotacization have also been found for educated Bahamian English (Hackert 2022: 366; Kraus 2017: 260–261) and several other varieties of English (Irvine-Sobers 2018; Meer et al. 2021).

Phonetically, the target of (non-)rhotacized NURSE in terms of vowel quality is less clear. Previous studies on variation of NURSE in Trinidad differ in their descriptive accounts and suggest a high degree of variation, both in TEC and, though somewhat less so, in standard TrinE. Earlier descriptions mostly rely on anecdotal evidence and are often not explicitly geared toward standard TrinE but focus on TEC (Wells 1982: 579; Winer 1993; Youssef and James 2008). In these works, TrinE NURSE is mostly described as the central low-mid vowel [ɜː], while variation between different back vowels is noted in TEC [oː ~ ɔ ~ ɒ ~ ʌ]. More recent studies rely on auditory (Deuber and Leung 2013; Wilson 2014) and acoustic analyses (Leung 2013), or a combination of anecdotal, auditory, and acoustic approaches (Ferreira and Drayton fc.). NURSE in present-day TEC mostly varies between [ɒː ~ ʌ] (Leung 2013: 134). Variation in NURSE in TrinE is observed along two parameters:

- **Vowel height**: While there is agreement that NURSE is generally realized as a central vowel, variation is found between low-mid [ɜː] (Deuber and Leung 2013; Wilson 2014) and high-mid [ɘː] (Deuber and Leung 2013; Ferreira and Drayton fc; Leung 2013.). Compared to realizations of NURSE in standard American English [ɚː] (Kretzschmar 2008), central high-mid productions are considerably raised and located higher in the vowel space.
- **Rhotacization**: NURSE may be non-rhotacized [ɜː / ɘː] or rhotacized [ɜ˞ː / ɘ˞ː] (Deuber and Leung 2013; Ferreira and Drayton fc.; Leung 2013; Wilson 2014).

Low-mid realizations, both rhotacized and non-rhotacized [ɜː ~ ɜ˞ː], have been observed in studies in the context of newscasts (Deuber and Leung 2013) and choral singing (Wilson 2014). High-mid productions [ə: ~ ə˞:] are reported in non-domain-specific, acoustic research (Ferreira and Drayton fc.; Leung 2013).[1] However, at this point, it is not clear whether the observed patterns might be indications of domain-specific tendencies or possible consequences of the different kinds of analyses employed (auditory vs. acoustic).

NURSE-rhotacization shows a high degree of sociolinguistic variation. Studies on speech production suggest that NURSE-rhotacization is conditioned by the factors age, gender, education or school type, social class, and speaking style – in accordance with the largely parallel effects of these factors on rhotacization in other traditionally non-rhotic postcolonial Englishes, both in the Bahamas (Hackert 2022; Kraus 2017) and elsewhere (e.g. Singapore, Hong Kong; Hansen Edwards 2016; Tan 2012):

- **Age**: There is a tendency for adolescents (and younger adults) to show higher levels of NURSE-rhotacization (see Ferreira and Drayton fc.: 11 for anecdotal observations). Similarly, Wilson (2014: 231, 338) observes rhotacization in school choir singers and younger audience members.
- **Gender**: Ferreira and Drayton (fc.: 11) argue that NURSE-rhotacization is led by female speakers. Likewise, rhotacization was particularly frequent in female singers and audience members in Wilson (2014), while a few cases also occurred in male speech.
- **Prestige school:** NURSE-rhotacization seems to be particularly associated with students (and teachers) from secondary schools popularly known in Trinidad as "prestige schools" (Ferreira and Drayton fc: 11–13; Wilson 2014: 338). Prestige schools are denominational schools, typically attended by the highest achieving students (Jackson 2010), the majority being from middle to upper-class backgrounds. Moreover, teachers at prestige schools may have higher levels of education (National Institute of Higher Education 2002: 33; 2017: 5). Schools of this type are associated with educational elitism and overt social prestige (Deuber, Hänsel, and Westphal 2021: 451).
- **Social class**: Relatedly, the feature is argued to vary according to social class, with (upper) middle-class speakers showing an increased tendency toward NURSE-rhotacization (Ferreira and Drayton fc.: 11).
- **Style**: Ferreira and Drayton (fc.: 13) indicate that NURSE-rhotacization shows stylistic variation and may occur in formal and conscious speaking styles.

---

[1] In contrast to Ferreira and Drayton (fc.), Leung (2013) does not report cases of rhotacized [ə˞:].

In sum, NURSE-rhotacization appears to primarily occur in the speech of younger (adolescent), female, prestige school speakers, and generally more so in formal speaking styles.

At the level of speech perception, (NURSE)-rhotacization is associated with local, endonormative social meanings, such as educatedness, ambition, and upward social mobility. At the same time, the feature may also be perceived as North American and pretentious (Deuber, Hänsel, and Westphal 2021: 451; Meer et al. 2019: 113). Similar exonormative associations with AmE influence were observed in other perception studies (Deuber, Hänsel, and Westphal 2021; Stell 2018: 128–130). More generally, these tendencies are reminiscent of the dualistic nature of social meanings often associated with supralocal changes (Villareal and Kohn 2021).

3 Research questions and hypotheses

The current study investigates the following research questions (RQ) and tests related hypotheses (H):

RQ1 What is the position of rhotacized and non-rhotacized NURSE in the acoustic vowel space?
  H1 NURSE will predominantly be realized as central high-mid [ɘː ~ ɚː], independently of rhotacization (Ferreira and Drayton fc.; Leung 2013); rhotacization will thus not coincide with a change in vowel quality toward AmE central mid [ɚː]. TEC variants [ɒː ~ ʌ] will be avoided (Leung 2013).
RQ2 How frequent is NURSE-rhotacization overall?
  H2 It will occur variably with high levels of inter-speaker variation (Deuber and Leung 2013; Ferreira and Drayton fc.: 11–13; Wilson 2014). The proportion of rhotacized productions will be well below that of non-rhotacized ones (Ferreira and Drayton fc.).
RQ3 What factors influence variation in the production of rhotacized NURSE?
  H3 These factors will be age, gender, prestige school, and style (Ferreira and Drayton fc.: 11–13; Wilson 2014).
RQ4 Which speakers and social groups are leading NURSE-rhotacization in apparent time?
  H4 Female adolescent speakers affiliated with prestige schools will be leading the change in apparent time (Ferreira and Drayton fc.: 11–13; Wilson 2014).

4 Method

4.1 Data

The present study was conducted in Trinidadian secondary schools. It involved a total of 100 speakers, 65 students and 35 teachers, who were recorded in a sociolinguistic interview context (see Table 13.1). The data were collected by the author during two field trips in 2015 and 2016. The speakers were recorded with Zoom H4n recorders equipped with external SHURE cardioid MX150B/C clip-on microphones using a 44.1 kHz sampling rate and 16-bit quantization. Recordings were usually made in quiet rooms provided by the different schools and had a good signal-to-noise ratio.

Table 13.1: Number of speakers across different groups.

		Age group (in years)						Total
		14–17	18–25	26–35	46–45	46–55	56–65	
Gender	F	25	10	14	7	3	4	63
	M	16	15	1	3	2	–	37
Prestige school	non-prestige	17	–	3	5	2	1	28
	prestige	24	25	12	5	3	3	72
Lived N. America	no	41	25	12	10	4	3	95
	yes	–	–	3	–	1	1	5
Total		41	25	15	10	5	4	100

The age groups split the speakers into students and teachers: The two youngest groups only include students (14–17, 18–25 years old), the others only teachers (26–35 to 56–65 years old).[2] Students in the two youngest groups were mostly aged 15–17 and 18–20 years old, respectively. While the gender distribution is approximately equal in the two youngest age groups, there is an imbalance toward females (82.9 percent) in the older ones, given that most secondary school teachers in Trinidad are female (Trading Economics 2016). Approximately two thirds of all speakers were affiliated with prestige schools and one third with non-prestige schools. Five teachers had lived in North America (United States or Canada) for a period of at least two years.

---

2 There was one female teacher (25 years old) in the 18–25-year-old group.

Speakers were sampled from nine secondary schools in various locations on the island. Most of them were located in the metropolitan region ranging from Port of Spain, the capital, to Arima, the most populous area in Trinidad. Two schools from San Fernando in the south and one school from the rural area on the northern coast were also included. The present study focuses on the two most formal speaking styles produced as part of the interview context. All respondents read out a text passage (reading passage style, REPA, 243 words) and a list of individual words (word list style, WL, 24 words). This was motivated by the aim of considering realizations of tokens that largely reflect the speakers' underlying norm, i.e. standard TrinE rather than TEC. The WL and REPA were designed with the aim of mapping a speaker's entire vowel space. Vowels were mostly presented with preceding and following obstruents and occasionally nasals; phonetic contexts with strong coarticulatory effects, such as /w, j,/ and [ɫ], and unstressed vowels known for undershoot were not included in the analysis (Thomas 2011: 159). Together, the WL and REPA contained four NURSE tokens, all of which occurred word-medially: three in a tautosyllabic consonant cluster in case of rhotacization – *hurt* (WL), *first*, and *birds* (REPA) – and one in singleton coda position – *journey* (REPA).

4.2 Processing

Automatic alignment was carried using the FAVE forced aligner (Rosenfelder et al. 2014) and followed by manual corrections for less well-segmented vowels, including rhotacized NURSE tokens, as shown in a systematic assessment of the segmentation quality (Meer 2020). Given that coarticulation was frequently observed in rhotacized NURSE productions, manual alignment followed the recommendations by Lawson et al. (2011: 80) for the segmentation of coarticulated vowels: The boundary between the vowel proper and the (more heavily) rhotacized portion of the vowel was placed at the point where an amplitude drop occurs in the acoustic signal due to the added approximant articulation.

4.3 Analysis

A combined acoustic-auditory approach was used to investigate rhotacization of the NURSE vowel. The first step of analysis was to provide an auditory coding. A total of 378 tokens were analyzed; this number excludes gross outliers in acoustic terms, which had previously been removed (see below). Rhotacization was coded using a binary coding system: "rhotacized" vs. "non-rhotacized," operationalized in terms of presence or absence of an r-colored vowel quality. The auditory analysis was complemented by visual inspection of broadband spectrograms in Praat. Lowering of the third formant and/or a close proximity of the second (F2) and third (F3) formant were taken as acoustic cues for auditory rhotacization (see below). The coding was carried out by the author together with two student assistants at the Chair of Variation Linguistics of the University of Münster, who were previously trained by the author in coding this variable based on auditory perception and visual spectrographic analysis. Each coder analyzed different sets of tokens. 10 percent of these tokens were subsequently re-checked by the author and an inter-rater agreement test was conducted. Inter-rater reliability, measured as percentage of agreements, of 92.3 percent was achieved.

The second step of the investigation was an acoustic analysis of NURSE. The study followed a protocol for semi-automatic acoustic phonetic analysis developed for the variety (Meer, Brato, and Matute Flores 2021). Specifically, formants 1–3 were extracted for all vowels produced by a speaker using TRINI-FAVE, a Bayesian vowel formant estimation method with speaker adaptation trained on TrinE (Meer, Brato, and Matute Flores 2021: 62–65). Given that hand measurements of TrinE vowels were initially required for its training, TRINI-FAVE was not used for formant extraction of 13 speakers in the sample. Following standard procedure in sociophonetics (Thomas 2011: 138–183), further post-hoc data processing was conducted. First, the raw acoustic measurements of all vowels were transformed to the equivalent rectangular bandwidth (ERB) scale to account for the nonlinear perception by the inner ear (Winn and Stilp 2019: 164–165). Second, to control for physiologically conditioned effects on formants, the ERB-transformed formant frequencies were subsequently normalized using z-transformation (Lobanov 1971). Despite TRINI-FAVE's overall high accuracy (Meer, Brato, and Matute Flores 2021), data reduction was carried out to avoid potential effects of erroneous measurements. Following common guidelines (Thomas 2011: 159), the 5 percent of vowel tokens that were the furthest away from the grand mean of each vowel class were removed. Prior to exclusion, however, the resulting vowel scatter plots were visually compared to ascertain that tokens to be excluded were indeed outliers.

Following research on the acoustic-auditory correlates of rhotacization, NURSE-rhotacization was investigated with a focus on two acoustic parameters: the degree of (1) lowering of F3 and (2) integration of F2 and F3, both of which are associated with auditory rhotacization (e.g. Heselwood, Plug, and Tickle 2010). F3-lowering was examined using z-normalized ERB formant measures. The integration of F2 and F3 was operationalized based on the distance between both formants: Δ(F3-F2). Following Heselwood, Plug, and Tickle (2010), Δ(F3-F2) was measured in non-normalized acoustic space (ERB), given that confounding physiological effects are limited as the distance metric is obtained on a per speaker basis. The measurement point was set to the midpoint of NURSE, i.e. the vowel proper. The primary reason for choosing this point was to avoid possible errors associated with reading formant tracks from the end of the vowel-rhotic sequence, where chaotic and unreliable formant tracks were often observed (see Figure 13.1; see also Stuart-Smith, Lawson, and Scobbie 2014: 75). Given that, in line with previous research on rhotacized monophthongs (e.g. Lawson et al. 2011: 78), the vowel proper was similarly affected by stable F3-lowering and the approximation of F2 and F3, this approach was warranted.

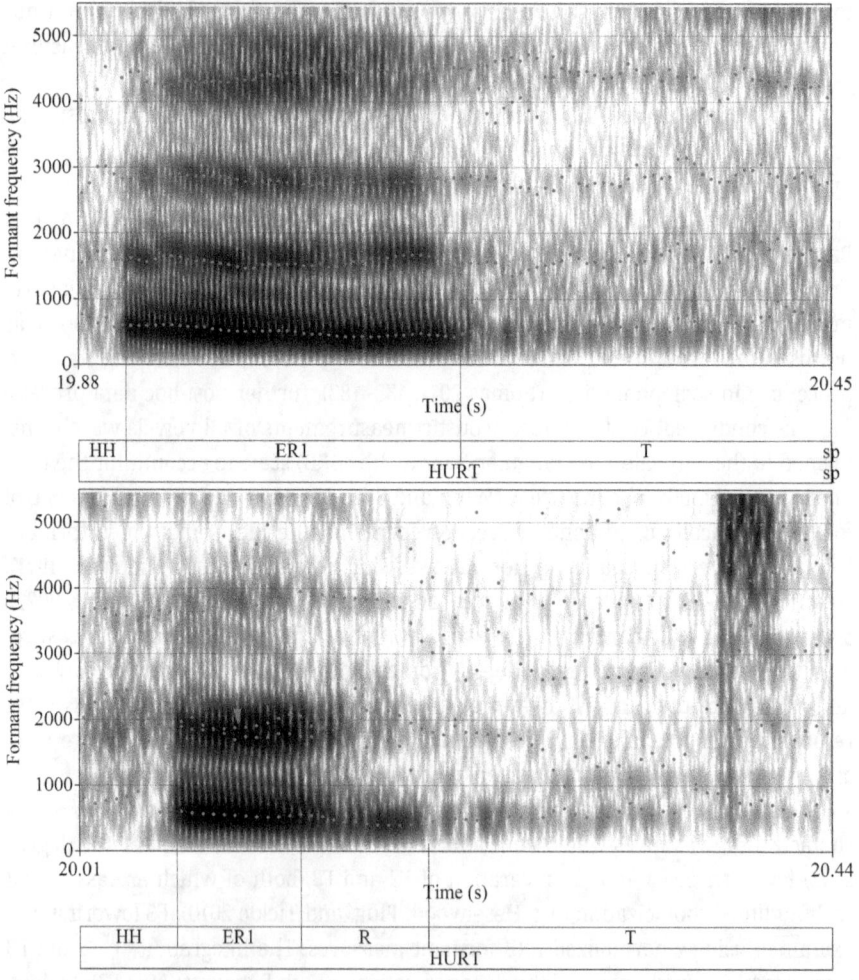

Figure 13.1: Exemplary non-rhotacized (above) and rhotacized (below) NURSE tokens in the word list style. The arrow shows the measurement point of F2 and F3 frequencies.

The statistical analysis focuses on the factors laid out in the hypotheses (i.e. AGE, GENDER, PRESTIGE SCHOOL, and STYLE; see Table 13.2). The study additionally examines the effect of longer stays abroad in the US or Canada (LIVED N. AMERICA; see Section 2.3). Previous sociophonetic research has further revealed that the (non-)occurrence of /r/ in a tautosyllabic consonant cluster is an important language-internal factor in conditioning variable rhotacization (e.g. Hackert 2022; Meer et al. 2021). CLUSTER is therefore also examined.

Table 13.2: Overview of factors under investigation and their levels.

Group	Factor	Levels	Effect type
Sociolinguistic	AGE	14–17, 18–25, 26–35, 36–45, 46–55, 56–65	fixed
	GENDER	female, male	
	PRESTIGE SCHOOL	prestige school, non-prestige school	
	STYLE	WL, REPA	
	LIVED N. AMERICA	yes, no	
Language-internal	CLUSTER	/r/ in tautosyllabic cluster, singleton /r/	fixed
Individual	SCHOOL	individual schools	random
	SPEAKER	individual speakers	
	WORD	individual words	

The effects of these factors are investigated drawing on a combination of (1) descriptive statistics, (2) non-parametric data analysis in the form of conditional inference trees and random forests for the categorical data to take into account existing imbalances and (quasi-)complete separations in the data (Tagliamonte and Baayen 2012; see Section 5.2.1), and (3) linear mixed-effects regression models for the acoustic data (see Section 5). All tree and regression analyses were run in IBM SPSS 27; random forests were grown in R using the Language Variation Suite interface (Scrivner and Díaz-Campos 2021). The conditional inference trees were computed using the chi-squared automatic interaction detection growing method, with the chi-square statistic being calculated using the likelihood-ratio method. Each tree was validated via 25-fold cross-validation. The tree analysis was complemented by random forest analysis where appropriate to avoid potential problems in fitting individual trees (Tagliamonte and Baayen 2012: 162). Best-fit linear mixed-effects models in the current study were based on a hypothesis-driven, manual, hierarchical model building strategy with the aim of model parsimony (Twisk 2006: 82; Winter 2020: 243–244). As regards the specification of the fixed-effects structure, models were built in a manual backward elimination process, starting with a full model including all fixed effects (main effects for all factors and interactions for AGE, GENDER, PRESTIGE SCHOOL) as well as all random effects for SCHOOL, SPEAKER, and WORD.

Model selection was informed by the two χ^2 likelihood parameters Akaike information criterion (AIC) and Bayesian information criterion (BIC). All linear models rely on the maximum likelihood (ML) estimation method (following Twisk 2006: 29), with degrees of freedom generated using Satterthwaite approximation. Prior to the specification of the fixed effects, the random intercept-slopes effects structure was determined following Twisk (2006: 82). However, no random slopes were fitted in the end, given that their inclusion consistently decreased model parsimony or resulted in non-convergence. Effects close to statistical significance are also reported to minimize potential Type II errors.

5 Results

5.1 (Non-)rhotacized NURSE in the acoustic vowel space

A visual comparison of the mean formant frequencies of rhotacized and non-rhotacized NURSE in the wider acoustic vowel space shows that the vowel – on average and independent of rhotacization – occupies a central to slightly fronted position on the F2 dimension (related to vowel frontness) and a near-high position on the F1 dimension (related to vowel height) (see Figure 13.2, left panel; $F1_{rhot.}$ = –0.96 zERB, $F2_{rhot.}$ = 0.27 zERB vs. $F1_{non-rhot.}$ = –1.00 zERB, $F2_{non-rhot.}$ = 0.22 zERB). NURSE is located higher in the vowel space than KIT but lower than both FLEECE and GOOSE and roughly between the latter in terms of F2, although slightly fronter than the absolute central position (at F2 = 0 zERB). Similarly, the observed vowel scatter shows heavy overlap between rhotacized and non-rhotacized NURSE (see Figure 13.2, right panel). For both variants, some variation exists between more central and somewhat fronted productions in terms of F2 and high-mid to near-high realizations regarding F1. However, no (non-)rhotacized token is in or near the central mid position (at F1 and F2 = 0 zERB) or in the lower back vowel space.

Statistical modeling generally confirms these tendencies. While a linear mixed model revealed that the difference between rhotacized and non-rhotacized NURSE in terms of F1 is still within the margin of statistical significance, $F(1, 259.5) = 3.9$, $p = .049$, the magnitude of this effect is exceedingly low (Δ = 0.04 zERB) and negligible regarding the degree of variation in the larger vowel space. Multivariate analysis of variance (MANOVA) and Pillai scores, formally known as the Pillai's Trace statistic, were used to quantify the degree of spectral (F1–F2) overlap observed between rhotacized and non-rhotacized tokens across all speakers (Hay, Warren, and Drager

2006). Pillai values range from 0 to 1, with 0 indicating complete overlap and 1 indicating no overlap between two vowel clusters. With a Pillai score of 0.004, the results of the analysis indicate almost complete spectral overlap between rhotacized and non-rhotacized tokens.

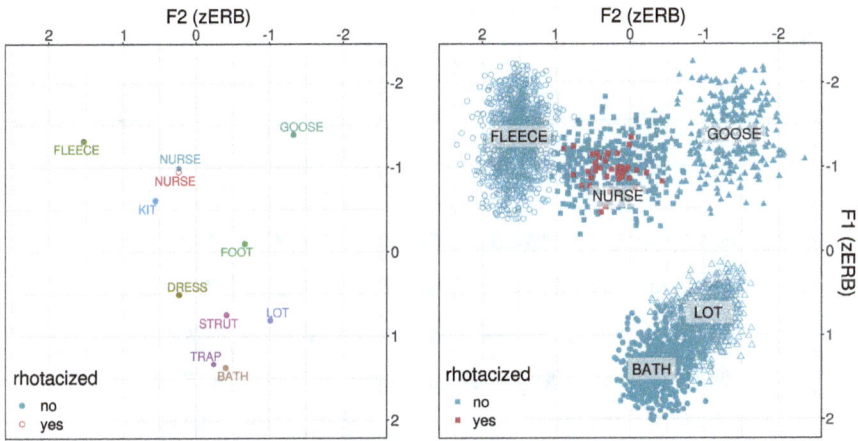

Figure 13.2: Variation of (non-)rhotacized NURSE in F1–F2 acoustic space (in z-normalized ERB). Left panel shows average formant frequencies in relation to several other monophthongs, right panel shows entire scatter.[3]

5.2 Sociolinguistic variation in NURSE-rhotacization

5.2.1 General distribution and variation patterns

Overall, NURSE-rhotacization is a minority phenomenon in the data. Approximately 12 percent of all tokens were rhotacized (see Table 13.3). The findings further show some degree of inter-speaker variation. While most speakers (79 percent) consistently produced non-rhotacized NURSE vowels, around one fifth (21 percent) showed rhotacization. However, most of these speakers (18 percent) were variably rhotacizing in that fewer than the four tokens for each speaker were rhotacized; only very few speakers showed categorical rhotacization (3 percent).

The distribution across different factors points to a high degree of sociolinguistic variation (see Figure 13.3). Importantly, the data show two (quasi-)complete splits. First, there is a complete separation of rhotacized and non-rhotacized tokens

---

3 Figure 13.2 was created using Visible Vowels (Heeringa and Van de Velde 2017).

Table 13.3: Overall distribution (in percent) for NURSE-rhotacization (rounded to the nearest whole number).

		Proportion
Tokens (n = 378)	rhotacized	12%
	non-rhotacized	88%
Speakers (n = 100)	categorical rhotacization	3%
	variable rhotacization	18%
	categorical non-rhotacization	79%

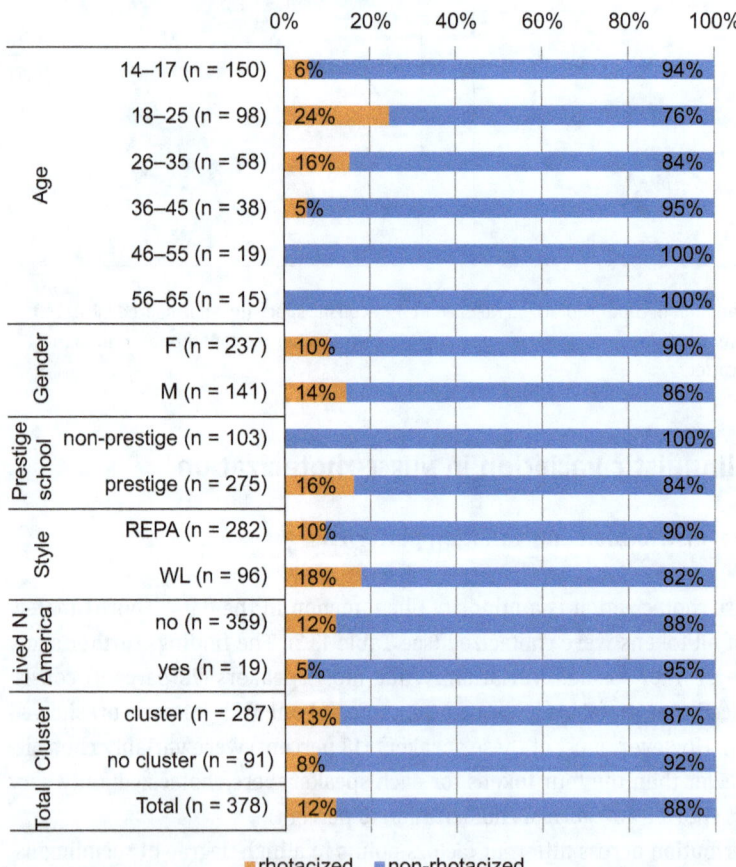

Figure 13.3: Distribution (in percent) of (non-)rhotacized NURSE tokens across sociolinguistic and language-internal factors (rounded to the nearest whole number).

depending on the school type: rhotacization solely occurred among speakers associated with prestige schools and never in speakers from other schools. Second, a quasi-complete age stratification was observed, such that rhotacized tokens were not produced among the two oldest age groups (46–55 and 56–65 years old) but only among the younger speakers (groups 14–17 to 36–45 years old). The 18–25-year-old group showed the highest rhotacization rate (24 percent), followed by the 26–35-year-olds (16 percent). Speakers aged 14–17 years old had approximately similar levels of rhotacization as the 36–45-year-olds (6 percent vs. 5 percent).

More gradual variation was observed for the other variables. Both male and female speakers showed NURSE-rhotacization, with the former having a slightly higher rate than the latter (14 percent vs. 10 percent). Higher overall levels of rhotacization were found in the WL compared to the REPA style (18 percent vs. 10 percent). Speakers who had lived in North America did not produce more rhotacized tokens than speakers who had resided in Trinidad all their life (5 percent vs. 12 percent). Additionally, NURSE-rhotacization was more often found in words with tautosyllabic coda clusters than tokens without clusters (13 percent vs. 8 percent).

5.2.2 Statistical modeling

Figure 13.4 shows the results of a conditional inference tree analysis that examined the power of the fixed-effects factors in predicting (non-)rhotacized NURSE. The tree model achieved a balanced accuracy of 70.8 percent,[4] which is generally considered sufficient or even high in linguistics (Winter 2020: 77). In line with the descriptive account of the distribution (see Section 5.2.1), the most prominent split separates non-prestige-school from prestige-school speakers, with the latter showing an overall rhotacization rate of 16 percent. The analysis further revealed significant age differences among prestige-school speakers. The tree indicates a three-fold split: (1) Speakers in the 18–25 and 26–35-year-old groups both have the highest levels of NURSE-rhotacization (22.8 percent); (2) the 14–17 and 36–45-year-old groups show intermediate levels (10.3 percent); (3) speakers older than 45 years old have zero rhotacization. The other factors were not significant and not included in the tree model.

In line with the individual tree, the random forest fitted to the data shows that AGE and PRESTIGE SCHOOL are the two most important variables in predicting NURSE-rhotacization (see Figure 13.5). However, in contrast to the tree model, AGE

---

4 To mitigate the imbalance of (non-)rhotacized token frequencies, individual cases were weighted by a factor representing the proportion of rhotacized/non-rhotacized tokens, which resulted in a considerable increase in the balanced accuracy rate. The procedure was also applied to the second tree analysis (Figure 13.6).

is attributed considerably more variable importance than PRESTIGE SCHOOL. The forest further revealed that STYLE, and to a lesser extent GENDER, have intermediate importance compared to the other variables. The lowest importance levels in comparison are attributed to CLUSTER and LIVED N. AMERICA.

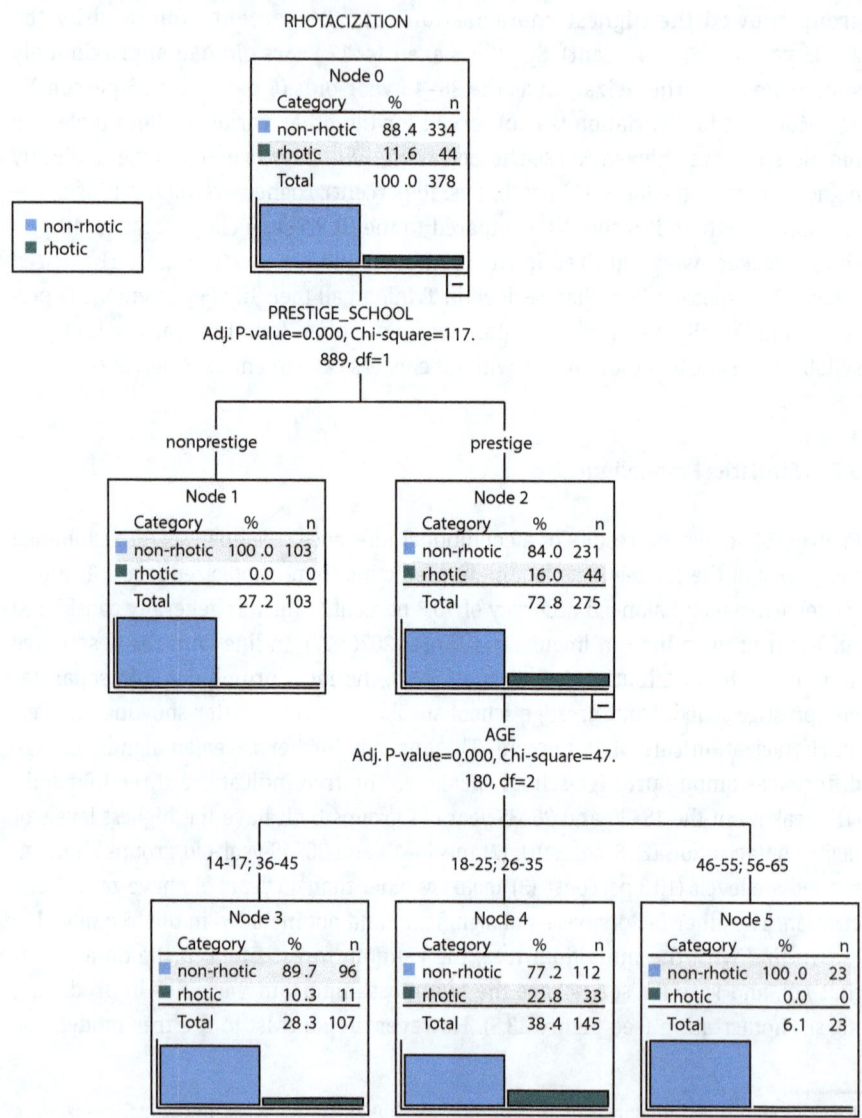

Figure 13.4: Conditional inference tree analysis for NURSE-rhotacization (only fixed effects).

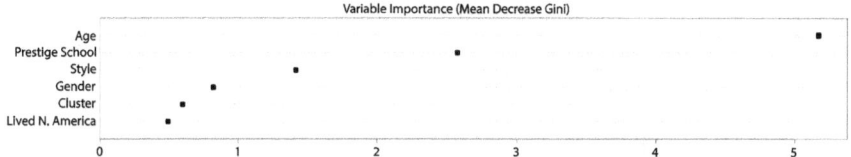

Figure 13.5: Random forest analysis for NURSE-rhotacization (only fixed effects).

The analyses of the fixed-effects predictors were complemented by a second conditional inference tree that also examined the random effects of SCHOOL and SPEAKER (as well as WORD) in predicting NURSE-rhotacization (see Figure 13.6). Apart from the broader effects identified above, the increased balanced accuracy of the tree (92.8 percent) indicates that rhotacization additionally shows individual school- and speaker-specific tendencies. While NURSE-rhotacization is a prestige school phenomenon, the feature is largely restricted to the schools with the indices D and G (overall rhotacization level: 23.5 percent). Both are elite-type schools located in Port of Spain. Specifically, among all the prestige schools in the sample, D and G are generally the most selective and highest performing, and their students often come from higher social classes. In line with the descriptive account above (see Table 13.3), the tree further shows high levels of inter-speaker variation among students and teachers affiliated with these schools (overall rhotacization level: 56 percent). Within this cluster of speakers, individuals were identified who showed more rhotacized than non-rhotacized productions, and their socio-demographic profiles were examined as a means to identify potential leaders of change. One 17-, three 18-, and two 26–35-year-old speakers formed part of this subgroup. Their gender distribution was balanced, and none of the speakers had previously lived in North America (with the exception of one teacher who had spent some years abroad in both Nigeria and the US). However, a qualitative content-analytic inspection of the interviews with these speakers revealed that most of them, including the students, had transnational contacts to the US, often in the form of networks with Trinidadian family members living there. The students commented that they had siblings, uncles and aunts, or other relatives in the US and reported relatively frequent visits to or from these family members. All students reported to have ambitions to go to university, two of them in the US, the other two in Trinidad. All of them indicated frequent engagement with (US) media, including US-based online streaming services, (predominantly) US TV, and platforms such as YouTube, Facebook, or Instagram, as well as (US) music. AmE was often commented to sound "normal," in the sense that they were well accustomed to hearing it. One student claimed that their language use was influenced by AmE.

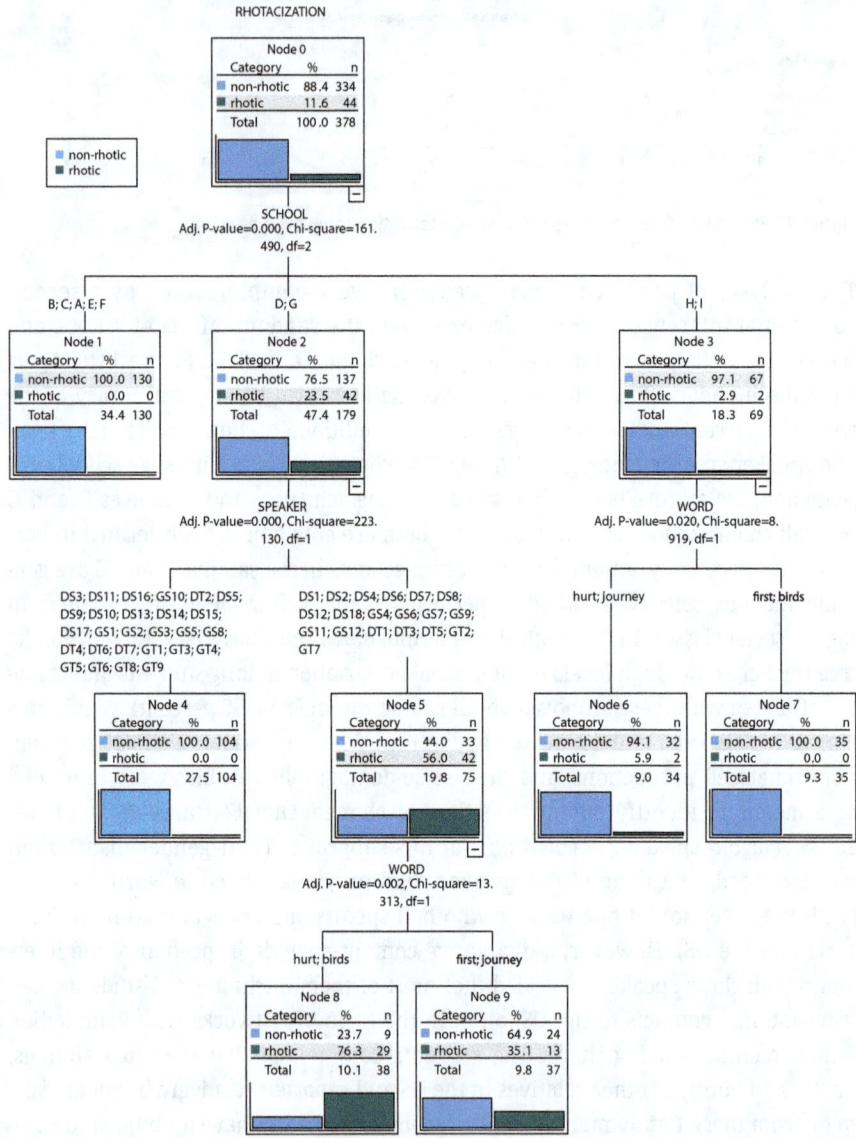

Figure 13.6: Conditional inference tree analysis for NURSE-rhotacization (fixed and random effects). Individual school indices: A–H. Individual speaker indices: school (A–H; first digit), teacher vs. student (T or S; second digit), and identification number (third digit).

5.2.3 Acoustic correlates of NURSE-rhotacization

Linear mixed-effects models revealed that PRESTIGE SCHOOL has a significant main effect on both F3 and Δ(F3-F2) (see Table 13.4). An additional significant effect on Δ(F3-F2) was found for GENDER. The effect of LIVED N. AMERICA on F3 was close to statistical significance. In contrast to the above findings (see Section 5.2.2), the two models did not include a significant effect of AGE. However, considering that the age-stratified distribution of F3 and Δ(F3-F2) was similar to that observed for NURSE-rhotacization as a categorical variable, age differences are also described in the following section to avoid Type II errors connected to possible limitations in statistical power due to the smaller number of speakers in the older age groups.

Table 13.4: Summary of best-fit linear mixed-effects models (Type III tests of fixed effects) for F3 and Δ(F3-F2). Levels of significance: $p<.05$ (*), $p<.01$ (**), $p<.001$ (***).

	F3				Δ(F3-F2)			
	dfn	dfd	F	p	dfn	dfd	F	p
Intercept	1	47.7	3.2	0.078	1	6.9	109.8	***
GENDER	–	–	–	–	1	94.9	4.2	*
PRESTIGE SCHOOL	1	12.5	5.4	*	1	11.2	8.1	*
LIVED N. AMERICA	1	95.5	3.5	0.066	–	–	–	–

The patterns of variation in the acoustic correlates generally resemble those for NURSE-rhotacization as a categorical dependent variable (see Figure 13.7). Prestige school speakers show both lower mean levels of F3 (−0.35 vs. 0.37 zERB) and lower mean Δ(F3-F2) distances (3.22 vs. 4.60 ERB). The magnitudes of the effects for GENDER and LIVED N. AMERICA are considerably smaller: Speakers who had lived in North America have slightly lower mean F3 (−0.16 vs. −0.03 zERB), and male speakers have a somewhat smaller Δ(F3-F2) distances than female speakers (3.56 vs. 3.62 ERB). Although the 18–25-year-old speakers show the greatest degree of F3-lowering, overall, relatively little age-stratified variation exists concerning F3 compared to the patterns for auditory NURSE-rhotacization. For Δ(F3-F2), by contrast, the distribution across age groups is in line with that identified above (see Sections 5.2.1–5.2.2) in that younger age groups show decreasing Δ(F3-F2) distances, with a minimum observed in the 18–25-year-olds. The other factors only showed minor (and non-significant) differences.

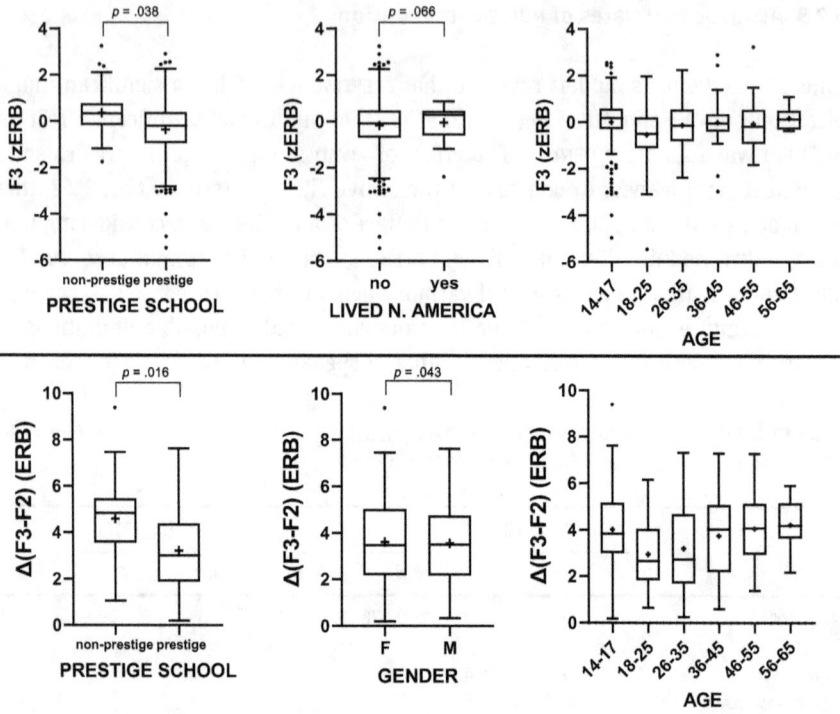

Figure 13.7: Acoustic correlates of rhotacization across PRESTIGE SCHOOL, LIVED N. AMERICA, GENDER, AND AGE: F3 in zERB (above) and Δ(F3-F2) in ERB (below). Tukey boxplots with means as dots, medians as lines, and significance levels.

6 Discussion and conclusion

Using auditory and acoustic data from 100 speakers, this study has investigated rhotacization of the NURSE vowel in TrinE, an apparent sound change that has previously been argued to be linked to younger speakers and AmE influence (Ferreira and Drayton fc.: 11). The results show that the first hypothesis (H1) concerning the position of (non-)rhotacized NURSE in the acoustic vowel space can partially be confirmed. Rhotacized and non-rhotacized NURSE were found to show heavy spectral overlap and occupy a central (though slightly fronted) position of the vowel space. Further, rhotacization did not coincide with a corresponding change in vowel quality toward AmE central mid [ɚː], and low back realizations associated with TEC [ɒː ~ ʌ] (Leung 2013) as well as low-mid [ɜː] (Deuber and Leung 2013; Wilson 2014) did not occur. However, although high-mid realizations of NURSE also occurred, NURSE was produced as a near-high vowel on average, approximately [ɘː ~ ɘ˞ː].

The findings further show that the second hypothesis (H2), i.e. that rhotacized NURSE will occur less frequently than non-rhotacized NURSE and with high levels of inter-speaker variation, can be generally confirmed. The observed overall rate of rhotacized tokens (c. 12 percent) combined with the observed levels of inter-speaker variation confirm reports in Ferreira and Drayton (fc.) of NURSE-rhotacization being an incipient sound change in TrinE.

As regards the third hypothesis (H3), the results partially confirm the influence of the factors AGE, GENDER, PRESTIGE SCHOOL, and STYLE (Ferreira and Drayton fc.: 11–13; Wilson 2014). However, GENDER and STYLE were largely not significant and have less predictive power in explaining NURSE-rhotacization. Variation in the feature by and large seems to be conditioned by AGE and PRESTIGE SCHOOL. At the same time, it was found that NURSE-rhotacization is a school- and speaker-specific phenomenon and that membership of larger, macro-level social groups alone (such as younger age groups or prestige schools) is not a sufficient predictor for variation and change in this feature.

The identified patterns of variation suggest that the fourth hypothesis (H4), regarding the leaders of rhotacization in apparent time, can be only partially confirmed. In contrast to previous observations, both in TrinE overall and the domain of classical choral singing (Wilson 2014; Ferreira and Drayton fc.) – and findings in variationist sociolinguistics more generally – NURSE-rhotacization in the education domain is not led by female speakers. Rather, it is led by both male and female speakers associated with prestige schools – not necessarily adolescents per se, if closely defined as speakers under the age of 18 years old, but younger speakers in the 18–25-year-old group. Speakers in this group are mostly 18–20 years old, i.e. they qualify as (late) adolescents in a broader sense, in accordance with how the label is frequently applied in the sociolinguistic literature (Tagliamonte and D'Arcy 2009). The adolescent peak observed here is thus in line with occasional observations in previous studies of the peak being located in slightly older age groups (17–19/20–29 years old; Labov 2001; Tagliamonte and D'Arcy 2009: 98). Additionally, the findings suggest that NURSE-rhotacization is not just led by younger prestige school speakers overall but speakers with specific affiliations to elite-type, high-performing prestige schools located in the capital, Port of Spain. These speakers further had some transnational contacts to the US, frequent engagement with (US) media, and ambitions to pursue tertiary education in both Trinidad and the US. On the regional level, the observed tendencies for TrinE show similarities to the parallel change toward rhotacized pronunciations in educated Bahamian English identified and described in Kraus (2017) and Hackert (2022) in that younger speakers show a relatively sharp increase in (NURSE-)rhotacization (Hackert 2022) and relatively few gender differences in formal speaking styles (Kraus 2017: 174–175). Language-internally, the findings further indicate that, in line with tendencies in the Bahamas (Hackert 2022; see also Meer et al. 2021), rhotacization might be more frequent in words with tautosyllabic coda clusters. However, given that this effect was rather weak and only identified in the random forest, further research is needed to investigate this.

An important and surprising result of this study is that Trinidadians who had lived in North America showed lower levels of NURSE-rhotacization than speakers who had resided in Trinidad all their life. Crucially, although speakers with more frequent NURSE-rhotacization had some transnational contacts to the US, this finding suggests that AmE influence is unlikely to be the only reason for increasing levels of rhotacization in apparent time (see Hackert 2022. for a similar argument concerning rhotacization in Bahamian English). Rather, what may be likely to play a role in this context is the dualistic nature of social meanings of (NURSE-)rhotacization in Trinidad (Deuber, Hänsel, and Westphal 2021: 451; Meer et al. 2019: 113). Apart from popular exonormative associations with "Americanness," it is conceivable that locally created, endonormative meanings of the feature with very positive connotations – "educatedness," "ambition," or "upward social mobility" – might lead younger speakers associated with prestige schools to adopt NURSE-rhotacization, especially perhaps in more formal or conscious speaking styles as observed here. This possibility is in line with the fact that the younger speakers with more rhotacized than non-rhotacized productions from the two elite-type schools all had ambitions to pursue tertiary education, including in the US. Indeed, previous research indicates that supralocal sound changes may be accelerated once these come to be associated with favorable local social meanings in addition to supralocal associations or stereotypes (Stuart-Smith et al. 2013: 527; Villareal and Kohn 2021). In the school context itself and potentially more so for students, NURSE-rhotacization could also be interpreted as an endonormative feature that may index belonging to prestige schools in addition to more general social meanings of educatedness or ambition. The observed variation for rhotacized and non-rhotacized NURSE in the acoustic vowel space further suggests that speakers do not draw on rhotacization to approximate an AmE vowel target but integrate this feature into their speech (cp. Kraus 2017: 278). That is, rather than coinciding with acoustic lowering toward AmE central mid [ɚː], rhotacization was combined with the distinct TrinE-specific realization of NURSE in a mid near-high position of the vowel space. More generally, considering speech production and perception jointly, variation in NURSE thus shows a possible blurring of exonormativity and endonormativity – a situation that may illustrate tendencies of multinormative orientation in the given context (see Meer and Deuber 2020).

The present study is, of course, not without limitations. (1) While a large sample of speakers was included, each speaker only produced a small number of NURSE tokens. An analysis of intra-speaker variation was thus beyond the scope of the study. (2) As mentioned above, the distribution of speakers was unbalanced across age groups, such that fewer older speakers were included. (3) Given that the study primarily draws on variationist and sociophonetic approaches, an analysis of NURSE-rhotacization in the tradition of Third Wave Sociolinguistics would allow more insights into the social evaluations and meanings of the feature and reasons for its adoption.

On a general level, the findings highlight the importance of studying adolescents and younger adults in tracking variation and change in Caribbean and other postcolonial Englishes. Including these speakers allows the researcher to observe incipient patterns of variation and directions of early changes that can otherwise go unnoticed. An inclusion of adolescents and younger adults may thus be helpful in scrutinizing potential translocal linguistic forces in the development of varieties of English in the Caribbean and other postcolonial contexts (Hackert 2022; Meer and Deuber 2020). Additionally, as the current study has shown, an analysis of adolescent language use may reveal patterns of variation specific to individual World Englishes contexts like Trinidad, such as variation in NURSE-rhotacization depending on the type of school. Scrutinizing adolescents has further helped in understanding the emergence of a new linguistic feature in an environment of potential interaction of exonormative (American) influence and endonormative developments, a situation that may also be found in other postcolonial contexts.

References

Ahlers, Wiebke & Philipp Meer. 2019. Sibilant variation in New Englishes: A comparative sociophonetic study of Trinidadian and American English /s(tr)/-retraction. *Annual Conference of the International Speech Communication Association (INTERSPEECH 2019)*. 291–295.

Deuber, Dagmar. 2014. *English in the Caribbean: Variation, style and standards in Jamaica and Trinidad*. Cambridge: Cambridge University Press.

Deuber, Dagmar, Eva Canan Hänsel & Michael Westphal. 2021. Quotative be like in Trinidadian English. *World Englishes* 40 (3). 436–458.

Deuber, Dagmar & Glenda-Alicia Leung. 2013. Investigating attitudes towards an emerging standard of English: Evaluations of newscasters' accents in Trinidad. *Multilingua* 32 (3). 289–319.

Ferreira, Jo-Anne & Kathy-Ann Drayton. fc. *Trinidadian English*. Author manuscript.

Gonçalves, Bruno, Lucía Loureiro-Porto, José J. Ramasco & David Sánchez. 2018. Mapping the Americanization of English in space and time. *PloS one* 13 (5). 1–15.

Hackert, Stephanie. 2022. The epicentre model and American influence on Bahamian Englishes. *World Englishes* 41 (3). 361–376. doi.org/10.1111/weng.12583

Hansen Edwards, Jette G. 2016. Accent preferences and the use of American English features in Hong Kong. *Asian Englishes* 18 (3). 197–215.

Hay, Jennifer, Paul Warren & Katie Drager. 2006. Factors influencing speech perception in the context of a merger-in-progress. *Journal of Phonetics* 34 (4). 458–484.

Heeringa, Wilbert & Hans van de Velde. 2017. Visible vowels: A tool for the visualization of vowel variation. *Proceedings of the Annual Conference of the International Speech Communication Association (INTERSPEECH 2017)*. 4034–4035.

Heselwood, Barry, Leendert Plug & Alison Tickle. 2010. Assessing rhoticity using auditory, acoustic and psychoacoustic methods. In Barry Heselwood & Clive Upton (eds.), *Proceedings of Methods XIII*, 331–340. Frankfurt: Lang.

Irvine-Sobers, G. Alison. 2018. *The acrolect in Jamaica: The architecture of phonological variation*. Berlin: Language Science Press.

Jackson, Clement Kirabo. 2010. Do students benefit from attending better schools? Evidence from rule-based student assignments in Trinidad and Tobago. *The Economic Journal* 120 (549). 1399–1429.

Kraus, Janina. 2017. *A sociophonetic study of the urban Bahamian Creole vowel system*. Germany: Ludwig-Maximilian University Munich PhD dissertation.

Kretzschmar, William A. 2008. Standard American English pronunciation. In Edgar W. Schneider (ed.), *Varieties of English: The Americas and the Caribbean*, 37–51. Berlin, New York: De Gruyter Mouton.

Labov, William. 2001. *Principles of linguistic change: Social Factors*. Hoboken NJ: Wiley-Blackwell.

Lawson, Eleanor, Jane Stuart-Smith, James M. Scobbie, Malcah Yaeger-Dror & Margaret A. Maclagan. 2011. Liquids. In Marianna Di Paolo & Malcah Yaeger-Dror (eds.), *Sociophonetics: A student's guide*, 72–86. London: Routledge.

Lenhart, Amanda, Kristen Purcell, Aaron Smith & Kathryn Zickuhr. 2010. *Social media and mobile internet use among teens and young adults*. Washington, D.C.

Leung, Glenda-Alicia. 2013. *A synchronic sociophonetic study of monophthongs in Trinidadian English*. Germany: University of Freiburg PhD dissertation.

Lobanov, Boris M. 1971. Classification of Russian vowels spoken by different speakers. *The Journal of the Acoustical Society of America* 49 (2B). 606–608.

Mair, Christian. 2013. The world system of Englishes: Accounting for the transnational importance of mobile and mediated vernaculars. *English World-Wide* 34 (3). 253–278.

Meer, Philipp. 2020. Automatic alignment for New Englishes: Applying state-of-the-art aligners to Trinidadian English. *The Journal of the Acoustical Society of America* 147 (4). 2283–2294.

Meer, Philipp & Dagmar Deuber. 2020. Standard English in Trinidad: Multinormativity, translocality, and implications for the Dynamic Model and the EIF Model. In Sarah Buschfeld & Alexander Kautzsch (eds.), *Modelling World Englishes: A joint approach to postcolonial and non-postcolonial varieties*, 274–297. Edinburgh: Edinburgh University Press.

Meer, Philipp, Michael Westphal, Eva Canan Hänsel & Dagmar Deuber. 2019. Trinidadian secondary school students' attitudes toward accents of Standard English. *Journal of Pidgin and Creole Languages* 34 (1). 83–125.

Meer, Philipp & Robert Fuchs. 2022. The Trini Sing-Song: Sociophonetic variation in Trinidadian English prosody and differences to other varieties. *Language and Speech* 65 (4). 923–957.

Meer, Philipp, Robert Fuchs, Anika Gerfer, Ulrike Gut & Zeyu Li. 2021. Rhotics in Standard Scottish English. *English World-Wide* 42 (2). 121–144.

Meer, Philipp, Thorsten Brato & José Alejandro Matute Flores. 2021. Extending automatic vowel formant extraction to New Englishes: A comparison of different methods. *English World-Wide* 42 (1). 54–84.

Meyerhoff, Miriam & Nancy Niedzielski. 2003. The globalisation of vernacular variation. *Journal of Sociolinguistics* 7 (4). 534–555.

National Institute of Higher Education, Research, Science, and Technology. 2002. *Profile of teachers in public secondary schools 1999–2000*. www.niherst.gov.tt/research/publications/publication-teacherprofiles.html (accessed 11 June 2021).

National Institute of Higher Education, Research, Science, and Technology. 2017. *Survey of Mathematics in secondary schools 2016*. www.niherst.gov.tt/research/publications/survey-of-mathematics-in-secondary-schools-2016.html (accessed 11 June 2021).

Orozco, Manuel. 2020. *Diaspora engagement mapping*: Trinidad and Tobago. https://diasporafordevelopment.eu/wp-content/uploads/2020/04/CF_Trinidad-and-Tobago-v.1.pdf (accessed 11 June 2021).

Republic of Trinidad and Tobago, Central Statistical Office. 2021. *Mid-year population estimate by age and sex 2005–2020*. https://cso.gov.tt/subjects/population-and-vital-statistics/population/ (accessed 11 June 2021).

Rosenfelder, Ingrid, Josef Fruehwald, Keelan Evanini, Scott Seyfarth, Kyle Gorman, Hilary Prichard & Jiahong Yuan. 2014. *Forced Alignment and Vowel Extraction (FAVE): Program Suite v1.2.2*. https://github.com/JoFrhwld/FAVE (accessed 11 June 2021).

Scrivner, Olga & Manuel Díaz-Campos. *Language Variation Suite (LVS)*. https://languagevariationsuite.shinyapps.io/Pages/ (accessed 11 June 2021).

Stell, Gerald. 2018. Representing variation in creole continua: A folk linguistic view of language variation in Trinidad. *Journal of English Linguistics* 46 (2). 113–139.

Stuart-Smith, Jane, Eleanor Lawson & James M. Scobbie. 2014. Derhoticisation in Scottish English: A sociophonetic journey. In Chiara Celata & Silvia Calamai (eds.), *Advances in Sociophonetics*, 59–96. Amsterdam: John Benjamins.

Stuart-Smith, Jane, Gwilym Pryce, Claire Timmins & Barrie Gunter. 2013. Television can also be a factor in language change: Evidence from an urban dialect. *Language* 89 (3). 501–536.

Tagliamonte, Sali A. & Alexandra D'Arcy. 2009. Peaks beyond phonology: Adolescence, incrementation, and language change. *Language* 85 (1). 58–108.

Tagliamonte, Sali A. & R. Harald Baayen. 2012. Models, forests, and trees of York English: Was/were variation as a case study for statistical practice. *Language Variation and Change* 24 (2). 135–178.

Tan, Ying-Ying. 2012. To r or not to r: Social correlates of /ɹ/ in Singapore English. *International Journal of the Sociology of Language* 2012 (218). 1–24.

Thomas, Erik R. 2011. *Sociophonetics*. Basingstoke: Palgrave Macmillan.

Trading Economics. 2016. Secondary education – teachers (% female) in Trinidad and Tobago. www.tradingeconomics.com/trinidad-and-tobago/secondary-education-teachers-percent-female-wb-data.html.

Twisk, Jos W. R. 2006. *Applied multilevel analysis*. Cambridge: Cambridge University Press.

UNESCO. 2018. Global flow of tertiary-level students. https://uis.unesco.org/en/uis-student-flow.

Villarreal, Dan & Mary Kohn. 2021. Local meanings for supralocal change. *American Speech* 96 (1). 45–77.

Wells, John C. 1982. *Accents of English*. Cambridge: Cambridge University Press.

Wilson, Guyanne. 2014. *The sociolinguistics of singing: Dialect and style in classical choral singing in Trinidad*. Münster: Monsenstein.

Wilson, Guyanne. 2023. British and American norms in the Trinidadian English lexicon. *World Englishes* 42 (1). 73–90.

Winer, Lise. 1993. *Trinidad and Tobago*. Amsterdam: John Benjamins.

Winford, Donald. 1978. Phonological hypercorrection in the process of decreolization: The case of Trinidadian English. *Journal of Linguistics* 14 (2). 277–291.

Winn, Matthew B. & Christian E. Stilp. 2019. Phonetics and the auditory system. In William F. Katz & Peter F. Assmann (eds.), *The Routledge handbook of phonetics*, 164–192. London: Routledge.

Winter, Bodo. 2020. *Statistics for linguists*: *An introduction using R*. London: Routledge.

Youssef, Valerie & Winford James. 2008. The creoles of Trinidad and Tobago: Phonology. In Edgar W. Schneider (ed.), *Varieties of English*: *The Americas and the Caribbean*, 320–338. Berlin, New York: De Gruyter Mouton.

Stefan Dollinger, Vanessa Chan, Kate Pasula and Anthony Maag

14 How linguistically tolerant or insecure are school-aged children? A matched-guise, gamified approach for 6- to 12-year-olds in Canada

Abstract: Children in Canada, a highly multicultural nation, are exposed to a variety of accented speech. This study examines the linguistic tolerance of 6- to 12-year-old children in Canada. A gamified and matched-guise approach to the written questionnaire method allows attitudinal insights for this young school-age group when their results are compared with those of young and mature adults. We test whether the respondents' multilingualism and age indicate differing sociolinguistic attitudes, judgements, and assessments of accented speech. The results show that the Standard Canadian English accent is preferred across all age cohorts. Counter to expectations, multilingual speakers are among the least tolerant of non-native accented speech which is consistent with the concept of linguistic insecurity (Preston 2013b). In terms of age cohorts, we found that 8- to 9-year-olds are more likely to be the least tolerant of all age groups. By contrast, children 7 years of age consistently proved to be the most linguistically tolerant as they rated the various accents highest for the attributes of "friendly," "interesting," "smart," and "right (correct)".

Keywords: language attitudes, matched guise, children, L2 varieties, Canadian English

1 Introduction

It is well known today in the sociolinguistic literature that people assess speakers based on their language and language use (e.g. Lippi-Green 2012; Preston 2013a, 2013b).[1] This widespread truism, which was not systemically studied before the

---

[1] The present paper was support by UBC Faculty of Arts COVID-19 student relief funding with matched funds from UBC's Department of English Language and Literatures (summer 2020). The three student authors are recent graduates with a bachelor's degree in English Language and Literatures (Chan, Maag) or B.A. students in that program (Pasula).

Stefan Dollinger, Vanessa Chan, Kate Pasula, Anthony Maag, University of British Columbia, Canada

https://doi.org/10.1515/9783110733723-014

1960s (e.g. Labov 1963; Lambert et al. 1960), has acquired a new level of urgency today. In a world that has become ready to decolonize and tackle hitherto impervious systems of discrimination, the way we speak, the "auditory minorities" as it were (see also Gluszek and Dovidio 2010: 216), is a new frontier that complements existing work of visual, ethnic, racial, and social minorities. While we indeed know a lot about the social evaluations of speech by adults – both younger and older – as well as teenagers through the plethora of studies in sociolinguistic frameworks, whether Labovian (e.g. Britain 2010; Kerswill 1994; Labov 2001, 2010; Tagliamonte and Jankowski 2019, to name but a few) or Prestonian (e.g. McKinnie and Dailey-O'Cain 2002; Preston 1989, 1999, 2013a), younger children have only relatively recently gained more sociolinguistic attention (e.g. D'Arcy 2019; Kinzler and DeJesus 2013; Smith and Durham 2019). Non-monolingual speakers have also been studied from additional vantage points in recent years (e.g. Barakos and Selleck 2019; Norton 2013; Tsinivits and Unsworth 2020).

The present paper aims to further the conversation by combining Preston's perceptual dialectology approach in a Lambert-inspired matched-guise design for young school-aged children in comparison to adults.[2] The goal is to address the question, if or when in their developments and to what degree children acquire their sociolinguistic assessments and judgements of accented speech. The setting is Western Canada, where the dominant accent is Standard Canadian English (StCanE), which will serve as one reference point in comparison with English accents of Cantonese, Mandarin, Finnish, and East Indian origin. Other reference points represent the multilingual milieus of the children, among other variables, to model and predict their sociolinguistically attitudinal responses as they are developed. The present study examines responses from children aged just under 6 to 12 years old, with comparative samples of adults that are usually their caretakers.

In the 1960s, the discovery of linguistic insecurity (Labov 1966; Owens and Baker 1984; Preston 2013b) led to new insights into the social dynamics of language variation. While linguistic insecurity, defined as "speakers' feeling that the variety they use is somehow inferior, ugly or bad" (Meyerhoff 2018: 192), has existed as a concept, it had taken a back seat to more behaviour-based data in the early period of sociolinguistics and now seems to be occasionally sidelined for the benefit of more neurological and cognitive points of view. We believe that in more cases than we might assume linguistic insecurity is an undervalued factor in shaping the linguistic behav-

---

[2] Our sincere thanks to the principals, parents, and pupils at St Patrick's Elementary (Victoria, BC), Maryview Elementary (Red Deer, AB), and Holy Family Elementary (Red Deer, AB) for granting us access to their communities; without their help, this study would have been impossible to conduct. As a result of their good will, pupils and parents from neighboring schools also contributed.

iour, attitudes, and conceptual thinking of entire speech communities (see e.g. Dollinger 2019 for Austrian German). In this light, Preston (2013b: 322) introduced a three-tier distinction of linguistic insecurity, which we will use in our interpretation. Preston's trichotomy is described as follows:

- *regional-personal insecurity* refers to people "who find their region (or group) incorrect" (Preston 2013b: 322) and who also personally feel their linguistic performance is lacking;
- *regional insecurity* refers to people who do not "find their own region (or group) relatively correct" (Preston 2013b: 322) but themselves feel linguistically secure;
- *personal insecurity* refers to people "who find their own area correct (perhaps even considerably so) but may find their own individual performances lacking" (Preston 2013b: 322).

Linguistic insecurity is a versatile concept that, in the present paper, will be used to interpret another concept that we label and construct in this paper as "linguistic tolerance," by which we understand the acceptance of otherwise stigmatized accents and linguistic variation more generally without social de-valuation. The present findings, framed in the context of relative linguistic tolerance vs. intolerance, might contribute to a further refined understanding of the social dynamics of language use in a world that is still globalizing, notwithstanding the recent hiccups of a pandemic. In local and non-local contexts, the question of membership and identities, as they are linked with language, is increasingly relevant. Preferential vs. dispreferential treatment of certain accents show possible biases in Canadian society, a society that is, per federal legislation, considered as multicultural (since 1988) and bilingual (English and French, since 1969). The positive messages of tolerance are countered, for instance, by the inexistence of effective Indigenous language legislation or the lack of its implementation. Canada's approximately 60 First Nations languages have, by and large, no legal status in the country and ongoing English-French linguistic hegemony tends to sideline Canada's other 250+ immigrant and heritage languages. It is in this context that we aim to ascertain the degree of linguistic tolerance of young speakers as they enter the Canadian school system, which is generally their first exposure with "official" Canadian language policies.

2 Literature review

The research literature on language acquisition in children and the accompanying attitudinal, perceptual, and cognitive angles are reference points for our study and complements the social perspective, which we are most interested in.

The perception of different accents of a given language and their different social assessments is a vexing question and one that might provide an indicator for tolerance levels. When dealing with children, the developmental angle – at which age are children neurologically and cognitively able to distinguish varying accents – is most relevant.

There are two quite disparate approaches in the study of accent perception. First, an attitudinal, language-perceptual angle highlights the social indexicality of accent features. This approach has been explored in sociolinguistics since Labov (1963, 1966) and has figured prominently in the study of language and social expectations and evaluation since Lambert et al.'s (1960) study in matched-guise format. This perspective has seen a distinct focus in Preston's (1989, 1999, 2013a) perceptual dialectology. The common thread in this socially inspired perspective is that accent study has largely focused on adults or teenagers (e.g. Cristia et al. 2012; Lippi-Green 2012).

The second perspective is informed by a neurological and developmental angle, which is often referred to as neural or cognitive processing (e.g. Jiang 2018). It seeks to establish at which point in the cognitive-neurological development humans are able to physiologically and cognitively distinguish between different accents and/or understand unfamiliar accents. Naturally, in this line of research, toddlers and even babies are studied and tested. They are then often compared to the adults' skills in discriminating between various accents. The working assumption in this framework is that in order to compare like with like, the neural and cognitive abilities of the age groups to be compared must be matched (e.g. Jusczyk and Aslin 1995; Polk and Sundra 2012).

While the attitudinal approach tends to be constructivist – we interpret certain accents in certain contexts as a proxy for attributes that we socially assign to groups – the processing approach tends to treat the varying and developing skill levels in accent discrimination as an absolute, physiological, and cognitive phenomenon that the language learner has to acquire (e.g. Cristia et al. 2012 for an overview; e.g. Bent 2018; Durrant et al. 2015; Kinzler, Corriveau, and Harris 2011). Lalonde and Holt (2016), for instance, look at participants' understandings of words and situations as a measure of their brains' abilities to process information in difficult and/or altered situations. Reviews suggest that perceptual processing research tends to view accents as a form of obstacle that our cognitive processing needs to overcome with time and practice (e.g. Adank et al. 2015; Alter and Oppenheimer 2009). We do not take this view but rather see accents of any kind as a signal that adds more information about the speakers and their identities.

Adank et al.'s (2015) review conducts a neurobiological comparison of unfamiliar accent processing with effortful processing (i.e. processing of audio with background noise, time compression, etc.). They find that the processing of accented speech uses similar parts of the brain as effortful processing (Adank et al. 2015: 3). Perceptual processing is still relevant to our accent tolerance and attitude research, however. The *hedonic fluency hypothesis* "encapsulates the general principle that people [prefer] easily processed stimuli" (Alter and Oppenheimer 2009: 228); thus, accents that are harder to process may be less well-liked (for more see Reber, Schwarz, and Winkielman 2004, cited in Alter and Oppenheimer 2009). This is a claim we would like to scrutinize in our data. Alter and Oppenheimer (2009: 228) also recognize an assimilation effect when they summarize that "people are more easily able to retrieve stimuli from memory after repeated exposure, which induces feelings of positivity".

2.1 Processing accents: Neurological cut-offs

Cristia et al. (2012: 12) stipulate that children have a harder time with perceptual processing than adults. The research also suggests that children improve with time and development (Cristia et al. 2012: 8). Lalonde and Holt (2016), for instance, compare 6- to 8-year-old children with adults at three increasingly difficult levels of perceptual processing. Unlike the children who were equally affected by the impairment implemented by the researchers at all levels, the adults in the study were affected only for tasks that required more complex perceptual processing. Similarly, it was found that preteens and teens differed in their abilities to process unfamiliar accents in quiet and noisy situations when compared to adults and to each other (Bent 2018). Preteens 11 to 12 years of age are, as the study found, able to process accents at "adult-like" levels only up to the point of familiar, native accents in noisy contexts (Bent 2018: 1400); the 14- to 15-year-olds, by contrast, were performing at adult-like levels up to non-native accents in quiet settings (1406). This data suggests that our age cohort, up to age 12, face developmental restrictions in processing ability and are not yet at the adult levels of sound and accent discrimination.

2.2 Monolingual bias in the processing literature

The literature regarding accent tolerance and attitudes, especially pertaining to school-aged children, is faced with possible limitations in its theoretical framework in that monolingual North American speakers are often implied as the benchmark (e.g. Dollinger 2019 on Jiang 2018). While studies with a multilingual focus do exist (e.g. Bratož, Pirih, and Štemberger 2019), they tend not to be conducted in language acquisition frameworks. Additionally, accent tolerance research, such as Dewaele and McCloskey (2015), usually looks to multilingual contexts, where accents are the result of interference from the speakers' first language and are not considered as an organically developed way of identity expression as a World Englishes perspective would yield. Second language processing is, according to Jiang (2018: 15), mainly concerned with three recurrent themes: acquirability, L1–L2 interference, and age effects. While we do not rule out possible age effects or interferences between the languages and acquisitional sequences, we do point out that many of these models are inherently based in monolingual target performances, which limits alternative interpretations of the data. Our data suggest, however, that the responses of children aged 6 or older may be indicative, first and foremost, of social dimensions of accents and dialects and only in a second instance of acquisition and processing sequences that are cognitively and neurologically conditioned.

Durrant et al. (2015: 448), building on Albareda-Castellot, Pons, and Sebastián-Gallés (2011), suggest that the accent processing literature should explore multidialectal individuals as a special form of monolingualism that shares some of the challenges of bilingual (and/or multilingual) individuals in the processing of information. In their study, they found that multidialectal (but still monolingual) infants take more time than their monodialectal peers to spot errors in the auditory stimuli (Durrant et al. 2015: 457), which shows that the focus of monodialectal infants might be skewed compared with multidialectal ones, who treat variation as something "normal" that does not deserve special attention.

Sociolinguistic research suggests that children make attitudinal and social indexing decisions based on their perceptions. Children aged 9 to 10 in both the northern and southern parts of the United States were found to say that northern accents were smarter and sounded more "in-charge," while southern American accents were "nice" (Kinzler and DeJesus 2013: 1154). In other words, the 9- to 10-year-olds have the expected social bias and stereotypes displayed by adults already internalized. Younger children, by contrast, tend to prefer their local dialect, as seen with children from Illinois (Kinzler and DeJesus 2013: 1151). This not only demonstrates an ability to differentiate some basic accent features from a very young age, but it also suggests the impact of stereotypes in social indexing. Compared to their younger counterparts (ages 5–6), 9- to 10-year-old children were more likely to answer similarly to adults regardless of whether a positive or negative reading of their local, familiar accent, was elicited. Wagner, Clopper, and Pate (2014: 1081) have evidence to show that children's home language dialect, e.g. Austin, Texas, non-ethnic English, is not seen as different from the larger regional dialect (e.g. Southern US English), but as "simply within the noise tolerance" of one another. The children in their study manage to tell home dialect speakers apart from EFL-accented speakers (Wagner, Clopper, and Pate 2014: 1074). In Stamou, Maroniti, and Griva (2015: 224), Greek children (average age of 6 years old) were given semi-structured interviews with video clips from the popular media. It was found that children tended to prefer hegemonic presentations, such as from characters with standard accents over characters with rural or otherwise marginalized accents. In light of these data, which seem to show a subtle yet clear bias towards a monolingual view of standards, we aimed to construct a questionnaire that mitigates this effect to a minimum.

3 Participants

For the present study, we developed an online written questionnaire (WQ) with a gamified approach for use with 6- to 12-year-old children and adults in two locations in British Columbia (BC) and Alberta, Canada. In total, 87 responses (65 children and 22 adults) were usable, which fall into the following age cohorts (Table 14.1):

Table 14.1: Useable responses in gamified WQ.

Age	≤6	7	8–9	10–12	20–29	30–50	Total
Number of participants	16	9	22	18	12	10	87

More than 40 respondents did not complete the survey and, therefore, were removed from the study. Parents and caregivers, after having given consent for the study, were asked to let the children go first and to not provide assistance. The caregivers were subsequently encouraged to complete the survey on their own. WQs represent special challenges when applied to young school children (e.g. see Bratož, Pirih, and Štemberger 2019 on writing WQs for children). In order to mitigate these problems, the WQ was tailored for 6- to 12-year-olds and gamification was employed wherever possible with the overall aim of creating a questionnaire that was both age-appropriate and enjoyable. Adult guardians were encouraged to participate in the same survey only in a second round. A pre-testing phase preceded the start of data collection, in which we tested the WQ on 6 elementary-school children in the think-aloud protocol format (Dollinger 2015: 248). The WQ takes approximately 20 minutes to complete and consists of 45 questions.

Ethically, as well as logistically, working with young school-aged children presents a special challenge, which we sought to address via the school context. First, principals were asked to consent to their school partaking in the gamified WQ; we recruited one school from Victoria, British Columbia and two from Red Deer, Alberta. Second, legal guardians were presented with a consent page about the survey, which was followed by agreement to participate (assent) from the child as shown in Figure 14.1:

Hello kids! We are researchers who want to learn more about what you think about the language that you hear in your town. By language we mean the words, sounds and the way people speak in English.

We invite you to be part of a study! It's up to you if you want to answer our questions. You can stop at any time. No one will be mad at you if you choose to stop. If you do the survey, your answers will help us find out things about language.

Can we ask you some questions about language?

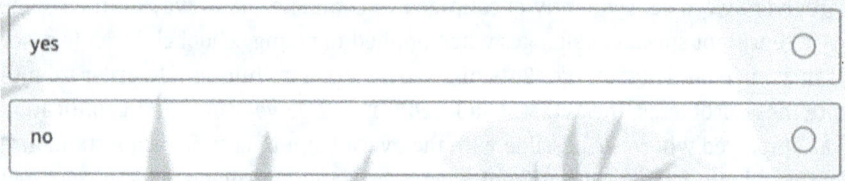

Figure 14.1: Child-focused "agreement" question. Note: consent can only be given by legal guardian (not shown here; available at the beginning of the survey, see footnote 3).

4 Methodology

A jungle-themed story with animated characters, as seen in Figure 14.2, was presented in a matched-guise format for the first part of the survey.[3] A character

---

3 See www.academia.edu/63385965/ for the text of the story.

named R. Jaguar leads the participant through the survey as the narrator speaking Standard Canadian English. We decided to make the third-person narrator use a standard accent in order to have an easier time with the interpretation, though we are well aware that this choice, in itself, presents a certain priming effect. It would, therefore, be most interesting to repeat the study with R. Jaguar using a non-standard accent.

All audio cues were presented with female voices, and the monkeys represent cues in Cantonese, Mandarin, Finnish, and (East) Indian accents. The monkeys are identical except for the pattern on the bandanas around their necks to eliminate any visual bias (see Figure 14.2). Each bandana pairs with an accent: Cantonese (striped bandana), Mandarin (plaid bandana), Finnish (solid bandana), Indian (polka-dotted bandana). Participants were also given a visual reward for completing the survey in the form of an image of a "pot of gold" mentioned in the story.

Figure 14.2: Left to right: Narrating character R. Jaguar; Monkeys with closed mouths (1) Striped: Cantonese, (2) Plaid: Mandarin, (3) Solid: Finnish, (4) Polka-dotted: Indian Accent; Pot of gold featured at the end of the survey.

The precise audio-visual cues can be accessed online,[4] where the survey is live for inspection.[5] Note that we no longer monitor, inspect, or download any submissions as the survey is officially closed. After listening to a monkey tell one part of the story, the children were asked to answer three sets of questions about each monkey. The first set reflects accent perceptions (e.g. Lippi-Green 2012; Preston 2013a) and had the following star rating format (Figure 14.3):

---

4 Jaguar: www.academia.edu/video/k3dz0j
   Cantonese monkey: www.academia.edu/video/le60gk
   Mandarin monkey: www.academia.edu/video/jZKOE1
   Finnish monkey: www.academia.edu/video/1N3vAl
   Indian monkey:www.academia.edu/video/jXv8yl.
5 ubc.ca1.qualtrics.com/jfe/form/SV_cNEjcZaGeqYw8w5 (accessed 15 April 2021).

How much does the monkey sound:
(more stars is more)
friendly
easy to understand
interesting
cute
smart
right ("correct")

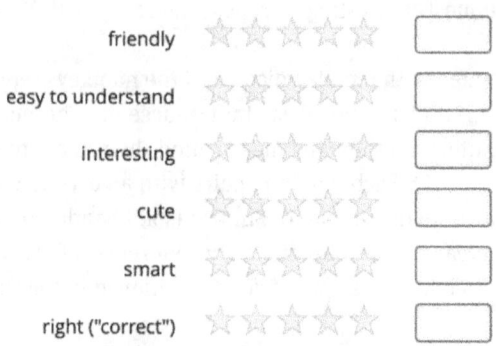

Figure 14.3: Star rating answer response.

The stars translate into the scores 1 (lowest) to 5 (highest), which we will see in the reporting charts, i.e. an average of 1.5 stars is represented as a score of 1.5 on the y-axis (see Figures 14.7 and 14.8). We are aware of the context-dependent and performance-related dimensions of comprehensibility and intelligibility (Munro and Derwing 1995, 2011, 2020) that this simplified answer format cannot consider. Similar critique may be voiced over the following two questions, which target the domains of identity and self-identification via categorical or binary choices. For the second and third questions, children were presented, respectively, with binary "yes" or "no" and categorical "yes," "no," and "maybe" answer formats (Figure 14.4).

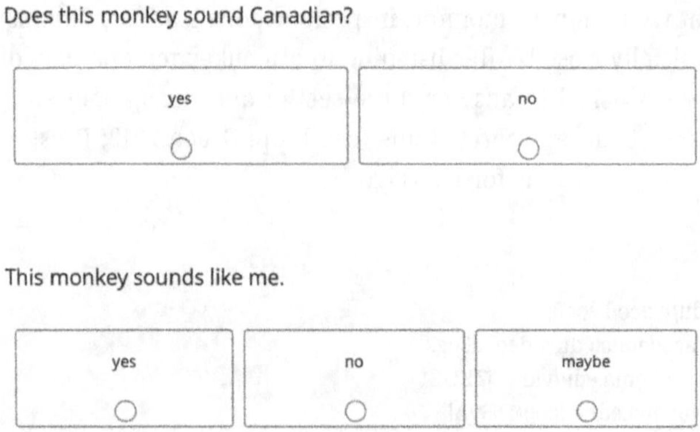

Does this monkey sound Canadian?
yes
no
This monkey sounds like me.
yes
no
maybe

Figure 14.4: Identification questions.

When I hear someone speaking a language that I don't understand I feel:

I feel............................	Interested	Not Interested	Neither
I feel............................	Annoyed	Not Annoyed	Neither
I feel............................	Scared	Not Scared	Neither
I feel............................	Happy	Unhappy	Neither

Do you think it's cool when people speak more than 1 language?

- Yes, absolutely
- Yes
- No
- I don't know

Figure 14.5: Multilingualism attitude questions.

We were aiming to elicit what "counts," in the sense of identity construction (e.g. De Cillia et al. 2020; Wodak et al. 2009), as a Canadian accent, which prompted us to use a binary choice. For the direct self-identification in the next question, "this monkey sounds like me," the category "maybe" was included to allow for more subjective (mis)matches of idiolects, gender constructions, and the like. This set of three kinds of questions – star ratings on six dimensions, Canadian-ness ("sounds Canadian?") and personal oral identification ("sounds like me?") – is repeated for each of the four monkeys. At the end of the story, the children are asked the same three sets of questions about the narrator, R. Jaguar, using the same format as the monkey-related questions.

After the gamified matched-guise portion of the written questionnaire, children are asked about their own exposure to languages. They are asked "what language(s) they speak in the settings and locations of "at recess," "in class," and "at home," followed by the languages spoken by adults in their home: "What language(s) do your parents (adults you live with) speak?" and to "click on all languages that either your mom, dad, or any adult who lives with you uses". Children were able to select from seventeen different preset languages (in the random order offered): French, Farsi, Mandarin, Hindu, English, Urdu, Punjabi, Spanish, Tagalog, Italian, Cantonese, German, Inuktitut, Cree, First Nations languages, Portuguese, and Arabic, with the option to provide any languages not listed: "Language(s) not listed. Please write the language(s) down" in a text entry box. Personal attitudes towards multilingualism were polled in two questions, as shown in Figure 14.5.

The first question assessed four dimensions, from the neutral "interested," to the more biased "annoyed," "scared," and "happy" categories, and is followed by a positively couched question on the "coolness" of speaking more than one language. Finally, the last question targets the role of identity and language in Canada in regard to Canadian English (Figure 14.6).

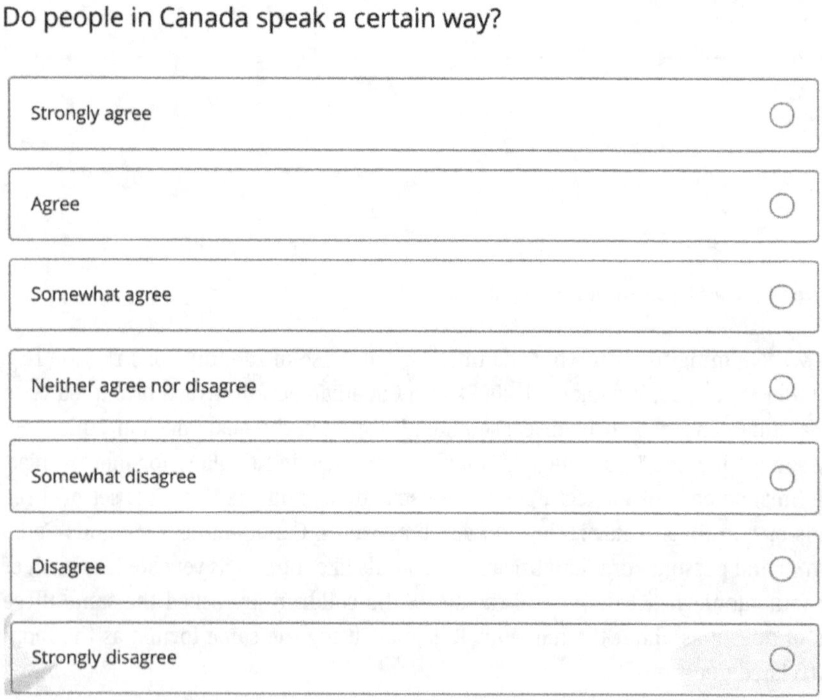

Do people in Canada speak a certain way?

- Strongly agree
- Agree
- Somewhat agree
- Neither agree nor disagree
- Somewhat disagree
- Disagree
- Strongly disagree

Figure 14.6: Canadian English question.

The target of this question was to assess if and to what degree the national variety of English is perceived as part of a Canadian identity. In a previous study on adults, 81% at least "somewhat agreed" with the statement that there was a "Canadian way" of speaking English, while 59% "strongly agreed" or "agreed" (Dollinger 2020: Table 4.5).

5 Results and discussion

This section presents a range of analyses from the original survey that we organize in three sections. The first section introduces our method of visual presentation of our findings (5.1), followed by the aggregate results of the "star" questions on how friendly, intelligible, interesting, cute, smart, and right ("correct") the four non-standard accented monkeys and the Standard Canadian English jaguar sounded (Section 5.2). The third section, 5.3, addresses if and to what degree the question of "identity" is reflected in the accent preferences, which, finally in Section 5.4, we will link with the multilingual vs. monolingual milieu (home setting) that the children come from. Section 5.5 discusses a likely bias in the data elicitation process relating to gender.

5.1 Explaining the charts

The idea of intelligibility is a highly dynamic category that is dependent on a number of factors. Social Accommodation Theory offers a nuanced perspective on intelligibility (e.g. Coupland and Giles 1988; Giles 1977), as does L2 pronunciation and comprehensibility research (e.g. Munro and Derwing 2020). Figure 14.7 shows the expected preference of Standard Canadian English across all age cohorts, as the standard dialect with overt prestige in Canada. Only the pre-teens, ages 10–12, score the standard dialect under 4.5 on a scale from 5 (fully intelligible) to 0 (not intelligible). Note also that the young adults, ages 20–29, score this dialect, with a score of 5, the maximum score for all respondents.

We use the intelligibility dimension in Figure 14.7 to illustrate the way we present our results in aggregate format. Along the x-axis, each of the age groups (including the comparative adult samples) are shown with the number of respondents used, e.g. age cohort 6 and younger has 16 respondents, while 10- to 12-year-olds have 18. The rating (i.e. number of stars given) on intelligibility is indicated along the y-axis, from 1 (star) to 5 (stars). Each line on the graph, therefore, represents

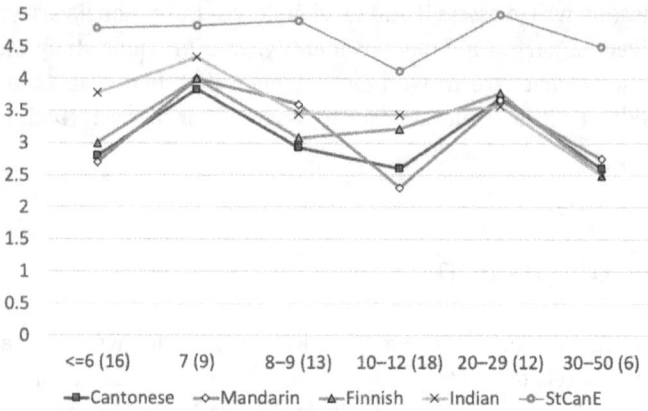

Figure 14.7: Intelligibility, "easy to understand".

the mean of ratings relating to a particular accent by the whole range of age groups studied. Each of the figures in Figure 14.8 below match the format described here.

5.2 Intelligibility

Two important results can be gleaned from Figure 14.7; these results have been verified as statistically significant with t-tests. First, the 7-year-olds are particularly tolerant of each of the non-standard accents compared to most of the other age groups. 7-year-olds, on the whole, display more linguistic tolerance than our comparative adult samples in terms of ease of understanding. When evaluating the Mandarin-accented monkey, for instance, the 7-year-olds ranked higher (mean = 4.000) than the 10- to 12-year-old respondents (mean = 2.273; t = 2.348, df = 13.459, p = 0.035). This pattern emerges for Cantonese, Finnish, and Indian-accented monkeys in like fashion when compared to the 30- to 50-year-olds (see Table 14.2).

Table 14.2: 7-year-olds vs. 30–50-year-old adults on the intelligibility of non-standard accents.

	Mean of 7 y/o	Mean of 30–50 y/o	T-Value	Degrees of freedom	P-Value
Cantonese	3.833	2.444	2.375	9.740	0.040
Mandarin	4.000	2.750	2.308	6.012	0.060
Finnish	4.000	2.875	2.618	8.673	0.029
Indian	4.333	3.000	2.823	10.047	0.018

By contrast, we found that 8- to 9-year-olds are more likely to be the least tolerant of all age groups. We therefore see a remarkable disparity in immediately adjacent age groups: the "super tolerant" 7-year-olds, and the very intolerant 8- to 9-year-olds, linguistically speaking. This does not mean, however, that all 8- to 9-year-olds must necessarily be linguistically intolerant, although their age group certainly is. The 8- to 9-year-olds, for instance, found the Mandarin-accented monkey more easy to understand than their 10- to 12-year-old peers (t = 2.46, df = 13.394, p = 0.028) and the 30- to 50-year-old adult group (t = 3.403, df = 23.32, p = 0.0024).

5.3 Little angels (the tolerant 7-year-olds) and sceptics (the 8- to 12-year-olds)

Figure 14.8 is an overview of all six dimensions of the star-rating exercise. Dimension 1, "easy to understand," shown in Figure 14.8 (top middle), was already introduced in Figure 14.7 to explicate the visual approach and facilitate readings of the graphs. From Figure 14.8, it seems that there are two windows of opportunity, as we would like to call them, in which people are especially linguistically tolerant. The first is at the the age of 7; we can see that from Figure 14.8 (top middle, bottom right, bottom middle, top right, top left), and even in Figure 14.8 (bottom left) if we allow for a little more scatter.

The 7-year olds are, for some reason, attitudinal angels: they are tolerant in that they understand the accents with ease and find them friendly, cute (which we used in place of "beautiful"), smart, right ("correct") and – with some scatter – interesting. These very positive assessments – from a humanistic, inclusionary view – fall off in the 8- to 9-year-olds and further in the 10- to 12-year-olds. While we lack data from teenagers, the second window of opportunity occurs with the young adults, the 20- to 29-year-olds, that are more tolerant. Older middle-aged adults (our oldest age group) from 30–50 are generally highly critical, particularly for correctness (right), which reflects their roles as parents.

Other noteworthy observations include that the Cantonese accented English, which is generally less widely appreciated in the data, scores unusually high in the dimension of "smartness" (Figure 14.8, bottom right). This may be a reflection of stereotypes of the diligent Hong Kong Canadians, who have traditionally outnumbered Mandarin speakers in Canadian locales. Importantly, Finnish and Indian accented English are generally at the bottom of the pack, as seen in the results from the categories of "friendly," "interesting" (only for Finnish), "cute," "smart," and especially "right ('correct')" and, again most importantly, have ratings that decrease with age from the general peaks of appreciation and tolerance in the 7-year-olds. Against this backdrop, it is obvious that the Standard Canadian English accent, which is spoken by almost

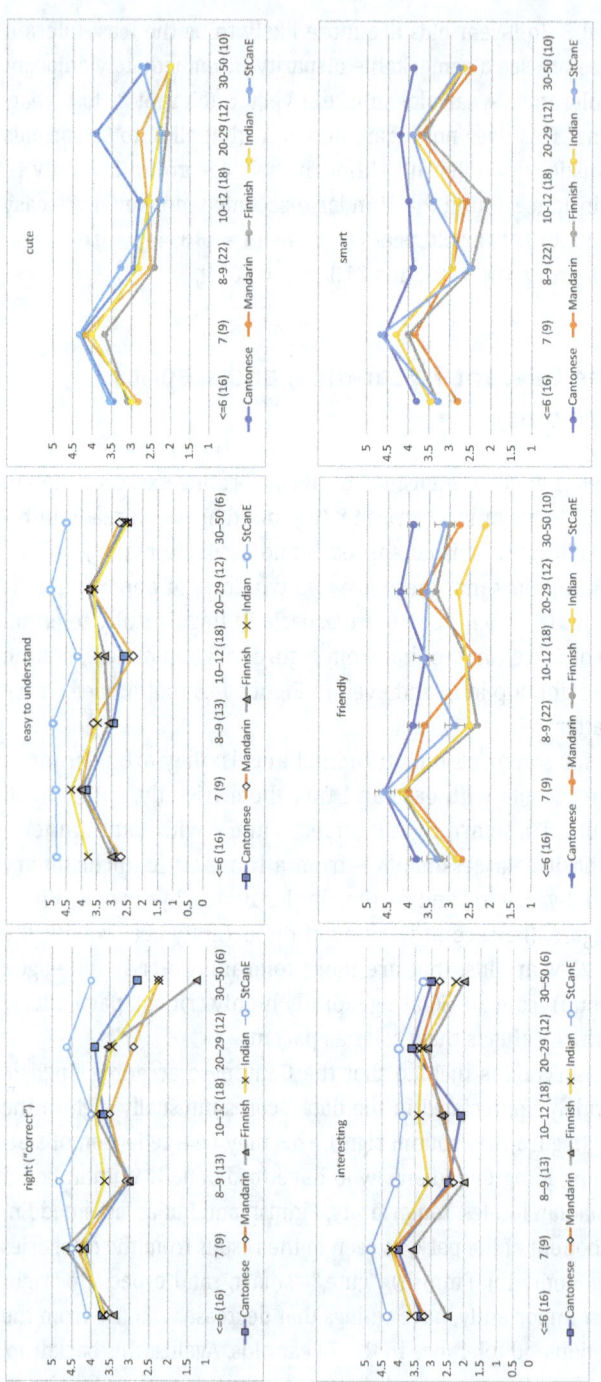

Figure 14.8: Six dimensions of attributes in matched-guise accent task.

40% of the population (Dollinger 2020: 60), is viewed across all age groups as the accent that is most "easy to understand," most "interesting," and most "right (correct)".

In order to compare the general attitudes of each age group, we combined the Cantonese, Mandarin, Finnish and Indian accent scores as non-standard varieties. These results were then compared against those for StCanE in Table 14.3. The 6-year-olds and those younger are more sceptical of non-standard accents, which may be rooted in a lack of exposure before going to school (Canada as a "cultural mosaic" of quite autonomous ethnic groups). Remarkable, however, is the change in comparison to the next age group. The 7-year-olds generally rank the non-standard accents higher than all older age groups, while the preteens, 10–12 years old, rank them the lowest among the children. The collective average ratings of the Cantonese, Mandarin, Finnish, and Indian accents combined are as follows:

Table 14.3: Average scores of non-standard accents vs. standard accent by age group (lower = less standard).

Age	≤6	7	8–9	10–12	20–29	30–50
Non-stand. accents	3.07	4.04	3.27	2.89	3.68	2.59
StCanE	4.8	4.83	4.91	4.13	5	4.50

We saw earlier in Table 14.2 that the difference between assessments of intelligibility in non-standard versus the standard accent is the smallest in the 7-year-olds, and the highest in the older adults. This may be indicative of more tolerance in the 7-year-olds on the one hand and the least tolerance in the older, middle-aged adults. In Table 14.3, a more general assessment of the tolerant 7-year-olds and more "intolerant" or discriminating older children, younger children, and middle-aged adults is replicated in all six dimensions polled: "friendly," "easy to understand," "interesting," "cute," "smart," and "right ('correct')," see Figure 14.8. With the possible exception of "interesting," where the answers are more heterogeneous among the 7-year-olds, this age group appears to display quite coherent behavior: they consider speakers with non-standard accents as smarter than, on average, the other age groups (Figure 14.8, bottom right), friendlier (Figure 14.8, bottom middle), and more "right (correct)" (Figure 14.8, top left).

This data suggests that the widely reported onset of a preference pattern towards the standard variety in the first two years of schooling (e.g. Day 1980: 29 between the ages of 5 and 7; Kaiser and Kasberger 2021: 145 between the ages of 6 and 8) is complemented in our data by highly favorable assessments of non-standard accents in the 7-year-old Canadian children. The appreciation of non-standard accents comes after two years of schooling – in Canada, children start school at 5 –

which seems to complement Day's (1980) finding that Year 2 in school, age 6, leads to a linguistic orientation favouring the standard. This reported "clear tendency in favour of the standard variety between ages 7 and 9" (Kaiser and Kasberger 2021: 150) is complemented in our data by an appreciation of non-standard accents, an appreciation that wanes in ages 8–9 and 10–12. The Canadian 7-year-olds linguistic appreciation is reminiscent of Kinzler and DeJesus' (2013: 1151) children from the non-standard speaking US South, where children "are exposed to both dialects [standard and non-standard] and they therefore view both types of speech as equally favorable". In the Canadian context, the difference is that the environment is more akin a US Northern context, with local norms close to the standard. Going back to Preston's distinction of linguistic insecurity from the beginning, we see that "regional insecurity" is high in the US South, which would explain the original bi-dialectal tolerance in Kinzler and DeJesus (2013). In Canada, however, that regional insecurity would be expected to be low, yet the tolerance of non-standard dialects is, in contrast to Kinzler and DeJesus data on the US North, rather high. The differential might indicate a different conceptualization of non-native accents in Canada and the (northern) US.

5.4 Identity formation as "Canadian"

Social evaluations of how Canadian-sounding the non-standard accents are varies by age group. Fisher exact tests show that age is a statistically significant factor when respondents were determining whether Cantonese ($p = 0.009$ for 7-year-olds vs. 8- to 9-year-olds); Finnish ($p = 0.039$ for 10- to 12-year-olds vs. 30- to 50-year-olds), and Indian ($p = 0.045$ for 6-year-olds vs. 20- to 29-year-olds) accents sounded Canadian. For the Cantonese-accented monkey, age was a statistically significant factor for respondents aged 7 versus those aged 8–9 ($p = 0.009$). Respondents aged 8–9 were significantly less likely to consider the Cantonese-accented monkey Canadian (age 7 "no" n = 3, age 8–9 "no" n = 18). These results suggest a cut-off between the 7-year-olds and the older children, 8–9 and above, who have a more exclusive conceptualization of what sounds are "Canadian" and which are not. We suggest that it is here, in the 8- to 9-year-olds, that an element of auditory prescriptivism, which is characteristic of a much older demographic, begins to emerge (i.e. the 30- to 50-year-olds or older adults). While the 7-year-olds are the most tolerant, the older children no longer are, not until they reach young adulthood, aged 20–29, where a second window of relative tolerance seems to open up.

The Finnish-accented monkey was most contested as Canadian. There is a statistical difference between the 7-year-olds and 8- to 9-year-olds ($p = 0.021$) and between the 7-year-olds and 10- to 12-year-olds ($p = 0.025$); in each case, the older children were less likely to say the Finnish-accented monkey sounded Canadian.

Curiously, the statistically significant difference between the 8- to 9-year-olds and the 10- to 12-year-olds with the 30- to 50-year-olds (p = 0.033 and p = 0.04, respectively) demonstrates that the older children are even more critical than the middle-aged adults and, of course, very different from the tolerant 7-year-olds.

One question was how Canadian-ness or Canadian identity might be reflected in the six-dimension questions. We know from previous work in Vancouver that a large majority of adults, 69%, considered their "Canadian English is part of their Canadian identity" to be at least "somewhat correct," while about half all respondents, 46%, responded that this statement was "very correct" or "correct" for their situation (Dollinger 2020: Table 4.5). Most consistently across all age groups, the Standard Canadian English speaker, the jaguar, was rated as the most "interesting" voice. This is unusual, as, in our assessment, the standard speaker would be the most "boring" as the one who does not divert from the norm. This leads us to question what the respondents understood by "interesting" across all age groups, whether the text the jaguar read, which was by far the longest text, interfered with the assessment of the attribute "interesting," or whether the jaguar's lab coat and difference from the monkeys made her stand out.

5.5 Linguistic insecurity, linguistic tolerance, and *habitus multilingualis*

Linguistic insecurity is a factor within English Canada, though there is some evidence that it has decreased since the late 1970s (Dollinger 2015: 253, Figure 7.2; Gulden 1979; Owens and Baker 1984). Linguistic tolerance is, according to some writers, a key characteristic of the Canadian social make up. Chambers (1986: 3) went so far as to declare the Canadians as laissez-faire when it comes to which standard variety is enforced (revolving around Canadian, US American, or UK), as an expression of linguistic tolerance: "there is a sense in which the notion of standards is alien to – perhaps even repugnant to – our national character. [. . .] In one sense – and this is the one, I think, that turns us off – a standard connotes an imposition by some authority on one's behaviour or activities". Perhaps, Chambers' reasoning could be put on a more testable footing by assuming that if Canadians are to a good degree multilingual, linguistic tolerance would be encouraged and with it a more flexible interpretation of standards, rather than the concept of standard being seen more generally as repugnant.

Figure 14.9 captures the self-assessment of respondents' answers on the dimensions of "sounds Canadian?" (binary choice) and "sounds like me?" (yes, no, maybe). It indicates a clear demarcation between identification with Standard Canadian English (29%) and the non-native accented Englishes (6% to 0%). It can be seen that the vast majority does not identify with these accents, with 94% selecting "no" for Indian and 88% for Cantonese ("no" values are the remainder to 100, e.g. Indian sounds like me: yes 6% and maybe 6% = 88% do not identify with East-Indian accented English).

The data suggests a notable identification with StCanE, as there is at least four times the positive response rate compared with the non-standard accents (29% identification with StCanE vs. between 0% and 7% identification with non-native accents). In regard to respondents' answers to accents sounding Canadian ("sounds Canadian?"), a prominent distinction exists between StCanE and the non-native English options. StCanE (at 69% considered as "Canadian") is at two-and-a-half times the value of the second highest ranked accent (Mandarin at 26%). The data shown in Figure 14.9 appears to indicate a distinct attitude of what sounds "Canadian". While we do not adopt a concept of "halo" that children allegedly bestow onto adult native speakers that was introduced by Kinzler et al. (2011: 110), we do identify a certain bias towards a StCanE accent which we attribute to the forcefulness of standard language ideology in Canada.

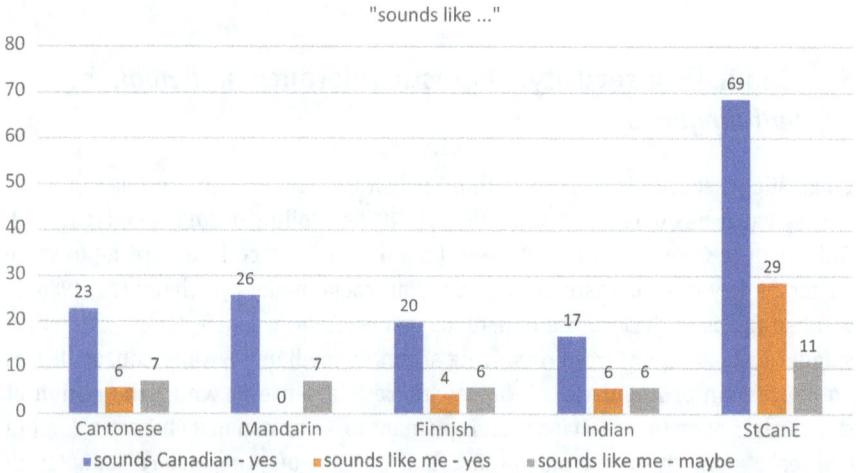

Figure 14.9: Self-assessment: sounds like me; sounds Canadian (in %).

An interesting aspect can be seen when Figure 14.9 is correlated with monolingual English vs. multilingual family practices and households. For the purposes of this paper, the multilingualism of respondents was determined based on the number of reported languages spoken "at recess" and "at home," and the multilingualism of the home environment was determined based on whether the reported languages spoken "by adults in the home" (i.e. the care takers) were or were not only English. Table 14.4 offers some examples of the classification process from both the surveyed locations of Greater Victoria, BC and Red Deer, Alberta.

Table 14.4: Multilingualism vs. monolingualism of the respondents and the home.

		Survey data			Reclassified data	
Age	Location	Language(s) at recess	Language(s) at home	Language(s) of adults at home	Multilingual respondents	Multilingual Home
≤6	Victoria	English	English	English, Punjabi, Hindi	monolingual	multilingual
8–9	Saanich	English	English, Cantonese	English, Cantonese, Mandarin, Dutch	multilingual	multilingual
≤6	Saanich	English	English	English	monolingual	monolingual
8–9	Saanich	English	English, Punjabi	English, Punjabi	multilingual	multilingual
7	Red Deer	English	English	English	monolingual	monolingual
7	Oak Bay	English	NA	English, Cantonese	monolingual	multilingual
7	Red Deer	English	English	Tagalog	monolingual	multilingual
8	Red Deer	English, Hindi	English, Hindi	Hindi	multilingual	multilingual
10–12	Red Deer	English	English	English	monolingual	monolingual
10–12	Red Deer	English	English, Mandarin	Mandarin	multilingual	multilingual

The data, correlated with monolingual and multilingual attributes, offers a most interesting finding, which is quite counter to expectations. We do, as might be expected, find differences between monolingual and multilingual speakers in the data. They are, however, in a different direction as one might assume. Respondents who spoke more than just English at recess or at home were more likely to judge the Cantonese and Finnish-accented monkeys more negatively than monolingual English speakers. Likewise, respondents who lived with an adult who spoke more than just English were also more likely to judge the Cantonese and Finnish-accented monkeys more negatively. In the cases of the Mandarin-accented and Indian-accented monkeys, multilingual respondents and monolingual respondents tended to rate their accents as sounding *not* Canadian. Multilingual individuals were also less likely to find the Cantonese-accented monkey Canadian-sounding than their monolingual peers (p = 0.005) and in homes with multilingual adults, the Cantonese monkey was still less likely to be evaluated as Canadian-sounding (p = 0.049). Similar results were found for the Finnish-accented monkey in multilingual individuals (p = 0.008) and in multilingual homes (p = 0.024). These findings are consistent with Dewaele and McCloskey's (2015: 234) study on multilingual individuals' attitudes towards foreign accents, which are that multilingual speakers who knew more languages and at higher levels are more negative about the foreign accents of others and themselves, presumably because of "higher expectations". These expectations may be seen as an effect of a monolingual norm that leaves no one unaffected. It is as if a *habitus monolingualis* is seen as an ideal norm among highly proficient multilinguals.

5.6 Possible stimuli bias

Respondents, when asked if the jaguar sounded Canadian or "like me" (i.e. like the respondents), viewed the Standard Canadian English-speaking jaguar differently depending on gender. In both cases, female respondents were more likely than male respondents to consider the jaguar Canadian (Fisher Exact, p = 0.012) or like themselves (p = 0.011). This result may reveal a possible bias in our testing to account for respondents taking the "like me" question literally and identify the female voices as the cues rather than the accent. The effect can be seen in the data as such, i.e. affecting both the jaguar and monkey, that children's identifications align by gender, not accent. Table 14.5 shows the results of a logistic regression modelling run with a comparable difference between males and females in the sample. We modelled the linguistic assessment of the Finnish monkey for sounds "right ('correct')," the one accent considered as the least correct one by adults, 30–50, with age, gender, and self-assessments of sounding like the Standard Canadian, Indian, Finnish, Mandarin and Cantonese monkeys (Table 14.5). To our surprise, self-assessment did not produce significant differences, while gender did.

At present, we find a possible gender bias in our data as perhaps the weakest point of our study design, which is why we refrain from commenting on that aspect. We leave this open for further study: are girls or boys more or less tolerant of foreign accents and what is their contrastive developmental route, if any?

Table 14.5: Logistic regression modelling: significant (<0.05) and near-significant (<0.10) results for those who assess Finnish-English as sounding "right (correct)".

Call: glm(formula = Fin_right ~ age * gender + StCanE_like.me + Ind_like.me + Fin_like.me + Man_like.me + Can_like.me, data = jungle)

	Estimate	Std. Error	t value	p value
(Intercept)	6.8435	2.0414	3.352	0.00207
age30–50	−1.9595	1.0683	−1/834	0.07593
genderM	−2.4152	1.0721	−2.253	0.03126
age10–12:genderM	2.6156	1.4888	1.757	0.08851
age30–50:genderM	2.7412	1.4732	1.862	0.07199
age7:genderM	2.8931	1.6473	1.756	0.08861

6 Conclusion

This brings us to the conclusion of our present 87-respondent-based study. The gamified approach utilized in this study provided us with a means for expanding linguistic research on the less examined populations of young school-aged children. The findings reveal how 7-year-olds' assessments in (almost) all of the six dimensions – "friendly," "easy to understand," "interesting," "cute," "smart," and "right ('correct')" – are more tolerant than both younger and older age groups. The difference between the non-standard accents compared with the standard Canadian English accent was found to be the smallest among the 7-year-olds (with the highest often found in the older adults). The 7-year-olds, or rather their stage in the social-cognitive development, shows a remarkably high degree of linguistic tolerance and seemingly low linguistic insecurity, which presents itself as a possibly fortuitous window in our school systems for prophylactic intervention. If we manage to prolong, to the degree possible, this linguistic tolerance into the older age groups, we will likely generate (even) more tolerant teenagers, young adults and, above all, mature adults (who are remarkably linguistically intolerant). In comparison to the older age cohorts, differences in sociolinguistic judgements of accented speech are considerable between the 7-year-old children and older or younger children/adults (besides the second window of relative tolerance at age 20–29).

This paper has also detected a statistical significance between monolingual and multilingual English speakers in our western Canadian setting. The finding that the multilingual speaker is less tolerant towards L2-accented Englishes than monolingual speakers is worthy of note. It suggests that some standard language ideologies – meaning that there is only one preferred and normative, codified form – permeates the language competencies and affects even those who might, as a result of their own socialization, know better. Such greater societal bias may be reflected in respondents who speak more than just English ("at recess" or "at home") – the mainstream language in our western Canadian setting –, who judge the Cantonese- and Finnish-accented monkeys more negatively than monolingual English respondents. This finding suggests a multilingual bias as well as what we termed *habitus monolingualis,* by which we mean a negative multilingual habit in the form of a harsher application of the standard language ideology that is being applied by those speakers who managed to maintain more than one code (English) in their lives at or near full-competence levels across all domains (speaking, comprehension, writing, reading). This suggested *habitus monolingualis negativus,* as it were, should be tested further and, if confirmed, would contribute to a more complete description and theorizing of the many positive multilingual habits, *habitus monolingualis positivus,* that are today, fortunately, frequently pointed out in the literature.

The standard language ideology, the belief that only one form or use in a set of variants can be correct (Cameron 2012; Milroy and Milroy 1999), is also clearly applicable in western Canada. The association that one particular function must have one particular and exclusive form may be stronger than average in the highly proficient, educated multilinguals that participated in our study. There is an important distinction to be made between low-education and high-education (what is often called "elite") multilingualism (cf. Barakos and Selleck 2019), along the lines of which our data would warrant further investigation. Even in our context of Canada's international generally highly regarded multicultural make-up, respondents across all age groups, from ages 6 and younger to the 50-year-olds, indicate a considerable preference for the Standard Canadian accent in the domains of "easy to understand," "interesting," and "right('correct')" – the latter with the notable exception of our tolerant 7-year-olds, who raise the otherwise stigmatized Finnish accent even above StCanE in that domain (Figure 14.8, top left).

We like to think that the 7-year-olds offer the best window of opportunity to instil the beauty of linguistic variation into young minds. This window might also explain why older students are more language-ideologically biased; after all, this is what Canadian (and generally western) schools teach at that age: "proper" writing and a spelling mistake is often presented as a problem. Our results, if they are proven to hold, might have profound pedagogical consequences, perhaps going so far as to delay the enforcement of the standard language ideology until *after* age 7.

This is not the paper to propose concrete interventions. Yet such interventions would need to be the inevitable goal of research along the lines of our paper. As "interventions introduced in the United States have focused on the stigmatized individual as opposed to the stigmatizer or the threatening environment" (Gluszek and Dovidio 2010: 229), it is high time to address structural problems in language education in school and beyond. Moving away from the native-speaker as the norm and towards more objective comprehensibility standards should no longer be considered extra "flavour". Such norms allow for expressions of individual identities which are, as our 7-year-olds suggests, not negatively viewed per se, though they are essential in our ways of communicating with one another.

References

Adank, Patti, Helen E. Nuttall, Briony Banks & Daniel Kennedy-Higgins. 2015. Neural bases of accented speech perception. *Frontiers in Human Neuroscience* 9 (558). 1–7.

Albareda-Castellot, Bàrbara, Ferran Pons & Núria Sebastián-Gallés. 2011. The acquisition of phonetic categories in bilingual infants: New data from an anticipatory eye movement paradigm. *Developmental Science* 14 (2). 395–401.

Alter, Adam L. & Daniel M. Oppenheimer. 2009. Uniting the tribes of fluency to form a metacognitive nation. *Personality and Social Psychology Review* 13 (3). 219–235.

Barakos, Elisabeth & Charlotte Selleck. 2019. Elite multilingualism: Discourses, practices, and debates. *Journal of Multilingual and Multicultural Development* 40 (5). 361–374.

Bent, Tessa. 2018. Development of unfamiliar accent comprehension continues through adolescence. *Journal of Child Language* 45 (6). 1400–1411.

Bratož, Silva, Anja Pirih & Tina Štemberger. 2019. Identifying children's attitudes towards languages: Construction and validation of the LANGattMini Scale. *Journal of Multilingual and Multicultural Development* 42 (3). 234–246.

Britain, David. 2010. Language and space: The variationist approach. In Jürgen Erich Schmidt & Peter Auer (eds.), *Volume 1 Theories and methods: An international handbook of linguistic variation*, 142–163. Berlin & New York: De Gruyter Mouton.

Cameron, Deborah. 2012. *Verbal Hygiene*, 2nd edn. London, UK: Routledge.

Chambers, Jack K. 1986. Three kinds of standard in Canadian English. In William C. Lougheed (ed.), *In search of the standard in Candian English*, 1–19. Kingston, Ontario: Queen's Univeristy.

Coupland, Nikolas & Howard Giles. 1988. Introduction: The communicative context of accommodation. *Language & Communication* 8 (3/4). 175–182.

Cristia, Alejandrina, Amanda Seidl, Charlotte Vaughn, Rachel Schmale, Ann Bradlow & Caroline Floccia. 2012. Linguistic processing of accented speech across the lifespan. *Frontiers in Psychology* 3. 1–15.

D'Arcy, Alexandra. 2019. Exploring the dynamics of language change through the lens of community, caregiver, and child. Paper presented at the Annual Meeting of the American Dialect Society (ADS), New York City, 5 January.

Day, Richard R. 1980. The development of linguistics attitudes and preferences. *TESOL Quarterly* 14 (1). 27–37.

De Cillia, Rudolf, Ruth Wodak, Markus Rheindorf & Sabine Lehner. 2020. *Österreichische Identitäten im Wandel: Empirische Untersuchungen zu ihrer diskursiven Konstruktion 1995–2015* [Austrian identities in flux: empirical investigations into their discursive construction 1995–2015]. Wiesbaden: Springer VS.

Dewaele, Jean-Marc & James McCloskey. 2015. Attitudes towards foreign accents among adult multilingual language users. *Journal of Multilingual and Multicultural Development* 36 (3). 221–238.

Dollinger, Stefan. 2015. *The written questionnaire in social dialectology: History, theory, practice*. Amsterdam/Philadelphia: John Benjamins.
Dollinger, Stefan. 2019. Review of Nan Jiang. 2018. Second language processing: An Introduction. New York & Abingdon: Routledge. *English World-Wide* 40 (1). 109–114.
Dollinger, Stefan. 2020. English in Canada. In Cecil Nelson, Zoya Proshina & Daniel Davis (eds.), *Handbook of World Englishes*, 2nd edn., 52–69. Malden, MA: Blackwell-Wiley.
Durrant, Samantha, Claire Delle Luche, Allegra Cattani & Caroline Floccia. 2015. Monodialectal and multidialectal infants' representation of familiar words. *Journal of Child Language* 42 (2). 447–465.
Giles, Howard. 1977. Social psychology and applied linguistics: Towards an integrative aproach. *ITL – International Journal of Applied Linguistics* 35. 27–42.
Gluszek, Agata & John F. Dovidio. 2010. The way *they* speak: a social psychological perspective on the stigma of nonnative accents in communication. *Personality and Social Psychology Review* 14 (2). 214–237.
Gulden, Brigitte K. 1979. *Attitudinal factors in Canadian English usage*. Victoria: University of Victoria MA thesis.
Jiang, Nan. 2018. *Second language processing: An introduction*. New York & Abingdon: Routledge.
Jusczyk, Peter W. & Richard N. Aslin. 1995. Infants' detection of the sound patterns of words in fluent speech. *Cognitive Psychology* 29 (1). 1–23.
Kaiser, Irmgard & Gudrun Kasberger. 2021. Children's sociolinguistic preferences: The acquisition of language attitudes within the Austrian dialect-standard continuum. In Anna Ghimenton, Aurélie Nardy & Jean-Pierre Chevot (eds.), *Sociolinguistic variation and language acquisition across the lifespan*, 129–160. Amsterdam: John Benjamins.
Kerswill, Paul. 1994. *Dialects converging: Rural speech in urban Norway*. Oxford: Clarendon Press.
Kinzler, Katherine D. & Jasmine M. DeJesus. 2013. Northern = smart and Southern = nice: The development of accent attitudes in the United States. *The Quarterly Journal of Experimental Psychology* 66 (6). 1146–1158.
Kinzler, Katherine D, Kathleen H. Corriveau & Paul L. Harris. 2011. Children's selective trust in native-accented speakers. *Developmental Science* 14 (1). 106–111.
Labov, William. 1963. The social motivation of a sound change. *Word* 19 (3). 273–309.
Labov, William. 1966. *The social stratification of English in New York City*, 1st edn. Cambridge: Cambridge University Press.
Labov, William. 2001. *Principles of linguistic change. Volume 2: Social factors*. Oxford: Wiley-Blackwell.
Labov, William. 2010. *Principles of linguistic change. Volume 3: Cognitive factors*. Oxford: Wiley-Blackwell.
Lalonde, Kaylah & Rachael Frush Holt. 2016. Audiovisual speech perception development at varying levels of perceptual processing. *The Journal of the Acoustical Society of America* 139 (4). 1713–1723.
Lambert, Wallace E., Richard C. Hodgson, Robert C. Gardner & Samuel Fillenbaum. 1960. Evaluational reactions to spoken languages. *Journal of Abnormal and Social Psychology* 60 (1). 44–51.
Lippi-Green, Rosina. 2012. *English with and Accent: Language, ideology, and discrimination in the United States*. 2nd ed. London: Routledge.
McKinnie, Meghan & Jennifer Dailey-O'Cain. 2002. A perceptual dialectology of Anglophone Canada from the perspective of young Albertans and Ontarians. In Daniel Long (ed.), *Handbook of perceptual dialectology, Volume 2*, 277–294. Amsterdam: John Benjamins.
Meyerhoff, Miriam. 2018. *Introducing sociolinguistics*, 3rd edn. London & New York: Routledge.
Milroy, James & Lesley Milroy. 1999. *Authority in Language: Investigating Standard English*, 3rd edn. London: Routledge.

Munro, Murray J. & Tracey M. Derwing. 1995. Foreign accent, comprehensibility, and intelligibility in the speech of second language learners. *Language Learning* 45 (1). 73–97.
Munro, Murray J. & Tracey M. Derwing. 2011. The foundations of accent and intelligibility in pronunciation research. *Language Teaching* 42 (4). 476–490.
Munro, Murray J. & Tracey M. Derwing. 2020. Foreign accent, comprehensibility and intelligibility, redux. *Journal of Second Language Pronunciation* 6 (3). 283–309.
Norton, Bonny. 2013. *Identity and language learning: Extending the conversation*. Bristol: Multilingual Matters.
Owens, Thompson W. & Paul M. Baker. 1984. Linguistic insecurity in Winnipeg: Validation of a Canadian index of linguistic insecurity. *Language in Society* 13 (3). 337–350.
Polka, Linda and Megha Sundra. 2012. Word segmentation in monolingual infants acquiring Canadian English and Canadian French: Native language, cross-dialect, and cross-language comparisons. *Infancy* 17 (2). 198–232.
Preston, Dennis R. 1989. *Perceptual dialectology: Nonlinguists' views of areal linguistics*. Dordrecht, NL: Foris.
Preston, Dennis R. 1999. *Handbook of perceptual dialectology, Volume 1*. Amsterdam & New York: John Benjamins.
Preston, Dennis R. 2013a. Language with an attitude. In Jack K. Chambers & Natalie Schilling (eds.), *The handbook of language variation and change*, 157–182. Malden, MA: Blackwell.
Preston, Dennis R. 2013b. Linguistic insecurity forty years later. *Journal of English Linguistics* 41 (4). 304–331.
Reber, Rolf, Norbert Schwarz & Piotr Winkielman. 2004. Processing fluency and aesthetic pleasure: Is beauty in the perceiver's processing experience? *Personality and Social Psychology Review* 8 (4). 364–382.
Smith, Jennifer & Mercedes Durham. 2019. *Sociolinguistic variation in children's language: Acquiring community norms*. Cambridge: Cambridge University Press.
Stamou, Anastasia G., Katerina Maroniti & Eleni Griva. 2015. Young children talk about their popular cartoon and TV heroes' speech styles: Media reception and language attitudes. *Language Awareness* 24 (3). 216–232.
Tagliamonte, Sali A. & Bridget L. Jankowski. 2019. Golly, gosh, and oh my god! What North American dialects can tell us about swear words. *American Speech* 94 (2). 195–222.
Tsinivits, Danai & Sharon Unsworth. 2020. The impact of older siblings on the language environment and language development of bilingual toddlers. *Applied Psycholinguistics* 42 (2). 325–344.
Wagner, Laura, Cynthia G. Clopper & John K. Pate. 2014. Children's perception of dialect variation. *Journal of Child Language* 41 (5). 1062–1084.
Wodak, Ruth, Rudolf de Cillia, Martin Reisigl & Karin Liebhart (eds.). 2009 [1999]. *The discursive construction of national identity*, 2nd edn. Translated by Angelika Hirsch, Richard Mitten & Johann W. Unger. Edinburgh: Edinburgh University Press.

Naashia Mohamed
15 Caught between languages and cultures: Exploring linguistic and cultural identity among Maldivian adolescents

Abstract: This chapter draws on theories of language attitudes and identity to describe identity struggles faced by Maldivian adolescents as they shift from their indigenous language to the more globally powerful English language. Following British colonialism in the Maldives, the English language attained an indelible role in the country's educational system in particular and its society in general, causing language to be an important aspect of the identity construction of Maldivians. Based on the findings of a mixed methods study, this chapter illustrates how young people in this context have strong views regarding hierarchies of languages and language varieties present in the community. Their language use indicates that their preference for English overshadows their use of the Dhivehi language in many domains, despite the official status of Dhivehi. They consider the English language to be a passport to progress and look to the English of Inner Circle countries as the ideal to be attained to earn social status and prestige, while othering those who do not fit into their self-determined label of an English speaker. The findings suggest that prestige planning measures are necessary to protect and promote the Dhivehi language in the Maldives.

Keywords: language attitudes, language identity, World Englishes, Maldives

1 Introduction

The concepts of language, power, and identity are inherently related (Bourdieu 1992; Norton [2000] 2013; Norton and De Costa 2018). The power we ascribe to languages and our linguistic behaviour manifest who we are, how we define reality, and how we draw boundaries between us and others (Wodak 2012). This chapter

---

Acknowledgements: The study was made possible through a grant awarded by the Maldives National University. The author wishes to acknowledge the contributions of Waleeda Easa, Aminath Zahir, and Sana Farooq to the project, particularly during the data collection phase.

Naashia Mohamed, University of Auckland, New Zealand

focuses on the dialectic relationship between language and identity, describing how Maldivian adolescents' identities are impacted through the language hierarchies in society, focusing in particular on the power imbalance between Dhivehi, the national language of the Maldives, and English. Drawing on data gathered from young people aged between 12 and 17 years, this chapter shows how adolescents in one of the world's smallest countries position themselves as a result of the English-mediated access they gain to the world.

The transitional period of adolescence is a time when self-categorisation and identity development are at their peak (McCarty et al. 2009), and given the connectedness of today's world, it is also a time when young people are easily exposed to and influenced by global trends and practices. As Peterson (2020) notes, there is strong social pressure for young people around the world to become comfortable with using English at an increasingly young age. To be part of the computer-mediated communication, English "is a modern-day necessity" that has become a practical choice at the expense of other languages (Peterson 2020: 4). Pressures from both formal (e.g. school) and informal (e.g. online interests) sides expose young people to English from an early age and cause them to "have an integrated and personal relationship with the language" (Peterson 2020: 5), affecting their sense of self and their association with others.

Understanding language attitudes in young people is vital to gain insights into language change over time (Coupland 2014). Children not only form attitudes about languages from a young age but are aware of ideologies and attitudes present in their surroundings (Habib 2016), and these in turn influence their own beliefs and behaviours. As Wright (2004) notes, a laissez-faire approach means that languages with power and prestige will take over in situations of contact. It is particularly pertinent to contexts like the Maldives where the indigenous language, although given official status, is a minority language on the global scale. Efforts to preserve the language can begin by understanding the attitudes young people have towards it and other languages used in the society, including English.

Language is not just a tool for communication, but embodies the histories, cultures, values, beliefs, and identities of its speakers (Pennycook 2002). A national language is often seen as a key mechanism for enhancing cohesion and preserving the identity of a nation state (Coleman 2015). The emergence of global languages such as English has unsettled the cultural capital (Bourdieu 1997) of other languages. In an age of unprecedented globalisation, the economic, political, social, and cultural power and prestige afforded through competence in English cannot match the benefits of speaking a language that is ranked lower on the social scale (Morrison and Lui 2000), and as a consequence, individuals may engage in identity management to affiliate with languages and cultures that are considered to be more powerful (Giles, Bourhis, and Taylor 1977). The process of deterritorialization of languages and cultures as a consequence of globalisation has made identity management even more possible, as individual speakers can operate in a trans-national framework which has been considerably enhanced by the development of new media and technology (Craith 2007). Tsui (2005) describes how the features of globalisation – interconnectivity, intensity, immediacy and multidimensionality of knowledge generation, transmission, and interaction – have been brought about by the mediational effect of technology and language. As Tsui argues, societies need to re-examine the mediational tools with which they are equipped in order to respond to changes brought about by globalisation and consider how their language policies and patterns of language use are impacting its people.

By examining the patterns of language use among young people and their own descriptions of their affiliation to the communities represented by these languages, the study presented in this chapter makes a significant contribution to the fields of sociolinguistics and World Englishes as it documents how learners redefine their identities and claim ownership of English. It addresses a contextual gap as relatively few studies have focused on language identities and attitudes of young people in non-European contexts where English is studied widely but has no administrative status. Even fewer studies examine how language attitudes can impact language maintenance in contexts where English as a global language has become a threat to the future of a small national language (Thordardottir 2021). By incorporating a range of methodological approaches, including a survey, interviews, and narrative tasks, this chapter intends to move beyond a linguistic analysis of the language variety used in this context, to focus on the sociolinguistic realities urged by Kachru (1997) in an attempt to understand how learning English has affected these young people's everyday language behaviour, ideologies, and identities.

2 The context of the Maldives

Following its colonial legacy, English became firmly entrenched in the linguistic landscape of South Asia (Lange 2019), and the effects of globalisation served to further heighten its role in the linguistic ecology of this multilingual region. The rich multicultural mosaic of South Asia makes a sharp contrast to the relative linguistic, cultural, and religious homogeneity of its smallest and least populous member: the Maldives. The Maldives is an archipelagic country comprised of 1190 islands dispersed over 90,000 square kilometres with a land area of just under 300 square kilometres. It has a population of approximately 400,000 of which 15%

are expatriate residents (National Bureau of Statistics 2014). The geographical nature of the Maldives allowed for limited opportunities of language contact and may partly explain why it remained monolingual in Dhivehi for a long period of time. Dhivehi, of Indo Aryan descent, is almost exclusively spoken in the Maldives[1] and has a unique script called Thaana. Although it has significant Persian, Urdu, and Sinhala overlay (Gnanadesikan 2016), due to religious affiliation, Dhivehi is heavily influenced by Arabic. Furthermore, contemporary Dhivehi uses an increasing amount of loanwords from English. Although contact with the English language occurred mainly as a result of being colonised and governed by the British for 77 years until 1965, the global language did not leave a significant mark on the language of Maldivians until relatively recently (Meierkord 2018), when it became a mainstay of the education system.

During the mid-twentieth century, the rudimentary education system of the Maldives was overhauled and modernised to follow a British model of schooling with the intention of accelerating national development to maximise social and economic progress (Latheef and Gupta 2007). The English language was introduced into the school curriculum first as a subject in the late 1950s and then shortly afterwards as the medium of instruction in 1961 (Mohamed 2019), leading it to be accepted by the inhabitants as the nation's second language even though there is no official recognition of this status. Today, in addition to the educational domain, the English language plays a crucial role in tourism and trade and is visible everywhere on signage. A nativised variety is on the verge of development and the prominence of English has left an indelible mark on the identity of Maldivians (Mohamed 2020).

3 Theoretical framework

A sense of identity is an integral aspect of one's self-understanding and provides a meaning-making lens through which to view the world and our place in it. Previous research emphasises that identities are complex, multiple, and dynamic social constructs (Norton 2013), which include both individualistic perspectives of the self as well as a collective perspective of group affiliations (Oyserman, Elmore, and Smith [2003] 2012). As individuals, we construct, negotiate, perform, and accomplish self-attributed identities through our discursive practices, and in our in-

---

[1] The only other community that uses Dhivehi as their primary language is the Maliku people on Minicoy Island of Lakshadweep, India. However, the Lakshadweep Administration refers to Dhivehi as Mahl.

teractions with others (Blommaert 2006). But identities are also other-ascribed. This aspect of our identities affords us membership in groups or limits our rights to participation in them (Preece 2016), which can gain us legitimacy (Kramsch 2021) and in turn, affect our own sense of belonging.

Language is one of the vehicles through which we construct identity. Language allows us to represent ourselves and denote our characters, our personalities, and our own individualities. Joseph (2016: 19–20) succinctly summarises the interaction between language and identity: "Identities are manifested in language as, first, the categories and labels that people attach to themselves and others to signal their belonging; second, as the indexed ways of speaking and behaving through which they perform their belonging; and third, as the interpretations that others make of those indices".

Traditional descriptions of the relationship between language and identity stem from Tajfel's (1981) theory of social identity and intergroup conflict. Scholars of this tradition (e.g. Fishman 1991; Skutnabb-Kangas and Philipson 1989) associate a strong emotive and spiritual connection between an individual and their native language. Others highlight the performative aspect of identity and argue that they are negotiated (Bucholtz and Hall 2005) through the use of communicative practices (Kroskrity 1999). Tracy (2002) offers an alternative compromise, suggesting that identities are multiple: some are stable while others change through interaction; some arise through group membership while others are the result of individual personalities.

Language attitudes are central to understanding identity and are practised through language use (Bokhorst-Heng and Caleon 2008). Busse (2017: 567) describes language attitudes as "a summary evaluation of a language which can have favourable or less favourable tendencies". Bartram (2010) notes that several scholars offer tripartite structures of attitudes. Baker (1992), Cargile et al. (1994), and Ladegraad (2000) are among those who describe language attitudes as consisting of cognitive, affective, and conative constituents. The cognitive aspect of language attitudes relates to knowledge and beliefs about and experience with languages, language varieties, and language use. For example, hearing a person speak can trigger associations about their personality, group affiliation, and individual attributes that may be stereotypical. The affective component addresses emotions, evaluations, and opinions about language varieties, their speakers, and one's own language use. The conative component is associated with how linguistic behaviour and decision making are influenced by the interlocutor, auditor, context, and topic of interaction.

Ladegaard's (2000) study with Danish adolescents established a clear relationship between attitudes and sociolinguistic behaviour suggesting that attitudes are likely to predict broad patterns of sociolinguistic behaviour. However, it is not only language that a hearer may react to. Cargile et al. (1994) suggest that a speaker's paralinguistic behaviours as well as non-linguistic aspects of the communication, such as the physical features of the speaker, affect the evaluation of the interlocutor. An individual's language attitudes are shaped by societal views, group membership, and family background (Masgoret and Gardner 2003). Attitudes towards languages can vary based on perceptions of social status or group solidarity (Dörnyei and Csizér 2005). A distinction can also be made between instrumental and integrative attitudes (Baker and Wright [1993] 2017). Instrumental attitudes relate to viewing a particular language as a positive influence on achieving a goal, whereas integrative attitudes relate to an intrinsic desire to become associated with the speech community of that language.

Some studies point to the relationship between attitudes and age. Sharma (2016) highlighted how peer influence is a strong factor in affecting adolescents' language attitudes, more so than parents and teachers. Gardner (1985) showed that attitudes towards learning an additional language become less positive with age. Cargile et al. (1994) report that adolescents identify increasingly more with local sociolinguistic ideals across teenage years. Price and Tamburelli (2020: 209) found that in their study of Welsh-English bilinguals, adolescents are drawn to English because of the symbolic social status it affords. Regardless of their level of competence in the two languages or their confidence in using them, the participants in their study found more appeal in English as it was seen "as an emblem of youth culture" (Price and Tamburelli 2016: 209). Kircher (2016) found this to be also true in the context of Canada, regardless of the language background of the learner.

Previous studies of the interaction between language, identity, and power in World Englishes contexts have highlighted how English can be both an empowering and disempowering tool. Kachru's (1985: 16) conceptualisation of World Englishes through his Three Circle Model captured the power of "norm-providing" native speaker varieties of the Inner Circle that served as models for the Outer and Expanding Circles. He questioned the superiority of native speaker varieties and drew attention to the inequalities of perception between the three speech groups (Buschfeld and Kautzsch 2017). The power dynamics between so-called native and non-native speakers is evident in Zacharias (2012) in the context of Indonesian learners of English. The participants of the study regarded themselves as being part of the elite in Indonesian society because their English user status repositioned them as being educated. However, when in the company of native English speakers, they saw themselves as being linguistically incompetent and felt disempowered. These learners rated their national identity unfavourably as it branded them as non-native speakers of English and therefore identified them as being inferior to native speakers.

However, this characterisation of deficit and disadvantage was not always evident in studies of young people in Outer or Expanding Circles. Huang's (2011) examination of English learners in Taiwan and Sung's (2015) study of English learners in Hong Kong showed that participants generally used positive metaphors to describe their L2 self-development through learning English and saw themselves as legitimate speakers of English and not as adoptees of a "borrowed identity" (Seidlhofer 2003: 23). Similarly, Sicam and Lucas' (2016) study of English-Filipino high school students revealed high positive attitudes towards both of their languages, seeing clear roles and benefits of both of their languages.

Nevertheless, most studies recognise the prestige afforded by English. Jahan and Hamid's (2019) highlight the social privilege gained through access to English in Bangladeshi society. The prestige of English and its association with modernity are echoed by Lanza and Woldemariam's (2014) analysis of the Ethiopian linguistic landscape. Similarly, Fei et al.'s (2012) study with Malaysian undergraduates illustrates how language was an identity marker that simultaneously raised the social status of English users in some contexts while they were considered "less Malay" by other groups in the same society. In multilingual Singapore, Bokhorst-Heng and Caleon (2008) found that young people did not necessarily associate English with notions of status or solidarity, but regarded English as having utilitarian value.

These studies highlight the significance of power relationships in identity construction as a result of language learning. The following sections will draw on these theoretical concepts as they describe the identity negotiation processes young Maldivians engage in in the context of language and culture.

4 Methods

Scholars of language attitudes have used three main approaches to studying this primarily psychological construct (Garrett 2010). The direct approach involves asking people to directly articulate their attitudes towards a language phenomenon. The indirect approach uses more subtle techniques, such as matched guise tests, to determine language attitudes. The societal treatment approach involves sourcing data from the public domain, such as media texts, advertisements, language policy documents, etc. and inferring attitudes from these sources. This study utilised the first approach, by eliciting attitudes and identity from young people in this context.

A total of 1587 students from 19 different schools participated in this study. They were aged between 12 and 17 years and included both males (48.8%) and females (51.2%). While there was representation from different geographical regions of the country, the majority of participants (81.9%) were residents of the capital island, Malé. Three sources of empirical data were used. Questionnaire responses from all 1587 participants documented participants' demographic background, patterns of language use, self-reported levels of competence in their languages, and attitudes towards their languages. From those who completed the questionnaires, 40 participants (28 girls and 12 boys) self-selected to provide written narratives, and a further 20 participants (11 girls and 9 boys) opted to do one-to-one interviews.

Participants who chose to do the written narrative task were provided with two prompts and asked to choose one. This was an untimed task without a restriction on the number of words and conducted at school, as an after-school activity, with feedback provided to students on their writing. The first prompt was: "If you could live anywhere in the world, where would you choose to live and why? You may choose where you already live, or somewhere completely different". The second prompt was: "How would you describe a typical Maldivian of today? Explain how similar or different you think you are to that typical Maldivian and discuss reasons why that may be". Participants wrote an average of 502 words in response to these prompts.

The semi-structured interviews focused on unpacking participants' beliefs about language and culture, their positionality, and their language learning experiences. They were conducted by three researchers who shared the participants' ethnicity and language backgrounds. The interviews were audio-recorded and transcribed for analysis. The interview duration ranged from 35–77 minutes.

Each method of data collection offered participants the option of proceeding in either Dhivehi or English. While the language option was provided largely for reasons of equity and for the ease and comfort of participants, their choice of language also indicated their linguistic preferences. The majority of respondents (82%) opted to complete the questionnaire in English. None of the students who completed the narrative task wrote in Dhivehi, even though they were explicitly given the choice and prompts were provided in both languages. Most participants (70%) who were interviewed also stated that they wished to be interviewed in English, although in reality most of the interviews were translingual dialogues.

The questionnaire responses were analysed using descriptive statistics and thematic analysis (Braun and Clarke 2006) was used to examine the two qualitative sources of data. The next section describes the findings from these analyses.

5 Findings

The first sub-section presents the findings from the analysis of the survey and the second sub-section presents the results from the narrative tasks and interviews. All names used are pseudonyms.

5.1 Quantitative findings

One aim of the study was to explore the patterns of language use and to identify language preferences for everyday interactions. Table 15.1 shows the language used most frequently by the questionnaire respondents when speaking with family and friends.

Table 15.1: Language used most frequently when speaking with family and friends.

	Grandparents	Mother	Father	Siblings	Friends outside school	Friends in school
Dhivehi	1435 (90.4%)	1430 (90.1%)	1428 (90.0%)	902 (56.8%)	690 (43.5%)	707 (44.5%)
English	21 (1.3%)	135 (8.5%)	134 (8.4%)	642 (40.5%)	629 (39.6%)	855 (53.9%)
Other[2]	25 (1.6%)	19 (1.2%)	19 (1.2%)	24 (1.5%)	46 (2.9%)	20 (1.3%)

These figures indicate that both Dhivehi and English featured prominently in participants' everyday oral language use. The rate of use of Dhivehi declines, but only by a miniscule amount, from grandparents to the parent generation and declines more significantly to the group of siblings and friends. As these respondents attended English-medium schools, they were required to use English to communicate within the school environment. This may explain why a higher percentage of respondents reported using English more frequently than Dhivehi when speaking with friends in school. However, the use of language for writing in everyday life was different, as shown in Table 15.2.

---

[2] On the survey, questions to specify language offered three choices: Dhivehi, English, and Other. Respondents were invited to state what the "Other" language was. Responses throughout the survey (i.e. not just for this question) included Arabic, Hindi, Korean, and Malayalam. However, not all respondents who chose the "Other" option specified the language in every instance.

Table 15.2: Language used most frequently when interacting through writing with family and friends.

	Grandparents	Mother	Father	Siblings	Friends outside school	Friends in school
Dhivehi	1320 (83.2%)	1120 (70.6%)	1136 (71.6%)	703 (44.3%)	530 (33.4%)	447 (28.2%)
English	43 (2.7%)	451 (28.4%)	433 (27.3%)	842 (53.1%)	1019 (64.2%)	1117 (70.4%)
Other	28 (1.8%)	16 (1%)	16 (1%)	17 (1.1%)	34 (2.1%)	18 (1.1%)

The preference for Dhivehi still prevails when communicating with parents and grandparents. However, there is now a clear preference for English over Dhivehi when interacting with peers and siblings. While expected to be less frequent than oral communication, writing in everyday life would typically involve the use of text messaging or computer-mediated communication. This is likely to be more common among younger populations, and given the lack of ease in using Dhivehi for technology as Thaana is not an in-built feature or always compatible with all applications, it is unsurprising that English seems to be more frequently used among the younger generation.

Table 15.3 shows participants' self-evaluation of their fluency in their languages. The questionnaire required participants to indicate agreement or disagreement with statements such as "I can read fluently in this language". Participants were specifically asked about Arabic as well as Dhivehi and English. Given that Arabic is typically used in the community for religious purposes (mainly in reading

Table 15.3: Self-evaluation of language fluency.

	Reading fluency	Speaking fluency	Writing fluency
Dhivehi	1371 (86.6%)	1352 (85.2%)	1288 (81.2%)
English	1255 (79.1%)	1141 (71.9%)	1253 (79.0%)
Arabic	611 (38.5%)	127 (8.0%)	452 (28.6%)
Other	137 (8.6%)	167 (10.5%)	118 (7.4%)

the Qur'an and for academic study of the Qur'an) and not as a language of communication per se, it was not expected that participants would be able to speak the language.

Participants were also asked to state what they felt was their strongest language; the language they used the most; and the language they had the most confidence using (see Table 15.4).

Table 15.4: Self-evaluation of language competence.

	Strongest language	Most used language	Most confidence in using
Dhivehi	517 (32.6%)	1214 (76.5%)	1297 (81.7%)
English	1055 (66.5%)	360 (22.7%)	446 (28.1%)
Other	15 (0.9%)	10 (0.6%)	13 (0.8%)

These results appear almost contradictory and are highly interesting, depicting an example of colonial cringe – dismissing one's own language and culture as being inferior to the language and cultures of other countries. Previously shown solid rates of individual competence in and identification with English, as well as extremely high rates of self-reported daily usage are in stark contrast to the low confidence in using English seen here. This points to a gap with regards to feeling legitimacy in using the language. This relates to the low level of confidence expressed by participants in the qualitative components of the study as well, where students were reported to have suffered from ridicule for using accented English.

One part of the questionnaire required respondents to rate statements about Dhivehi and English on a five-point Likert scale ranging from 1 = Strongly Agree to 5 = Strongly Disagree. The mean values for each statement are shown in Figure 15.1 (see Appendix 15.1 for a detailed table of this data).

The results shown in Figure 15.1 suggests that there is a greater affinity towards English. Students for example claim "liking" English better than Dhivehi, feel that their "real self comes out" more when they speak English, and use English more in everyday use such as for telling the time. Students felt that it was important for Maldivians to speak English perfectly than they felt it was necessary to speak Dhivehi perfectly.

To determine if there was a difference in the attitudes of the participants towards Dhivehi and English, a paired samples t-test was used to compare participant responses in these conditions. As shown in Table 15.5, there was a significant

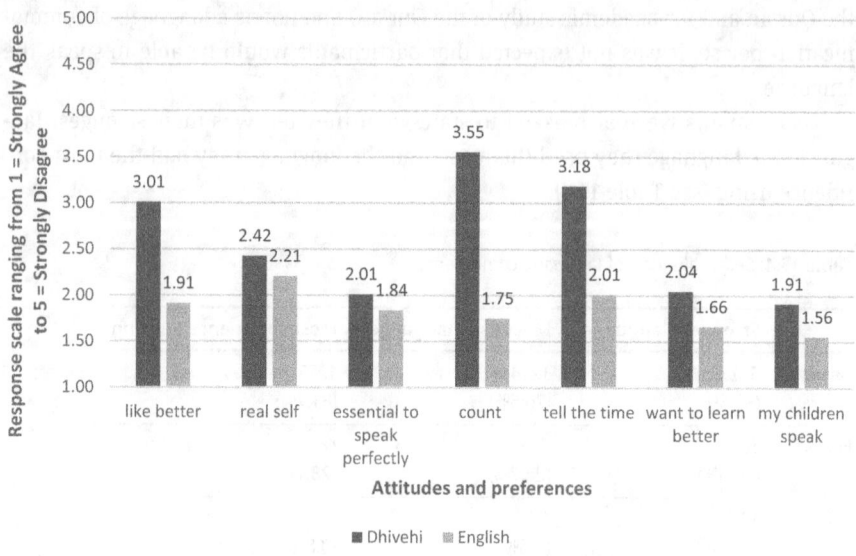

Figure 15.1: Attitudes towards Dhivehi and English.

Table 15.5: Paired samples t-test.

		Mean	Std. Deviation	t	df	Sig. (2-tailed)
Pair 1	I like Dhivehi better than I like English – I like English better than I like Dhivehi	1.08845	1.60771	26.054	1480	.000
Pair 2	My real self comes out more when I speak in Dhivehi – My real self comes out more when I speak in English	.20158	2.13123	3.691	1522	.000
Pair 3	It is essential for Maldivians to speak Dhivehi perfectly – It is essential for Maldivians to speak English perfectly	.15333	1.62837	3.647	1499	.000
Pair 4	I usually count in Dhivehi – I usually count in English	1.80680	2.06623	33.878	1500	.000
Pair 5	I usually tell the time in Dhivehi – I usually tell the time in English	1.08774	2.41609	17.396	1492	.000
Pair 6	I want to learn and be able to use Dhivehi better than now – I want to learn and be able to use English better than now	.38360	1.37903	10.816	1511	.000

Table 15.5 (continued)

		Mean	Std. Deviation	t	df	Sig. (2-tailed)
Pair 7	When I am a parent, I want my children to speak Dhivehi well – When I am a parent, I want my children to speak English well	.35003	1.33459	10.148	1496	.000

difference (p <.001) between the attitudes towards Dhivehi and English in each of these conditions, indicating that adolescents in this study had more positive attitudes towards English than Dhivehi.

5.2 Qualitative findings

In the narrative writing tasks, two views of the Maldives and its people were evident. One was a traditionalist view of the country where students wrote about the natural beauty of the islands and the simple island lifestyle of rural Maldivians who were viewed to be uneducated and have a limited understanding of English but a strong community spirit and looked out for each other. The second was a more contemporary view of the Maldives which did not project its people in a very positive light. Those who held a contemporary view of the Maldives wrote about how people typically "lived beyond their means" (Paree, age 16), are "obsessed with politics" (Nisha, age 17), selfish, tech-savvy, and code-switch effortlessly. Some argued that the carefree lifestyle where people are "genuinely kind and neighbours took care of each other" (Jud, age 16) is a mere fantasy created by tourist brochures because the reality is quite different. One participant wrote about how Maldivian youth "desperately want to be Western but are unable to let go of tradition" and that as a result, "they are kind of lost in between" (Hadi, age 15). Interestingly, several students wrote about Maldivians from an etic perspective, as if they were not part of this cultural group. They drew contrasts between themselves and Maldivians, often painting a not too positive picture of Maldivians. Contrasting the two polarised views of Maldivians, one student wrote:

(1) "I am proud to be Maldivian but I am not a typical traditional Maldivian. I am a true Maldivian of the modern age with developed thinking and a knowledge of the world because I read, and I travel and I speak English" (Insha, aged 16).

Several participants explained that they lived in the Maldives not out of choice and looked forward to living elsewhere when they had the means to emigrate. They wrote about experiencing other people and cultures during holidays and listed Inner Circle countries such as the United Kingdom, the United States, Australia, and Canada as their preferred countries to live in. For two participants, the appeal of such Western countries lay in the "beautiful people with very white skin" (Zaid, age 15). But for most participants there were other attractions, such as their association with modernity:

(2) "They have the technology, the fashion, the knowledge, the know-how of everything we need. Their people are nice and friendly and respect each other. I have been to other countries on holiday and I always wish that Maldives was more like that" (Lubna, age 16).

These comments suggest a level of naivety and an adherence to the common belief in other pastures being greener than their own. The young people in this study seem to equate culture with tradition and appear to be largely unfamiliar with the history, customs, and literature of the Maldives. Jabir (age 14), for example, equated Maldivian culture with wearing *libaas* or *mundu*[3] and climbing coconut trees. Another participant (Kulsum, age 15) acknowledged that she had never seen or participated in a "real" festival or celebration such as Eid, nor had she any knowledge of traditional games or songs and professed to not reading books in Dhivehi because "they are boring and uncool".

Culture was also seen to be a deterrent for modernity, and as an aspect of history:

(3) "Culture and traditions are something in the past. We need to look ahead and move forward if we want Maldives to develop and modernise" (Faheema, age 15).

Despite their largely negative attitudes towards Maldivian culture and its people, many participants expressed pride in Dhivehi because "it's our own language," which is "not spoken anywhere else in the world" (Aara, age 13). One participant commented that "it is pretty neat to think that we are very special to have our own language" because it is not a distinction that every society has (Owais, age 14). However, many participants felt that because the language is not used outside of the country, it has little value. Some associated Dhivehi with a by-gone era.

---

3 *Libaas* is the traditional dress of Maldivian women, and *mundu* is the sarong that men wear.

(4) "Only old people use Dhivehi. Even when I have to speak in Dhivehi, I use a lot of English words" (Dhanish, age 14).

Dhanish went on to express feeling forced to have to speak Dhivehi. His use of English words when speaking Dhivehi was a way for Dhanish to signal his youth and distinguish himself as being separate from users of Dhivehi, whom he believed were from an older generation.

In contrast, English is seen to be their passport to better opportunities. Many participants referred to how English has "opened [their] eyes to the world" (Eiman, age 16), or how exposure to Western cultures through the media has impacted their identity.

(5) "I can easily say that this is all due to learning English. English helped me to become aware of the world. The books and films and everything we see on TV has made me into who I am today. If I had only focused on Dhivehi, I would have been very ignorant because there is nothing in Dhivehi. Nothing. To go ahead in life, we have to use more English, be more English" (Laila, age 16).

Similar integrative attitudes towards learning English were echoed by several interview participants who stressed the need to "be like them" (Dhanish, age 14).

(6) "I have always wanted to be the best. So far, I have always achieved every ambition I have had. I want to be a doctor, a neurosurgeon. I can only do that by going abroad to study. Maybe in England or America. So, I want to speak like them, so that when I get to go, I will be like one of them. This is why I pay so much attention to excelling in English" (Mahir, age 17).

One interview participant used her social media following as a way of explaining her own membership in an English-speaking community. She noted with pride that most of her social media accounts had followers who were not Maldivians and were English speakers. She talked about how English enabled her to reach out to such a wide audience from around the world, and that for her, the boundaries of geography were blurred.

(7) "I can speak to anyone anywhere in the world with an internet connection. English does that for you. . . . You can't do that with Dhivehi. And [with Dhivehi] there is also a sense of having to do things a certain way, like you don't have the freedom to do things your own way. . . It is more restrictive" (Raisa, age 17).

Such comments suggest that these young people feel that English is liberating and gives them the ability to express themselves freely. It was also clear from participants' comments that there is a preference for Inner Circle Englishes as these are seen to be far superior to other varieties. Some participants, for example, remarked that it is "essential to go to somewhere like the UK where real English is spoken" (Kulsum, age 15). Their bias towards British and US American English is most likely due to their exposure to these cultures through popular media and a schooling system that encourages them to follow British English models.

One student commented on how she could not take her English teacher seriously as he had "a strange accent" (Nabila, age 15), which she did not believe was appropriate for an English teacher. There were also comments to indicate that some students distanced themselves from their idea of a typical Maldivian because in their view typical Maldivians knew very little English or spoke "broken English" (Insha, age 16).

(8) "There is this girl in my class who joined our school last year. She came from [name of rural island]. I would say she is a typical Maldivian because she likes all the typical Dhivehi stuff. Even watches Dhivehi films (grimaces). She doesn't do very well in school as she can hardly speak any English" (Dhanish, age 14).

Comments such as this indicate that there appears to be an urban-rural divide in the use of Dhivehi and in the practice of cultural traditions. The affiliation with Inner Circle English shows the high regard these young people have for US American and British Standard English and how they attribute a lower status to any localised varieties.

A few students expressed their unhappiness about not being more competent in Dhivehi and not having a better awareness of Maldivian culture. They felt that it was because "so little time was spent on learning that" in school (Owais, age 14). As Dhivehi is used in only two subjects out of the nine that they study at school, they naturally spent less time using the language. Given the amount of time students spend at school, some reported that they are "actually more comfortable using English" (Aara, age 13).

In addition to the time factor, participants alluded to the main focus of school being on excelling in the end of school examinations. In such an exam-centric educational environment, Dhivehi just could not compete, they explained.

(9) "[The IGCSE[4] exams are] all you ever hear about, from the time you start school. Everyone aims to get to the Top 10.[5] And whatever subject you do, you need [English] to get there. To do well. . . . Being good in Dhivehi will not get you into the Top 10" (Rabia, age 15).

Another reason why young people in this context seemed to distance themselves from Dhivehi was the participants' perceived grammatical rigidity of Dhivehi. Participants commented on how there were "just too many rules" (Faheema, age 15) about writing in Dhivehi which make it less user-friendly. Dhivehi is also seen to be difficult to incorporate into computer-mediated communications. When young people spend a lot of time communicating through this medium, it is unsurprising that they are more drawn towards English because of its accessibility. For some participants, English was their "default language" (Faheema, age 15) which they automatically use in every domain, unless they are specifically asked to use Dhivehi.

The interviews also make clear that tensions exist in society about language preferences and language use. Despite participants' increased use of English and seeming preference for English, many lack the confidence in using both languages. Several interview participants referred to feeling inadequate because of their experiences of being ridiculed by teachers, peers, and family members for using "foreign accents and wrong pronunciation" (Jabir, age 14) or "ungrammatical English" (Laila, age 16). Some talked about how this insecurity in English was not a result of something they had personally experienced but through being an observer when others were subjected to such humiliation. This suggests that there is a high expectation for English to be used accurately, and an inability to use English well (whether perceived or real), is a way to lose face. One interview participant explained his experience of this:

(10) "No one will laugh even if you make mistakes in Dhivehi or use English words when speaking in Dhivehi. They might think you are arrogant for using English words but they won't laugh at you. But if you make mistakes in English, then people see it as [something] bad about you. You have failed" (Ghufran, age 13).

---

4 The International General Certificate of School Education examinations offered by Cambridge International Examinations Board are how all Maldivian students are assessed at the end of formal compulsory schooling at the age of 16.
5 The Ministry of Education selects the students who achieve the best results in the IGCSE exams every year and the students who achieve these awards get selected into the best high schools as well as receive scholarships for further study.

In a similar vein, another participant made reference to taking private lessons from a native speaker to "remove [their] accent and sound more English" (Jud, age 16). These comments suggest the strong recognition of Inner Circle varieties as being the norm to aspire to and an unwillingness to recognise their own language use as being equally legitimate.

In summary, these results show that both the quantitative and qualitative data paint the same picture. Adolescents in this context report using both Dhivehi and English in their everyday lives but have a clear preference for English over Dhivehi. Similarly, the results show comparatively higher rates of English usage and competence and indicate a pattern of language shift. These participants hold hybrid identities and associate themselves with both the English-speaking communities in Inner Circle countries and, to a lesser extent, the Maldivian people. There appears to be some conflict between their stated identities and their reported behaviours. The next section will discuss these results in light of the literature.

6 Discussion and conclusions

This chapter contributes to the growing body of work on children and adolescents in World Englishes. Understanding the views and behaviours of young people is essential to appreciate the vitality of a language and predict its future (Ehala and Niglas 2006). This study has examined a group of Maldivian young people's perceptions of their linguistic and cultural identities, with the aim of advancing our understanding of identity construction and language attitudes in an Expanding Circle World Englishes context.

This study shows that adolescents in the Maldives place a high importance on learning English. They recognise the economic value of the language and how this translates into greater opportunities. They are also cognizant of the power associated with languages in general, and in particular, Standard Varieties of English, and aligned themselves with the desired social status achieved through English. This supports the contention that attitudes are learned, not innate (Masgoret and Gardner 2003). It is likely that they were influenced by the attitudes of others (parents, teachers, media) and became socialised to thinking of Standard Varieties as being superior to other varieties. Although much of the literature on World Englishes point to the formation of glocalised varieties (Pennycook 2010), in this study the strong preference was for an exonormative standard variety of English. Accented English was noted as being incorrect and unacceptable, even when this was used by teachers.

This is not to say that the young people participating in the present study did not value Dhivehi. They did appreciate that they were the guardians to a language that is not spoken in any other context. Yet, because of this uniqueness, they doubted that Dhivehi could be relevant in the modern world. This is reminiscent of the conflict highlighted by Thordardottir (2021) in her analysis of Icelandic adolescents who were more interested in learning English than Icelandic. In both cases, the young people are caught up in two worlds and seek to express the duality of their linguistic identities.

The hybrid nature of these adolescents' identities is not new and is in line with the findings of other studies that have explored identity construction (Cunningham and King 2018; Sung 2015). These young people saw themselves as being caught in-between the two worlds they inhabited, both in terms of language as well as culture. The seemingly contradictory findings of rating English higher than Dhivehi in terms of language competence and frequency of use but lower than Dhivehi in terms of their confidence in using the language may be attributed to their conflicting identities.

Significantly, however, these participants did not see themselves as being deficient because they were non-native speakers of English. Rather, most participants saw themselves as legitimate users of English and ascribed to themselves membership in their imagined communities of English speakers. They saw the English language as an empowering tool that placed them on par with others who used the language globally. This was not necessarily a "borrowed identity" (Seidlhofer 2003) or one that marked them as being different from other users of English. In fact, these participants clearly felt a sense of ownership of English and described the feeling of being able to use English to interact with others globally as liberating, supporting the notion that language is no longer fixed to a certain location (Blommaert 2010; Kubota 2016).

Nevertheless, the data also shows evidence of quite negative attitudes towards their indigenous language. It may be that these young people are so invested in the perceived power of English that they view Dhivehi as holding them back from realising the promise that the global language provides. It may also be possible that because the study was conducted in the school context where English is dominant, participants were affected by the association of the setting with English. Perhaps the direct elicitation of language attitudes used in this study triggered participants to respond in ways that they believed to be appropriate, to articulate the attitudes that they think they ought to have, rather than the ones they actually do have.

Young (2017) argues that indigenous people feel threatened by outside languages as they see the language to be a hegemonic influence that threatens their culture and identity as a group. In the case of these young Maldivians, however, they have not formed a stable identity to associate themselves firmly with the language and culture of their people. They simultaneously state their pride in their heritage and imply that Dhivehi is dispensable because they fail to see the economic value of the language. This suggests that there is a mismatch between explicit and implicit attitudes (McKenzie and Carrie 2018), where the positive attitudes towards Dhivehi are explicitly asserted, but negative attitudes are inferred from their reported actions and beliefs.

This study makes clear that in contexts like this, there needs to be a greater awareness about the way in which languages interact with each other and an appreciation for both the local and the global needs to be established. As Canagarajah (2005) argued, it is essential to reclaim the local in the light of the pressures and discourses of globalisation. Reiterating Canagarajah's (2005) arguments, both May (2014) and Young (2017) asserted that all languages – regardless of their status on the global scale – influence our identity and serve as linguistic vehicles for social and economic mobility. The findings from this study lend support to this claim that one particular language does not index a person's identity and that identities are continually recreated based on context and interlocutor.

The language attitudes and patterns of language use uncovered in this chapter point to the broader language change taking place in the Maldivian context. With young people claiming ownership of English and redefining their identities, this study indicates that, if Dhivehi is to thrive among young people, there is a need for Dhivehi to become more relevant to youth culture (for example, making Thaana more accessible for computer-mediated communication) and for its prestige to be raised so that young people see greater value in learning to use it well and become eager to invest in its use. The lax attitude towards Dhivehi may be enhanced by the fact that the language is not seen as being at risk or portrayed as a minority language, which it is on a global scale. As Thordardottir (2021) argues, countries with small national languages will require state backing to ensure that the language survives the current threat of English and a young generation that is drawn to the appeal of the global language.

The chapter highlights the importance of understanding adolescents' language identities and attitudes as a shifting, complex and multifaceted processes that impact language use at both an individual and societal level. Future research in this context could explore the process of attitude formation and the factors that influence that process.

Appendix 15.1

Attitudes towards Dhivehi and English – Likert scale 1: Strongly Agree; 2: Agree; 3: Neutral; 4: Disagree; 5: Strongly Disagree

Statements	Mean	SD
I like Dhivehi better than I like English.	3.01	1.47
I like English better than I like Dhivehi.	1.91	.99
My real self comes out when I speak in Dhivehi.	2.42	1.35
My real self comes out when I speak in English.	2.21	1.30
It is essential for Maldivians to speak Dhivehi perfectly.	2.01	1.33
It is essential for Maldivians to speak English perfectly.	1.84	1.10
I use a mix of Dhivehi and English in my normal speaking.	2.07	1.31
I usually count in Dhivehi.	3.55	1.35
I usually count in English.	1.75	1.07
I usually tell the time in Dhivehi.	3.18	1.53
I usually tell the time in English.	2.01	1.25
I want to learn and be able to use Dhivehi better than now.	2.04	1.17
I want to learn and be able to use English better than now.	1.66	.94
When I am a parent I want my children to speak Dhivehi well.	1.91	1.11
When I am a parent I want my children to speak English well.	1.56	.93

References

Baker, Colin. 1992. *Attitudes and language*. Clevedon: Multilingual Matters.
Baker, Colin & Wayne E. Wright. 2017 [1993]. *Foundations of bilingual education and bilingualism*, 6th edn. Bristol: Multilingual Matters.
Bartram, Brendan. 2010. *Attitudes to modern foreign language learning: Insights from comparative education*. London: Continuum.
Blommaert, Jan. 2006. Language policy and national identity. In Thomas Ricento (ed.), *Language policy: Theory and method*, 238–254. Oxford: Blackwell Publishing.
Blommaert, Jan. 2010. *The sociolinguistics of globalization*. Cambridge: Cambridge University Press.
Bokhorst-Heng, Wendy D. & Imelda Santos Caleon. 2008. The language attitudes of bilingual youth in multilingual Singapore. *Journal of Multilingual and Multicultural Development* 30 (3). 235–251.
Bourdieu, Pierre. 1992. Thinking about limits. *Theory, Culture & Society* 9 (1). 37–49.
Bourdieu, Pierre. 1997. The forms of capital. In Albert Henry Halsey, Hugh Lauder, Phillip Brown & Amy Stuart Wells (eds.), *Education, culture, economy and society*, 46–58. Oxford: Oxford University Press.
Braun, Virginia & Victoria Clarke. 2006. Using thematic analysis in psychology. *Qualitative Research in Psychology* 3 (2). 77–101.

Bucholtz, Mary & Kira Hall. 2005. Identity and interaction: A sociocultural linguistic approach. *Discourse Studies* 7 (4–5). 585–614.

Buschfeld, Sarah & Alexander Kautzsch. 2017. Towards an integrated approach to postcolonial and non-postcolonial Englishes. *World Englishes* 36 (1). 104–126.

Busse, Vera. 2017. Plurilingualism in Europe: Exploring attitudes toward English and other European languages among adolescents in Bulgaria, Germany, the Netherlands, and Spain. *Modern Language Journal* 101 (3). 566–582.

Canagarajah, Suresh. 2005. Dilemmas in planning English/vernacular relations in post-colonial communities. *Journal of Sociolinguistics* 9. 418–447.

Cargile, Aaron C., Howard Giles, Ellen B. Ryan & James J. Bradac. 1994. Language attitudes as a social process: A conceptual model and new directions. *Language and Communication* 14 (3). 211–236.

Coleman, Hywel (ed.). 2015. *Language and social cohesion in the developing world*. Colombo: British Council. www.teachingenglish.org.uk/sites/teacheng/files/pub_language%20and%20social%20cohesion.pdf (accessed 20 January 2022).

Coupland, Nikolas. 2014. Language change, social change, sociolinguistic change: A meta-commentary. *Journal of Sociolinguistics* 18 (2). 277–286.

Craith, Máiréad Nic. 2007. *Language, power and identity politics*. Basingstoke: Palgrave Macmillan.

Cunningham Una & Jeanette King. 2018. *Language, ethnicity, and belonging for the children of migrants in New Zealand*. SAGE Open 8 (2). 1–11.

Dörnyei, Zoltán & Kata Csizér. 2005. The effects of intercultural contact and tourism on language attitudes and language learning motivation. *Journal of Language and Social Psychology* 24 (4). 327–357.

Ehala, Martin & Katrin Niglas. 2006. Language attitudes of Estonian secondary school students. *Journal of Language, Identity, and Education* 5 (3). 209–227.

Fei, Wong Fook, Lee King Siong, Lee Su Kim & Azizah Yaacob. 2012. English use as an identity marker among Malaysian undergraduates. *The Southeast Asian Journal of English Language Studies*. 18 (11). 145–155.

Fishman, Joshua A. 1991. *Reversing language shift: Theoretical and empirical foundations of assistance to threatened languages*. Clevedon: Multilingual Matters.

Gardner, Robert. 1985. *Social psychology and second language learning. The role of attitudes and motivation*. London: Edward Arnold.

Garrett, Peter. 2010. *Attitudes to Language*. Cambridge: Cambridge University Press.

Giles, Howard, Richard Yvon Bourhis & Donald M. Taylor. 1977. Towards a theory of language in ethnic group relations. In Howard Giles (ed.), *Language, ethnicity, and intergroup relations*, 307–348. London: Academic Press.

Gnanadesikan, Amalia E. 2016. *Dhivehi. The language of the Maldives*. Berlin & Boston: De Gruyter Mouton.

Habib, Rania. 2016. Identity, ideology, and attitude in Syrian rural child and adolescent speech. *Linguistic Variation* 16 (1). 34–67.

Huang, Ju Chuan. 2011. Attitudes of Taiwanese scholars toward English and Chinese as languages of publication. *Asia Pacific Journal of Education* 31 (2). 115–128.

Jahan, Iffat & Obdaidul M. Hamid. 2019. English as a medium of instruction and the discursive construction of elite identity. *Journal of Sociolinguistics* 23 (4). 386–408.

Joseph, John E. 2016. Historical perspectives on language and identity. In Siân Preece (ed.), *The Routledge handbook of language and identity*, 19–33. Abingdon: Routledge.

Kachru, Braj. B. 1985. Standards, codification, and sociolinguistic realism: The English language in the Outer Circle. In Randolph Quirk & Henry Widdowson (eds.), *English in the world: Teaching and learning language and literatures*, 11–30. Cambridge: Cambridge University Press.

Kachru, Braj. B. 1997. World Englishes and English-using communities. *Annual Review of Applied Linguistics* 17. 66–87.

Kircher, Ruth. 2016. Language attitudes among adolescents in Montreal: Potential lessons for language planning in Québec. *Nottingham French Studies* 55 (2). 239–259.

Kramsch, Claire. 2021. *Language as symbolic power*. Cambridge: Cambridge University Press.

Kroskrity, Paul V. 1999. Identity. *Journal of Linguistic Anthropology* 9 (1–2). 111–114.

Kubota, Ryuko. 2016. The multi/plural turn, postcolonial theory, and neoliberal multiculturalism: Complicities and implications for applied linguistics. *Applied Linguistics* 37 (4). 474–494.

Ladegaard, Hans J. 2000. Language attitudes and sociolinguistic behaviour: Exploring attitude-behaviour relations in language. *Journal of Sociolinguistics* 4 (2). 214–233.

Lange, Claudia. 2019. English in South Asia. In Daniel Schreier, Marianne Hundt & Edgar W. Schneider (eds.), *The Cambridge handbook of World Englishes*, 236–262. Cambridge: Cambridge University Press.

Lanza, Elizabeth & Hirut Woldemariam. 2014. Indexing modernity: English and branding in the linguistic landscape of Addis Ababa. *International Journal of Bilingualism* 18 (5). 491–506.

Latheef, Mohamed & Amita Gupta. 2007. Schooling in Maldives. In Amita Gupta (ed.), *Going to school in South Asia*, 112–125. Westport: Greenwood Press.

Masgoret, Anne-Marie & Robert C. Gardner. 2003. Attitudes, motivation and second language learning: A meta-analysis of studies conducted by Gardner and associates. *Language Learning* 53 (1). 123–163.

May, Stephen. 2014. *The multilingual turn: Implications for SLA, TESOL and bilingual education*. New York: Routledge.

McCarty, Teresa, Mary Eunice Romero-Little, Larisa Warhol & Ofelia Zepeda. 2009. Indigenous youth as language policy makers. *Journal of Language, Identity, and Education* 8 (5). 291–306.

McKenzie, Robert & Erin Carrie. 2018. Implicit–explicit attitudinal discrepancy and the investigation of language attitude change in progress. *Journal of Multilingual and Multicultural Development* 39 (9). 830–844.

Meierkord, Christiane. 2018. English in paradise: The Maldives. *English Today* 34 (1). 1–10.

Mohamed, Naashia. 2019. From a monolingual to a multilingual nation: Analysing the language education policy in the Maldives. In Anthony J. Liddicoat & Andy Kirkpatrick (eds.), *The Routledge international handbook of language education policy in Asia*, 414–426. Abingdon: Routledge.

Mohamed, Naashia. 2020. First language loss and negative attitudes towards Dhivehi among young Maldivians: Is the English-first educational policy to blame? *TESOL Quarterly* 54 (3). 743–772.

Morrison, Keith & Icy Lui. 2000. Ideology, linguistic capital and the medium of instruction in Hong Kong. *Journal of Multilingual and Multicultural Development* 21 (6). 471–486.

National Bureau of Statistics. 2014. *Maldives population and housing census 2014*. Malé: Ministry of Finance and Treasury.

Norton, Bonny. 2013 [2000]. *Identity and language learning: Extending the conversation*, 2nd edn. Bristol: Multilingual Matters.

Norton, Bonny & Peter Ignatius De Costa. 2018. Research tasks on identity in language learning and teaching. *Language Teaching* 51 (1). 90–112.

Oyserman, Daphna, Kristen Elmore & George Smith. 2012 [2003]. Self, self-concept, and identity. In Mark R. Leary & June Price Tangney (eds.), *The handbook of self and identity*, 2nd edn., 69–104. New York: Guilford Press.

Pennycook, Alastair. 2002. Language policy and docile bodies: Hong Kong and governmentality. In James W. Tollefson (ed.), *Language policies in education: Critical issues*, 91–110. Mahwah: Lawrence Erlbaum Associates.

Pennycook, Alastair. 2010. The future of Englishes: One, many, or more? In Andy Kirkpatrick (ed.), *The Routledge handbook of World Englishes*, 673–688. Abingdon: Routledge.

Peterson, Elizabeth. 2020. *Making sense of bad English*. Abingdon: Routledge.

Preece, Siân. 2016. Introduction: Language and identity in applied linguistics. In Siân Preece (ed.), *The Routledge handbook of language and identity*, 1–16. Abingdon: Routledge.

Price, Abigail Ruth & Marco Tamburelli. 2020. Welsh-language prestige in adolescents: Attitudes in the heartlands. *International Journal of Applied Linguistic* 30 (2). 195–213.

Price, A. & Tamburelli, M. (2016). Minority language abandonment in Welsh-medium educated L2 male adolescents: Classroom, not chatroom. Language, Culture and Curriculum 29(2). 189–206.

Seidlhofer, Barbara. 2003. *Controversies in applied linguistics*. Oxford: Oxford University Press.

Sharma, Devyani. 2017. World Englishes and sociolinguistic Theory. In Markku Filppula, Juhani Klemola & Devyani Sharma (eds.), *The Oxford handbook of World Englishes*. Oxford, New York: Oxford University Press.

Sharma, D. (2016). Interaction: Talk and beyond Series Introduction. *Journal Of Sociolinguistics* 20 (3) 335–335. 10.1111/josl.12177

Sicam, Faith Patricia M. & Rochelle Irene G. Lucas. 2016. Language attitudes of adolescent Filipino bilingual learners towards English and Filipino. *Asian Englishes* 18 (2). 109–128.

Skutnabb-Kangas, Tove &Robert Phillipson. 1989. 'Mother tongue': The theoretical and sociopolitical construction of a concept. In Ulrich Ammon (ed.), *Status and function of languages and language varieties*, 450–477. Berlin & Boston: De Gruyter.

Sung, Chit Cheung Matthew. 2015. Exploring second language speakers' linguistic identities in ELF communication: A Hong Kong study. *Journal of English as a Lingua Franca* 4 (2). 309–332.

Tajfel, Henri. 1981. Social stereotypes and social groups. In John C. Turner & Howard Giles (eds.), *Intergroup Behavior*, 144–165. Oxford: Blackwell.

Thordardottir, Elin. 2021. National language in a globalised world: Are L1 and L2 adolescents in Iceland more interested in learning English than Icelandic? *Journal of Multilingual and Multicultural Development*.

Tracy, Karen. 2002. *Everyday talk: Building and reflecting identities*. New York: Guilford.

Tsui, Amy. 2005. Language policy, culture and identity in the era of globalization. In *International Association of Teachers of English as a Foreign Language (IATEFL) 2005 Conference Selections*, 41–51. Cardiff, 5–9 April.

Wodak, Ruth. 2012. Language, power and identity. *Language Teaching* 45 (2). 215–233.

Wright, Sue. 2004. *Language policy and language planning: From nationalism to globalisation*. London: Palgrave Macmillan.

Young, Richard. 2017. World languages, World Englishes and local identities. *World Englishes* 36 (4–5).

Zacharias, Nugrahenny T. 2012. EFL students' understanding of their multilingual English identities. *Electronic Journal of Foreign Language Teaching* 9 (2). 233–244.

Part IV: **Summary and discussion**

Simone E. Pfenninger
16 Conclusion and envoi: Language acquisition at the intersection of sociolinguistics and World Englishes research

1 Introduction

The current volume puts the integration of two research paradigms – World Englishes (WEs) and language acquisition research – on the theoretical and methodological agenda. This focus on how WEs research can inform studies on the acquisition of English by children in different acquisitional settings (and how acquisition research can inform the former) is long overdue and represents a site for more critical and holistic quantitative and qualitative analyses.

In the introduction of this book, the editors post some of the issues which an evolving theory and practice of WEs analysis needs to address: adopting an acquisition-inspired approach that has the potential of transforming the relationship between WEs research, sociolinguistics, studies on child first language (L1) acquisition and second language (L2) learning; shifting away from classifying and describing linguistic entities as static and clearly delimitable varieties (like Outer or Expanding Circle Englishes) to the evolution and development of these varieties; moving further toward socially and contextually sensitive mechanisms of analysis through a variety of psycholinguistic, corpus-linguistic, ethnographic, and sociolinguistic methodologies; and seeking to understand how the interacting parts of a linguistic system and the interaction of the system as a whole with other systems give rise to new patterns of behavior, variability, and change.

I return to some of these issues here, exploring current and ongoing challenges in investigating humans as inherently complex systems from a linguistic perspective. As Moulder, Martynova, and Boker (2022) rightly point out, the set of all emotions, behaviors, and cognitive processes that define individual human experiences at any given time is immense. Within different individuals, these defining factors are also sensitive to external influences – and they vary from person to person as well as within a single individual across time and context, and at both short and long-time scales. These compounding influences interact with one

---

Simone E. Pfenninger, University of Zurich, Switzerland

https://doi.org/10.1515/9783110733723-016

another to create multiple nonlinear relationships between all variables that define how an individual is experiencing life at any given moment. Such a discussion is particularly timely in WEs research in the light of the recent wave of language shifts towards English as an L1, which has reached many of the third diaspora L2 English-speaking former colonies of the British Empire (Buschfeld and Ronan, this volume). It is also a research agenda from which others can draw when capturing the complex acquisitional realities most children are faced with in today's globalizing and multilingual world. Specifically, in what follows, I will look at the aims of the book and highlight the converging findings. I will also discuss issues that surfaced in the analyses and call attention to questions which, it is hoped, future research can tackle.

2 Perspectival shifts in World Englishes and language acquisition research

At first glance, there appear to remain important differences between WEs and language acquisition research, foremost among these being the fundamental difference that language acquisition tends to focus on the cognitive and socio-psychological processes at the individual level of learners of English as an L1 or L2, while the WEs paradigm focuses on the language as used by a larger community of speakers – or, as Buschfeld and Schneider (this volume: 134) put it, "the products of societal language acquisition such as Singaporean English (SingE) and other postcolonial varieties of English". As such, WEs scholars have placed a premium on the second and third diaspora L2 English-speaking former colonies of the British Empire, where English is mainly acquired on the basis of contact-induced L2 language input. In second language acquisition (SLA) or L1 child language acquisition research, very few studies have investigated the acquisition of English in one of the L1 English-speaking settler communities. What is more, sociolinguistically informed studies of L1 and L2 acquisition constitute a rather recent development (see e.g. the field of second dialect acquisition). On the other hand, according to the contributors in this book, current models of the evolution of WEs do not explicitly address children and young adolescents despite the pivotal role they play in the diffusion of innovative linguistic variants in language and dialect contact situations.

This volume essentially argues that this difference may be overcome – or is, in fact, only a fundamental difference on a superficial level. After all, as Buschfeld and Schneider (this volume) note, the only differences lie in the particular contexts on which they focus and the stage of the language acquisition process with which they are mainly concerned. One could add that just like WEs scholars, language acquisition researchers also strive to model more general processes beyond the individual, such as cognitive functioning. Also, in both SLA research and the WEs paradigm, scholars have started conceptualizing phenomena as complex and dynamic, thus emphasizing the multiple elements and/or agents engaged in interaction in any given system as well as the continuous and often non-linear changes systems go through (see Section 3).

SLA and child bilingualism researchers can also profit from a joint approach as they often use convenience samples that are not representative of the immigrant population under investigation, as those samples are strongly biased toward the more educated (DeKeyser 2013). There may be good reasons for these practices (see e.g. Pfenninger and Singleton 2017), but they place severe limits on the statistical generalizability of the relevant findings – such as when a convenience sample, not obtained randomly, does not represent, for example, a variety of socioeconomic levels. As the editors point out in Chapter 1, WEs scholars who put these generalizations to the test by applying them to English in multilingual, multicultural, and heterogeneous contexts (e.g. in the global south) improves our understanding and representation of the current English(es) and the emerging new generation of English speakers. That said, such a joint approach requires willingness and ability on the part of WEs scholars and acquisition researchers to cross boundaries and unite with disparate conceptualizations and methodologies. The chapters in the current volume recognize the importance of this, as illustrated in the following examples.

Buschfeld and Schneider's (this volume) study is a good example that the individual-collective divide can be bridged and indeed needs to be bridged in order for us to fully understand the heterogeneity and development of the English language and the emergence of new generations of native speakers in formerly nonnative contexts. The authors compared the acquisition of English past tense marking by simultaneous bilingual English-Chinese children aged 2–12 in Singapore, Hong Kong, and the US, and monolingual children who acquired English in the US. Investigating data extracted from various corpora such as the CHEsS corpus (Children's English in Singapore; Buschfeld 2020) and the CHILDES database, Buschfeld and Schneider's findings suggest that important differences exist between past tense marking in the different scenarios, i.e. differences in the acquisitional outcome and route taken by new native speakers and traditional native speakers of English. This has important implications for language acquisition research, particularly SLA, where the fraught nature of "scrutinized nativelikeness," in the sense of monolingual nativelikeness, has been debated for decades (see e.g. Birdsong 2005). The criterion of "scrutinized nativelikeness" is faced with several major empirical objections. For instance, the notion of nativeness implies in its usual conception that there is a clearly defined level of language proficiency that characterizes native speakers; in reality, however, native speakers of a language display a considerable spectrum of divergence from the idealized norms that are supposed to be associated with them (Dąbrowska, Becker, and Miorelli 2020) – even "typical" L1 development does not result in a stable native language system (see Kasparian and Steinhauer 2017; Pakulak and Neville 2010; Tanner and Van Hell 2014). In part, this variability is due to the changes of the native language in response to learning and using an L2 (Bialystok and Kroll 2018; Perani and Abutalebi 2005). It has always been widely accepted that there are variable outcomes for L2 learning, particularly when it comes to multilinguals (Baum and Titone 2014; Bialystok and Kroll 2018; Pierce et al. 2017). As is clear from research into multicompetence and translanguaging, knowledge of every active language in a person's repertoire influences every other language in that repertoire, and so in a speaker of more than one language, "scrutinized nativelikeness" will quite simply never be found. According to Bialystok and Kroll (2018: 909) the "age of acquisition alone is insufficient to capture this variation," which resonates with Buschfeld and Schneider (this volume: 152), who conclude Chapter 7 by stating that the observed differences between the monolingual children, the Singaporeans, and the rest of the bilingual corpora "cannot be explained on the basis of age".

Another example of the integration of WEs and language acquisition research is Ronan and Buschfeld's Chapter 9, which brings together the results of two independent corpus studies – a synchronic investigation of the development of English from L2 to L1 in Singapore and a diachronic analysis of the mechanisms in the large-scale language shift in Ireland – both of which compared adult and child data to trace potential changes initiated by bilingual children in language contact and change scenarios. On the one hand, triangulation was used as an argument to seek convergence, corroboration, and correspondence of results from the two studies (and methods) and to obtain more valid conclusions about the role of children and adults in language change. Another purpose of the integration of the two studies was complementarity, as the Irish data was used to enhance and clarify the results from the Singapore study, or, in the authors' (this volume: 181) words, to "predict [. . .] the linguistic future of Singapore". Zooming in on subject pronoun realization, the Singapore study found that while zero subjects emerge as the result of language contact and naturalistic L2 acquisition in adult L2 Singapore English, these linguistic features in the child generation not only represent a salient feature in the input (including cross-linguistic influence from the other languages the children speak), but they also correspond to the typical characteristics of early language acquisition. Similarly, in child bilingualism research, Fernández, de Souza, and Carando (2017) suggest the following mechanisms: (1) Cross-linguistic interactions in (sequential) bilinguals leads to (2) changes in the L1 grammar as a function of exposure to the

L2, which in turn contributes to (3) long-term novel representations in the linguistic competence repositories. As for (1), SLA has a relatively well-established tradition of investigating the consequences that acquiring and regularly using an L2 may have on L1 and vice versa (Cook 2002; Pavlenko and Jarvis 2002). The (written) Irish English data set discussed in Chapter 9, where the focus was on perfect use (the *after*-perfect and the Medial Object Perfect, MOP), was then used to illustrate the endpoint of language shift, considering that Ireland has experienced large-scale language shift towards English. This potentially foreshadows the future of SingE, where the children in the school system are also confronted with the more standard realizations of the language and the governmental opposition to the nonstandard realizations of SingE. Idiosyncratic findings aside, their two studies have jointly uncovered evidence of a point earlier made in the diachronic linguistics literature (e.g. Thomason 2013): even if adults may be the primary innovators, an innovation will not become a change in a community's main language unless it is eventually acquired by children during L1 acquisition.

Chapter 8 (Regnoli and Brato) provides compelling evidence of how cross-fertilization of research fields can improve methodological rigor. Proceeding from the assumption that language contact between English and a syllable-timed language such as French leads to an emerging variety of English that is more syllable-timed than British English or American English (AmE), the authors carried out sociolinguistic interviews with 9 children aged 9–11 with different language backgrounds in an English-medium primary school in Yaoundé, Cameroon, so as to identify variability in the rhythm of Cameroon English. Despite the small sample size, they were able to detect fine-grained rhythmic differences between the children's group and the adults' group. Regnoli and Brato's (this volume: 171) study benefited from the integrative approach to both language acquisition and WEs research on the one hand, and WEs and variationist sociolinguistics on the other, inasmuch as their results pointed to "emerging bilingualism at the expense of the local languages". Importantly, the authors (this volume: 172) made some valuable remarks about the potentially problematic adoption of data collection methods tested in Western contexts, suggesting that "collection methods other than the Labovian approach should be taken into consideration in WEs research and should be informed by the language acquisition paradigm".

The status of languages is another illustration of the nexus of SLA and WEs. For instance, Hansen Edwards (this volume) analyzes what learners are acquiring and using (and resisting) in Hong Kong. Her work on the complex linguistic situation in Hong Kong makes us aware that any research on SLA within a WEs and/or multilingual context needs to examine the status of English vis-à-vis other languages in the language ecology, to understand the status and use of a local variety in that given context. Hansen Edwards' main argument is that there is a need to incorporate sociocultural, sociolinguistic, and socio-political theory into any framework of SLA to account for language acquisition and use within WEs and/or multilingual and multidialectal contexts, in particular language ecology shifts due to sociopolitical changes. She (this volume: 228) even goes as far as to argue for a new theoretical framework that "incorporates an analysis of the impact of social movements on youth language acquisition and use in multilingual societies".

Taking a slightly different approach to analyzing the "effects" of Content and Language Integrated Learning (CLIL) in a non-postcolonial context (Turkey) – a notoriously difficult enterprise – Köylü and Dikilitaş (this volume) decided to adopt Schneider's (2012) Dynamic Model. CLIL is a method in which school subjects are taught in a target language different from the mainstream school language, thereby extending foreign language exposure and providing a motivational basis for purposeful communication. Such an intensive language learning experience can lead to substantial progress in an L2 in a relatively short amount of time, for both children and adults and for early and late starters. The evidence, however, is conflicting in the SLA literature: while numerous studies (e.g. Dalton-Puffer 2011; Ruiz de Zarobe 2011) have confirmed the benefits conferred on CLIL/immersion learners versus non-CLIL learners, there has been some questioning of conclusions drawn from CLIL research (e.g. Bruton 2011; Cenoz, Genesee, and Gorter 2014). Particularly because of the diversity of CLIL programs and the lack of conceptual clarity, it has been difficult for SLA researchers to provide a clear characterization of CLIL programs. Drawing on learner varieties of English within the broader WEs paradigm allows Köylü and Dikilitaş to account for the lingua franca status of the target language (English as a lingua franca, ELF) in the setting in question, as well as the interplay between ELF and CLIL. Their results revealed that both CLIL and non-CLIL students displayed typical characteristics of learner Englishes as English as a Foreign Language (EFL), English as a Second Language (ESL), and ELF within the WEs paradigm: simplified vocabulary made of a large proportion of high-frequency words. Furthermore, the authors explain their non-significant differences between CLIL and non-CLIL classes in terms of Edwards' (2016) notion of "foundation-through-globalization". Reintroducing the "Foundation phase" of Schneider's Dynamic Model as "foundation through globalization," Edwards (2016) postulates that language contact appears in the ever-growing exposure to English through the internet, travel, and popular culture (in short: globalization) rather than through colonization in non-postcolonial countries.

In fact, many scholars in this volume emphasize the global status, ubiquity, and cachet of English as an international language, one that is heavily promoted by educational and other institutions as well as by popular culture, the internet, scientific knowledge mobilization, mass media communication, and social media. For instance, Jocuns and Jocuns (this volume) investigated family language policies promoting Thai and English elective bilingualism in Thailand, with a special emphasis on perceptions of the status of Thai English as a variety and the practices involved in using it. Thai English makes for an interesting case as it does not fit the standard English varieties model: "while features are identifiable, they most certainly are not uniform," according to Jocuns and Jocuns (this volume: 60). Thai speakers of English rarely speak to one another in English, which naturally has an impact on bilingual practices at home, as well as ideologies, attitudes, and identity construction (although the latter is not specifically examined in Chapter 4). All five families in Jocuns and Jocuns' (this volume: 77) study are acutely aware of the importance of English for their child's education, perceiving it a language that increases learning, opportunities, overall educational benefits, and, more generally, "a language that one cannot live without," although there were no conscious, official policies about language use in their homes, i.e. the implemented practices, were "fluid" rather than "fixed". Some parents reported a change in perception from seeing English as "a language of opportunity" to a "language of necessity" (Jocuns and Jocuns, this volume: 70). Importantly, Jocuns and Jocuns developed a complex theoretical framework that is sensitive to the intricate network of linguistic repertoires, discourses in place, and family language policies. To this end, they drew on nexus analysis (Scollon and Scollon 2004), which focuses on social action as a unit of analysis in a combination of ethnographically focused micro and macro data, global stances towards English (Rose and Galloway 2019), child bilingualism (notably insights from studies on child-directed speech, e.g. De Houwer 2020, 2021), and conceptualizations of multilingualism from the translanguaging literature (Blackledge and Creese 2010; García and Wei 2014).

Similarly, in Ong and Ting (this volume), we learn about parental home language policies and parental beliefs in Malaysia that influence children's simultaneous dual language acquisition in favor of English, an unofficial language which was introduced to Malaysia by the British in 1771. Initially perceived as "a vehicle for upward mobility" (Ong and Ting, this volume: 40), providing access to jobs in the civil service, and scholarships in the UK, English permeates many areas in today's Malaysian society. In Ong and Ting's descriptive case study, the children ended up speaking English as their main language irrespective of the Chinese-English bilingual language policy at home and despite their regular contact with Chinese dialects. Studies such as these are a good example of the phenomenon that the globalization of, and status enjoyed by, English in our otherwise richly multilingual world has a significant impact on socio-political ideologies and educational agendas at local, national, and transnational levels – and these ideologies and agendas in turn have inescapable repercussions for L1/L2 language learning motivation at the individual level. Indeed, the increasing stature and "market share" held by English in additional-language curricula and as a medium of education worldwide have perceived – and also real – consequences for the vitality and standing of many other languages and dialects (such as Chinese dialects in Malaysian society), and for interest in learning those languages, whether "big" or "small" (i.e., less commonly spoken or taught), indigenous, heritage, or "foreign". Within these socio-political and institutional structures, there may be different priorities accorded to different languages, and there may be more valued and less valued forms of bilingualism or multilingualism (in this connection, see Blommaert's (2011: 251) discussion of "multilingualism of the elite" vs. "multilingualism of the poor").

This resonates with Mohamed's Chapter 15 (this volume: 354, 349), which explores the extent of identity struggles present in Maldivian adolescents as they shift from their indigenous language Dhivehi, which they deem "dispensable" because they fail to see the economic value of the language, to the more globally powerful English language, which they consider to be "a passport". Drawing on data gathered from young people aged 12–17, Mohamed's chapter shows how adolescents in one of the world's smallest countries position themselves as a result of the English-mediated access they gain to the world. She cites Wright (2004), who cautioned that a laissez-faire approach towards ideologies and attitudes influencing children's beliefs and behaviors means that languages with power and prestige may take over in situations of contact: "Efforts to preserve the language can begin by understanding the attitudes young people have towards it and other languages used in the society, including English" (Mohamed, this volume: 336). This is important insofar as we can read in the SLA literature that attitudes are learned (i.e., influenced by the attitudes of others, such as parents, teachers, media) rather than innate (Masgoret and Gardner 2003).

Other chapters in this volume also conceptualize their studies within the framework of bilingual L1 acquisition – and many (e.g. Schmalz, this volume) emphasize that understanding language attitudes in young people is vital to gain insights into language change over time (see also Coupland 2014). Understanding the views and behaviors of young people is essential to appreciate their perceptions and attitudes, as well as their construction, negotiation, performing and accomplishing of self-attributed identities through discursive practices and in interaction with others, all of which can point to broader language change taking place (Blommaert 2006). That questions of language use in diaspora contexts are inevitably questions of language and identity is shown by Wilson (this volume), who investigated the use and awareness of selected Trinidadian and Standard American English phonological features and lexical items by Trinidadian-heritage children in the USA. The five participants aged 4–9 had become culturally hybrid, "living in the in-between," constructing an identity additional to the one they were immersed in and performing linguistically, "[f]or sounding Trinidadian is important to the children" (Wilson, this volume: 30). Wilson's study is also a great example of how group membership may fluctuate over time as social identity is shifting and complex. The parents of the children were acutely aware of "the effect of the AmE speech community" (attending school, joining Girl Scout troops, and playing on sports teams) on their children's speech (Wilson, this volume: 31). Similarly, in (child) bilingualism research, studies on "split, hybrid, mixed" (Menard-Warwick 2008: 635) identities and feelings of difference linked to language switching and shifting abound. For instance, Pavlenko (2006: 29) points out that many bi- and multilinguals "perceive the world differently, and change perspectives, ways of thinking, and verbal and non-verbal behaviours when switching languages". While some of them may enjoy their hybridity and the relativity of their existence, others still "may feel that they inhabit distinct and at times incommensurable lifeworlds and experience pain and anguish over this condition" (Pavlenko 2006: 29).

Similarly, Chapter 12 (Vowell, this volume) focuses on a population of temporary migrants who have received very little attention in the field of WEs, that is, Third Culture Kids (TCKs). Using sociolinguistic interviews with seven children and adolescents between 5 and 18 years old who have grown up as TCKs in Hong Kong, Vowell analyzes the results against the backdrop of theories from the fields of TCK research, second dialect acquisition, new dialect formation, and WEs. This allows her to identify the varying degrees of multiple influences reflected in her participants' speech; she (this volume: 274) concludes accordingly: "the cultural homelessness experienced by TCKs is reflected in their linguistic homelessness" as they use features from a mixture of sources. Second dialect acquisition research sheds light on Vowell's (this volume: 275) observation that "older children acquired more localized lexical items" in that older age has been found to provide an advantage for the acquisition of localized lexical features in the SDA literature (Starr et al. 2017).

One ramification of the various inter- and transdisciplinary studies in this volume is an increasing awareness of the need for a broader focus in phenomenological conception and research, which helps curb the linguistic fields' tendency to perpetuate their comfortable narrowness. Another potential effect is a realization of the need to view phenomena as part of a larger system where multiple forces mutually interact, adapt, and constrain. A further consequence is an evolving perception of the need to transcend the fields' internal and external "boundaries" and to seek collaboration in order to achieve systems thinking.

3 Focus shifts from states and products to dynamic processes

As the editors write in Chapter 1, the field of WEs has been complexified and widened in scope by including new speaker groups. Specifically, efforts have been made to account for the ever-increasing *dynamism* of the diffusion of English into new territories and contexts. For instance, what has been identified as problematic about Kachru's (1985) Three Circles model is that it is too static, imprecise, and superficial, i.e. it captures neither the heterogeneity of speech groups, nor transitions from one type of English to another, and does not account for diachronic developments (Buschfeld, Kautzsch, and Schneider 2018). This is where Schneider's (2003, 2007) Dynamic Model comes in, which has received wide acclaim and application in the WEs literature, although some suggestions for modifications and extensions have been made (Buschfeld and Kautzsch 2017). The investigation of English as a dynamic and evolving concept has offered a new understanding of the nature and role of English around the globe, which is one of the reasons for the development of Buschfeld and Kautzsch's Extra- and Intra-Territorial Forces Model (EIF Model; 2017).

The study of L2 acquisition has also significantly evolved in line with the person-in-context view and dynamically oriented approaches to L2 learning, most notably complex dynamic systems theory (CDST, see e.g. Hiver and Al-Hoorie 2019; Larsen-Freeman and Cameron 2008; Verspoor, Lowie, and van Dijk 2008). While not all acquisition researchers subscribe to CDST approaches, the insight that interactions between the variables that contribute to the explanation of SLA often go beyond rigid linear relationships will hardly be disputed anymore. What is more, SLA researchers have long questioned treating individual learner differences as modular, stable, and context-independent traits (see Serafini 2017), arguing for consideration of the multiple ways individual differences and their sub-components dynamically interact with one another and with the external environment.

It is thus not surprising that several chapters in this volume aim to draw on key conceptual insights and methodological tools afforded by an ecological perspective in order to elucidate the complex ways that patterns of language variation, use and acquisition develop over time through dynamic, reciprocal interactions with context, conceived on both micro- and macrolevels. Describing the world of Third Culture Kids, Vowell (this volume) refers to Blommaert's (2013: 10) point that superdiversity – a characteristic of the TCK environment according to Vowell – "is driven by three keywords: mobility, complexity and unpredictability". Furthermore, complex systems are characterized by patterns and mechanisms of change that occur on various interdependent time scales, such as short-term versus long-term processes (van Geert 2008; van Geert and Fischer 2009). For language this means that change at the individual level may be a relatively short-term change, but at the speech community level it might represent a relatively long-term change. It is likely that the two levels are related to one another, in that developmental changes at the individual level are related to historical changes in language and vice versa.

Meer (this volume) investigated sociophonetic variation and change in adolescent and adult speakers of Trinidadian English, the English spoken in the Caribbean island of Trinidad (100 speakers, 65 students aged 14–25 and 35 teachers aged 56–65 in nine secondary schools). One of the surprising findings of his study is that the American English influence – e.g. through stays in North America – is unlikely to be the only reason for increasing levels of rhotacization in apparent time: "Apart from popular exonormative associations with 'Americanness,' it is conceivable that locally created, endonormative meanings of the feature with very positive connotations – 'educatedness,' 'ambition,' or 'upward social mobility' – might lead younger speakers associated with prestige schools to adopt NURSE-rhotacization, especially perhaps in more formal or conscious speaking styles as observed here" (Meer, this volume: 302). Both macro-level social variables such as age, gender, prestige, and style and micro-social variables such as speaker-specific effects had predictive power in explaining variation and change in NURSE-rhotacization. This exemplifies the usefulness of linear mixed effects regression models, which have been extensively applied in SLA (see Pfenninger and Neuser 2019 for a discussion of this).

Other studies such as Schmalz's (this volume: 209) analysis of the changes in the norm orientation in 62 10- to 14-year-old children in St. Kitts in the Eastern Caribbean are asking similar questions about so-called "complex attitudinal situations," i.e. situations that are "complex both concerning the attitudes towards the locally spoken Creole varieties, as well as the different varieties of English". Schmalz's results demonstrate, inter alia, an attitudinal change in process towards more pronounced levels of "multinormativity," which, according to Meer and Deuber (2020: 288), is defined as "a stable and systematic multidimensional orientation involving several coexisting norms" in which no single "standard emerged as a superordinate norm" (2020: 281). Schmalz's work makes us aware that language attitudes of speakers of all age groups need to be taken into consideration to understand changes in norm orientation better. This is particularly important in the light of the ever-changing re-negotiations of the status of exonormative and endonormative varieties (see also Hackert 2016) and their dynamic, reciprocal interaction with context.

Such observations cry out for more longitudinal studies that allow the modelling of the dynamic acquisition processes and show the way in which variation at a single point in time is tied to longitudinal development – ideally including repeated measurements and a high density of observations relative to the rate of change in order to reveal the degree and patterns of variability. In this connection, researchers working within a complexity tradition in SLA have promoted the use of longitudinal quantitative analyses using intensively sampled natural language data from a small number of learners (e.g. Verspoor and Behrens 2011). As mentioned above, L2 development often proceeds nonlinearly, which makes it important to demonstrate the path the metric follows over the course of development, collecting multiple data points per learner over a period of time. Overall, SLA studies have shown that longitudinal datasets prove critical to unveiling the dynamics of interactions, shedding light, in particular, on how the micro ecosystem provide affordances (or lack thereof) for linguistic and pragmatic synchrony, social solidarity, and, not least, creative expressions and adaptations of one's linguistic and cultural identity. To give an example from this book, Hansen Edwards (this volume) analyzed longitudinal data obtained over a period of 6 years via 2000 surveys and 60 interviews with young adults aged 15–36+, trying to capture the complex interplay among language(s) (varieties), attitudes, identity, and politics that is unfolding in Hong Kong as the political landscape changes. Including multiple measurements between 2014 and 2020 allows her to observe a period of rapid change in acceptance of Hong Kong English (HKE) in Hong Kong, which can only be explained when considering both the changing status and role of English vis-à-vis Cantonese, English, and Putonghua within Hong Kong's sociopolitical context and language policies, attitudes towards the colonizing power, and sociodemographic background.

The findings outlined in this envoi also illustrate how systems are nested within each other, and how we can investigate them at any level of granularity, from the micro-level of neurons in the human brain to the macro-level of human society and anything in between. Accordingly, it is argued in the SLA literature that we can only investigate the development of an individual's language system(s) in a meaningful way if we consider the elements that constitute the system itself, its interactions with other characteristics of the individual, and the context in which the individual functions. For instance, in language, linguistic subsystems interact, but they also interact with non-linguistic systems, such as the social and physical context in which they are used (van Geert and Verspoor 2015). Interdependency means that connected components cannot be treated as independent variables or independent components; for example, a child's current linguistic skill is dependent on the environment.

Along those lines, Vida-Mannl (this volume) focuses on the role of, perceived, and actual use and acquisition of English(es) in Singapore, investigating the dynamics and complex interactions of language ideologies and their reproduction within a society, the social groups that immediately affect the prestige, and contexts of use of English, including policymakers, teachers, and parents who are naturally concerned with the practical or theoretical implementations of L1 or L2 acquisition. Vida-Mannl thus includes a wealth of influences, notably the home language of the families under study, the L1(s) of the caretakers and their children, as well as their age, sex, ethnicity, highest level of education, and current occupation. Her analysis of parental statements concerning their home language use and their children's language acquisition, use, and exposure to English in Singapore relies on frequencies, statistical independence, and conditional inference trees to show interrelations and dependencies between the three dependent variables (use, acquisition, and exposure to English(es) in Singapore) and twelve independent variables. Relating complexity to the perspectives in this chapter, the individuals (perceived) language use can be seen as a complex adaptive system at the micro level, as can interpretations, attitudes, and beliefs about properties, meanings, functions, and use of (a) communal language at the macro level. Governmental language policy influences the language attitudes of Singaporeans and causes the reproduction of language ideologies at the meso level, i.e. on a societal and domestic level. This offers a holistic framework for investigating micro and macro level analyses.

Framed in the context of attitudinal and social indexing decisions, Dollinger, Chan, Pasula, and Maag (this volume: 309) focus on the "social dynamics of language use" by studying the linguistic tolerance of 6- to 12-year-old children in Western Canada – a notoriously under-researched age group in sociolinguistic studies on linguistic insecurity, linguistic tolerance, and social evaluations and judgements of accented speech. Via a written questionnaire completed by 87 respondents (65 children and 22 adults) who rated accents of Cantonese, Mandarin, Finnish, and East Indian origin as opposed to Standard Canadian English as the dominant accent, the authors found that 7-year-olds displayed more linguistic tolerance than their adult comparative samples, while the 8- to 9-year-olds were the least tolerant of all age groups. Appreciation of non-standard accents is thus a highly dynamic phenomenon and influenced by a variety of linguistic variables, such as multilingualism, socio-affective variables, such as identity formation, and contextual variables, for instance the onset of mandatory schooling.

Studies such as these make us aware that multilingual proficiency is dynamic, and language systems influence each other in multilingual cognition, and beyond that, like other complex systems they interact with their environment. For language systems at any scale, the crucial environments are social. Once we accept the need to contextualize our analysis, we have to face the issue of the size and type of environment we admit into our framework. Furthermore, we have to ask ourselves what the contextual factors are that are part of the environmental frame of reference for the system in question, its dynamic actions, and its patterned outcomes. How can we define, delimit, and empirically capture what is meant by context at all (see also Ushioda 2015).

Against this backdrop, the present volume has made important inroads into the issues raised by the editors in Chapter 1. Recognizing the complexity of WEs, scholars, sociolinguists, and language acquisition researchers alike are turning to correspondingly sophisticated methods to analyze and statistically evaluate data, as several chapters in this book demonstrate. With advancing statistical techniques, linguists can study important relationships between linguistic processes, features, and forms that conform to the main premises of complexity theories.

References

Baum, Shari & Debra Titone. 2014. Moving toward a neuroplasticity view of bilingualism, executive control, and aging. *Applied Psycholinguistics* 35 (5). 857–894.
Bialystok, Ellen & Judith F. Kroll. 2018. Can the critical period be saved? A bilingual perspective. *Bilingualism: Language and Cognition* 21 (5). 908–910.
Birdsong, David. 2005. Interpreting age effects in second language acquisition. In Judith F. Kroll & Annette M. B. de Groot (eds.), *Handbook of bilingualism: Psycholinguistic approaches*, 109–127. New York: Oxford University Press.
Blackledge, Adrian & Angela Creese. 2010. *Multilingualism: A critical perspective*. London & New York: Bloomsbury Academic.
Blommaert, Jan. 2006. Language policy and national identity. In Thomas Ricento (ed.), *An introduction to language policy: Theory and method*, 238–254. Oxford: Blackwell Publishing.
Blommaert, Jan. 2011. The long language-ideological debate in Belgium. *Journal of Multicultural Discourses* 6 (3). 241–256.
Blommaert, Jan. 2013. *Chronicles of complexity: Ethnography, superdiversity and linguistic landscapes* (Critical Language and Literacy Studies 18). Bristol: Multilingual Matters.
Bruton, Anthony. 2011. Is CLIL so beneficial, or just selective? Re-evaluating some of the research. *System* 39 (4). 523–532.
Buschfeld, Sarah. 2020. *Children's English in Singapore: Acquisition, properties, and use*. Oxon & New York: Routledge.
Buschfeld, Sarah & Alexander Kautzsch. 2017. Towards an integrative approach to postcolonial and non-postcolonial Englishes. *World Englishes* 36 (1). 104–126.
Buschfeld, Sarah, Alexander Kautzsch & Edgar W. Schneider. 2018. From colonial dynamism to current transnationalism: A unified view on postcolonial and non-postcolonial Englishes. In Sandra C. Deshors (ed.), *Modeling World Englishes: Assessing the interplay of emancipation and globalization of ESL varieties*, 15–44. Amsterdam: John Benjamins.
Cenoz, Jasone, Fred Genesee & Durk Gorter. 2014. Critical analysis of CLIL: Taking stock and looking forward. *Applied Linguistics* 35 (3). 243–262.
Cook, Vivian J. 2002. Background to the L2 user. In Vivian J. Cook (ed.), *Portraits of the L2 User*, 1–28. Clevedon, UK: Multilingual Matters.
Coupland, Nikolas. 2014. Language change, social change, sociolinguistic change: A meta-commentary. *Journal of Sociolinguistics* 18 (2). 277–286.

Dąbrowska, Ewa, Laura Becker & Luca Miorelli. 2020. Is adult second language acquisition defective? *Frontiers in Psychology* 11.

Dalton-Puffer, Christiane. 2011. Content-and-language integrated learning: From practice to principles. *Annual Review of Applied Linguistics* 31. 182–204.

De Houwer, Annick. 2020. Harmonious bilingualism: Well-being for families in bilingual settings. In Andrea C. Schalley & Susana A. Eisenchlas (eds.), *Handbook of Home Language Maintenance and Development: Social and Affective Factors*, 63–83. Berlin & Boston: De Gruyter Mouton.

De Houwer, Annick. 2021. *Bilingual development in childhood*, 1st edn. Cambridge University Press.

DeKeyser, Robert M. 2013. Age effects in second language learning: Stepping stones toward better understanding. *Language Learning* 63 (Supplement 1). 52–67.

Edwards, Alison. 2016. *English in the Netherlands: Functions, forms and attitudes* (Varieties of English Around the World G56). Amsterdam: John Benjamins.

Fernández, Eva M., Ricardo Augusto de Souza & Agustina Carando. 2017. Bilingual innovations: Experimental evidence offers clues regarding the psycholinguistics of language change. *Bilingualism: Language and cognition* 20 (2). 251–268.

García, Ofelia & Li Wei. 2014. *Translanguaging: Language, bilingualism and education*. New York: Palgrave Pivot.

Hackert, Stephanie. 2016. Standards of English in the Caribbean: History, attitudes, functions, features. In Elena Seoane & Cristina Suárez-Gómez (eds.), *World Englishes: New theoretical and methodological considerations*, 85–112. Amsterdam: John Benjamins.

Hiver, Phil & Ali H. Al-Hoorie. 2019. *Research methods for complexity theory in applied linguistics*. Bristol: Multilingual Matters.

Kachru, Braj B. 1985. Standards, codification and sociolinguistic realism: The English language in the Outer Circle. In Randolph Quirk & Henry G. Widdowson (eds.), *English in the world: Teaching and learning the language and literatures*, 11–30. Cambridge: Cambridge University Press.

Kasparian, Kristina & Karsten Steinhauer. 2017. When the second language takes the lead: Neurocognitive processing changes in the first language of adult attriters. *Frontiers in Psychology* 8.

Larsen-Freeman, Diane & Lynne Cameron. 2008. Research methodology on language development from a complex systems perspective. *The Modern Language Journal* 92 (2). 200–213.

Masgoret, Anne-Marie & Robert C. Gardner. 2003. Attitudes, motivation and second language learning: A meta-analysis of studies conducted by Gardner and Associates. *Language Learning* 53 (1). 123–163.

Meer, Philipp & Dagmar Deuber. 2020. Standard English in Trinidad: Multinormativity, translocality, and implications for the Dynamic Model and the EIF Model. In Sarah Buschfeld & Alexander Kautzsch (eds.), *Modelling world Englishes: A joint approach to postcolonial and non-postcolonial varieties*, 274–297. Edinburgh: Edinburgh University Press.

Menard-Warwick, Julia (2008). The Cultural and Intercultural Identities of Transnational English Teachers: Two Case Studies from the Americas. *TESOL Quarterly* 42 (4). 617–640.

Moulder, Robert G., Elena Martynova & Steven M. Boker. 2022. Extracting nonlinear dynamics from psychological and behavioral time series through HAVOK analysis. *Multivariate Behavioral Research*.

Pakulak, Erik & Helen J. Neville. 2010. Proficiency differences in syntactic processing of monolingual native speakers indexed by event-related potentials. *Journal of Cognitive Neuroscience* 22 (12). 2728–2744.

Pavlenko, Aneta. 2006. Bilingual selves. In Aneta Pavlenko (ed.), *Bilingual minds: Emotional experience, expression, and representation*, 1–33. Clevedon: Multilingual Matters.

Pavlenko, Aneta & Scott Jarvis. 2002. Bidirectional transfer. *Applied Linguistics* 23 (2). 190–214.

Perani, Daniela & Jubin Abutalebi. 2005. The neural basis of first and second language processing. *Current Opinion in Neurobiology* 15 (2). 202–206.

Pfenninger, Simone E. & David Singleton. 2017. *Beyond age effects in instructional L2 learning: Revisiting the age factor.* Bristol: Multilingual Matters.

Pfenninger, Simone E. & Hannah Neuser. 2019. Inferential statistics in data analysis. In Heath Rose & Jim McKinley (eds.), *The Routledge handbook of research methods in applied linguistics.* New York: Routledge.

Pierce, Lara J., Fred Genesee, Audrey Delcenserie & Gary Morgan. 2017. Variations in phonological working memory: Linking early language experiences and language learning outcomes. *Applied Psycholinguistics* 38 (6). 1265–1300.

Rose, Heath & Nicola Galloway. 2019. *Global Englishes for language teaching*, 1st edn. Cambridge: Cambridge University Press.

Ruiz de Zarobe, Yolanda. 2011. Which language competencies benefit from CLIL? An insight into applied linguistics research. In Yolanda Ruiz de Zarobe, Juan Manuel Sierra & Francisco Gallardo del Puerto (eds.), *Content and foreign language integrated learning: Contributions to multilingualism in European contexts*, 129–154. Bern: Peter Lang.

Schneider, Edgar W. 2003. The dynamics of New Englishes: From identity construction to dialect birth. *Language* 79 (2). 233–281.

Schneider, Edgar W. 2007. *Postcolonial English: Varieties around the world.* Cambridge: Cambridge University Press.

Schneider, Edgar W. 2012. Exploring the interface between World Englishes and second language acquisition – and implications for English as a lingua franca. *Journal of English as a Lingua Franca* 1 (1). 57–91.

Scollon, Ron & Suzie Wong Scollon. 2004. *Nexus analysis: Discourse and the emerging Internet.* New York: Routledge.

Serafini, Ellen J. 2017. Exploring the dynamic long-term interaction between cognitive and psychosocial resources in adult second language development at varying proficiency. *Modern Language Journal* 101 (2). 369–390.

Starr, Rebecca Lurie, Andre Joseph Theng, Kevin Martens Wong, Natalie Jing Yi Tong, Nurul Afiqah Bte Ibrahim, Alicia Mei Yin Chua, Clarice Hui Min Yong, Frances Wei Loke, Helen Dominic, Keith Jayden Fernandez & Matthew Tian Jing Peh. 2017. Third culture kids in the Outer Circle: The development of sociolinguistic knowledge among local and expatriate children in Singapore. *Language in Society* 46 (4). 507–546.

Tanner, Darren & Janet G. Van Hell. 2014. ERPs reveal individual differences in morphosyntactic processing. *Neuropsychologia* 56. 289–301.

Thomason, Sarah G. 2013. Innovation and contact: The role of adults (and children). In Daniel Schreier and Marianne Hundt (eds.), *English as a contact language*, 283–297. Cambridge: Cambridge University Press.

Ushioda, Ema. 2015. Context and complex dynamic systems theory. In Zoltán Dörnyei, Peter D. MacIntyre & Alastair Henry (eds.), *Motivational dynamics in language learning*, 47–54. Bristol, England: Multilingual Matters.

Van Geert, Paul. 2008. Nonlinear complex dynamical systems in developmental psychology. In Stephen J. Guastello, Matthijs Koopmans & David Pincus (eds.), *Chaos and complexity in psychology: The theory of nonlinear dynamic systems*, 242–281. Cambridge: Cambridge University Press.

Van Geert, Paul & Kurt W. Fischer. 2009. Dynamic systems and the quest for individual-based models of change and development. In John P. Spencer, Michael S. C. Thomas & James L. McClelland (eds.), *Toward a unified theory of development: Connectionism and dynamic systems theory reconsidered*, 313–336. Oxford: Oxford University Press.

Van Geert, Paul & Marjolijn Verspoor. 2015. Dynamic systems and language development. In Brian MacWhinney and William O'Grady (eds.), *The handbook of language emergence*, 1st edn., 537–556. Sussex: John Wiley & Sons, Inc.

Verspoor, Marjolijn, Wander Lowie & Marijn van Dijk. 2008. Variability in second language development from a dynamic systems perspective. *The Modern Language Journal* 92 (2). 214–231.

Verspoor, Marjolijn H. & Heike Behrens. 2011. Dynamic systems theory and a usage-based approach to second language development. In Marjolijn H. Verspoor, Kees de Bot & Wander Lowie (eds.), *A dynamic approach to second language development: Methods and techniques*, 25–38. Amsterdam: John Benjamins.

Wright, Sue. 2004. *Language policy and language planning: From nationalism to globalisation*. London: Palgrave Macmillan.

Index

accent 7, 14, 15, 22, 30, 31, 71, 73–77, 207, 212, 213, 215, 216, 221, 273, 284, 308, 310–312, 315, 317, 319–323, 326, 328–330, 350, 352, 373
acoustic phonetic analysis 160, 161, 284, 288–290, 292–293, 299–300, 302
acquisition 3–5, 7, 30, 38, 41, 42, 49, 64, 78, 86, 88–95, 100–104, 134–139, 142, 144, 147, 149–154, 164, 171, 172, 178, 181, 187, 199, 205–208, 227, 249, 256, 258, 272–276, 312, 361–364, 368–374
– acquisitional settings 134, 138, 139, 153, 361
– bilingual first language acquisition 41, 42, 187
– first language acquisition 2, 3, 41, 92, 154, 185, 187
– language acquisition 2–7, 14–16, 38, 41, 53, 61, 62, 72, 84, 86, 89, 92, 94, 101–106, 120, 128, 133–154, 163, 164, 171, 172, 178, 181, 183, 185–188, 197, 200, 227–251, 361–374
– second dialect acquisition (SDA) 3, 256, 258, 264, 272, 274–276, 362, 369
– second language acquisition (SLA) 2–4, 7, 84, 120, 127, 139, 163, 187, 227, 228, 245–251, 362, 363, 365, 366, 368, 370–372
adolescent peak 281–282, 301
African Englishes 6, 17, 18, 33, 134, 137, 159, 164, 170
after-perfect 189–194, 365
age-grading 185, 186, 198, 221

bilingualism 45, 51, 53, 54, 59–65, 68, 71, 77, 78, 89, 139, 151, 165, 171, 180, 191, 198, 199, 208, 235, 239, 244, 247–249, 251, 363–365, 367–369
– bilingual 4, 5, 41–43, 47, 49, 52, 63–66, 103, 134–136, 138–141, 145, 147, 149, 152, 160, 164, 171, 191, 197–199, 233–238, 244, 245, 309, 367
– bilingual children 4, 43, 47, 49, 52, 62–64, 136, 139, 143, 145, 151, 153, 178, 364
– bilingual language acquisition 41, 62, 73, 77, 139, 197
– bilingual parenting 64
– elective bilingualism 59–63, 68, 76–78, 367

Cameroon English (CamE) 6, 159–172, 179, 365
Canada 6, 7, 13, 15, 19, 208, 280, 287, 291, 307–331, 340, 348, 373
– Canadian English 15, 75, 308, 315, 318, 319, 321, 325, 328, 329, 373
Caribbean 6, 13–16, 20–22, 30–32, 163, 205, 206, 209–211, 213, 215–218, 220–222, 280–282, 303, 371
– Caribbean diaspora 13–16, 21, 22, 30, 32, 33
Children 1–7, 13–33, 37–54, 62–63, 65, 67–73, 75–78, 83–106, 133–141, 143–147, 149, 151–154, 160, 162–172, 178–183, 185–188, 197–199, 205–222, 229, 255, 256–259, 261, 264, 268, 269, 272–276, 307–331, 336, 346, 347, 355, 361–369, 371, 373
– child-directed speech 136, 145, 163
– child language 4, 5, 33, 61, 62, 84, 101–105, 133–154, 179, 181, 362
– early childhood literacy practices 61
Chinese 4, 5, 37–54, 75, 87–91, 93, 99, 134–143, 146, 147, 149, 151–153, 179, 181–183, 212, 229–233, 235–244, 247, 251, 363, 367, 368
– Chinese descendant 37–54
– Chinese dialects 38–40, 43, 45–48, 50–53, 90, 367, 368
CLIL. *See* Content and Language Integrated Learning (CLIL)
code-mixing 42, 43, 47, 48, 52, 53
complexity 5, 7, 111–129, 139, 192–194, 209, 228, 258, 370, 372–374
– lexical complexity 5, 111–129
– syntactic complexity 5, 111–129
conditional inference tree (ctree) 92–93, 142, 147–150, 182, 183, 186, 193, 194, 196, 291, 296–298, 373
Content and Language Integrated Learning (CLIL) 5, 111–129, 366
corpus linguistics 4, 117, 128, 133, 140, 145, 280, 283, 361
Creole 4, 14–16, 30, 31, 208–210, 212, 213, 215–217, 219–221, 282, 283
ctree. *See* conditional inference tree (ctree)

data collection 3, 23, 67, 68, 114, 121, 128, 154, 172, 234, 241, 313, 342, 365
– elicitation 6, 20, 140, 164, 181, 319
– gamified approach 164, 307–331
– matched guise 307–331, 341
– open-ended questionnaires 43, 45, 230
– questionnaire 4, 43, 91, 214, 313, 342
– story telling tasks 22–24, 141
– word list task 115, 123, 164, 272, 288
Dhivehi 7, 336, 338, 342–355, 368
diachronic turn 2, 35, 200, 364, 370
dialect 3, 14–16, 38–40, 43, 45–48, 50–53, 62, 90, 163, 186, 192–197, 208, 211, 212, 249, 251, 256–259, 272–276, 312, 319, 324, 336, 362, 367–369
– dialect awareness 48, 51, 208, 368–369
– dialect maintenance in the family 38, 45–47, 62
domains 5, 7, 38–41, 45–52, 63, 117, 124, 137, 209, 210, 282, 285, 301, 316, 330, 338, 341, 351
Dynamic Model 2, 112, 138, 162, 228, 248–251, 260, 275, 366, 370

EFL. *See* English as a Foreign Language (EFL)
EIF Model. *See* Extra-and Intra-territorial Forces Mode, extra-and intra-territorial forces (EIF)
ELF. *See* English as a Lingua Franca (ELF)
English as a Foreign Language (EFL) 1, 5, 68, 111–129, 312, 366
English as a Lingua Franca (ELF) 1, 5, 60, 67, 68, 111–129, 312, 366
English language learning 38, 39, 44, 45, 49–51, 62, 68–70, 118, 250, 337, 349, 352, 353
ethnic language 38, 39, 41, 51, 87–93, 179–180
Extra-and Intra-territorial Forces Mode 2, 210, 249, 251, 260, 264, 275, 370
– extra-and intra-territorial forces (EIF) 256, 260, 370

family 4, 5, 16, 38, 41, 45–47, 50, 59–78, 88, 147, 257, 273, 275, 297, 308, 326, 340, 343, 344, 351, 366, 367

Global Englishes 5, 41, 59–78, 105, 260, 367
globalisation 33, 38, 260, 336, 337, 354
global north 3
global south 3, 4, 363

Hong Kong 4–6, 43, 46, 66, 134, 138–142, 147, 151–153, 227–251, 255–276, 285, 321, 341, 363, 365, 369, 372
– Hong Kong English (HKE) 6, 138, 227, 233, 239–251, 256, 259–260, 262–265, 272, 274, 275, 372

ICE corpora. *See* International Corpus of English (ICE)
identity 6, 7, 14–16, 24, 29–33, 39, 40, 44, 45, 138, 221, 227–251, 257, 312, 316–319, 324–325, 335–355, 367–369, 372, 373
indigenous (IDG) community 1, 18, 39, 41, 160, 260, 309, 336, 353, 368
Inner Circle 1, 212, 256, 258, 260, 340, 348, 350, 352
International Corpus of English (ICE) 2, 178, 180–182, 185
international school 257–260, 262, 264, 273
Intra- and Extra Territorial Forces Model 2, 370
IrE. *See* Irish English (IrE)
Irish English (IrE) 178–179, 188–196, 198, 365
island 19, 87, 206, 208, 210–212, 220, 281–282, 288, 337, 338, 342, 347, 350, 371

language attitudes 4, 6, 91, 102, 103, 106, 199, 205–222, 228, 230, 251, 336, 337, 339, 340, 341, 352–354, 368, 371, 373
– attitude acquisition 4, 6, 91, 199, 205, 206, 207, 228, 371, 373
– attitudinal change 206, 209, 216, 220–221
– parental language attitude 83–106, 199
language change 4, 6, 106, 163, 171, 178–188, 197, 199, 200, 206, 222, 280, 336, 354, 364, 368
language identity 235–236, 246, 249, 337, 340, 354
language ideology 5, 63, 76, 83–106, 326, 329, 330, 372, 373
language learning 5, 52, 63, 121, 250, 341, 342, 366, 367
– English language learning 38, 39, 44, 45, 49–51, 62, 68–70, 118, 250, 337, 349, 352, 353
– informal language learning 32, 89, 336
language policy 4, 5, 39, 49, 50, 52, 59–78, 84, 89–91, 103–106, 139, 151, 180, 249–251, 309, 337, 341, 366, 367, 372, 373

- family language policy 4, 5, 59–78, 367
- home language policy 5, 62, 64, 89–91, 367
language shift 6, 38, 177–200, 352, 362, 364, 365
language use 1–6, 13, 30, 37–54, 62, 63, 70, 72, 78, 83–106, 114, 138, 166, 188, 189, 192, 197, 230, 244, 248, 283, 297, 303, 307, 309, 337, 339, 342–344, 351, 352, 354, 367, 368, 373
- home language strategies 38, 39, 45, 49–51
- home language use 5, 89–92, 373
logistic regression 142, 328, 329
L1 and L2 English 4, 6, 126, 127, 135, 137, 153, 178, 180–181, 188, 362, 373

Malaysia 4, 5, 37–54, 341, 367, 368
Maldives 4, 6, 335–338, 347, 348, 352
matched-guise 7, 307–331, 341
medial object perfect (MOP) 189, 190, 192–194, 196, 365
mixed-effects model 291, 299, 371
MOP. *See* medial object perfect (MOP)
mothers 5, 19, 20, 25–29, 32, 35–54, 67, 70, 72, 73, 87–89, 92, 93, 95–100, 102, 103, 138, 151, 229, 273
multiethnolect 256, 258, 275
multilingualism 46, 62, 66, 89, 90, 317, 318, 326, 327, 330, 367, 368, 373
- multilingual 3, 5, 6, 37–54, 64–66, 136, 139, 160, 171, 208, 228, 249–251, 311, 325–330, 341, 365–367, 369, 373
- societal multilingualism 91, 330, 373
multiliteracy practices 5, 59–78
multinormativity 210, 216, 302, 371
- multinormative orientation 210, 302, 371

native speaker 105, 112, 116, 117, 119, 126–128, 134, 135, 138, 140, 141, 149, 152, 153, 198, 326, 330, 340, 352, 363, 364
- new native speakers of English 134, 149, 153, 363
- traditional native speakers of English 134, 138, 149, 152, 153, 363
neoliberalism 64, 78
new dialect formation 197, 256, 258, 259, 272, 275, 276, 369
norms 3, 7, 43, 136, 163, 164, 171, 185–187, 206, 209, 210, 216, 221, 239, 258, 275, 276, 283, 288, 324, 325, 328, 331, 340, 352, 364, 371

- community norms 3
- language norms 3, 43, 136, 163, 171, 206, 209, 340, 364, 371
North America 286, 287, 295, 297, 299, 302, 311, 371

Outer Circle 1, 256, 258, 259, 260, 340, 341, 361

past tense marking 5, 88, 102, 134–139, 141–143, 147, 148, 150, 152, 153, 363
perceptions 3, 4, 6, 38, 60, 62, 70, 102, 103, 138, 180, 205, 209, 215, 247, 249, 280, 281, 283, 286, 302, 310, 312, 315, 340, 352, 367–369
phonological variation 4, 14, 17–18, 24–27, 160, 161, 170, 368
political engagement 227–251
postcolonial 2, 3, 66, 102, 134, 147, 153, 160, 162, 171, 172, 180, 228, 248–251, 280, 285, 303, 362
- postcolonial Englishes (PCEs) 2, 66, 162, 228, 248–251, 285, 303
post-colonial English. *See* postcolonial, postcolonial Englishes (PCEs)
prestige 7, 84–86, 151, 152, 188, 205, 208, 216–221, 235, 239, 259, 262, 272, 273, 276, 280, 283, 285–287, 291, 292, 295–297, 299–302, 319, 336, 341, 354, 368, 371, 372
- covert prestige 220–221
- overt prestige 216–221, 259, 272, 319
- prestige schools 7, 283, 285–287, 291, 292, 295–297, 299–302, 371

random forest 291, 295, 297, 302
rhoticity 6, 256, 262, 263, 270–271, 273
- rhotacization 280–281, 283–286, 288–303, 371
- rhotic 17, 24, 25, 262, 263, 270–273

St. Kitts 4, 6, 205–222, 371
settler (STL) community 18, 137, 260, 362
Singapore 3–6, 66, 83–106, 134, 137–147, 151–153, 163, 177–200, 248, 249, 257, 285, 341, 362–364, 372, 373
- Colloquial Singapore English 5, 84, 86–94, 97, 101–105, 198, 351
- Singapore English (SingE) 5, 6, 66, 84, 86–89, 91, 105, 134, 137–138, 142, 151, 152, 178–181, 185, 187, 188, 198, 285, 362, 365

– Singlish 89, 90, 151, 198
– Standard Singapore English (SSE) 5, 84, 87–93, 101, 104, 105, 198
SingE. *See* Singapore, Singapore English (SingE)
SLA. *See* acquisition, second language acquisition (SLA)
social meanings 206, 281, 283, 286, 302–303
social movements 6, 227–229, 249, 366
sociophonetics 164, 280, 283, 289, 291, 303, 371
solidarity 206, 209, 214, 218–221, 248, 340, 341, 372
spectrogram 166, 289
speech rhythm 6, 159–172
standard 4, 5, 14, 16, 17, 39, 60, 61, 71, 83–106, 135, 137–140, 142, 149, 161, 162, 167, 169, 170, 189, 192, 193, 196, 198, 206–208, 210–213, 215, 216, 220, 221, 262, 280, 283, 284, 288, 289, 308, 315, 319, 321, 323–326, 328–331, 352, 365, 367, 368, 371, 373
– Standard English (StE) 5, 16, 60, 83–106, 189, 191–197, 199, 208, 211, 216, 220, 282, 283, 350, 367
– standard language ideology 5, 85–87, 104, 326, 329, 330
status 1, 37, 39–41, 53, 60–63, 65, 68, 69, 78, 112, 116, 137, 139, 147, 152, 180, 188, 192, 198, 206, 210, 214–222, 227, 229, 234, 236, 247, 248, 250, 251, 264, 309, 336–338, 340, 341, 350, 352, 354, 365–367, 371, 372
superdiversity 255, 256, 258, 264, 275, 276, 370
suprasegmental variation 17

Thailand 4, 5, 59–78, 367
– Thai English 60–62, 65–68, 71–77, 367
Third Culture Kids (TCKs) 6, 255–276, 369, 370
translanguaging 5, 62, 64, 66, 71–73, 76–78, 364, 367
Trinidad 4, 6, 16, 18–21, 26, 28–31, 206, 208–210, 212, 213, 220, 280–288, 295, 297, 301–303, 371
TRINI-FAVE 289

United States of America (USA) 4, 14, 16, 19, 20, 30, 51, 206, 368
– US 5, 6, 13, 14, 16, 19, 32, 33, 134, 138–141, 147, 149, 152, 153, 212, 213, 215–221, 260, 280–284, 287, 291, 297, 301, 302, 312, 324, 325, 330, 348, 350, 363
– US English 5, 6, 134, 151, 212, 312, 350, 363
US American linguistic influence 280, 282–283, 301–302

variationist sociolinguistics 171, 301, 365
vowel 6, 7, 17, 23, 25, 26, 88, 160–162, 166–168, 258, 262, 263, 265–273, 279–303
– NURSE 7, 17, 24, 263, 271, 279–303, 371

word frequency 115, 121
written L2 development 5, 113–114, 125–128, 372

zero subject 88, 101, 179, 181, 183, 185–187, 364
– zero subject pronoun 179, 183, 186, 187, 364

www.ingramcontent.com/pod-product-compliance
Lightning Source LLC
Chambersburg PA
CBHW061928220426
43662CB00012B/1837